Also by Julia Markus

J. Anthony Froude

J. ANTHONY FROUDE

The Last Undiscovered Great Victorian

A Biography by

Julia Markus

SCRIBNER

New York   London   Toronto   Sydney

SCRIBNER
1230 Avenue of the Americas
New York, NY 10020

SCRIBNER and design are trademarks of Macmillan Library Reference USA, Inc.,
used under license by Simon & Schuster, the publisher of this work.

For information about special discounts for bulk purchases,
please contact Simon & Schuster Special Sales:
1-800-456-6798 or business@simonandschuster.com

DESIGNED BY ERICH HOBBING

Text set in Berthold Baskerville

Manufactured in the United States of America

1   3   5   7   9   10   8   6   4   2

Library of Congress Cataloging-in-Publication Data

Markus, Julia [date]
J. Anthony Froude: the last undiscovered great Victorian: a biography/by Julia Markus.
p. cm.
1. Froude, James Anthony, 1818–1894. 2. Historians–Great Britain–Biography.
3. Novelists, English–19th century–Biography. 4. Biographers–Great Britain–Biography.
5. Diplomats–Great Britain–Biography. I. Title.

DA3.F9M37 2005
823'.8–dc22
[B]
2005048990

ISBN-13: 978-0-7432-4555-5
ISBN-10: 0-7432-4555-5

CONTENTS

You pronounce his name *Frood*.
—Thomas Carlyle, private letter

All mention of Frowde
Is henceforth disallowed,
Nor shall any one now de-
Scribe him as Froude-ee.
For he swears by the rood,
That his name it is Froude.

Published in newspapers throughout America,
on Froude's first visit, after he quickly corrected
reporters who mispronounced his name.

J. ANTHONY FROUDE

Character is a Victory, not a gift.
—J.A.F.

Sliding Toward Tasmania

*H*e had been nothing but trouble for his father, a thorn in the archdea-con's side. Now he sat alone at the Exeter College high table, after the other diners left, listening to the crackle in the fireplace and staring at nothing in front of his eyes. He had taken off his scholar's gown, which lay in the chair next to him. He wore good worsted trousers that emphasized his long, lanky, athletic legs, and a dark gray jacket of a softer material that fit well and hung fine from his shoulders. It was the understated elegance of Oxford tailoring that proclaimed him a young man of some importance while discreetly draping the fire in his belly. He was tall, almost six feet, quite good-looking, with a long, pale face, strong nose, and cleft chin. His black hair was rather long and parted on the left side and his eyebrows emphasized his large dark eyes, which glowed with intellect and vivacity. Missing was the signature smile on his lips, commented upon by those who knew him through his life. Myste-rious, that smile. The fact that it was missing while he sat there alone was proof, perhaps, that it was a smile used to reflect the smiles he met or to defend himself when people around him were far from smiling.

James Anthony Froude was thirty years old that February of 1849, and Anthony—as he was called—had just destroyed the future that fronted him. He had not dined at the hall, nor been there the afternoon when his

1

newly published book, *The Nemesis of Faith,* was thrown into the flames—hellfire presumably meant for its author.

It was all over. His career, his life in Oxford, any chance of reconciliation with his father. Ashes. He knew his rebellious novel—about a Church of England cleric who doubted the divinity of Jesus Christ and had an affair with a sad married woman—would cause an uproar at Oxford. But Anthony could have no idea that the book would burst past the small, inbred community that nurtured him for the last twelve years and become a cause célèbre in the world at large—read in the English-speaking world, debated in France, admired in Germany. It would make him famous in forward-thinking communities, and infamous everywhere else. Everyone who was anyone would talk about it, write about it to friends, or pen an opinion for the newspapers. *The Nemesis of Faith* would become the most relevant book of its day, speaking out to the wrenching religious doubts of an entire generation.

This would be Anthony's last night at Exeter College, sitting alone and dejected at the high table. A few years before at the same table he had stirring conversations with the visiting American poet and philosopher Ralph Waldo Emerson—a man who had long since given up his ministry in the Second Church Boston and set out on a spiritual quest. In Emerson, Anthony met a truly original thinker. Added to that, the American was a close personal friend of the author whose works were indelibly altering Anthony's views: Thomas Carlyle, by the 1840s an increasingly world-famous figure. In these men Anthony discovered a power and earnestness at least equal to that of the most brilliant of the Oxford churchmen: "With this difference: that I was no longer referred to books and distant centuries but to present facts and the world in which I lived and breathed."

The emotional and intellectual kinship that Anthony felt for Emerson was enhanced by Emerson's face, which so resembled John Henry Newman's, who had attempted to bring Anthony to a different light: "Lead kindly Light, amid the enduring gloom, Lead thou me on." The future Cardinal Newman's poem is still sung, but Newman was no longer leading Anthony on. Emerson encouraged the doubt-ridden, emotionally torn Anthony in a new direction. Inspired him to go into the wilderness over his long vacation from his students, his Oxford, to go back to Ireland, not as a tutor or a traveler this time, but in a Thoreau-like manner, just to *write.* Which he did. After all, it was 1848, the year of revolution all through Europe, and Anthony was a radical, a Red, thoroughly believing that everything was wrong and on the eve of great change.

Well, now it was 1849, and after all the Sturm und Drang and European bloodletting of the previous year, nothing much had changed, except Anthony was true to his own inclinations, wrote down exactly how he felt for everyone to read, and for that, in Oxford in 1849, one must face the consequences.

He thought he was ready. Had written offhandedly, debonairly, of his coming downfall to his friends the poets Arthur Clough and "Matt" Arnold. And to that Cambridge man, Charles Kingsley, the Low Church cleric who (unlike Anthony and his friends) stuck to his religious calling. Anthony knew what the future would bring. Exile and cunning. He would leave England; after many inquiries he'd found a post directing a school in Tasmania—a new British colony then called Van Diemen's Land. His disappointed father was willing to finance his youngest child one last time, with the vague hope that immigration to the colonies might make a man of Anthony yet. All this before *The Nemesis of Faith* was published.

Anthony considered himself more than ready to give up his fellowship, the possibility of a church living, England itself. Though he was steady—and quite witty—in anticipation, his bravado buckled when the rector of Exeter College did not want to shake his hand, even if it was only to say good-bye. Couldn't Rector Richards appreciate his honesty—an honesty the rector himself urged of Anthony?

As usual, Anthony was callow when it came to consequences—half naive, half devil-may-care—a youngest son in this as in everything. He purposely published *The Nemesis of Faith* not only under his own name but with his title: J. A. Froude, M.A., Fellow of Exeter College, Oxford. The rector, who had protected Anthony two years earlier when Anthony published his autobiographical *Shadows of the Clouds,* under the pseudonym Zeta, now had more explaining to do, more irate letters to answer, other hands to shake.

Not for the first time in his life, Anthony brooded over his fate.

The father Anthony could not please was the Archdeacon Robert Hurrell Froude (1769–1859), a well-to-do, landed clergyman and important Devonshire church administrator who was fifty years old when Anthony, his youngest child, was born at Dartington Parsonage. There are no memorials to the Venerable Archdeacon of Totnes. His marble or bronze bust cannot be found among other Devonshire archdeacons commemorated at Exeter Cathedral. No mention, either, that he fathered three sons of genius, each of whom brought something new to the nineteenth century before receding into its very texture: Hurrell, the theologian who along with John Henry Newman rocked the Church of England; controversial Anthony, the prose artist and historian who, at great expense to his self-worth, would raise the art of biography to the modern standard; and William, the scientist, engineer, and first naval architect, who invented the bilge keel, used to steady every commercial and warring ship in the seas, and who was considered "the greatest of experimenters and investigators in hydrodynamics" well into the twentieth century.

The parsonage of Anthony's birth was among the calm and beautiful rolling hills of Dartington, above the thriving town of Totnes, the highest navigable point of the River Dart. Age-old Totnes came into its own in Elizabethan times, when this charming inland port was the center for exporting cloth to France and importing wine. Anthony's father was raised there. Should he take a stroll along the high street today, the Venerable Archdeacon of Totnes would certainly be astounded by the life-size Buddha in the window of the Eclectic Englishman. Small shops thrive on both sides of the winding hill of a main road, selling crystals and incense and herbal cures and the best fudge, as a later generation searches for organic truth and variations of sixteenth-century fruit still flourishing in the trees behind Totnes's picturesque church. The Old Forge, across the bridge above the River Dart, no longer uses its dungeons as the temporary prison for Puritans caught on their way to Plymouth, the resident blacksmith ready and able to custom-make their shackles. Instead it is an inn serving an excellent breakfast and sporting a hot tub for its guests.

Nineteenth-century Totnes and environs, squeezed in between Henry VIII and the New Age, was a less emphatic place, though quite vulnerable to the power struggles between church and state ripe at the time, keeping the archdeacon busy both as church administrator and advisor to the famous High Church Archbishop of Exeter, Henry Phillpotts.

Anthony was born long past the days when his tall, distinguished father was a snappy dresser and renowned horseman. At Oxford he had leapt the turnpike gate on Abingdon Road without displacing one of the pennies placed strategically between his limbs, his seat, and his horse. But the archdeacon had no fond memories of his youth. "Those were the days when I was an ass," he cautioned his youngest son. Though he never fell into debt or other irregularities he did have a weakness for his appearance. "I laugh when I think of it," Anthony wrote, for the old man he knew was completely indifferent to such things.

Still, the archdeacon retained the good bearing and good looks of the Froude men—if not an interest in fashion. He had married Margaret Spedding, a beautiful and brilliant woman from a very good, intellectually distinguished family—particularly in the area of science. A remarkably handsome couple, they balanced one another. Margaret, a born writer, mingled a love of virtue with psychological insight in her daily journal. The archdeacon prided himself on duty, practicality, horse sense, stables. He was the first to admit that he was not a man of theory, not that he downplayed a philosophical mind like that of his wife or the Oxford men who at times sought his advice. Although he wasn't a man to show his feelings, one can see them in the sketchbooks he left behind, vital drawings and washes of churches, churchyards, tracery, trees, and the surrounding sea. The couple were quite happy in those early days, before they realized Margaret Spedding brought tuberculosis to the marriage.

There was nothing but joy when their first son was born on March 25, 1803. Richard Hurrell (known as Hurrell) and thirteen months later, Robert. "Hurrell and Robert, being my father's eldest children and therefore nearer to him in age, were his companions in the sense which the rest of us never were. They were both interesting boys, tall, handsome, and brilliant. They shared my father's leisure, and went with him into the hunting field, to which he still gave such time as he could afford. They had my mother's influence to moderate and guide them and keep open the affectionate understanding between father and children." These two oldest were sent to Eton. "They were not particularly studious, but they were light, bright, and popular, Hurrell showing signs of real genius. The relations between them and my father and mother were of unbroken affection and confidence, a confidence which from the difference of age, especially after my mother's death, could not be extended to the rest of us."

There was a space of four years in which the couple enjoyed their first two sons before four more children arrived—John, Margaret, Phillis, William—one a year, then a breathing space of four years before the birth of daughter Mary. Finally, after another four years, on Shakespeare's birthdate, April 23, Anthony was born in 1818. As a child he wondered if his white-bearded father knew the patriarch Abraham in biblical days.

His old and remote paterfamilias had never known a father himself and was raised in a household of women. Anthony recalled:

"My grandmother who had country blood in her veins, considered of

5

later years that she had made a rash mesalliance. I have heard her say that she was a fool to marry. She had everything a young woman could desire; a kind father, an ample property. Her picture had been painted by Sir Joshua. What could have possessed her? It can be alleged only in her excuse that she was very young, scarcely turned sixteen when she so committed herself. In five or six years, she was left a widow with four children, three girls and a son the Archdeacon my father, who was born after my grandfather's death. She survived her husband more than sixty years, and lived, as she used to tell us children with pride, to be a great grandmother. She removed in her widowhood to Totnes, where she brought up her family on a narrow income with care and thrift, care so excessive that in her later years it developed into a disease. On her death, my father found hoards of gold secreted about the house in which she lived—*goold* she called it—and was rather ashamed of the sack of sovereigns which he was obliged to carry to the bank."

Anthony, the last of eight children, would never know mother love. "My mother was already in a decline when I was born. I was a sickly child and was christened privately at home as it was not supposed that I could live to be taken to church. My mother had nursed my brothers and sisters. Me she could not nurse. I was consigned to a healthy young woman of the parish who had lost her own baby, and to her I believe I owe it that I survived and still survive." About a month and a half before Anthony turned three, his mother died.

The archdeacon dealt with the grief of his wife's death, the burden of a last infant, and the tuberculosis poised to ravage his children, with the strongest resource in his arsenal—silence. His wife's effects were all disposed of (perhaps he felt that could exterminate contagion) and Anthony never heard him speak of her again. The fact that the dreaded disease came from his wife's line was etched into that silence. The archdeacon became more severe and silent as circumstances turned his life into unrelenting duty, not the least responsibility for a weak, overly fearful infant son born long after the others, a son who would remember nothing of his mother, except, at times, a far-off whisper that might have been her voice.

Anthony's first memory was of being struck for dirtying his baby frock. "We were a Spartan family. Whipping was always resorted to as the prompt consequence of naughtiness." When Anthony's spinster aunt Mary, who had nursed her consumptive sister Margaret, stayed to take care of the motherless family, she woke the sickly toddler at dawn each day, brought him outdoors, and dipped him into a gravel pit filled with ice-cold water in order to toughen him, improve his health. His father approved, as did his oldest brother, Hurrell, fifteen years Anthony's senior, and the pride of the Froude name. Hurrell Froude—tall, slender, with black curly hair and coal black eyes of bright intensity, Byronic in looks and repartee—was a born leader, known for his romantic imagination and otherworldly piety. His brilliance lit up his pious nature, his words sparked thunderclaps.

"My father was infinitely proud of Hurrell and let him do as he pleased. I worshiped him, but I cannot say that I think his educational experiments were always successful. He thought that I wanted manliness. A small stream ran along the fence which enclosed our garden. I remember Hurrell once when I was very little taking me by the heels and stirring the mud at the bottom with my head. Another time I have a vivid recollection of being put overboard into deep water out of a boat in the river again to make me bold, which it didn't make me at all."

Young Anthony had an escape from early-morning baths in gravel pits, from a bullying, pious brother, and a remote, punishing father, when he was sent to Buckfastleigh School, hardly a five-mile stroll from his home. Even so, the eight-year-old was forbidden to return to the parsonage except during school holidays. His father had the peculiar idea that a child should not consider that he had a home. Perhaps banishment was a blessing. For the schoolmasters and the schoolchildren were not punishing. Better yet and quite uncharacteristically, at this school, "bullying was by common consent treated as a public crime." This was particularly helpful to Anthony, since he suffered from a hernia, which prevented him from fighting and "taking part in the rough games of the playing field."

At Buckfastleigh even the punishment meted out for bullying was considered tame—for the times: "A lad who was guilty of persecuting any smaller boy was made to kneel with bare back on the schoolroom floor, and was flogged, buffeted we called it, every boy striking him one blow with a knotted handkerchief. I can see a poor boy now on his knees, with tears in his eyes, suffering more from the shame than the pain of the blows."

Of course, it was de rigueur that the teaching at the school was "quickened into effectiveness by the vigorous and frequent application of the cane," particularly since the more severe whippings, called birchings, were infrequent and resorted to only for such "disgraceful offences" as theft or lying. Canings, birchings, floggings, were all hallmarks of a young gentleman's education.

Away from the family, Anthony, who hadn't been a particularly accomplished toddler—he was born to a household of brilliant siblings—flourished intellectually, learned Latin rapidly, and found a special aptitude for Greek. His enthusiasm for classical study was boundless and he was soon in a class all his own. "Before I was eleven I had read all the *Iliad* and the *Odyssey* twice over."

The child could recite hundreds of lines of Greek, commit hundreds more to memory on short notice, a talent for which, at home on holiday, he was rewarded. But this precocity turned into a curse. A shilling did not compensate for the fact that he now had "the misfortune to be considered a genius," to be advanced beyond his age, and "to encourage expectations." During school vacations he "must work, work, work without pause or relief." It was drudgery year in and year out. "It did me no good. I was forced like a sickly plant in a hot-house: a bad preparation for the rough weather I was soon to face."

Even Hurrell, who had frightened the wits out of his baby brother with ghost stories and harsh teasing, wrote to their brother William when Anthony was nine: "I think I can explain to you the allusion Aunt Mary makes at Att's promotion. For a day or two before I left home news was brought us that he had been put up into the class above him. I am afraid he is being pushed on beyond his age so much that it will make him stupid, for I am sure it is not a good thing for boys in general to live so much among fellows much older than themselves."

The archdeacon, the "sensible, strong, practical" churchman who "never spoke even in private of feeling or sentiment, and never showed any in word or action," thought differently, and expected return on his shilling. His youngest son was the last of a large family and must pull his own weight in the world, make his own living. Anthony must study, study, study, in order to be eligible for early admission to public school (private school, in American parlance) and from there to early admission on scholarship to Oxford. With the expectation that Anthony would follow in his father's clerical profession, the boy was sent to Westminster at the age of eleven.

If the brutality of English public school education—around the time Dr. Arnold (Matt's father) was reforming Rugby—was to be described in one word, that word would be *Westminster*. It was an absolutely dreadful school in that respect, considered so at the time. Physical punishment was extreme, causing enrollment to drop year after year. To send a precocious eleven-year-old there, one who did so well on entrance exams that he was placed among boys sixteen and seventeen, was a terrible cruelty. His father was advised to allow Anthony to board at one of the many houses in the vicinity catering to younger students, but the archdeacon and Aunt Mary refused to shield the boy, deciding that being thrown in with the older set would be good for the child's character.

At eleven, physically frail and weak, intellectually overdeveloped, the boy was sent to live in one large and dismal dormitory room with thirty-nine boys much older and stronger than he, upperclassmen bred to systematic bullying: "The rule was that we were to learn by suffering." The dormitory was kept so cold that in the winter the boys put water on the stone floors so that they could slide on the ice that formed. The "fagging" system, in which the younger is servant/slave to the older, turned Anthony's young life into a living hell far worse than being plunged into gravel pits or having one's head used to stir mud at Dartington Parsonage: "I had my legs set on fire to make me dance. When I had crawled to bed, I have been woke many times by the hot points of cigars burning holes in my face." Simply put, he was brutalized and came to see himself as a victim of fate. In his first novella, *Shadows of the Clouds,* he wrote that his life was "as hard, and the treatment as barbarous as that of the negroes in Virginia," and he fleshed out the method of his torture, of how the older boys would stalk the college at midnight, stop by his bed as he slept, how one would hold him down while another burned him with his cigar until his face was scarred and blistered for weeks. He was not exaggerating. His own son, Ashley, would write way into the twentieth century that the best said of his father's education was that he survived it.

He was made to swallow brandy punch till he was drunk, and at meals the sixteen-year-olds kept the meat for themselves and gave this weak child the bones. He couldn't defend himself, either physically or emotionally. No father or older brother or friend had taught him how. Only a friendly cook at a nearby boardinghouse kept him from starving. The code of honor was never to tell on another boy. He took to lying, invented "excuses of illness" that were easily found out. The headmaster thought he was trying to escape lessons, "instead of the young tyrants up the college stairs." Anthony later wondered if the headmaster would have made any changes even if he knew the truth. As it was, his behavior was constantly complained of to his father.

After three years Anthony, fourteen and still frail for his age, could not return; he had suffered what we would consider a severe nervous breakdown. He could hardly speak *at all,* not to mention that he had lost his fluency in Greek and Latin along with his good clothes, sold to keep the bigger boys in stationery. Younger boys' buying the older boys school supplies was such a standard practice that most fathers opened accounts for their sons with local shops to facilitate the trade-off—but not the archdeacon.

He could not tell his father the truth when he arrived at the parsonage mute and in tatters, that he sold his clothes for protection money. Of course his father *knew* his best clothes were gone, *knew* he spent all his money, no matter how Anthony equivocated. Both Hurrell and the archdeacon considered him a cowardly, unmanly boy, a liar and a cheat. And so he was—to himself as well—though a softer later era might allow for extenuating circumstances. Without putting too fine a point on it, by attempting to wiggle out of an unbearable situation, Anthony was learning how to survive. And a survival skill once learned is rarely forgotten.

His father did not leave it to Hurrell but beat him himself for his lies, his tattered state, and academic failure. Punishment not prevention was the "old-fashioned principle" he was raised by, described in *Shadows of the Clouds:* "If a boy goes wrong whip him. Teach him to be afraid of going wrong, by the pains and penalties to ensue—just the principle on which gamekeepers used to try to break dogs." Don't attempt to talk to him, reason with him, offer him advice on how to control the impulses that boil up in *all* boys. Simply beat the boy out of him. Unfortunately, with the human animal the consequences could be disastrous, for untutored youths began to believe they *deserved* their whippings, "as if they could have helped doing what they did in a way dogs cannot."

The archdeacon envisioned an academic career and then a clerical living for his youngest son, and was bitterly disappointed by Anthony's failure at Westminster. As always he met adversity with silence. When his favorite daughter died of tuberculosis, his parishioners were amazed to find him at church as usual, conducting services, while she was laid out at home. He was in his midsixties, having to deal with the dreaded disease he never named, as well as with a wretched fourteen-year-old who was taciturn and told lies.

All Anthony saw was a distant father, a severe old man who despised him. At home under his father's roof, he was an outcast in the midst of plenty. The tailor was no longer allowed to make new clothes for him. His coat was refashioned out of his brothers' throwaways. No wonder his favorite Bible story was Joseph and his coat of many colors.

The father punished the wayward boy with silence. Anthony no longer seemed to have a tongue in his mouth, so no one was allowed to talk to Anthony, either. Daily he was made to feel worthless. Silence was lifted only to tell the boy time and again that he would not go to Oxford but instead would be apprenticed to a trade. Anthony considered that option good enough for such an unworthy son as himself. And in any case, it hardly mattered. He was broken. His self-worth had been beaten out of him and his chief consolation was that he was sure he would soon die. His exceedingly handsome and equally good-natured brother Robert, the next to oldest, who had treated him kindly, and whom he loved dearly and trusted, had died of tuberculosis when Anthony was ten, and signs of the dread disease were evident in Hurrell. "My complexion, my sickly body," Anthony wrote, "marked me for a certain victim." He looked forward to his death, adding yet another flaw to his character—self-pity.

Yet at fourteen, stuck in Dartington Parsonage, waiting to die, he witnessed one of the most important religious movements of the nineteenth century. At Oxford, brother Hurrell had met classmate John Henry Newman, a young man from a more pedestrian background, who was using his highly developed intellect to find his way to God. They were both young churchmen at Oxford, both with brilliant clerical and scholarly careers ahead of them, and they became best friends. Much later in the century, a follower and biographer of Newman would have a dream that he was at a dinner party with a veiled woman beside him whose conversation was so enticing that he told her, "I have never felt such charm in any conversation since I used to talk with John Henry Newman at Oxford." She raised her veil: "I am John Henry Newman."

At Oxford, Hurrell and Newman were joined by Hurrell's former Oriel College tutor John Keble. Keble considered himself a country cleric, though he was also a distinguished don and author of the lauded book-length poem *The Christian Year.* Not a household in English-speaking Christendom lacked a copy of that celebrated work, in those days. The three, Hurrell, Newman, and Keble were writing a series of "Tracts for the Times." These tracts were intent on purging the Protestant elements of the Church of England, and thereby returning the church to its earlier authoritarian, Catholic roots. Particularly the tracts upheld the supremacy of church over state, as before Henry VIII. What had begun among the dons and fellows of Oxford, in a cloistered, clergy-ridden university town, would soon rock the Church of England to its foundations, altering perception and practice. The Oxford Movement, it would be called, and those churchmen, some young, some already eminent, became known as Tractarians.

Hurrell and Newman were often at Dartington Parsonage to consult with the practical archdeacon, Keble often writing to him to make sure there was nothing heretical in their tracts before each was published. Anthony was privy to these conversations.

Anthony listened to Hurrell, who hated the very idea of marriage and would not have the word uttered in his presence, talk at home against the Anglican practice of allowing priests to marry. Reform was needed. Newman, as charismatic, delicate, and brilliant as the dream of him, would write in his autobiography that he had a revelation at the age of fifteen that he would never marry. Hurrell's radical opinion of returning the Anglican clergy to celibacy struck a chord with him, just as all of Hurrell's ideas on restoring earlier church practices influenced Newman. When Hurrell's youngest sister Mary became engaged, Hurrell wrote revealingly to Newman, "Mary is going to be married to a very nice fellow down here. If he was not a parson I should have no kind of objection to it, but as it is they will have trouble in the flesh."

It had been to the Protestant elements in the Church of England that Anthony was raised. His father had always been "an excellent parish priest of the old sort, with strong sense, a practical belief in the doctrines of the Church of England *as by law established,* which no person in his right mind would think of questioning." The archdeacon taught his children that their business in life was to work and to make honorable positions for themselves, that religion was the light to see their way along the road of duty.

That religion of Anthony's childhood, described nostalgically in *The Nemesis of Faith,* was no introduction to otherworldly theological speculation, but was a series of "healthy young Sundays; they were all bright." The walk to church in one's Sunday clothes through the woods and meadows, the sense of special meaning among the congregation, the prayers said together, the music, even the long sermons had a Sunday shine to them when recollected. "The sacredness of Sunday is stamped on the soil of England, and in the heart of every Englishman; and all this by the old Sundays we remember the first ten years of our lives." But then: "Just as I was leaving off being a boy, we fell under a strong Catholicising influence at home, and I used to hear things which were strange enough to my ear."

His father always left the theorizing to Hurrell and Newman, admitting readily that he was no philosopher, and maintaining his stance as a nuts-and-bolts church administrator. The archdeacon was a busy man, overseeing his lands, modernizing the roads of his district, advising the

Archbishop of Exeter at a time when the politicians were keen to eliminate the sinecures of the churchmen. He was more than proud and justified when Hurrell, along with Newman and Keble, came together on a political matter and defeated the reelection of Robert Peel, at the time an odious radical member of Parliament, later the Conservative prime minister. To Anthony's father, the Oxford Movement, initiated by his son, his son's best friend, and his son's former tutor, offered the hope of something quite practical, a return to the church's authority over the ever-expanding liberalism of the state.

However, listening to brother Hurrell and Newman talk was a form of shock treatment to Anthony, who had a theoretical mind and realized how much of what they called a return to Anglo-Catholicism was dangerously close to Roman Catholicism. The thrilling, disconcerting conversations jolted him back to his books. He began reading once more in his father's library, and the archdeacon, remote but watchful, saw some hope for his wayward son: "If Anthony falls into good company I feel sure that his conduct will be everything a parent can wish, but he wants that manliness of character which enables a lad to steer a strait course if he meets clever lively companions that would lead him out of it," he wrote Keble. Carefully, and with more concern than Anthony was privy to, the archdeacon found a suitable tutor for his impressionable son in a town close to Oxford.

However, the archdeacon had greater concerns at the time. Advanced signs of tuberculosis—cough, fevers, the extraordinary shine of the eyes—were evident in Hurrell, as much as Hurrell and all who loved him wished to deny them. As soon as Anthony was sent off to be tutored, the archdeacon and John Henry Newman accompanied Hurrell to Italy in the hopes it would improve his health—a trip immortalized in the later Cardinal Newman's spiritual autobiography, *Apologia pro Vita Sua*—and in the inspired unpublished sketches of the archdeacon's.

For Hurrell there was Italy, and later Barbados, but in February 1836, in the dead cold of winter, he came home to Dartington Parsonage through a terrific snowstorm. "From day to day almost we could perceive that his body was wasting and his strength giving way," the archdeacon informed Keble. "Oxford and the friendships he had formed there, seemed to be always in his thoughts, but I cannot trust myself to say more. To me he was not only a most affectionate son, but my companion and familiar friend, entering into my pursuits and amusements, and guiding me by his advice when I needed it. I pray God Almighty to support me through this heaviest of earthly trials."

So weak had Hurrell become toward the end that he hadn't strength enough to clear his throat. On a cold winter Sunday the grieving father observed a sudden difficulty in Hurrell's breathing, a failed attempt to swallow, an attempt to speak, and then, after a slight struggle, suffering was over. At the age of thirty-three, Hurrell drowned in his father's arms. "My dear son died this day," the archdeacon wrote, describing the scene to Newman.

Then he swiftly moved on to practical matters. Son William, silent William who would always mediate family affairs, would be going up to collect things from Hurrell's rooms at Oxford. "It will be desirable perhaps if the rooms are not considered too good for an undergraduate that Anthony should be permitted to take them. But William will talk to you on the subject—& if likely to succeed speak to the Provost." And, of course, Newman was to take anything he wished in order to remember Hurrell.

A week later the archdeacon explained to Newman why he wrote on practical matters the very evening of Hurrell's passing ("our separation," he called the death). We find in his spare words an essential glimpse into the character of the Archdeacon of Totnes, as revealing as the sketchbooks he left behind him, devoid of people, filled with a glorious—yet exact—rendering of place: "I could not trust myself nor can I now, to touch on my own sorrows."

Later, Anthony, too, would see beyond the paternal severity that so marked his childhood, to the suffering and anxiety for him and his siblings that lay beneath it. Discipline and horse sense marked the way that this "high and dry" church administrator and landed gentleman kept his sanity and did his duty as year after year God tested him the way he tested Job. "May God in his Mercy," the archdeacon prayed out loud to Newman, turn sufferings into spiritual profit.

"All the manuscripts I can find will be delivered to you by William," the Archdeacon continued. Hurrell's journal "is very interesting to myself as bringing to my recollection many passages of his life, and a progressive picture, as it were, of his mind, when his thoughts and pursuits began to shew promise of his advancement to everything that was good." Hurrell's memorial would be four volumes of his literary remains, a collection of journal entries, prayers, thoughts, letters, essays, sermons, partially financed by the archdeacon and edited by Newman with the help of John Keble. And so the archdeacon occupied himself, as Anthony entered Oxford: "It is one of my few consolations whenever his loss occurs to me, & it is hardly ever out of my mind—to turn to letters & journals that almost bring back to me the reality of bygone days."

These religious daybooks of Hurrell's (the practice of keeping a journal he learned from his mother) are full of morbid self-examination. Hurrell describes how he humiliates his flesh, how he fasts—painful to read, the relentless starving of his own tubercular body. He atones for nameless sins, among them an avalanche of confused feelings for one of the boys he tutors at Oxford. What should be included, what excluded, what might the public misinterpret? The archdeacon senses danger, but as always, leaves such decisions to the philosophic minds of Oxford. In unpublished letter after letter he tells Newman and Keble to decide. His role is to finance the publication of the *Remains of the Reverend R. Hurrell Froude* (and to wait anxiously for the reviews).

Newman committed Hurrell's fasts, his self-flagellations, his exaggerated sense of his own worthlessness to print, did not edit out the more startling practices (or the young boy). He had to be aware that such thoughts and practices seemed less those of a young and promising Church of England cleric who tragically died before his promise could be fulfilled than those of a Roman Catholic monk (circa the Middle Ages). To many, Hurrell Froude's *Remains* were scandalous. They called out, *Beware! The Papists are coming!*

The archdeacon was appalled by the criticism. To him Hurrell, in his self-enforced celibacy, his exaggerated sense of sin, his humiliation of the flesh, was simply the saintliest of Church of England clerics. There was nothing but piety in his avoidance of girls and his detestation of marriage. "I take shame to myself," he wrote to Keble, "for the little share I can claim in laying a foundation for such genuine piety as marked the latter years of his life." Whenever Anthony got in trouble (which was often) he was advised by his father, John Keble, and by scientifically minded brother William to reread the *Remains*. "We adored Hurrell," Anthony insisted. "He was sparkling brilliant, moved as a sort of king in the element which surrounded us."

The contrast between how the archdeacon fathered his oldest and his youngest son is quite remarkable. When Hurrell was an undergraduate and needed money at Oxford, he could write flippantly: "You might as well have answered my most agreeable & interesting letter at an earlier period, but to pass over any little cause of complaint which I may keep in store for a future occasion, hereby I give notice that I am safe arrived at Keble's [then his Oxford tutor] without a farthing, which may suggest to you the propriety of supplying that deficiency at any rate soon."

Hurrell could joke with his father, jolly him out of anything, even before he matured into a churchman. In that maturity, the archdeacon appears to have found the father, the "companion and familiar friend" he had never known. Arriving home from Oxford late one cold January night, thirty-year-old Hurrell "found on getting upstairs that my Father had got out of bed to receive me. I sat up with him till one—& drank brandy & water—no bad thing under such circumstances."

Newman, too, was devoted to Hurrell, never coming to grips with his dark side, even as he used the *Remains* to further radicalize the English church through Hurrell's monklike practices and confessions. Overlooked was the sadistic streak in Hurrell, a true cruelty that terrorized Anthony as a child. It had homoerotic nuances that appeared, judging by the *Remains,* to frighten Hurrell as well.

Anthony had been just two when Hurrell, a young man of seventeen, was forced by illness home from school to Dartington Parsonage. "A letter of my mother's at the beginning of his *Remains* described how he had terrified his baby brother by acting wolf to him," Anthony wrote. "The baby was myself, sufficiently inclined already to imaginative alarms, and he continued to amuse himself with playing half seriously upon my fancy. His own mind was distinctly inclined to believe in the supernatural. Perhaps he thought that we could not be too early imbued with the same disposition."

Hurrell caused grief not only to baby Anthony but to his other siblings and, most important, to his dying mother. The letter she wrote to an imaginary, impartial "Sir" was actually meant for Hurrell's eyes and was given to him. Later, as he matured into a churchman, that letter haunted him. He kept it with his journals, read it often as a repentance, a mortification, and Newman understood that it had to begin the *Remains*. It's worth a reading today, testifying as it does to Margaret Spedding's literary ability and psychological insight—both passed on to Anthony—and to Hurrell's problematic character. The lines that are not in italics in the last paragraphs are revealing lines that Newman silently excised:

> *Sir, I have a son who is giving me a good deal of uneasiness at this time, from causes which I persuade myself are not altogether common; and having used my best judgement about him for seventeen years, I at last begin to think it competent to the case, and apply to you for advice.*
>
> *From his very birth his temper has been peculiar; pleasing, intelligent and attaching, when his mind was undisturbed, and he was in the company of people who treated him reasonably and kindly; but exceedingly impatient*

under vexatious circumstances; very much disposed to find his own amusements in teasing and vexing others; and almost entirely incorrigible when it was necessary to reprove him. I never could find a successful mode of treating him. Harshness made him obstinate and gloomy; calm and long displeasure made him stupid and sullen; and kind patience had not sufficient power over his feelings to force him to govern himself. His disposition to worry made his appearance the perpetual signal for noise and disturbance among his brothers and sisters; and this was impossible to stop, though a taste for quiet, and constant weak health, made it to me almost unsupportable. After the statement of such great faults, it may seem an inconsistency to say that he nevertheless still bore about him strong marks of a promising character. In all points of substantial principle his feelings were just and high. He had (for his age) an unusually deep feeling of admiration for everything which was good and noble; his relish was lively, his taste good, for all the pleasures of the imagination; and he was also quite conscious of his own faults, and (untempted) had a just dislike of them.

On these grounds I built my hope that his reason would gradually correct his temper, and do that for him which his friends could not accomplish. Such a hope was necessary to my peace of mind, for I will not say that he was dearer to me than my other children, but he was my first child, and certainly he could not be dearer. This expectation has been realized, gradually, though very slowly. The education his father chose for him agreed with him; his mind expanded and sweetened; and even some more material faults (which had grown out of circumstances uniting with his temper) entirely disappeared. His promising virtues became my most delightful hopes, and his company my greatest pleasure. At this time he had a dangerous illness, which he bore most admirably. The consequence of it obliged him to leave his school, submit for many months to the most troublesome restraints, and to be debarred from all the amusements and pleasures of his age, though he felt, at the same time, quite competent to them. All this he bore not only with patience and compliance, but with a cheerful sweetness which endeared him to all around him. He returned home for the confirmation of his health, and he appeared to me all I could desire. His manners were tender and kind, his conversation highly pleasing, and his occupations manly and rational. The promising parts of his character, like Aaron's rod, appeared to have swallowed up all the rest and to have left us nothing but his health to wish for.

After such an account, imagine the pain I must feel on being forced to acknowledge that the ease and indulgence of home is bringing on a relapse into his former habits. I view it with sincere alarm as well as grief, as he

17

must remain here many many months, and a strong return, at his age, I do not think would ever be recovered.

I will mention some facts to show that my fears are not too forward. He has a near relation [Aunt Mary] who has attended him through his illness with extraordinary tenderness, and who never made a difference between night and day, if she could give him the smallest comfort; to whom he is very troublesome, and not always respectful. He told her, in an argument, the other day, that "she lied, and knew she did," without, (I am ashamed to say) the smallest apology. I am in a wretched state of health, and quiet is important to my recovery, and quite essential to my comfort; yet he disturbs it, for what he calls "funny tormenting", without the slightest feeling, twenty times a day. I have not had a single meal today in peace, nor been long quiet even in my own room without being obliged to rouse myself to quell some disturbance made by him. *At one time he kept one of his brothers screaming, from a sort of teasing play, for near an hour under my window. At another, he acted a wolf to his baby brother, whom he had promised never to frighten again* & at another he revived a dirty practice at his first school which I am ashamed to mention & made his brother submit to a disgusting result which all the servants knew & talked of. *All this worry has been kept up upon a day when I have been particularly unwell* which I have pleaded many times in vain. He cannot think it pretense for I am to look at but a spectre whose days (whether to be passed in pain or peace) any one would say were not likely to be many.—Light as my body is become he sees many times that I have hardly strength to drag it about. *He also knows at the same time very well, that if his head does but ache, it is not only my occupation, but that of the whole family, to put an end to everything which can annoy him.*

You will readily see, dear sir, that our situation is very difficult, and very distressing. He is too old for any correction, but that of his own reason; and how to influence that, I know not. *Your advice will greatly oblige, a very anxious parent.*

M.F.

P.S. I have complained to him seriously of this day, and I thought he must have been hurt; but I am sorry to say that he has whistled almost ever since. If he cannot be induced to keep peace around me I must leave the house—but what a distress will that be from such a cause!—So unfeeling & from such a quarter!

It could not have been easy for the seventeen-year-old Hurrell to watch his mother die, and confined at home, ill himself, see in her wasting his own future. When his brother Robert had died on Good Friday 1828, he wrote to friend Sam Wilberforce (the future Anglican bishop known as "Soapy Sam"): "My brother's death was indeed a great shock to me at first, & I believe affected me rather with fright than sorrow." In that very long letter, Hurrell switched to pencil in order to implore Sam not to "be vexed with me for suspecting you. . . . Oh pray my truest love be as usual and believe how fondly . . . I love you. Wont you my own love write me a little note to tell me *all* you *did* and *do* feel."

Hurrell's anger and cruelty while his mother lay dying expressed his own fear of death, as well as revealing the blame his father buried: It was the mother's line that brought tuberculosis into the family. Still, even in the best of moods Hurrell teased his sisters unmercifully. There was a part of him he could not control. And the brothers he terrorized were bully's meat—the youngest, Anthony, hardly two; scientifically minded William just ten; brother John, who became an alcoholic before succumbing to tuberculosis, thirteen. Perhaps it was John whom Hurrell exposed to the dirty practices and disgusting results mentioned in the mother's letter.

But that was then. Less than two months after Hurrell's death in 1836, Anthony entered Oxford. Newman was able to do what the archdeacon asked and in time procured for Anthony the rooms at Oriel once occupied by the archdeacon himself, in his horsy days, and so recently cleared—if they ever could be—of Hurrell's remains. Anthony refused them.

No doubt Hurrell's tragic death released something in Anthony. It was only at college, away from his former connections, that he was surprised to find: "I had grown from a boy to a young man. I was tall, not ill-looking, and fairly strong. I could talk. I, who had been always snubbed and kept down, found myself suddenly free." A passerby at Oxford would come upon him outside Oriel College, taller than those gathered around him, his wit and vivacity obviously placing him at the center of a circle of newfound friends who were enjoying his conversation.

Or as he phrased it in *Shadows of the Clouds:* "He was an acute observer and a ready talker, talents always valued and rewarded in life, and he passed at once with a bound into a person whose opinion was to be received, whose advice was often asked, on serious subjects." This remarkably sudden change "did him good and evil." For at the same time, letters came from home, his father constantly "reminding him of what he had been! suspecting him, threatening him," so that he experienced the same evil that injured him when he was a precocious child reciting half *The Iliad* by heart: "His talents were outrunning the rest of him."

Freedom had turned eighteen-year-old Anthony giddy; he "rode and boated and played tennis" with his lively newfound friends and they influenced him just as his father feared. His friends smiled at him. He smiled back. He drank and gambled with the best of them, became a very affable fellow. "I seemed just what everybody wished, hence it was all *seem* with me, I *was* nothing."

He certainly did not want to go home during his long vacations: "Home was still the place of discipline and authority; all the amusements were at college. At college there was no 'you must' or 'you must not:' at home there was nothing else."

He preferred joining a small group of students and a tutor and going on a reading party. "Reading party" was a euphemism, he wrote, a "courtesy" to render such summer trips respectable, an "honourary title" for unbridled fun. Anthony wished for as much fun as possible, as soon as possible, for should his father find out his youngest child was in debt again—just a single debt, the archdeacon emphasized—he would be taken out of Oxford immediately and apprenticed to a trade (the old threat). After his second year at Oxford, he went on a reading party that changed his life.

Anthony chose the one that would take up residence around Thirlmere in the Lake District, and not without reason, for he had already met the Bushes—James Bush was a school friend and his father, the Reverend James Bush, was a man of singularly interesting character, at least to Anthony, who spent many a week happily at his home. Much younger than the archdeacon, this clergyman was a close friend to *all* his children. To Anthony he became "benevolence full, prompt, active, without a tinge of maudlin in it, yet so extensive that it could reach to sympathy even with a broken flower." What he found in the Reverend Bush was paternal *kindness*.

Empathetic understanding was not the Reverend Bush's only appeal. For the twenty-year-old Anthony was attracted to his daughter Harriet, three years Anthony's senior. Here again, Anthony was far from Hurrell, who abhorred girls and who in his undergraduate days went on reading parties supervised by the Reverend John Keble without a female's ever getting in striking distance of the boys' unbridled fun. Hurrell did, however, write home to tell his mother that John Keble reminded him of her. (Keble himself married a friend, his cousin, when he was in his forties, for the particular reason that marriage, which Hurrell and Newman opposed, was something *he* believed a Tractarian parson in the Church of England should support.)

Harriet was a beauty, with an oval face, long curls, full lips, and large eyes as compassionate as her father's actions. "Lakes, mountains, waterfalls, and moonlight on the water, produced their natural effects in a love affair," Anthony would write in *Shadows of the Clouds*. But this was not only first love in the romantic sense; it was the first time in his life that Anthony felt himself the *object* of love. Being loved opened him up to his own self-worth, as he humbly remembered more than a half century later:

"The details are of no consequence to anybody, yet every feature is photographed in my own memory, and forms and must always form while I continue myself an inseparable part of me. The sense of being valued by another made me set a value on my own life. I had something to care for, something which made it worth my while to distinguish myself. I had an object in the future. Every faculty that I had, brightened up as if the sun were suddenly shining."

A thunderbolt from the parsonage sent in the clouds. Anthony was making an ass of himself, his father wrote, and must cut off the attachment or else come home immediately, for there could be no engagement or marriage, *ever*. There was insanity in the Bush family, he informed his son. The archdeacon's reason shows how he was haunted by the shadow of hereditary illness. He was at the same time standing in the way of brother William's engagement because he was sure there was tuberculosis in that woman's family. And earlier, his hauntingly beautiful and rebellious daughter Phillis defied him by marrying John Spedding, her first cousin on her mother's side. She died of tuberculosis a year before Hurrell, who wrote to Newman that "Her fate has been a strange and melancholy one but it is no use talking," adding, her passing "seems to have been for the best." Twenty years later, the archdeacon would write of his favored grandson, Phillis's son Edward: "Just at the age of manhood & with every promise of his becoming a very valuable person he has been lost us, as his dear mother was . . . by a rapid decline." There was no end to the ravaging of his family.

It would take a dispassionate observer to realize that by thwarting his children's relationships, the stern father was thrusting about irrationally, attempting to save them—and his grandchildren—from his own life. All Anthony could think when ordered to disavow Harriet: Not again! Every time something good happened to him, a dreadful letter from home. He saw his father as a nemesis, an inescapable tragic fate, and he became once more what he had been in earlier years, the sacrificial victim. Terribly upset and confused by the letter, he had, at the same time, a profound fear of his father. At twenty he was as afraid of him as he had been when we was twelve—and was *deeply* ashamed of his cowardice, as he confessed in *Shadows of the Clouds*. He was constantly being "over threatened." His father was so old that he forgot boys take things literally, that *"the fear which is without love"* was "the very worst, the very most fatal feeling a child can be brought to entertain towards his father." Distraught and confused, Anthony turned to his tutor in the reading party, who advised him to set the matter of hereditary insanity directly to the Reverend Bush.

The Reverend Bush assured the Archdeacon of Totnes in writing that insanity did not run in the family, giving an acceptable account of the uniqueness of Harriet's grandfather's illness. The archdeacon relented in a return letter, one which he expected Anthony to read and then personally deliver to the Reverend Bush. Yes, Anthony could continue to court Harriet, but the barb this time was that his father pointed out every one of his son's faults—his gambling, his drinking, his lying, his unmanliness—assuring Harriet's father that his son was an unsuitable suitor. Overjoyed at the permission to continue the relationship, Anthony managed to lose the letter as he rushed to the Bushes—a self-serving accident he was the first to realize.

Returning to Oxford engaged to Harriet, he was a "new man." He got rid of his "expensive friends"—there were no more wine parties, no gambling. He did have gambling debts as well as outstanding bills that came to over four hundred pounds. His generous yearly allowance—worked out between his father and Newman—was little more than half that. Rather than tell his father, who had threatened expulsion, he secretly asked to borrow money from a friend. Then he reluctantly returned to the parsonage for Christmas 1838, writing to Oxford scholar Mark Pattison—five years his senior and the eventual prototype for George Eliot's pedant Casaubon—that he envied his older friend's ability to spend the vacation at college. "There is nothing at all to do at home except read and that I might as well do at Oxford." The "Blue Devils" pursued him at Dartington Parsonage, as he sat there by the fire writing this letter. His "worthy brother" William was sitting next to him, grumpily.

Anthony couldn't imagine what William had to be upset about. He was having a successful engineering career, his mentor the great cigar-chomping and audacious Victorian visionary I. K. Brunel. He had just returned from seeing his fiancée, his father finally allowing the match:

"My impression was that you had heard something of the love affair that hung heavily about William for two years," the archdeacon wrote to Keble. "With a hope that the disappointment might wear away, I have carefully avoided noticing in him the occasional depressions of spirits that I could not fail to observe, and for which I was at no loss for a cause. In herself the Lady is everything a father could approve, and my consent would not have been wanting for a moment but for fears that the malady so sadly manifested in my family, was constitutionally prevalent in hers." But carefully ignoring his son's condition hadn't remedied William's despondency: "My opposition will be withdrawn—all this I have told William in the last few days."

Like his father, William kept his feelings to himself. When he was seventeen, Hurrell, eight years his senior, cautioned: "You know one of the things with which we have always found fault, has been your great closeness about your pursuits, so that we are quite in the dark about you and hardly know you at all."

"I can't get anything out of him," Anthony complained of William to Pattison. Of course he realized "he and my Governor are more or less sulky with me for having spent rather more money than I should have done at Oxford, and accordingly wanting my bills paid." In fact, the archdeacon had found out that behind his back his son had secretly attempted to borrow money from a friend, but Anthony did not confide this: "I am sure I don't wonder at my Governor. Wouldn't I have a rage if a son of mine was to come upon me to pay his bills, but I don't quite consider that brothers have an equal claim to be sulky with one." Actually, William had attempted to mediate: "He is a good fellow, for though he may be rather cool to me, he has talked over my father, and made no end of excuses. Poor me, I was trying what I could do to clear myself last term, but found the attempt hopeless. I don't think any one gains wisdom except by experience, and that is often dearly bought; however, if the Archdeacon will clear me, I shan't do the like again in a hurry, I know."

He could not wait to get back to Oxford: "For here I am the youngest of the family and always shall be if I live to be a hundred." Only in his postscript does a hint of his fear surface beyond the bravado of his tone: "By the bye I heard you had taken your father in hand; how do you get on with the Old Man, is he tough?"

Anthony's Old Man was. Once returned to Oxford, he received the full impact of his father's silent fury, recorded vividly in *Shadows of the Clouds*. One need only take the liberty of changing back the fictive names—that's how close to the skin Anthony's first novella was: "The

Archdeacon Froude throughout the Christmas vacation was gloomy and reserved. Except in the common interchange of morning and evening greetings, he never spoke to Anthony at all, and even the rest of the family could only conjecture what he intended to do. . . . He reserved the expression of his anger till Anthony had returned again to college, and then it began to stream down upon him in letters. Still Anthony went on, kept to his resolution and worked harder and harder. . . . But letter came after letter, each darker than the one before."

The threatening letters might have gone on for a series of months until "came one containing an enclosed copy of what he believed it would be his duty to send," a letter in which he made Harriet's father privy to all of his son's faults. Anthony was sure denunciation was inevitable. Naively and at the same time self-destructively, Anthony copied out his father's harsh letter and then wrote a longer one to the humane Reverend Bush. This remarkably kind man, who saved kittens from drowning no matter the jeers of neighborhood boys, could be approached. To him Anthony was able to reveal his former weaknesses: his gambling, his cowardly lies, his drinking, his lack of purpose, and how he had changed all of that since he met Harriet. The empathetic clergyman was shocked into a severity that equaled the archdeacon's. Harriet was forced not only to break the engagement but swear to her father she would not speak another word to Anthony Froude until she herself was a respectably married woman.

"I am not exaggerating when I say that I was stunned and stupefied almost as if I had been struck by lightening," Anthony wrote a full fifty years later. He suffered a more perplexing breakdown than he had at fourteen when he returned home in tatters from Westminster. Being deprived of Harriet's love left him bitter, self-pitying, and passive: "Months passed by before I could collect myself to throw off the leaden torpor into which I had been plunged."

He fled Oxford. His father sent William after him, and William, eight years older than Anthony and recently married, found him sulking in a small room in Jersey: "One thing which by all accounts seems to dwell much in Anthony's mind," William explained to the archdeacon, "and which probably encourages him in his want of openness, is the notion that he is treated by us all as a child; and this notion makes him stuffy at home and break out into wildness elsewhere—perhaps a younger son *is* a little liable to be thus treated, and especially one who like Anthony has never done much in proof of manliness—and indeed one hardly knows how to treat him as a man."

Anthony himself was deeply conscious that his outward amiability among his friends—such as his nonchalant letter to Pattison—did not disclose what he thought was "perhaps" his "real self," reflected in his shameful fear of his father.

William reported to Keble that Anthony refused to return to his father's home and would battle it out in his own way. "He seems indeed sorry; & aware that he is not what he must acknowledge he ought to be, but he seems more sorry about the *discomfort* of being under a cloud, than as the *cause* of it."

Both Keble and William advised him to read his brother's *Remains:* "He tells me, he has read Hurrell's journal, sometime ago. I trust that when he does so again it may be with more seriousness & attention—but it seems to me that every time one reads ineffectually what ought to stir one to exertion, one's mind becomes less capable of being acted upon by it."

Anthony's refusal to return to Dartington Parsonage ended in a compromise. He went instead to Bristol, where William, chief engineer on the Bristol and Exeter Railway, was living with his new wife. There he made a decision to find solitary quarters somewhere, study hard, and eventually become independent of his family by taking pupils. William found there were many things Anthony said that showed he wished to improve his character, but he was shocked by his brother's resolution to cut completely from their father. Deliverance came in the form of a letter—not from Keble, or anyone in his family, but from a friend, one who Anthony had assumed would agree with him and offer him support. William supposed:

"The writer must be a very clever manly sort of fellow, who however has not lived as he felt he ought, but who has lately been thinking more seriously of his own position—He seemed to think A's resolution so shocking—& his ways of thinking of himself so unmanly, & expressed his thoughts so well & kindly, that coming as it did from an unexpected quarter his reproof produced a very remarkable effect & as far as one can judge, a most happy one—And in consequence A. immediately began by doing that which was the first thing to be done—he wrote a very proper letter to my Father making full submission; & stating his intention, with full mistrust of his power of adequately performing it, to do whatever he should order."

Within the week the archdeacon abruptly replied to Anthony's long letter: "Return thither next Friday."

"He showed me the letter," William commented. "My Father *appeared* to speak—more roughly—less kindly rather, than I know he feels." But that was always the case between the archdeacon and youngest son.

If Hurrell's *Remains* did nothing to engage Anthony, the advice of Hurrell's former tutor John Keble was silently resented. He would never see in Keble the brilliance he found in Hurrell and Newman. In his classic memoir of the Oxford Movement, "The Oxford Counter-Reformation," written years later, in 1881, Anthony would record: "I remember an instance of Keble's narrowness extremely characteristic of him. A member of a family with which he had been intimate had adopted Liberal opinions in theology. Keble probably did not know what those opinions were but regarded this person as an apostate who had sinned against light. He came to call one day when the erring brother happened to be at home; and learning that he was in the house, he refused to enter, and remained sitting in the porch." The insult was not erased by the passing of time.

But return thither to his father Anthony did in the late 1830s. At Dartington Parsonage one cold night, "I went out into the wood and in the darkness walked up and down, reviewing my past life, observing where I had laid myself open to the enemy, and determined to defy him." (Lest we forget, "the enemy" in the nineteenth-century sense was the devil.) While still feeling the leaden effects of the loss of Harriet's love, which led to suicidal urges, that night in the woods he came to his resolution. "I had trifled with life. I would trifle with it no longer. I would not be a slave, a pipe for Fortune's finger to sound what note she pleased upon. There may have been something stilted in this, but it was real, too, for it did represent a definite turning point in my small history."

Anthony's rebellion from his father made him lose precious time at Oxford. The first-class degree that he had "faintly" dreamed of while courting Harriet was beyond hope, but he did better than the authorities expected and "got a fair second, and was made to feel that in future competitions I might still recover my place." In *Shadows* he recorded, "He was learning, not for college honours, but to *know;* to make himself a man, and to raise himself above the beings whose play thing he had been so long."

Except for William with a first in mathematics, Hurrell and Anthony, like the archdeacon himself, placed a fair second. Still, Anthony's promise was noted and Newman, spokesperson for his father, encouraged him to wait on at Oxford after graduation, until a fellowship opened.

The whole system Anthony was born to presupposed he would become a clergyman, as his father and Hurrell before him. To enter

Oxford in those days one must be a member of the Church of England and must subscribe to the Thirty-Nine Articles of that church. To stay on after graduation as a fellow, one must eventually take deacon's orders, for a fellowship at Oxford was the first step in a clerical career.

For an educated man who had to make his own living, there were, as Anthony phrased it in *The Nemesis of Faith,* only three professions, "the three black Graces": A man could become a lawyer, a doctor, or a professional clergyman. It was a man's world Anthony was born into, but when gender determines destiny, not only women are thwarted. Gentlemen, too, had their options narrowly channeled.

It was usual for aspirants to fellowship to stay at the university until a vacancy opened up, supporting themselves by tutoring, but as Anthony phrased it, an accident threw a tutorship in Ireland his way, which he preferred. As he prepared to travel, brother John, who hated the practice of law and was threatening to follow his drinking buddy, famed animal painter Edwin Henry Landseer, into a life of art, lay dying.

John was the third son, but as usual it was the fourth son, William, who acted as the conciliator in the family. William Froude inherited from his father not only silence in adversity, but a defined sense of duty. It was he who obtained a leave from his work to return to Dartington Parsonage, and as his father wrote to Keble, "by his unremitting and affectionate attention he did all that could be done to spare me from fatigue and give ease to his brother." John died in March 1841, leaving the archdeacon with only his two youngest sons and his oldest daughter: "Dear Margaret too took her share of nursing & bore all with her usual fortitude." Even after Margaret married, she stayed by her father, while bringing yet another writer into the family, her son, William Hurrell Mallock, born in 1849, the year his uncle Anthony published *The Nemesis of Faith.*

With the loss of his fifth child to tuberculosis, the archdeacon did express his grief, admitting to more than an ordinary share of afflictions: "Each successive blow reviving the recollection and suffering of former ones have indeed borne heavily upon me, but I thank God that I have learnt in this severe school to bow to his will. To me the day is fast approaching when all that has given joy here will be as nothing."

In the same letter to Keble, the old man's thoughts, characteristically, turned to Anthony, who he wrote had the good fortune to be recommended to the Reverend Cleaver in Ireland as a tutor to his son, preparing for Oxford. It was a prestigious position in a very good family; the Reverend Cleaver's father was the Lord Archbishop of Dublin: "My fear is that they may overrate him & so feed the conceit that wants to be subdued."

Off Anthony sailed to Ireland. The archdeacon perhaps would have been less approving had he known how evangelical the Cleavers' household was. In this happy family, religion spoke to the individual heart—directly! Revelation was accepted as personal reality. "Christ was with us and about us," benevolently present. "There was no narrowness."

Anthony, personally, had never been in contact with a man like Cleaver, knowing evangelicals only through Hurrell's ridicule, and through the itinerant representatives of Bible societies that occasionally knocked at the parsonage door. There was no copy of Bunyan's *Pilgrim's Progress* in his father's library, and Anthony, future author of *Bunyan,* didn't read him until he was grown. Evangelical Protestants were regarded as amiable but silly people without learning, judgment, or accurate knowledge—"generally ridiculous." For Anglicans the practical commands of religion were accepted as rules of life, but religion itself was seldom spoken of directly. Tract 80 itself reiterated that religious subjects ought not to be generally talked about.

Now for the first time Anthony was exposed to what he considered "a purely spiritual religion," where the teachings of the New Testament were adopted as principles of life that were carried into the everyday details, into ordinary thoughts and actions. The Bible itself was openly discussed and was interpreted according to individual understanding. "My residence with Mr. Cleaver produced an indelible effect upon me." Anthony, though still basically a Tractarian, would never again believe that "the grace of God was confined to the ministrations of the Catholic Church," as his brother and Newman taught.

While Anthony was tutoring in Ireland, Newman published Tract 90, in which he ascertained that the Thirty-Nine Articles of the Church of England could be reconciled with Roman Catholic doctrine. It was vehemently censured as popery. Newman's audacious leaps of logic caused even more controversy than the publication of Hurrell's *Remains.* "It was considered dishonest, and its author was spoken of in terms which I could not bear to hear. I ventured to say that Newman was incapable of dishonesty, that whatever his opinions he was a pure and saintly person."

Anthony went further, explaining to the Reverend Cleaver that it was a historical fact that during Henry VIII's reign, the liturgy and the articles were constructed in a way that would allow both Catholics and Protestants to attend the same church services. Though he was historically correct, it was too dangerous a view to be accepted in Ireland, where Protestants and Catholics stood as irreconcilable antagonists. It was considered a great threat in England as well, and those who said Newman was a Roman Catholic in disguise now had their proof, considering Tract 90 the most blatant sophistry. Newman would soon be forced to step down from the ministry of St. Mary's Church, Oxford.

Although Anthony's Tractarian beliefs were modified through his exposure to the Reverend Cleaver and his evangelical household, he rigorously defended Newman's position. This is a good example of why he never could escape controversy. Froude was as capable of explaining the benefits of evangelical Protestantism to Newman (who had fled it), as he was of defending John Henry Newman's radical Anglo-Catholicism to Cleaver. His Oxford-trained mind constantly incorporated or shifted among the many sides of the same issue, which in itself might not be considered a character flaw. But to defend Tract 90 to Irish Protestants showed an almost constitutional inability to look ahead to consequences. "Mr. Cleaver very naturally was unwilling to leave his son in my hands, and it was decided, though I believe with mutual regret, that we should part."

Characteristic of Anthony to believe he and Mr. Cleaver parted with mutual regret. Maybe they did, maybe they didn't. Amiable Anthony, always careless of the effect of his words on others, went merrily on his way, making a short tour of Ireland before returning to the Cleavers, packing up, and going home. He was not about to leave Ireland ahead of his ward, for then his father would know he'd been sacked. As it was, his tour allowed the archdeacon to remain in the dark, the archdeacon informing Keble that his son was returning to England with the Cleaver boy, who was about to enter Oxford.

Right before leaving Ireland, Anthony described what he called a memorable incident. At Bray, a few miles from the Cleavers', Dr. Edward Pusey and his children were vacationing. Pusey, Newman, and Keble were the three most prominent Tractarians, "the triumvirs who became a national force, and gave its real character to the Oxford movement." Hurrell, of course, had been at the start of the movement, "the foremost of the party; the flame." Dr. Pusey had known Mr. Cleaver years ago when both were undergraduates at Christ Church. Anthony called on the vacationing Pusey. "I begged him in Mr. Cleaver's name to come over and dine with him. He came rather unwillingly."

At the dinner there was another guest, Robert Daly, who used Pusey's presence as an occasion to thunder out vehemently against the Tractarians.

Pusey said little and let the storm roll by. Anthony helped out by amiably directing Daly's wrath toward himself and his own Anglo-Catholic position. But when Daly extolled Martin Luther's break from the Roman Catholic priesthood, Pusey could no longer contain himself and said he could not submit his judgment to Martin Luther, a man who had not only broken his own vows but had induced a nun to break hers! With that Daly thumped his fist down hard enough to make the dinner table jump. "Sir, I declare before Heaven it was a vow more honoured in breach than in the observance."

Pusey had just about enough and fled as soon as he could, probably regretting that he had allowed the young Froude to convince him to attend. Daly followed, and at the head of the stairs shouted out after him, "We are glad to see you here, Dr. Pusey. We respect your learning and your character, but we want no more Popery, Dr. Pusey, no more Popery. We have enough of our own."

Anthony returned to Oxford in 1842 to find that Tract 90—Newman's bold attempt to reunite the Anglican Church with earlier Catholic practice—had filled the air with electricity. Still, the Oxford Movement by then had its own head of steam and was sweeping with it the most brilliant of Anthony's generation—Anthony included. His own impulse was still to go along with it, and Newman's personality would have recovered its complete hold over him had not the evangelical Protestantism that he experienced in Ireland held him back—somewhat.

As he recalled so many years later in his remarkable "The Oxford Counter-Reformation," it was Newman the man who was so attractive to him and to so many of Anthony's generation. In Newman they met a human being whose mind was all-encompassing. He was interested in everything that went on in science, politics, literature. There was nothing narrow about him, and he had a genius when it came to relating to young men. At St. Mary's, Anthony and his classmates had heard him preach in that gentle, low voice, Sunday after Sunday. He would take a character from scripture and through him speak to the students "about ourselves, our temptations, our experiences." He seemed to address the most secret consciousness of all his listeners. When he spoke of Christ on the cross, the Crucifixion itself was as palatable to the congregation as it was to the priest who evoked it. Newman never exaggerated, he never was "unreal," he never talked just to be smart or witty. "He was lightness itself—the lightness of elastic strength." He told the students what he believed. "He did not know where it would carry him." It eventually carried him over to Rome. But before Newman left the Church of England, *Credo in Newmannum*—belief in Newman—had been the call of Anthony's generation. Anthony was convinced that as a young man he had been more a Newmanite than a Tractarian.

By the time he returned from Ireland another mind was influencing him as well. By then he was reading Thomas Carlyle: *History of the French Revolution; On Heroes, Hero-Worship and the Heroic in History; Past and Present.* "Emerson followed and I found myself addressed by thinkers of a power and earnestness at least equal to the most brilliant of the Churchmen, with this difference: that I was no longer referred to books and distant centuries but to present facts and the world in which I lived and breathed."

The old ways were obsolete. One could not rely on the outdated, outward forms of traditional Christianity, Carlyle wrote. New clothes were needed for old truths. The great gifted men of every generation had the ability to see the truth manifest in the life around them and speak of it in their own terms, dressed in the garb of their times. "The natural, Carlyle said, was the supernatural; the supernatural, the natural."

"The question which Carlyle asked of every institution, secular or religious, was not, Is it true? but Is it alive? Truth can be but one." But truth is clothed differently at different times and in different places; one could find it "in the Norse Gods, in Mahomet, in Luther and Knox." No one institution encompasses it for all times.

Carlyle was writing about transcendental thought, about German literature, but "Oxford knew nothing of Goethe, knew nothing of modern languages outside of England. Even of English literature it was in almost absolute ignorance." Oxford was completely invested in theology, and to Oxford, Anthony returned. In the spring he won the highly prestigious Chancellor's Prize for an English essay—he wrote about the influence of political economy on the development of nations. In the summer he was elected (Devonshire) Fellow of Exeter. If he had been wise enough to continue where this path led, he later recalled, he would have had an easy road before him.

For of the "three black Graces," the clerical profession was still the most compatible, especially for someone like Anthony, who was now a fellow and preferred no other way of life. The caveat was that to maintain a fellowship at Oxford, one had eventually to take deacon's orders. He knew that his Carlylean ideas and doubts made him an unlikely candidate for eventual priesthood, yet he was able to rationalize. The established Church of England was a *national* institution, as well as being a "profession" for many a young man. A voluntary religious community might expect its members and clergy to agree with all its doctrines. But a church established by law, like the Church of England, could not expect universal agreement with a specific and narrow interpretation of its tenets. It intentionally demanded "latitude." Many of his fellows had the same religious doubts as he but accepted ordination in that spirit. These fortunate men "never repented at all, and rose to deaneries and bishoprics."

However, by starting out on that convenient road without real conviction, in order to become an Oxford scholar, Anthony made what he considered—and which was—*the* great mistake of his life. Rationalizing that the extreme broadness of the Anglican Church would allow him his increasing religious doubts, he took deacon's orders and became the Reverend J. A. Froude. He remained a fellow, tutoring students, reading, thinking, and assisting Newman in researching and writing *Lives of the English Saints*.

As he proved in Ireland, Anthony had an enormous respect for Newman, whom he would always consider one of the two great geniuses of his century—Carlyle the other. And, indelible for Anthony, Newman had been *kind* to him. Anthony later understood that the concern was offhanded—a debt to the archdeacon, a testimony to his undying love of Hurrell, a token of his abiding friendship with William. Still, it remained significant for Anthony, who knew no kindness in his early years, and as a result he would always be able to separate his great admiration for the man from his growing disagreement with almost everything Newman came to represent. Newman could not return the favor. To him Anthony would become as reprehensible in the future as he was irksome during the Oxford years.

Anthony was to write on Saint Patrick and Saint Neot for *Lives of the English Saints*. By then, Newman was living in nearby Littlemore among a group of young male acolytes. Mark Pattison described the scene in his *Memoirs:* "Newman had bought some land at Littlemore, and turned a row of single-roomed cottages into cells connected by a sort of cloister; had built a library for his very considerable collection of patristic literature, and got some of his young disciples to join him in a kind of semimonastic life." The place came to be nicknamed the Monastery. Froude could have gone to speak with Newman there or spoken with him when he came to Oxford, but in many ways he remained shy of the great man, though he certainly spoke his mind in many a letter.

He wrote that he despaired of making a historical case either for Saint

Neot or any of the Alfred legends connected with him. What he proposed doing was to throw all the legends together. He would state the
truth, that all anyone knew of Saint Neot and his miracles (including his
sweet-smelling corpse) was the tradition of his monastery, recorded a
hundred years after the saint's death. What he planned to do was to
bring the accounts at his disposal together in a way that gave a sort of
"poetical justification rather than an historical one." Which in fact he did.

"I suppose now," Froude wrote in his memoir of the movement
forty years later, that the object of *Lives of the English Saints* was "to recommend asceticism, and perhaps to show that the power of working
miracles had been continued in the Church until its unity was broken.
But no such intention was communicated to us." For Anthony, joining
the project was an opportunity to throw himself into a study of medieval
literature and to glean from the monks' accounts what human life had
really been like in England during a period only visible to the contemporary in what remained of medieval churches and monastic ruins.
No doubt Carlyle's *Past and Present,* with its dynamically imaginative
presentation of that lost world, was also an inspiration to him.

His study of the saints' lives quickly led him to a tangle of perplexities.
The accounts of miracles were recorded gravely as real facts, without
grace or imagination. "The sublime and ridiculous mixed together
indiscriminately, with the ridiculous largely predominating. Was it possible that such stuff could be true? or even intended to be taken for truth?
Was it not rather mere edifying reading for the monks' refectories; the
puerile absurdities thrown in to amuse innocently their dreary hours?"

He could only justify these accounts by realizing that "There is a class
of composition which is not history, and is not conscious fiction—it was
produced in old times; it is produced in our times; it will be produced
wherever and as long as society exists—something which honestly
believes itself to be fact, and is created, nevertheless, by the imagination."
These stories were actually legends, never examined carefully because
it would be sin to doubt them. "For an intending biographer this was a
serious discovery."

He couldn't repeat what he found in the saints' lives, for he hadn't the
faith to believe these stories. Many years later a spiritualist would tell him
that he himself could work a miracle if he had faith. "But, alas! I had
none." The life of Saint Patrick caused him inner turmoil as it presented unsurmountable obstacles. He could not believe that Saint Patrick
once lit a fire with icicles, changed a Welsh man into a wolf, or floated to
Ireland on an altar stone. "I thought it nonsense." He wondered if there

really was a Saint Patrick or if "Patricius" was actually a medieval title rather than the name of a single man. Although he did complete the life of Saint Neot, he soon realized Newman's project would have to go on without him. Still, having come in contact with the actual primary records intensified his religious doubts. "I was compelled to see that in certain conditions of mind the distinction between objective and subjective truth has no existence."

It brought him to a clear understanding that there were several kinds of truth. The abstract truth of pure mathematics, the psychological truth of a drama like *Hamlet,* the edifying truth of a moral tale. He also presaged the truth that Jung would elucidate, "of a legend which has sprung up involuntarily out of the hearts of a number of people, and therefore represents something in their own minds."

Finally, however, there was the "dull truth of plain experienced fact, which has to be painfully sifted out by comparison of evidence, by observation, and, when possible, by experiment." These facts were not absolutes but at all times open to revision and correction. This was forgotten by the hagiologists. "It is forgotten, for that matter, by most historians." It would never be forgotten by J. A. Froude, who would pay a great price in late-Victorian England for *not* turning Thomas Carlyle's pilgrimage on this earth into a saint's life.

Not only was Saint Patrick giving Anthony pause, many strange reports about Newman were flying about Oxford. "I do not know whether I have any right to say what I am going to say. I am afraid you will think me impertinent," Anthony wrote to him. People were saying that *Lives of the English Saints* was intended to lead them away from the Church of England. Anthony assured these critics that "the Author of them" had no idea of leaving the Anglican faith. Still, he couldn't account for his own misgivings: "I have no wish to intrude where I have no business—only am I at liberty in what I write to take my own line? I cannot write a Life of St Patrick without at best taking some notice of the present state of the work he has left behind him. Am I allowed to regard the question as I have always been taught to regard it? If not, I had rather not go on. I had rather avoid expressing a different opinion till I have a better right to have formed one. I cannot go straight unless I know the point to which I am bound. You have always been so very kind to me, that I am sure you will forgive me if I have said anything I ought not."

On the same day, November 9, 1844, Newman replied—but not easily. The draft of the letter at the Birmingham Oratory is filled with

34

scratched-out sentences and illegible reconsiderations, but it begins clearly enough: "My dear Anthony, You have no need to apologize for your note. I am an Editor, I have no direct control over the series of Lives of the Saints." Twenty years later Newman printed a clear draft of the letter in his *Apologia pro Vita Sua,* without disclosing to whom it was addressed. It stated, "I think the engagement between you and me should come to an end."

And twenty years after that he'd write in a private letter: "Froude I never took to." In "1844, he accused me of trying indirectly by means of the Lives of the Saints to hook him into the Tractarian party." Newman neither forgot nor forgave Anthony. Yet Anthony's concern was certainly not unfounded. For eleven months later, convinced the Church of England was in schism and that the Church of Rome was the *only* path to salvation, Newman did leave the Church of England. On October 9, 1845, he converted to Roman Catholicism. Fourteen months after that, in the Rome he once traveled to with Hurrell Froude and the Venerable Archdeacon of Totnes, John Henry Newman became a Roman Catholic priest.

The ensuing scandal appeared to justify those who accused Newman of being a Roman Catholic all along, and the Oxford Movement—or at least the first wave of it—collapsed around Newman's defection. Hurrell had once told Anthony and William that they would be free to go their own way on religious matters on that inconceivable day when Newman and Keble disagreed. When Newman went over to Rome, that day arrived.

Anthony thought of leaving Oxford. There were, after all, two black Graces left. Brother John had been a lawyer, but hated it. Perhaps medical school was an option; the new University College in London was nonsectarian. He spoke to his superiors but they told him it was impossible. Anthony had taken a fellowship, had "dipped his hand in Church ink" by becoming a deacon. The law of his country proclaimed that once a young man entered the Church of England, even before committing himself to priest's orders, all other learned professions were closed to him—permanently.

The Victorian age is often characterized as the time of great religious doubt, a time when the best and brightest turned away from the church. What is ignored or perhaps not understood is that in giving up a clerical life, a young, talented man such as Anthony gave up the chance of a professional life as well. Taking a fellowship, which included deacon's orders, was a legal as well as a religious commitment. An educated young man who changed his mind about becoming a clergyman had a perilous road ahead of him, particularly if he had to earn his own living. Many folded, just relied on the broadness of the church, and went on to clerical positions though they did not believe. Others became wanderers, outsiders, condemned to the fringes of society, plagued by religious insecurities in the way later generations would be plagued by existential ones.

Others became authors. "The men that write books, Carlyle says, are now the world's priests, the spiritual directors of mankind." In *The Nemesis of Faith,* Anthony's protagonist will exclaim, "Oh! how I wish I could write. I try sometimes; for I seem to feel myself overflowing with thoughts, and I cry out to be relieved of them. But it is so stiff and miserable when I get anything done. What seemed so clear and liquid, comes out so thick, stupid, and frostbitten. . . . Still, if there was a chance for me! To be an author—to make my thoughts the law of other minds!—to form a link, however humble, a real living link, in the electric chain which conducts the light of the ages!"

Staying on as fellow, Anthony tried his hand at writing essays. Then, at the age of twenty-seven, he wrote *Shadows of the Clouds* under the pseudonym Zeta. The brutal upbringing of Edward Fowler was narrated by an older and wiser tutor, and since Anthony looked at his life from this seemingly dispassionate point of view, he made the mistake of believing the moral and psychological overvoice he brought to his work turned the subjective into the universal. Canon Fowler could have been many a boy's severe, old-fashioned clergyman of a father. True enough. Yet he was also, without a shred of a doubt, the Venerable Archdeacon of Totnes.

Two things are extraordinary in Anthony's first fiction: its realistic depiction of physical punishment both at home and at school in the early Victorian period, and its plea to the fathers for psychological insight. *Shadows of the Clouds* contained Anthony's first love song to his distant father, perverse, perhaps, but still a plea for understanding.

For all its personal detail—or perhaps *because* of all its personal detail— it struck a chord in his society. It offered a startling reevaluation of the accustomed relationship between father and son: "If fathers could but know, or could but let themselves be taught, how many sleepless nights of anxiety they would save themselves—how many a naturally well-intentioned child they would save from sorrow and suffering and guilt, by but taking the trouble now and then to find a few kind words to express the real kindness which in their hearts they feel!" One kind, hearty word and our hero, tears in his eyes, would throw himself at his father's feet, "and his pains would have been at an end forever." The book caused the future George Eliot "a sort of palpitation that one hardly knew whether to call wretched or delightful." Its author was one of the "greater ones."

The all-knowing Benjamin Jowett, a year older than Anthony and a Balliol tutor at the time, considered the book well worth reading and instructive. "The purport of the book is to show that although in sermons etc we speak of man as a responsible free agent, yet there is another side of this truth not to be forgotten that he is under the dominion of circumstances too e.g. his education, the misunderstanding of his disposition by his friends etc." Though the book gave him a great interest in its author, Jowett wished certain personal things had been left out. "It is so very obviously the life of Froude that there is no mistaking it—the want of delicacy is certainly a great flaw in the book." If someone his own age considered the book indiscreet, one can only imagine the reaction of the archdeacon, who was cast as the severe, remote, threatening, punishing clergyman who sent his son to Westminster, where he was tortured, threatened to apprentice him to a trade, and did not allow him the woman he loved: "It is always the same, he cares for none of us. I believe he would think himself well rid of us if we were dead."

From a biographical point of view, the book is extraordinarily illuminating in that the upbringing of Ned Fowler differs from Anthony's lived life only in the characters' names. From a historical point of view, it pinpoints the abuses of public school education and the relationship of father and son with an accuracy and lack of restraint unparalleled at that time.

For years the archdeacon and William, as well as the ubiquitous Keble, kept urging Anthony to read and reread Hurrell's *Remains.* These journals of Hurrell's, which the archdeacon enthusiastically published, were a daily, uncensored, fluctuating account of a morbid young man's thoughts, sins, prayers, mistakes, fasts, feelings. The archdeacon considered the *Remains* a saint's life, though many in England were scandalized by Hurrell's unbridled, Romanish confessions. That unsparing psychological focus on one's flawed self, which Hurrell inherited from his mother, is evident all through the *Remains,* and one sees it as well in *Shadows of the Clouds.* Had Hurrell been a novelist, he probably would have been as confessional as Anthony.

Benjamin Jowett realized the connection between the brothers and quipped quite perceptively that he was actually reading a new edition of "Froude's remains." In a sense, that was what both of Anthony's early novels were. The self-revealing, confessional aspects of *Shadows* capture the whisper of the mother's voice as amplified through the unflinching consciousness of the oldest brother. One doubts Anthony's father read it that way. The archdeacon was as closemouthed and severe as ever, as he bought up every copy of *Shadows of the Clouds* he could find in order to get it off the market.

Meanwhile, at Oxford, Anthony's unpublished letters to the rector of Exeter College show him not as the hero of a new day but equivocating, denying, wiggling out from under the accusation that he was, in fact, the Zeta who wrote *Shadows of the Clouds*. Affable, smiling Anthony was reacting to the rector as if the head of the college were his father, one he did not want to lose. The rector had always been *kind* to him, had always appreciated his genius.

Anthony answered the accusations against him too cleverly by half, in an Oxford-speak that allowed him to deny authorship of *Shadows* at the same time as he wiggled out of taking further religious vows—priest's orders—*because* of the erroneous accusation. The italics are mine, added to pinpoint dancing angels.

"I have seen the Book to which you refer, & several reviews of it," he wrote to the rector. "I cannot say I think they have any of them given the true Idea of the Book and *if I had written it* I should not think it inconsistent in me to apply for Testimonials for the priest's orders."

However, "I could easily conceive an objection might be felt toward the author of such a book; and *what I should do in case it was so, would be what I do now* in the present instance, that is, withdraw the application [for priest's orders] which I made to you."

Somehow Rector Richards chose not to see through Anthony's lies—that Anthony was Zeta (brother Hurrell and Newman had written poetry, *Lyra Apostolica*, together as Beta) was as plain as the nose on his face. He smoothed things over with letters to the more outraged former fellows, and Anthony, in his late twenties, was reprimanded yet allowed to stay at Oxford, as long as he denied authorship, which he had to do in writing:

"As I am not aware that anything in my conduct has been matter of scandal or prejudice to the college, I can only thank you for your admonition and trust it will always be as little necessary as it is at present. You have my full authority for saying that *no Bookseller or other person has any right to give the authorship of the book you speak of to me.*"

The equivocations in these unpublished letters point to the fact that Anthony's first venture as an author did little to correct the moral cowardice that he portrayed so vividly in it. Instead, as Zeta, Anthony did somersaults on the head of a pin, retained his fellowship, and avoided taking the inevitable priest's orders.

"I had much talk with Emerson. I told him that he was in part responsible for my present state of mind, that I thought of giving up my profession and my fellowship. He did not advise. He did not dissuade, but characteristically he urged the propriety of doing nothing in a hurry. He recommended me to study the Vedas. I should find myself on a mountain peak from which I could look round and down on the turmoils and troubles of the lower world. I asked him if anything would grow on those mountain peaks. It did not seem to be of such importance to him whether anything would grow or not."

The mountain peak Froude chose was Killarney. He returned to southern Ireland and far from the locale of his discontent, like Thoreau (who sent him books); deeply inspired by conversations with Emerson and the writings of Carlyle, he obeyed the impulses of what both of these mentors called the inner man. Out of his moral morass came *The Nemesis of Faith,* or as Arthur Clough phrased it, "a new book of religious biography—auto or otherwise." For Anthony, the writing of the book itself brought him extraordinary relief. With it came psychological clarity. "I had thrown off the weight under which I had been staggering. I was free, able to encounter the realities of life without vexing myself further over the unanswerable problems." The book presented an exact picture of his own mind. "It was a mood, not a treatise."

"When the manuscript was completed I left my Killarney hermitage and went back to Oxford, but I had by this time made up my mind that Oxford was no longer the place for me; not Oxford nor indeed England, for I could not go on with my profession. If I was to begin a new life, it must be in some freer country, where the then unpardonable stain of relinquishing orders was not held to be so heinous."

He wrote to friend Charles Kingsley not to hold against him that he was thinking of retreating from England and hiding out in the colonies. There was a school being started at Hobart Town and he had applied for a position. If he was accepted, he'd teach for a few years and then quietly become a settler. He had few prospects in England, and he would eventually be glad of the change. He acknowledged that leaving England was cowardice and selfishness before Charles had a chance to make the accusation. Still, he wanted to give up his fellowship, he wanted to drop the *Reverend* from his name. He confessed to *hating* the Thirty-Nine Articles of the Church of England. He told the rector himself that he hated chapel. He had to make a living somehow and he couldn't do it at home because of his clerical disability.

Anthony was not the only doubt-ridden young man of his generation who looked to the colonies for a new path, who wished to "quietly slide into a settler." His friend the poet Arthur Clough dreamed of going off with him. And a few years later, Robert Browning, whose best friend Alfred Domett had abruptly left for New Zealand in 1842, would write *Bishop Blougram's Apology,* a long poem in which the cure for a self-conscious and doubting literary man would be to pick up his farming tools and emigrate. The colonies in the 1840s were perceived by many a young man as a way past the confines of the three black Graces and the dogmas of their national church toward a brave new world, where one would be able to find useful work and escape fruitless speculation.

During Christmas recess, Anthony was back at Dartington Parsonage, where he found the archdeacon willing to finance his emigration to Tasmania. "I sail in the middle of March for Van Diemen's Land, the land of green trees, and opossums, of kangaroos and cherry trees, whose fruit grows inside out."

Froude's break from Oxford was hardly the complete rebellion of a free mind that it has been made out to be. Unpublished letters, as well as the Yearly Register of Exeter College, point to Anthony's shifts and turns, the confusion and immaturity below his surface of certainty. There was a painful callowness that he, in certain moods, was the first to acknowledge. Even after *The Nemesis of Faith* was published, after he left the high table where we first found him watching the fire that earlier that day consumed his novel, he continued to write to the rector of Exeter, as one might to a father, explaining, edifying, always hoping that if enough ink flowed the older man would *understand* his book and the crises of faith rampant among the younger generation.

Still, *The Nemesis of Faith* was a farewell to the road he was expected to take. And he ensured himself against backtracking. This time he would not allow himself the temptation of signing himself Zeta; he would sign his name and his Oxford affiliation to it. The book was to be a revolution in itself, but such a book by a deacon of the church, by an archdeacon's son, by Hurrell Froude's brother!

The rector had a board and alumni to contend with. Word of *Nemesis* circulated before publication, and right after Ash Wednesday services in 1849, Edward Hawkins, provost of Oriel College, rushed to find it, read the first eighty pages and some pages at the end of the book, and breathlessly report its contents to the worried rector.

The big question was whether Froude held the ideas of his protagonist Markham Sutherland. Froude seemed to. But Hawkins had skimmed and still hoped it was not so. Sutherland denied the divinity of Jesus Christ. He disputed the goodness of a God cruel enough to subject man to an eternal hell. In fact, he denied eternal future punishment for man's sins, in the manner of Thomas Paine and Lord Byron. Hawkins thought it best to send the book to the rector without delay, before it was published. Whatever the rector decided to do would be wise and Christian.

The hero of the novel was indeed like Anthony, a man of the cloth who no longer believed in the divinity of Jesus Christ or the exclusivity of Christianity as the only way to salvation. But they differed in an essential respect. Sutherland, with all these doubts, went on to take priest's orders, and his ensuing tragedy was a cautionary tale. Anthony's novel of 1849 was a defining moment of the times, exposing and articulating the religious and professional doubts felt by an entire generation. It was also heresy.

"What I have written I have written," Anthony responded coolly at first to the rector's inquiry. But in the next line he equivocated, apparently leaving his fate in the rector's hands: "If you think it convenient now you are quite at liberty to say on Monday that I have ceased to be a Fellow of the College. Yours as much as you will let me be, J.A. Froude."

There were those in the college and among the alumni who would have refused Froude the privilege of resigning. Some would have had a public trial, prosecuted him for perjury, for willful violation of the terms of his oath. Lawyers were consulted. They advised that perjury would not be easy to prove. Letter after letter was written and received by the rector on the subject of legal prosecution. He informed Anthony that responsibility for resignation was Anthony's, not his. There was nothing the rector was "at liberty to say on Monday": "In regard to the act of resigning your fellowship, I do not feel that I can in my situation offer you any opinion."

"I am sorry my ignorance of the proper form to be observed should have caused you further inconvenience," Anthony replied tersely and handed in a formal resignation. The same day it was received, the rector responded in kind that Anthony had "ceased to be a Fellow of the Coll."

But the business still wasn't finished. Only eleven days later, on March 10, 1849, could the rector write: "I have removed your name, agreeably by your request from the book of the College. It is most painful to me not to be able to say that I regret severing the last of the ties that have connected us. I would add more, but I do not feel equal to writing more—& saying all I wish to say to you."

By then the scandal had gone beyond Oxford. The British newspapers had picked it up and there was a media storm—"dust storm," Anthony called it—about such a blasphemer being allowed to teach in the colonies. On the same day on which the rector accepted his resignation, Anthony, about to clear out of Oxford, made the mistake of responding to press criticism, writing to the *Morning Herald* in a most indignant manner: "Sir, I have seen an article in your paper reflecting in no measured language on my appointment to a school in Van Diemen's Land. You have not read my book (at least I hope you have not); you have contented yourself with the extracts you have seen in a newspaper, and unwisely committed yourself to adopt its comments. My book is a book of pure fiction." He demanded an apology.

Fleet Street was not impressed. Froude's letter "proves very fully that he did not study casuistry under Mr. Newman for nothing." His words were nothing more than "the old Tractarian shuffle, taught and practiced in Mr. Newman's school." The book is *not* a fiction, it's a collection of fragments, impossible to read without realizing it as "a sketch of the author's own mind, a *manual of infidelity*."

The very integrity of the new University College, London, which sponsored Anthony's Tasmania appointment was questioned. The daily press allowed Anthony no wiggle room; the Hobart School offer was withdrawn. There was going to be no new home for the infidel in the land of opossums, kangaroos, and peculiarly constructed cherry trees.

Anthony was anxious to see the rector before quitting Oxford; in more than one letter he expressed his desire to return his keys and pick up his twenty-one-shilling deposit in person, so that he could shake the rector's hand before departing. He could not grasp the rector's refusal to see him. And once exiled from Oxford, Anthony still attempted to explain his work to him—to *enlighten* the older man: "The Hero is evidently from his very first Introduction a weak, if amiable man, and I wished to paint such a man struggling in the element of scepticism which (however older men may be ignorant of it) is, since Carlyle has written, the element in which all young men have moved."

He wanted the rector of Exeter College to understand that faith in God existed in Carlyle's work, and in all the really powerful literature of the day. In fact this retailoring of old truths by contemporary authors was more inspiring and offered young men better solutions to spiritual difficulties than the Church of England.

In *Nemesis,* Sutherland's mind was destroyed because the Church of England gave him no solution to his intellectual difficulties concerning specific doctrine. The conclusion that could fairly be drawn from his book, Anthony informed the rector, was that either the Church of England must offer a "more comprehensive philosophy of the Bible" or its strict theory of "Infallibility" must be given up. Above all, human duty and faith in God must rest on a broader and deeper basis than that of authority and tradition. If not, "the fate of M Sutherland will be the fate of thousands."

Anthony's novel was a cautionary tale, written as he struggled with the possibility of taking priest's orders himself, though like the protagonist of his epistolary novel, he no longer believed in Christ's divinity or in the exclusivity of Anglican salvation.

He was quite aware of the responsibility of writing such a book—and that the rector might consider it particularly presumptuous for a Froude to have written it. "But I felt what was in me, & I could not choose but say it. And nothing which has happened since & nothing which has been said has shaken my own conviction that I have done my duty. That it has given you pain I am most sorry—yet I am sure of this—that in a few years as you look back, and if God gives me life & strength you will see both this book and me, if not as I myself see them, yet in a very different light from that in which you now see them."

So used was the Oxford man to the debate of issues, so used was the Oxford man to *being* an Oxford man, that he could not realize the conversation was over. He had cut off a limb but still thought he could walk on it.

The archdeacon was disgraced by the book. His close associate, the Archbishop of Exeter, wrote to the rector with compassion for the "truly venerable" octogenarian. For he had suffered one of the heaviest afflictions of this world, "the consciousness of having given birth to one who perverts no ordinary endowments to the corruption of his fellow men—and to the more presumptuous defiance of his God!"

His father was at the end of his rope and disinherited Anthony. "Perplexed as I believe he was, he came to the wisest resolution possible," Anthony wrote years later. "As I had persisted in declining the established roads and choosing a way of my own, he determined that I should be made to feel the meaning of what I was doing. As I would not do what he had wished, I must be left in the water to find bottom for myself where I could."

The archdeacon would not support him, would not talk to him, write to him, or allow Anthony to return home. So sharp and clean was this separation that Anthony, in the first throes of liberation, felt no pain, only release. Nor did it matter that his former friends dropped him, some out of fear for their reputations, others out of repulsion for his advanced religious views. Completely cut off from his past, he no longer felt himself victimized. "The worst that could befall me seemed light by the side of the burden which I had got rid of." He had relied on what he believed to be true, turned his back on what Carlyle would consider hypocrisy and cant, and acted decisively. It was only then that Anthony realized he was not fated to follow his older siblings to an early grave. He was going to live.

"Having thrown *The Nemesis* out of me, I had recovered my mental spirits and I was able to face the future without alarm or misgivings." He found himself half amused by the fuss so small a creature had been able to make, and it encouraged him to think that if he could produce such effect, there must be something in him after all.

In those heady days, left entirely on his own, Anthony was not thinking of what he lost but of what he had gained.

Yes and No

*T*he newspaper "dust storm" that greeted *The Nemesis of Faith* might have cost Anthony Tasmania, but at the same time it turned him into a celebrity among those who saw the old world in new ways. The future George Eliot once again reviewed Froude, calling *Nemesis* a magical book, a true product of genius. "We are sure that its author is a bright particular star, though he sometimes leaves us in doubt whether he be not a fallen 'son of the morning.'" She was no less than delighted when she received a charming, flirty little note from the young rebel of the hour requesting her to reveal her person to him and, if she thought him a fallen star, to help him to rise.

A secret patron offered Anthony a two-year scholarship to study with the scientific theologians of Germany, and a hundred pounds were advanced him. He went to London to discuss the offer with the Prussian ambassador, Chevalier Bunsen, who had been greatly moved by the book, reading it straight through. The book had come to Bunsen's notice through twenty-six-year-old Friedrich Max Müller, who arrived at Oxford from Germany for three weeks in 1846 and, as his wife later recalled in her biography of him, stayed for the rest of his life. Son of a

German poet, godson of the musician Mendelssohn, and a brilliant pianist himself, the slight young man with the Grecian profile convinced the East India Company to support his books of translations of the Hindu Rig-Veda, an ongoing series published from 1849 to 1874 at the Oxford University Press, which had the font that could accommodate the undertaking. The greatest Sanskrit scholar of the century, Max Müller introduced comparative philology to Oxford and eventually became the first professor of the discipline there. His encompassing knowledge of other cultures was a breath of fresh air for Anthony during his last years at Oxford, and the two were to become lifelong friends. Max Müller was convinced that Anthony had authentic theological talent that was being stifled under the religious provincialism of Oxford. He sent *The Nemesis of Faith* to Bunsen, who more than agreed. "I cannot describe the power of attraction exercised upon me by this deeply searching, noble spirit: I feel the tragic nature of his position." Max Müller was right. Germany was where Anthony must go. In Bonn he would find the "most deeply thoughtful and most original speculative minds among our living theologians," not to mention that "the free atmosphere of thought would do him good."

While the Archbishop of Exeter considered Anthony a corrupter of his fellow man, Müller and Bunsen saw him as an enlightened man of the cloth who could keep to his theological calling even as he went beyond the narrow strictures of the Thirty-Nine Articles of Anglican faith.

In London, Anthony reported, the enthusiastic diplomat talked his ear off, making him feel as a bucket might under a pump that kept on pouring. But Anthony realized further theological studies, no matter how progressive, were not for him, and he returned the hundred pounds. Eventually he "dropped the Rev'd" in front of his name. A symbolic act, indeed, as he could not be legally divested. Nor was the clergyman in him completely extinguished either culturally or morally, though by the age of thirty-one, in the throes of his new freedom, he thought his past had all been dropped.

It was a Cambridge man, a poet, member of Parliament, and man about town, Richard Monckton Milnes—"Dicky"—who had secretly supplied the money for the German scholarship. The future Lord Houghton had been, along with classmate Tennyson, one of the Cambridge Apostles and knew and would know everyone who was anyone from Napoleon III to Swinburne (whom he brought out).

Dicky Milnes had his political career damaged by his unconventional behavior. When his eccentric, reclusive, and at the same time competitive father received a letter from Cambridge during his son's university days, he hoped it contained news of a first, but found instead that his son had just gone up in a hot air balloon. As an adult, the effervescent Dicky, short, not yet stout, minced about *hugging* his fellow MPs in greeting and mischievously inviting warring parties to his table. He was known for his outlandish wit, which at times covered up a first-rate intellect and serious political ambitions. He had followed the Tracts as they came out of Oxford, and, in his usual outrageous way, wrote a parallel tract of his own. He was also the foremost collector of literature concerning the physical punishing of young schoolboys by their masters, a subdivision of his extensive collection of finely printed pornography or, if you will, sadistic—"Sadic"—literature. He found a copy of *Shadows of the Clouds* that the Archdeacon of Totnes had not bought off the market and had it bound in leather. Perhaps in later years when Froude or Carlyle visited Dicky at Fryston, they saw it in his famed library.

Against the backdrop of the public school system that Froude exposed in *Shadows of the Clouds,* it is not surprising to find much sadomasochism in the adult population. "The English vice," the French called it. "Sensuality is a near relation of cruelty" is the way Froude phrased it in *Caesar; a Sketch* decades later.

Almost all Anthony's former friends shunned him; it damaged one's own reputation to be with him. The exception that proved the rule was Froude's close friend Charles Kingsley, another Cambridge man, now Low Church curate, Christian socialist, and popular novelist. They began a correspondence in 1845 when Anthony was thinking of a career as an author, and they both had shared interest in the policies, editorial decisions, and fate of the *Oxford and Cambridge Review.* Late in his life, Froude would remark to John Ruskin that there was something that remained unbroken in Kingsley, and one could find it in his poetry. One could also find it in his prose and in his life. His novel *Yeast: A Problem* preached that God gave us bodies to enjoy, that the sexual is a celebration of the spiritual, and that Christian marriage is an ultimate and sacred triumph of the unity of men's and women's physical and spiritual natures. Along with its haunting evocation of the plight of England's poor, and its many social and religious concerns, *Yeast* celebrated the type of eroticism that echoed Kingsley's own sexual nature. He had sadomasochistic tendencies that are not only hinted at in his novels but expressed in the hundreds of letters he wrote to his future wife, Fanny Grenfell, and the sketches he drew of them as naked lovers.

The correspondence between Kingsley and Fanny cancels forever the impression that Victorians lacked sexual imagination. What they needed, really, was a way of incorporating fleshly desires with religious beliefs. Prime Minister Gladstone was an example with his night prowls in London earnestly beseeching the prostitutes he befriended to change their ways, and going home to note his progress or to flagellate himself (small whip drawn in daybook) when, perhaps, he was tempted.

The Kingsleys' erotic fantasies were based on dominance and submission. Kingsley took the role of the sober priest who must determine the penance of the supple nunlike penitent kneeling in front of him clothed mainly in humility. Humiliation of the flesh and orgiastic pleasure were intertwined, religious aspirations and sexual appetites merged, driving Fanny to a state of frenzied frustration. Kingsley flagellated himself to obtain spiritual purity—as we have seen, not unusual at the time—though he did not expect self-flagellation from Fanny, who could hardly wait for the shared mortifications of married life.

"I am afraid when you are married that you will be disappointed," Kingsley wrote, "at the amount of bliss you expect when you find me asking you to labour cold and hungry, girded in sackcloth, and to sleep at night shivering on the hard floor." Erotic suggestion stimulated Fanny to such high nervous pitch that her doctors felt only marriage could save her.

Kingsley admitted to Fanny that not only had he visited prostitutes during his college years, but he had done so with Charles Blachford Mansfield, his early lover, lifelong friend, and the future inventor of benzol: "The first human being, save my mother, I ever met who knew what I meant. Remember, the man is the stronger vessel. There is something awful, spiritual, in man's love for each other." Kingsley told Fanny that had she been a man, "we should have been like David and Jonathan." But she wasn't a man. And Kingsley, though fascinated by the male nude and rough-hewn workingmen throughout his life, turned his unabashed sexuality toward his wife. (Fanny, in her important biography of her husband, omitted all mention of Charles Blachford Mansfield.)

One wonders how one would react today to a drawing of a clergyman and his wife bobbing naked on a wooden cross in the billowing sea, the sun rising on the two of them, their feet bound to the bottom of the cross, one outstretched arm each tied Christlike to the cross, the other left free to embrace, as facing each other, his legs straddling hers, they fornicate. In another drawing Kingsley and Fanny ascend naked to heaven in the same carnal and winged embrace, albeit not on a cross.

In Kingsley's novel *Yeast*, Lancelot Smith presents similar drawings to his beloved, Argemone. Sections of Kingsley's book were written around the time of Froude's *Nemesis,* but Kingsley had the common sense in his semiautobiographical novel to make his hero an artist, not a clergyman, even though Lancelot stuttered like Kingsley and was equally tall, gaunt, and homely in a way that apparently charmed women. While Lancelot's drawings were eventually buried with the unmarried woman he called his wife, Kingsley's drawings stayed in the family and survived.

Kingsley's unapologetic sexuality—his rather Lawrentian belief in the sanctity of the erotic—must have been a boon to Froude as he left Oxford. Fellows were not allowed to marry in Anthony's day, a stipulation that provided strong motivation for the marrying kind of deacon to take priest's orders quickly and give up Oxford as soon as a suitable living opened. Ironically, Anthony's own reluctance to take priest's orders had kept him in a sexual as well as a theological bind. In both *Shadows of the Clouds* and *The Nemesis of Faith,* the protagonist eventually becomes involved with a married woman—in the *Nemesis,* to particularly tragic results.

Anthony was not only handsome and brilliant but had a mixture of vulnerability and virility that appealed to women. His love of Harriet Bush thwarted, this immature and motherless young man, with his sophisticated mind and his desire to be understood, might have found some sort of sexual alliance, perhaps with a married woman as in his novels.

These affairs of the heart appear artificial in his novels; they cut from the realistic, autobiographical concerns of both books to pulp fiction. As Jowett phrased it privately: "If Froude really thinks he has a great truth to publish he cannot fancy that the right or useful way of publishing it is after the manner of a French novel."

Kingsley's sex scenes in *Yeast* appear equally artificial, yet they come straight from conviction: "What was her womanhood, that it could stand against the energy of his manly will! The almost coarse simplicity of his words silenced her with a delicious violence. . . . A strong shudder ran through her frame—the ice of artificial years cracked, and the clear stream of her woman's nature welled up to the light. . . . The sensation was new to her. Again the delicious feeling of being utterly in his power came over her, and she left her hand upon his heart, and blushed as she felt its passionate throbbings."

Such passages earned Kingsley the tag "muscular Christian." We use the Victorian term earnestly today without the accompanying wink and nudge.

Kingsley and Froude were inseparable in the months following the latter's expulsion from Oxford. With customary openheartedness, and at the expense of his reputation, the Reverend Charles Kingsley, five years married and the father of two young children, immediately invited his excommunicated and homeless friend to visit him. Not that Kingsley approved of *The Nemesis of Faith;* he thought the writing of it a mistake. He reassured his scandalized mother and clergyman father that the protagonist's views were not Kingsley's own, but attempted to bring his parents up to date, informing them that these were nowadays the ideas of "too many men."

Kingsley was a Christian activist, endlessly writing essays and books and preaching the sermons he wrote week by week. Only on Sundays, at the pulpit, was he able to overcome his lifelong stammer. At his parish at Eversley outside London, Kingsley hoed fields with the workingmen, visited the sick and the poor, attempted to improve sewage conditions and stem the scourge of typhoid, a great concern in *Yeast* as well. His was a profoundly personal as well as a professional commitment, and he reached out—human to human—to the hearts and fellow feelings of his congregation. On Palm Sunday 1859, he'd preach at Buckingham Palace for the first time, a short, simple, colloquial Protestant sermon, similar to those he delivered at Eversley. Queen Victoria immediately grasped the worth of the man she'd eventually appoint tutor to the Prince of Wales.

At home, Kingsley was active as well, playing with his young children, writing stories for them (among them *The Water-Babies,* still read today), and passionately loving his not undemanding and, sackcloth aside, quite expensive wife.

Fanny had been one of the six wealthy Grenfell sisters. Orphaned after the death of their father, a tin magnate, Fanny and the three of her siblings who remained unmarried resided together in a large house near Cambridge. They were independent women of means who dressed beautifully and, during the London season, were seen in the best of houses. At the same time, the maiden sisters formed themselves into a spiritual sisterhood; they espoused High Church tenets inspired by the Oxford Movement, most particularly by Dr. Pusey. They were Puseyites, pledged a nunlike virginity, to fasting, and to diligently studying and discussing the Tracts.

One of those elegant women was Fanny's oldest and most intellectual sister, Charlotte Grenfell. And she appeared at the Kingsleys' door soon after Anthony Froude arrived there in 1849. She had taken her

Puseyite convictions one step further and had gone over to Rome two years previously. She was on the verge of joining the order of Saint Sepulchrens when she met the handsome rebel at a time when he did not know his future direction.

There was a lot of Charlotte Grenfell in Argemone, the heroine of Kingsley's *Yeast*. Kingsley described her as that "sweet prude, tall and stately." In her boudoir, among her books, dried flowers, and religious statuettes, she fancied herself, "not unfairly," as very intellectual. It was Argemone's fictive sister Honoria, "tiny and luscious," with dark hair and eyes, "as full of wild simple passion as an Italian, thinking little, except where she felt much," who resembled Kingsley's wife—the only kind of woman he could really live with.

The fictional sisters were diametric opposites, Kingsley wrote, in everything except beauty, though even their beauty contrasted. The tall, stately character based on Charlotte appeared almost angry when she witnessed her sister spending her days about the village going from school to sickroom. Perhaps Charlotte like Argemone had a conscience that hinted that her duty, too, was among the poor, rather than among her luxurious daydreams. "But alas!"—Argemone would be indignant if she was accused of selfishness—"yet in self and for self alone she lived."

Though in life the Grenfell sisters were able to fast themselves "cross and stupefied, and quite enjoy kneeling thinly clad and barefoot on the freezing chapel-floor on a winter's morning," the sister based on Charlotte in *Yeast* had a "fastidious delicacy." She would have been revolted sitting, like her sister, beside the bed of a peasant's consumptive daughter in some reeking, stifling garret that housed as well the father, mother, two grown-up boys, not to mention a new-married couple and the sick girl's baby. "And of such bedchambers there were too many."

Charlotte herself remained very close to Kingsley's heart, despite his disapproval of her aloof intellectual nature and what he considered a certain distance from her womanhood. He encouraged Anthony's interest in his sister-in-law. The attraction between Charlotte and Anthony was filled with intellectual friction. They sparred concerning religion as Anthony slowly turned Charlotte from her Catholicism and the convent to thoughts of a domestic life, particularly given the example they had in front of their eyes. Emotionally, they may have been too similar. Both were high-strung, both searching for answers, both staying at another's home during a crucial juncture in each of their lives.

During the courtship it did not occur to Anthony that his long visit was harming Kingsley's reputation. Characteristically, he was grateful to

Kingsley for sticking by him and offering him refuge, but he didn't fully grasp the approbation with which such charity was regarded, nor the price a clergyman who stood up for him would pay: "I learnt afterwards that each day's post brought him letters of reproach, of menace, of exhortation, all on my account. But he never for a moment let me guess what he was bearing."

Then, an offer came out of the blue, one better suited to Anthony than theological studies in Germany. A wealthy Manchester solicitor and civic and educational leader, Samuel Dukinfield Darbishire, was stirred by Froude's books. He wanted to give him a start in his progressive city and invited Anthony to Manchester as a live-in tutor to a son whose health was delicate and to give lessons to his daughters and his wife as well. *The Nemesis of Faith* was hardly anathema to Unitarians like Darbishire, to whom religion was not based on Christ's divinity or eternal hellfire.

No other city in England could have offered Anthony the new vision of the future that Manchester presented. It was at the forefront of the industrial revolution, and while it inspired Friedrich Engels (whose father was one of the textile merchants there) to write *The Condition of the Working Class in England* (1845), to others it spoke of a burgeoning vitality. It was there that Anthony came in contact with forward-looking people, progressives, many of them Unitarians, such as vegetarian Frank Newman, estranged brother of John Henry Newman. Frank was an extraordinary linguist and scholar who was also active in advocating prison reform, women's rights, and antivivisectionism—concerns that were hardly priorities at Oxford. It had been Frank Newman, through his affiliation with University College, London, who had earlier secured the ill-fated Tasmania post for Anthony. Now Frank was attempting to secure him the editorship of the *Manchester Guardian*. Manchester with all its new money aimed at rivaling London as a journalistic as well as a cultural hub. Frank's help came after a quick outburst of anger over Froude's positive portrayal of brother John Henry in *The Nemesis of Faith*.

Manchester was proud to welcome Anthony Froude, to have him tutor their children: "The thoughts of the place were new, the occupations were new, from dreams and speculations I was awakened into the industrious turmoil of busy life and practically active men." He met businessmen, factory owners, journalists, laborers, crusaders, capitalists, rather than students and dons.

It was Mr. Darbishire who introduced him to the literary women of Manchester: Harriet Martineau, who considered Anthony the handsomest man she had ever met; Elizabeth Gaskell, who wrote so relevantly of her city, its captains of industry and its laborers; and Geraldine Jewsbury. Jewsbury, novelist, critic, and liberated woman, wrote to her beloved Jane Welsh Carlyle that she was going out that night with "the author of *Nemesis of Faith*, a very nice, natural young man though rather like a lost sheep at present. He had only been used to the Oxford part of the world, so that sectarians and unbelievers are strange to him." It was a more prescient remark than it might have seemed at the time.

Geraldine, that fiery redhead, about the same age as Anthony, had recently published her first novel, *Zoe* (begun with Jane Welsh Carlyle, but Jane dropped out). The novel concerns a doubting Roman Catholic priest who falls in love with a woman and has bodice-ripping sex with her in a burning chapel. In its portrayal of the religious doubts and insecurities of the times, it was a precursor to *Nemesis,* which the prolific Jewsbury reviewed in a long, encompassing essay.

A decade later, in London, Geraldine Jewsbury would become reacquainted with Anthony, both of their destinies intricately and ironically tied to Jane Welsh and Thomas Carlyle. But in 1849, literally short-sighted, Geraldine saw long into Anthony, noticing a certain ambivalence in his point of view, contiguous with a need to please. His eyes never looked at you, "though they *saw* you." According to Geraldine, he did not yet know how "to say Yes and No like a man," had not yet exorcized "the Jesuit element which made him try to be *both at once.*" How eager he was to pick out a book and entertain her and her friends with his charm and his spontaneous translations of the Greek poets. And he was so very handsome, with "a strange elfin beauty," she would write to one of her younger lovers manqué.

Geraldine had the eyes to see, but it is doubtful that she knew of the ambivalence in Anthony's engagement to Charlotte Grenfell. On the surface, it would appear that Anthony had become decisive when that engagement met an obstacle. Charlotte's entire family was dead set against the notorious and professionless man, and Charlotte wavered, needed more time to think. And perhaps her short-lived conversion to Rome still weighed on her. Anthony sent her an ultimatum, in the "strong man–submissive woman" tradition of Kingsley's fantasy life: Either she was to go against her wealthy family's wishes and marry him immediately or he would cut her free.

Fanny Kingsley resented Anthony's imperious tone to her sister and backtracked in her unique support of the union. Anthony did not waver. He wrote to Fanny that she was being unreasonable. He had already warned her that he intended to make his own way in life in all important matters. He was not going to wait for Charlotte's family to approve of him. (He didn't have to spell out that his own family wouldn't even speak to him.) In the long run it would save Charlotte the most pain to make a decision now, allowing no interference from the dictates of others.

One wonders if Anthony's words would have been so strong had there not been another woman in the picture, Mr. Darbishire's beautiful, intelligent, and musically gifted twenty-one-year-old daughter Marianne. Anthony, living with the Darbishires, was free to take long rides in the countryside with Marianne, to be her tutor and companion without any coy restraints. This ultimatum to Charlotte was reflective of Anthony's newfound determination; at the same time it was also Anthony's old way of leaving his choice in the hands of fate and of possibly wiggling out of things—that "Yes and No" element Geraldine gleaned. For Marianne Darbishire was most willing to embrace this man who was already part of the household. According to family legend, Mr. Darbishire made it clear that this could occur only after the engagement to Charlotte, which was temporarily in abeyance, ended permanently, with Charlotte granting Anthony an unconditional release.

During this temporary abeyance in his relations with Charlotte, Anthony traveled to Coventry to meet the future George Eliot. It had been Mary Ann Evans's enthusiastic review of *Shadows of the Clouds* as a work of genius that led Froude to have his publisher, John Chapman, send *The Nemesis of Faith* on to her in Coventry. There, while nursing her invalid father, she was translating *Das Leben Jesu,* a weighty product of the new German biblical criticism, treating Christ the man. She, like Froude himself, was searching for a more meaningful and contemporary spiritual identity, and she responded intellectually and emotionally to his second novel, beginning her review in the *Coventry Herald:* "On certain red-letter days of our existence, it happens to us to discover among the *spawn* of the press, a book which, as we read, seems to undergo a sort of transfiguration before us." It is as if we are "in companionship with a spirit, who is transfusing himself into our souls, and vitalizing them by his superior energy." Life itself "both outward and inward, presents itself to us for higher relief, in colours brightened and deepened—we seem to have been bathing in a pool of Siloam, and to have come forth reeling."

When Froude responded to her review of *Nemesis* with a flirty little note, her delight was no less intense. Her friend Mrs. Bray reports that she came gleefully rushing in to show her the charming note Froude had sent "naively and prettily requesting her to reveal herself. . . . Poor girl, I am so pleased she should have this little episode in her dull life."

Then, not a week after her father's death, and her own release from isolated duty, though she had not responded to Froude's request, there he was, staying with the Brays, specifically come to Coventry to meet her—face-to-face. Before they met, he planned to join her, the Brays, and possibly John Chapman on a trip to the Continent. One can only imagine how Anthony pictured the young woman who had such intelligence as well as such appreciation of his work that it made her reel. Chapman must not have informed him that her inner beauty had no outward correspondence. She was a very passionate woman with a particularly big, heavy, unlovely head, who was quite aware of the dichotomy between what she felt and how she was perceived by eligible men. She and Anthony conversed, but he certainly did not flirt; reality hung heavy between them. When he ended his visit, he immediately wrote to beg off the trip that they had planned, his excuse an ironclad one: He had become engaged.

Charlotte, in fact, did capitulate to her strong-minded lover, and soon the Darbishires were in the position of house hunting for Mr. Froude and his fiancée. "It is a secret that he is going to be married," Marianne Darbishire wrote to her sister; she herself picked out the drawing room carpet for his new home, as well as presenting him with one of her dog's new puppies: "We have taken such pains to teach it to answer to the name of 'James Anthony.' I assure you it sounds extraordinary to hear James Anthony called all over the house all day long!" But when James Anthony himself was no longer available for those long, unescorted rides in the countryside and intimate conversations, Marianne's tone flattened.

Another Mary Ann, Miss Evans in Coventry, was no stranger to the effect of her face. Eight years later, happily living in sanctified sin with the married George Lewes, she would publish her first fiction under the pseudonym of George Eliot, and perhaps have a bit of feminine revenge on fleet-footed Froude. She sent Anthony a copy of the book.

"Dear Sir, I do not know when I have experienced a more pleasant surprise than when on opening a book parcel two mornings ago I found it to contain 'Scenes of Clerical Life,'" Froude responded. "I do not know whether I am addressing a young man or an old, a clergyman or a layman. Perhaps if you answer this note you may give us more information about yourself."

No response.

Eight months later: "Sir. A shadow holds out a hand to me. I try to take it & it fades away. Who are you! I do not ask from curiosity—you send me your book. I tell you how much it has affected me & I express my hope that the George Eliot who has touched me so keenly may allow me to know in him something more than the writer of his volumes on my table. You send me no answer. Keep yourself to yourself if you please—but I should value your acquaintance beyond that of most men if I was so happy as to possess it."

Another six months: *Adam Bede* arrived at Froude's doorstep. By then he seems to have found her out: "Dear—Sir—or Madam. Sir, I presume you wish it thus, perhaps it is. At any rate since you prefer to remain unknown it is not for me or any one to pry into your concealment. I have but to thank you again for your second present." He went on to admit that though the novel stirred his heart with "passionate interest," the stark realism of the workingman's predicament in the modern world had not given him the pleasure George Eliot's more "remarkable" characters had. And George Eliot, though she did not reveal herself to him, responded with the old heady appreciation. His criticism did real good: "The same sort of good as one has sometimes felt for a silent pressure of the hand and a grave look in the midst of smiling congratulations."

Given the opportunity of taking a trip with one of the greats of his age, a soul mate, albeit she was as homely as he was handsome, Anthony had fled. He probably could have married Marianne Darbishire whether or not the family legend be true. And he was offered the chance to be set up in business in Manchester by Marianne's father. That path was entirely new, but business did not appeal to him. He was at his crossroads with many an option—aided by genius, celebrity, good looks. His ultimatum to Charlotte was partially a toss of the dice. But once Charlotte capitulated to his demand, Anthony's way was clear, and he did become as direct as one could wish.

Intellectual, high-strung Charlotte, just as Kingsley's self-interested Argemone, was beyond such mundane concerns as house furnishings. Anthony wrote to Fanny Kingsley trusting that they could now come to peace, "at any rate briefly," and asked her advice, Charlotte's "knowledge of what servants and kitchen apparatus she possesses extending no further than that she has her dinner daily. Do make me a list." Their house would be big enough for a few live-in students, *"which pays,"* Anthony informed his future sister-in-law, "but Charlotte disliked it. I don't wonder."

On October 3, 1849, not eight months after he left Oxford (and had met during that time at least three eligible and interested women), he and Charlotte Grenfell were married at St. Peter's Church, Eaton Square, Belgravia. He had, as he put it, conquered his wife "from Romanism and a convent." He inscribed her copy of *Nemesis:* "J.A.F to his dear wife, 1849." And she made notes on many a line.

More important, not long after the marriage, he wrote to a friend, quite revealingly, "I married with confined expectations, and as if in reward they have grown like the grain of mustard." In a sense he had married like many a rebellious young man—to bring himself back to reason—and indeed found that he was a man who needed to be married, to be sexually and emotionally settled, in order to come into his maturity. His new condition surprised him, made him happier than he thought he would be. Finally the rest of him was catching up with his intellectual abilities. "Froude is married and all the better for it, they say," Arthur Clough wrote to Emerson. Geraldine Jewsbury (friend to both Clough and Emerson) would write it was his wife who taught Anthony to stand firm and say yes and no like a man.

Anthony himself would more than agree. But he now had two people to whom he must prove himself, his unforgiving father and his well-bred wife. And one institution. As early as his wedding trip, passing through Oxford, he wished to "show Charlotte a thing or two." The new man he had become considered it extravagant—it would have provoked him if anything could at the time—when he found out that the rector would not allow him to enter his former college, any more than his father or William would come to his wedding. "I think Exeter College is unwise and ungraceful," he wrote with his characteristic obtuseness concerning his effect on others. At the same time, the rejection stung him to the quick.

One wonders how Froude's ideas might have developed had he remained in Manchester, that city of strong newspapers, progressive human rights advocates, industrialists, vegetarian scholars, women novelists, and Unitarians—that city of the new. But Charlotte soon found she could not bear Manchester any more than she could bear the thought of student boarders. The people were vulgar and insolent. And for her, London would be just as bad. Froude, who at first had been so energized by Manchester and its new ways, now used the marital "we" as he explained the sudden dissatisfaction. The couple, who wrote a few fables together during that period, decided on the country, hoping for harmony, a banding together against the maddened crowd: "We calculated that in some quiet country place we could live on £400 a year [Charlotte's allotment] without difficulty. I should be able to add by writing reviews, but I should be free to follow my own pursuits. We were determined to try."

They found a remote and charming cottage at Plas Gwynant in North Wales. It was spring when they first saw it. A cherry orchard was in full bloom outside the doorway. Mount Snowdon was directly overhead, "the peak two miles off as the crow flies," and there was a dramatic waterfall below them. That September, eleven months into their marriage, Charlotte gave birth to their first child, a new and promising Margaret, named after the mother Froude never knew, and they moved to their new home and writer's retreat. "It was the opening stage of a new existence for me, and if any good has since come out of me, the seeds of it were planted in those years."

"Do you know," he would write at the time, "in politics I have absolutely ceased to be a revolutionist. I can think of a millionaire without being bilious. I can believe a Red Republican to be both a fool and a rascal." He had been taken with French Communism, had read George Sand and Louis Blanc, "had made myself indignant over the inequalities of life, and half believed that a revolution would set them right." But in Manchester he had found captains of industry who took financial risks and provided for their workers, civic leaders who donated much time and money to the culture and educational improvement in their city. In the world, rather than at Oxford, he discovered how easy it had once been "to make crooked things straight on paper in one's room."

After he married Charlotte, not only his political but his spiritual difficulties "cleared away never to come back to me." It was not for him to solve the problems surrounding religion and morality. He let go of concerns he could not effect. Even though he expected church reform by and by, his religion became essentially that of the father who disowned him. "To me religion is presented under the form of the law of the land. I acknowledge it as I do the common law or the civil law, and so I left and so I leave a question into which I am not required to examine further." He had taken orders hastily. "I was sufficiently punished by the brand which shut me out from other professions. I must work as I could on the best road which was left open to me."

The best road left open to him was literature. His and Charlotte's withdrawal to a remote outpost in order to live simply and frugally on her small income and his writings mirrored—perhaps intentionally—the first years of the marriage of Jane Welsh and Thomas Carlyle, albeit with sexual release and the arrival of children.

* * *

Soon after Anthony had settled in Manchester, on a trip to London, his first cousin James Spedding—one of the original Cambridge Apostles and biographer of Bacon—had brought him to meet Thomas Carlyle, historian, essayist, seer. If Anthony expected praise he would not find it. He had written in *Nemesis* (among many passages of praise for Carlyle) that there was not one modern writer bold enough to answer the younger generation's questions concerning faith: "Carlyle! Carlyle only raises questions he cannot answer, and seems best contented if he can make the rest of us as discontented as himself." Carlyle huffed: Froude should burn his own smoke and not trouble other people's nostrils with it.

However, when Anthony came to the cozy and brightly furnished town house on 5 Cheyne Row, and walked out to the back garden where the tall, gaunt, fifty-four-year-old Carlyle, with his straw-colored hair, bright blue eyes, flushed cheeks, and pronounced underlip, was sitting smoking his pipe, and when he later took tea with Carlyle and wife, Jane, it struck him that "false sentiment, insincerity, cant of any kind would find no quarter, either from wife or husband; and that one must speak truth only, and if possible, think truth only, if one wished to be admitted into that house on terms of friendship."

Carlyle had expressed his opinion of *Nemesis* in a letter to a friend as not "worth its paper and ink," explaining in his exaggerated, Germanically influenced, over-the-top style, "What on Earth is the use of a wretched mortal's vomiting up all his interior crudities, dubitations, and spiritual agonising belly-aches into the view of the Public, and howling tragically, 'See!' Let him, in the Devil's name, pass them, by the downward or other methods, into his own water-closet, and say nothing whatever!"

Dyspeptic Carlyle, who daily fought a painful, losing battle with his own fiery innards—and did not suffer in silence—probably told Anthony straight out that the spiritual bellyaching of *Nemesis* was worthy of the crapper. "I did not admire him the less because he treated me— I cannot say unkindly, but shortly and sternly. I saw then what I saw ever after—that no one need look for conventional politeness from Carlyle—he would hear the exact truth from him and nothing else."

Anthony was immediately taken by forty-eight-year-old Jane Welsh Carlyle, as was every other young literary man and political refugee in London. "Her features were not regular, but I thought I had never seen a more interesting-looking woman. Her hair was raven black, her eyes, dark, soft, sad with dangerous light in mocking. She was fond of [cousin]

Spedding, and kept up a quick, sparkling conversation with him, telling stories at her husband's expense, at which he laughed himself as heartily as we did."

The main result of the visit was that the Carlyles did not write the young man off; he was invited back. And when he came back, the grumbling Carlyle always took time to see him.

No doubt during those visits, Carlyle spoke nostalgically of the early years of his marriage at the remote farm at Craigenputtock in southern Scotland—he often threatened to return there—while Jane continued to tell "sparkling" stories at Carlyle's expense: how at Craigenputtock she got to speak to Carlyle only while he shaved in the morning, learned to make bread and cheese in order to keep her sanity, and how, in the isolation of that godforsaken place, completely cut off in snowbound winter, she swore she could hear the cows breathing a quarter of a mile away.

But Carlyle had sat in his study off the kitchen of the crude stone farmhouse writing *Sartor Resartus,* as well as articles for the *Edinburgh Review,* run by one of Jane's devoted admirers, Francis Jeffrey, and through his writings—and Jane's small income—the couple earned enough to get by. It was because of those articles that Emerson, abroad after his first wife's death and his resignation from the Second Church Boston, tracked Carlyle down, and actually arrived at the hilltop of Craigenputtock—only fourteen miles outside Dumfries, yet to this day still difficult to find.

In northern Wales, Froude returned to the issues raised in *Nemesis* in a new way. He left fiction and spiritual autobiography behind him, as Carlyle strongly advised. No more crying out loud, no more partially French novels: "After what has been said of me I have felt I ought to say positively and publically not what I doubt but what I am sure of," he wrote to Rector Richards on his expulsion from Oxford, "and I am now writing a set of essays in which I shall state my own belief—in my own person." Nonfiction was the medium better suited to his voice. That was where his real talent lay. The impetus to Froude's art was a powerful need to be understood combined with a determination to make his own living.

"My first business was to establish a connexion with the editors of periodicals, and here I was fortunate beyond my hopes. New volumes were sent to me to review, my articles were accepted and well paid for, and I found myself able to follow the lines of my own studies and inclinations, throwing out essays as I went along. Parcels of books came to me from the London Library. Very much I had to do, to do what was wanted of me, and the working hours of the day were fully occupied." Within a year he was earning "a hundred and twenty or thirty pounds a year by scribbling," and realized this would increase.

"I was feeling ground under my feet," is the way he put it. He had been a sickly youth; he was now an active, athletic married man. Healthful physical exercise abounded. "The days began, winter and summer, with a plunge into the pool below the waterfall." He could walk up to the peak of Snowdon "in an hour and return in three-quarters." The lakes "swarmed" with trout for this ardent fly fisherman, who many a midnight found himself rather romantically "drifting in the moonlight throwing my fly into the rings which showed where a fish was rising." And there was game galore. In winter snipe and ducks in the marshes; on the hillside, woodcock and hare. All his life he shot sparingly, bagging only what he could use. In the summer, many a visitor: Matt Arnold; Oxford friend Max Müller, now courting Charlotte's niece Georgie; and Arthur Clough. The friends would climb to the snow line to ice their whiskey.

Out of season, "the hotels were empty; the tourists were gone like the swallows. All was silent, still, and solitary, yet it was hard to say whether the winter or the summer landscape was more beautiful or the life we led more enjoyable." As he wrote to friend John Parker Jr., encouraging a winter visit: "Mountains don't fall with the leaves."

But it was the arrival of his brother-in-law Kingsley that was always "the event of the season." Kingsley was as ardent a fly fisherman. There were very deep small lakes in the mountains, and the higher one went, the larger the trout:

"No boat could be carried up among the crags, so we climbed with our coracles upon our shoulders, the old British coracle, light to carry, safe if well handled, in the wildest water. If a storm came we could paddle on shore and stand it bottom uppermost on rock or wall and lie sheltered under it till the rain had done. So loaded like tortoises with rods and baskets we climbed the mountains, Kingsley pouring out theology, science, poetry, or the plans for his new novels.

"I can see him now, among the rocks at Llyn Edno, two thousand feet up and rarely visited, famous for mountain trout which no one could catch. He had hooked a fish almost at his first cast, which had dashed down into the depths so fiercely that he imagined he had hold of some uncanny demon of the lake. His first impulse, he told me, was to drop his rod and say 'Please don't.'"

Poet Clough "neither fished nor shot nor boated if he could help it; but we walked far and wide, and climbed Snowdon, and bathed in the mountain torrents, and talked of all things in heaven and earth." Clough visited on his way to Emerson in America. "When he left Oxford he had taken charge of the University Hall in Gordon Square, but it had not answered with him. The class of students were of rougher material than Oxford undergraduates. They had not understood him or he them."

Many of the most brilliant minds of the time were unsatisfied outside university walls, inept at the transition from gown to the grit of town. Anthony Froude was able to adapt. Without ever sacrificing the complexity of his thoughts, he was able to express his opinions with a strength, clarity, and relevance that interested, informed, and at times infuriated a wide readership.

More and more books were sent to him to review. In those reviews, well-developed essays on the subject under consideration, Anthony plotted his future course. Criticizing friend Emerson's *Representative Men,* he accused the American he respected of putting the cart before the horse, giving his audience full-blown great men without illuminating the path to greatness that his generation could emulate: "We have no biographies, no history which are of real service to us." No contemporary work gave his age a *"track"* to follow, a *real* path trodden by *real* men. To supply such a track became his purpose, and he succeeded in his most influential essay up to then: "England's Forgotten Worthies" of 1852. It was with this review-essay that he found his true calling.

"England's Forgotten Worthies" was a bold reassessment of the exploring seamen—some would say pirates—of the Elizabethan age. He had gone back to the English Reformation, which brother Hurrell and Newman deplored, and saw it from an opposite point of view. The swashbuckling Elizabethan explorers were so unheralded up to then, that at the beginning of the nineteenth century, when Richard Hakluyt edited five volumes of first-person accounts of their adventures, only 270 copies were sold. In Anthony's long review-essay of a new—if inferior—edition of that work, he made a sweeping claim: Hakluyt's five-volume compendium of the English seamen was "the Prose Epic of the modern English nation."

"They contain the heroic tales of the exploits of great men in whom the new era was inaugurated." They were not myths but "plain broad narratives of substantial facts, which rival legend in interest and grandeur. What the old epics were to the royally or nobly born, this modern epic is to the common people." Just as the apostles were poor fishermen, these sailors "the Joneses, the Smiths, the Davises, the Drakes," were heroes who came from the people. They "went out across the unknown seas fighting, discovering, colonizing," through their own courage spreading England's commerce and enterprise throughout the world.

Drake, Hawkins, Raleigh, were all from Froude's Devonshire. Later generations of these worthies had been Froude's early neighbors. Through the exploits of common men the modern world took shape. The Elizabethan seamen stood as an example of all the English character was and could be—when freed from domination by Rome.

The Oxford Movement, which his brother and Newman had founded, considered the Elizabethan age a decadent, degenerate one. They disparaged the English Reformation: "We had been told at Oxford that it was the most unfortunate incident which had destroyed the unity of the Church, that it had been a rebellion against the divinely given authority, that it was a schism promoted by corrupt and tyrannical princes, carried out by unprincipled and priestly renegades. I had not believed this." It was as if he were sent into his age of religious doubt and upheaval to bring to the English-speaking world a renewal of pride in the Reformation that had so affected the modern world and founded their modern English nation.

Scottish Thomas Carlyle could interrelate *Past and Present,* the medieval monk and modern dilemma, into a brilliant, colorful, riotous book of social criticism that penetrated the bloodstream of the England he adopted. "England's Forgotten Worthies" was more like a shot of adrenaline directly into English veins. It stimulated such poets as Tennyson, who became Anthony's friend, suggested "to Kingsley his brilliant novel *Westward Ho!*" and gave his contemporaries a *track* they could be proud to follow, finding in the hitherto neglected Elizabethan explorers not rogues but heroes who gave his countrymen a "real path trodden by real men."

About his personal happiness in Wales, Anthony expressed himself more haltingly to such friends from Oxford days as Mrs. Long, the wife of William Long, now Mayor of Bath: "The new man which I have put on has not learnt as yet to express itself readily in words, and I have been so intensely happy, and so intensely sensible, that I have seemed almost to have nothing to write about.

"We glide along," he told Mrs. Long. "Of course there are the minor ills: Babies cry, storms blow, rain pours, and chimneys smoke, maidservants fall in love and become troublesome, and alas sometimes do worse things. The nurse we brought from England took to drinking, and one night, instead of walking into her bed, took to romancing, and fancied herself a water nymph; nothing would satisfy her but sailing down into the waterfall."

The new nurse who replaced the water nymph manqué came from "a fashionable house in London" and had nerves requiring green tea, breakfasts in bed, and cake instead of bread. Add to this frightfully unsanitary cooks and sleepy housemaids. "Moreover, there are housebreakers about among the mountains, and alone as we are (they have paid us one visit) we have dogs sleeping in the house, and I have loaded pistols at my bedside."

When another daughter, Rose Mary, was born on May 6, 1852, Mrs. Long became her godmother. Rose Mary was a particularly beautiful child, like her mother, Anthony wrote, Charlotte penciling in "like her father!" "My second daughter was happily brought into the world, with singularly little suffering to anybody. We hope it will be the symbol of the life which is to be," he wrote to Clough. "People condole with me on the sex, and I rather consider myself to be congratulated. It is a far simpler business to educate a girl into a woman than a boy into a man in these unheroic times."

Anthony was surrounded by women—his intellectual, high-strung wife and his two adorable and loving daughters. He had never known such a benign female influence. His own sisters, Mary, Phillis, Margaret, had been contemptuous, taught through Hurrell's "funny tormenting" to consider the weakling baby of the family something of a butt of humor. He was constantly teased, mocked, discounted, neither mothered nor befriended by either his sisters or Aunt Mary, whose major contribution to his education was to accustom him to cold waters. To have had the responsibility of a newborn son while consciously defining his own manhood and attempting to reunite with his own father would have been far less simple. In fact, his first son, Pascoe Grenfell, born right after the years in Wales, would bring Anthony greater disappointment than he himself had ever afforded the archdeacon.

It was in Wales, pistols under his bed, daughters in the nursery, that he found his own way, his path to manhood. "All life, to be worth anything, must be under the control of reason," he had written as early as *Shadows*. It was here that Froude put Humpty Dumpty back together again. He believed his life *was* under the control of reason, was worth something, and he looked back on his first thirty years with a shame that fluctuated in intensity throughout his life. How he viewed his misspent youth would remain a constant barometer of his sense of self at any particular moment. Most often he flatly rejected what he had been, literally *hated* his former self—the cowardly boy, the callow rebel—and in one great heave believed he had cast it away. This was a psychological boomerang, though it would take more than thirty years for it to return and clobber him.

Charlotte's family got "over *the shock*" of her marriage within its first six months, and while the couple were in London "the supreme Grenfell, the August of Belgrave Square signed our forgiveness by his own presence." But Froude's own family would not forgive him. "Nothing is wanting now except that my own people should follow the example, but when that may be I cannot well even guess. In the meantime we are as happy as we can be without them, and that is really most happy, though of course it would *relieve* me of a load indeed if they came round. Something tells me that I shall not forfeit favour again with any more outrages as soon as I have got it back."

Actually, to reconcile with his father was the driving force behind the new man—both intellectually, in his writings on the sixteenth century, and emotionally. To his own mind he had made himself over and was now a respectable adult. But each attempt to visit was thwarted, even after the birth of Margaret and Rose Mary.

"I suppose that there must have been a contradictory element in the nature of the whole of us, or some force must have been at work which thwarts the purposes of the most prudent," Anthony would one day write of himself and his brothers. "My father's greatest desire was that his sons should each travel one of the great established professions. He distrusted and despised the conceit of originality, and strove from the beginning to impress upon us that only fools would attempt to mark out a line for themselves. On the bare ground of intelligence, the tracts laid down by the common sense of mankind were infinitely more likely to be right than the weak fancies of boys or men who imagined themselves wiser than other people. Yet so it has been, perhaps as a recoil from the emphasis with which these most real truths were driven in upon us, not one of us all has either taken his advice or followed his directions. Hurrell, with Newman, led the great Anglo-Catholic revolt, tried to unprotestantize the Church of England, and for themselves cut off any prospect of professional advancement as clergymen. Newman seceded to Rome and believed that Hurrell, had he lived, would have preceded him. It might have been so, but the Pope would have found him an unmanageable subject.

"Robert's nature was simpler and less aggressive. He, at least, might have fulfilled my father's hopes, but he died at twenty-four like my grandfather. John became a lawyer and succeeded to a considerable business, but he hated and neglected it. . . . My brother William won for himself a brilliant but again original position as a Naval Engineer. He, however, left the lines of his profession, created a new science of Naval Architecture, and worked alone, making precious discoveries on his own personal resources."

The Oxford legend of William Froude was that his scientific experiments left their marks on the outside and inside walls of his rooms at Oriel. The archdeacon was prouder of William's accomplishments than Anthony's description would allow (or that William himself realized). "William is a great comfort to me," the archdeacon wrote after Hurrell's death, and he closely followed his son's engineering career under I. K. Brunel, with whom William worked on the construction of the Bristol and Exeter Railway. Such assignments afforded him "the most advantageous means of professional improvement, while it keeps him in the center of good society & kind friends."

Early on the archdeacon voiced enthusiasm for a novel scheme. "Did I tell you that William is likely to be employed in an engineering speculation of great interest," he wrote to Keble. "It is known that under the bed of clay which fills the vale of the Thames . . . there is an inexhaustible stream of the finest water flowing freely through a thick stratum of gravel. The plan is to raise this to the surface by means of powerful engines."

William, however, would soon be back to experimenting in his own laboratory, giving up his managerial and engineering work under I. K. Brunel in order to return to Dartington Parsonage. The fourth son had become the oldest son and heir, one who had a defined sense of duty and a father in his eighties who needed help at home and with his business affairs. William, too, would soon inadvertently foil his father's expectations, but in a way that even Anthony would not commit to paper.

All Anthony's life he had stood on one side of the family's tragedies, too young and, at times, too self-involved to be of much help at home. William, eight years his senior, had not in his youth shared the intimacy the archdeacon had with his oldest brothers, Hurrell and Robert, though he had ten years of a mother. He, like Anthony, was sent to Westminster, not Eton, and to him, too, the archdeacon was distant, remote. Still, rather than draw close to young Anthony, William took on the paternal, disapproving air of Hurrell, but at the same time he was kind, often attempting to mediate between father and youngest son. Once again, during the years at Wales, it was William who sought to reconcile with

Anthony first and then to open the old man to receiving the prodigal son.

He hinted to Anthony by post that the family had "returned to kinder feeling" toward him and that matters at Dartington Parsonage were "mending slowly but surely." He planned to visit Anthony in Wales the spring of 1851. Either he did not make that trip or it turned out poorly. For that spring, Anthony wrote to Mrs. Long that he wished he could give up thinking of what was going on at Dartington Parsonage. But he couldn't. He realized that the only hope of softening his family's attitude was the passage of time, not anything at all that he could do, for whatever he did or did not do displeased them. They had made up their minds to be dissatisfied, no matter what. "We Froudes have a way of our own of laying hold of the stick by the burnt end, and making the worst rather than the best of everything—a process which would be at last irritating, if happily it did not make its own punishment."

Charlotte, his "wise wife," convinced him to burn another letter, a doleful one to Mrs. Long: "I had just had a disappointment in an expected amendment of matters at home, and I had let it all run out very needlessly to you." He was in a better mood now. His bad fits, which never came over him except when it came to his estranged family, were at least of brief duration.

After the birth of Rose Mary, he wrote to Clough: "There is a hope that at the end of an indefinite number of months or years the *Nemesis* may be forgiven by my own family, but it is too vague a prospect to occupy me." But occupy him it did, until Christmas of 1852, when through William's mediation and, as important, after the publication of "England's Forgotten Worthies," he was allowed home for the holidays. There was another reason as well. By then the perceptive but silent archdeacon had inklings of a growing schism in William's family beside which his youngest son's exploits paled.

William Froude's marriage to Kate Holdsworth was a particularly happy one; he and his wife had a close companionship, and they parented four children, two girls, two boys, not one of whom yet showed signs of the tuberculosis that the archdeacon once feared. But the harmony of this long marriage was threatened by a spiritual contagion that had as great a power to shatter whatever was left of the archdeacon's peace of mind.

"I was thinking of you this morning when I said Mass—Oh that you were safe in the True Fold!" John Henry Newman wrote to William's wife in an ongoing correspondence. Before and after her marriage, Newman encouraged Kate Froude, who was from a most prominent Dartmouth family, on her road to Rome. Kate only wavered because of the pain she knew it would cause her husband and her father-in-law. But Newman held out hopes not only for Kate's soul but that of William, and, of course, the children's.

Before Newman went over to Rome, William, too, was a "Newman-ite." His religious convictions were staunch. He considered quitting the Bristol and Exeter Railway when, because of the demands of the schedule, workers were asked to work, temporarily, on Sundays. But after Newman's defection, William thought for himself. He called himself a universal skeptic, believing that scientific proof was more credible than religious proof: "Not however because I think the former so very certain, but because the latter seems to me so very doubtful," he told Newman.

At Dartington Parsonage, William came to realize that he had "underrated the force of the fascination" his wife had for the Roman Church. As painful to him as her conversion would be, he never considered standing in her way, for he had no religious faith to offer in its place. William was as far from a stereotypical Victorian patriarch as a man could be. Should his wife become a Roman Catholic, he told Newman, it could not impair affection, but it would certainly cause "the end of that full community of thought and judgment in which affection has such scope." He responded to emotional distress much like his father: "I cannot trust myself to think or speak of it."

Conversion was no simple matter of individual conscience in those days; it opened chasms, splitting husband from wife, parent from child. Silent William felt himself more and more cut out of the life and interests of his wife. And Kate Froude faced a complex decision that was already altering her relationship with William, not to mention the distress and upheaval it would cause her aging father-in-law, with whom the family lived.

It made her ask Newman if she would still be allowed to attend family prayers at the parsonage if she converted. If she still would be able to join her children when they went to their grandfather's church on Sundays. Eventually she'd ask Newman if she could convert privately, without letting the aged archdeacon know.

Newman believed "the dear Archdeacon's difficulty" would be gotten over quickly. "You need be no trouble to him at all, I am sure." This he wrote of the Anglican clergyman he had known for years and with whom he and Hurrell once traveled to Rome. "Don't think I write coldly. You may be sure I don't *feel* so. And you may be sure I never separate the thought of William from you, and never can be unmindful of how much he undergoes, or with what sweet gentleness."

Kate wavered for some years, but as early as Christmas 1852, when Anthony's father relented and agreed to see his youngest son, there was already the hint of a Roman Catholic daughter-in-law at Dartington Parsonage. It was not lost on the sharply observant yet silent archdeacon. And once the mother, the old man realized, the children would follow.

"We are here and all is well," Anthony wrote to Mrs. Long from the parsonage at Christmas. "All is so well as if it never had been otherwise. My father is to me as kind as possible, and does not conceal his admiration of Charlotte. What can I say more?"

Early in the new year, Anthony and his family returned to Wales in time for a terrible winter. His children were half dead with influenza and Charlotte, too, was in bed with it. Their nursery maid had to go home because she was spitting blood. Added to this there was "a blighting North Easter, the whole country buried in snow and a sharp frost on top of it."

The children recuperated, but Charlotte's cough lingered, varying with the temperature. It was probably at this period that the opium prescribed for her condition was turning into a drug dependency, if one is to believe later family reports.

It was time to leave Wales. Matt Arnold wrote to Clough after having dinner with Froude in Devonshire in August that their mutual friend "had *softened* more than I can tell you" but was in "baddish spirits." When he visited Anthony later that same month in Wales, "I should like you to see Froude," he continued. "He goes to church, has family prayers—says the *Nemesis* ought never to have been published etc. etc.—his friends say that he is altogether changed," and if he had not exactly returned into the fold of the church, he was at any rate within the fold of the Christian religion. All this after he reconciled with his father.

Matthew Arnold saw Anthony's maturation in a more positive light than other friends: Anthony wasn't conforming; he was purifying his moral being. "All that was mere fume and vanity and love of notoriety and opposition in his proceedings he has abandoned and regrets. This is my view." Instead of beating the air, he was getting more and more literary. "May we all follow his example!"

Froude had reexamined his earlier motives, and found in them the same faults of conceit, immaturity, impressionability, desire to make a stir, that his father found in him. He would never truly forgive himself for exposing the archdeacon as he had in *Shadows of the Clouds*, and was only too aware of what the unpublished letters between him and the rector of Exeter concerning his authorship of the book revealed, a cowardice mixed with a callow bravado. About *The Nemesis of Faith* he felt differently. It was the *publishing* of it that was a mistake, not the writing of it or the ideas of it; it was the unmanly motives of his youth that caused Froude a lingering sense of shame. He would often say he hated what he had been through the age of thirty. He had his reasons.

Though his relationship with the archdeacon and William had improved, no doubt his mood was still "baddish" in November 1853 when the Froudes moved to the milder climate of Devonshire, to Babbicombe outside Torquay, close to both Dartington Parsonage and Charlotte's sisters. From there he acted as a conduit between his friend Max Müller and Charlotte's niece Georgie Grenfell, with whom Müller was in love. Charlotte's brother, Riversdale Grenfell, whom Anthony characterized as a particularly "odd person," opposed the match, and the couple were separated for long stretches of time. However, one of Georgie's sisters, Anthony reported, "said laughing the other day, 'if Mr. Müller were a lady Riversdale would want to marry him himself.'" Anthony advised Müller to "avoid Kingsley in this matter. Don't breathe it to him." Obviously Fanny Kingsley was not as supportive of the relationship as were sister Charlotte and Anthony.

On February 15, 1854, Anthony sent on a letter from Georgie to Müller. The future was Müller's to make, he wrote, encouraging him to be "firm and persistent": "My dear Müller everybody knows what your talents are. Show now what your *character is*. Don't do anything impulsive, it would be harmful to the cause." Not till the end of the letter did he tell his friend that on the previous night, after comparatively brief suffering, Charlotte "became the mother of a boy." Most likely placing the announcement last, as well as not putting in words that he had just become the father of a boy, was a form of modest understatement. Anthony's first son was named Pascoe Grenfell, after Charlotte's father. "Grenny" they called him. The birth did not seem to lighten Anthony's mood.

From Babbicombe, Anthony thanked a "dear Sir" for sending him books from the London Library, a *lending* library, founded by Carlyle and others. It "makes it possible for me to carry on my work so distant from the great repositories," he wrote, "my wife & in some respects my own health obliging me to live here. I should otherwise have had no alternative except to give it up."

*　　*　　*

Around this rather hectic, gloomy time, Anthony was afforded a stroke of luck. The publisher John Parker had come into the possession of a large collection of unpublished manuscripts relating to the reign of Henry VIII. The collector of them placed the trove in Parker's hand and commissioned him to find a writer capable of incorporating them into a new history of the period. Kingsley suggested Froude, as did the publisher's son and namesake, John Parker Jr., the editor of *Fraser's* and another of Froude's close friends. It would be difficult to think of a better choice than Froude for this reevaluation based on primary material, particularly since Froude's essays on the Reformation had been so well received. The opportunity was both auspicious and lucrative; Froude accepted.

The publisher John Chapman was beside himself. He had published two printings of *Nemesis* before Froude disallowed further editions, and the many important essays that had appeared in his *Westminster Review*. Since "England's Forgotten Worthies" was so successful, he and Froude had discussed the possibility of a multivolume history of Queen Elizabeth.

Debonair Chapman was in financial straits, as usual, and might have been counting on (or dreaming of) future profits from Froude's prose. He was trying, unsuccessfully, to sell *The Westminster Review,* edited with great force and less pay by Mary Ann Evans, who had moved to London after her father died. In fact, she lived for some months with Chapman, his wife, and his mistress, upsetting the triangular sexual balance of that household when she, too, became Chapman's mistress for a while. For a longer time her brains were at the service of that charmer's publishing exploits, and, ironically, it was she who published all of Froude's successful work for *Westminster*.

Chapman owed money to the Manchester set, to Harriet Martineau's brother James, to Frank Newman, and to Mr. Darbishire. Froude's defection to Parker would be a financial blow. But on the issue of who would publish the history, Froude was exceedingly direct, as direct as his good father might have been when seeing to the construction of better roads for his district or judging the worth of a new horse for his stables.

He wrote to Chapman: "With regard to my *History* which you suppose to be identical with that of which I have spoken to you, your mistake, I suppose, is not intentional, but it is not less real. It will consist of six volumes (if I complete it), the first two of which will contain the reign of Henry the Eighth, the second two the reigns of Edward and Mary, the remaining two that of Elizabeth. The four first volumes will, with the notes and appendices, take ten years, and these have nothing to do with what you speak of. I shall then only arrive at the subject of my original intention. But at all events, neither I nor any other writer of a book which he hopes to be valuable would compromise the prospects of it by committing the issue of it to embarrassment and crippled resources. I do not say this to wound you, but you must know as a man of business that there is but one course under circumstances of this kind."

He and Chapman had never discussed a history of Henry the Eighth, only of his daughter. The history of Henry would be based on manuscripts Chapman did not and could not possess, and he would be rather unreasonable if he thought Froude should abstain from a work that had no connection to Chapman at all and for which he had been offered a large price.

Not only that, Chapman spoke of "an heretical book" that had been refused by other publishers. "But the *Nemesis* was never refused and you do not pretend that you have lost by it," even though Froude withdrew it from print after the second edition. If his *History of England* proved successful, "the value of the copyrights which you already possess of my historical articles will more than indemnify you for any loss you may suppose yourself to have experienced. If it does not prove valuable you have escaped a bad speculation." He didn't suppose Chapman would have "anything further to say."

Chapman may have had a lot more to say to the Manchester circle; he might even have borrowed the money he owed them on the prospects of Froude's proposed history of Queen Elizabeth. In any case, there was an outcry among Froude's former friends in that city, and it pained Anthony to such a degree that some years afterward he could not broach the subject of this outcry with novelist Elizabeth Gaskell when they met. Still, Anthony had made the most important business decision of his life, though he could not have imagined at the time that he had just secured his financial future.

Intellectually, Froude had already found in the English Reformation a topic as deeply rooted in personal history as his earlier fiction, but this topic allowed his genius a larger canvas and a broader range. The exhaustive reexamination of King Henry VIII—which would wind up taking four volumes, not two—was a subject that could be said to have picked him. From the age of fourteen, he had heard time and again that the English Reformation was a most unfortunate incident, a rebellion against divinely given authority, a schism promoted by two corrupt and tyrannical forces who destroyed the unity of the Church by declaring themselves heads of it. That was what brother Hurrell and John Henry Newman thought, talked about, and wrote. Now Anthony was given the opportunity to confute the tenets of the Oxford Movement, which was leading many of his fellow countrymen into the arms of the Roman Catholic Church. No rash autobiographical novel this time. Instead, a thorough, fact-filled historical reassessment based on previously unavailable records and documents in England and later in Spain.

Psychologically and creatively, this master of English prose style had found his objective correlative. These historical volumes were the appropriate form in which to disagree with his dead brother and to attempt, yet again, to show Oxford that they had misread the intentions of he who had authored *The Nemesis of Faith*. Most of all, these volumes were a sort of love song to his father, one attempting to establish beyond doubt the legitimacy of the Church of England into which he and the archdeacon were born. Given the archdeacon's practical, nontheoretical bent of mind, he would not see his youngest son's ideas as a refutation of his beloved Hurrell's legacy, any more than he had previously seen the radical nature of Hurrell's intimate *Remains*.

The reign of Henry VIII as Froude presented it, using a plethora of hitherto unpublished primary sources, went beyond the issue of divorce and wife beheading to a perceptive study of the political necessity of England's separation from Catholic Europe. In all, his conclusions are quite similar to the way these issues are viewed and taught today. But in his day, Froude was again fighting the current, attempting to restore the reputation of a notorious king. The Tower aside, in Froude's *History,* Henry became England itself, the body politic, forced to rise up against the choke hold of the priesthood, the dominance of an Italian pope, a Spanish emperor. Through his political instincts and savvy, Henry, while still retaining the English church's essentially Catholic character, upheld the power of the modern state over the church.

Of course Froude had a Protestant bias. He upheld the Protestant elements of the Church of England, which his brother Hurrell and Newman had wished to strip away. This was exactly the love song Froude was singing. He was a historian who *did* realize that facts were building blocks which could be arranged—and rearranged—in many different ways. When they were relevant, he laid out his own opinions without disguise, having the ability standard in his times to use the first person when it applied. "I assume the Reformation was in the right, that the claims of the Pope to English supremacy were unjust." Clear enough. But any reader was free to agree or disagree with his interpretation, for the facts were all there. Large and fascinating excerpts from the voices of the times were the backbone of the study, quoted and paraphrased on most every page of the many volumes. His copious footnotes were filled with translations of interesting primary material. The documents were there for the reader to accept, challenge, or reinterpret.

No other historian at that time relied on primary material to such an extent or in such a way. And as unique was his method of describing controversial events. If it was a matter of Roman Catholic abuse, it was substantiated through Roman Catholic observers and recorders of it; Protestant abuse substantiated through Protestant observers and records.

This was history, and at the same time this was riveting literature. The upheavals of the English Reformation were presented with a realism that some of his critics considered too graphic. Flames once more licked the feet of the Catholic monk or the Protestant reformer as the volumes progressed. The martyrs went to the stake with gunpowder hidden in their armpits, in hopes the wood would be dry enough for the fire to rage upward and quickly dispatch them to disparate heavens. The old battles and the old issues were fleshed out with skill and color—and with too much enjoyment, his critics opined.

In successive volumes, the reader experienced political necessity becoming a moral imperative in order for England to free itself from foreign domination. Catherine of Aragon, for example, cast away by Henry: "Let us compensate the queen's sorrows with unstinted sympathy; but let us not trifle with history, by confusing a political necessity with a moral crime."

Froude countered the tendency in many of his fellow Victorians to ignore both the Reformation and the changes it set in motion by imitating and incorporating medieval and Gothic elements in their art, architecture, and poetry. For him the enormous *change* from medieval times held up a mirror in which the nineteenth century could see itself reflected darkly:

"The paths trodden by the footsteps of ages were broken up; old things were passing away, and the faith and the life of ten centuries were dissolving like a dream. Chivalry was dying; the abbey and the castle were soon together to crumble into ruins; and all the forms, desires, beliefs, convictions of the old world were passing away, never to return." The feudal days of "merry old England" were "all gone—like an unsubstantial pageant faded; and between us and the old English there lies a gulf of mystery which the prose of the historian will never adequately bridge."

The very purpose of his history was to track the transition from those unreclaimable times to the present. While many of Froude's fellow artists looked to medieval "Pre-Raphaelite" art for their metaphors, Froude looked for his in the rise of the modern state.

The first two volumes were published on Froude's thirty-eighth birthday and the critics carped. The one constant in Froude's long life would always be controversy. He was dogged by critics, led by one who waited in ambush for each pair of volumes as they were published, and then in the most condescending and contemptuous way shredded them to pieces in *The Saturday Review,* treating the Oxford-educated author as if he were some half-educated schoolboy in need of a good whipping.

E. A. Freeman (remembered mainly for these attacks rather than his own historical work on the Norman period) avowed he knew little about the Reformation and didn't need to know much to criticize Froude. He insisted he had no personal animosity against this man he did not know, that his hatchet jobs were merely intellectual sport, "a strong sense of amusement in bowling down one thing after another." At the same time he wrote in the margins of one of his review copies: "May I live to embowel James Anthony Froude." Freeman was far from Froude's only critic, or his most perceptive one, yet his persistence and his venom allow him to stand as the universal prototype for every author's worst nightmare—the critic from hell.

"Freeman was a man of considerable learning, and of an ill temper even more considerable," Lytton Strachey wrote in 1931. "Naturally enough Froude's work, so coloured, so personal, so obviously written by somebody who was acquainted with the world as well as Oxford, acted like a red rag on the professor. He stormed, he stamped, his fiery and choleric beard shook with indignation. He declared that the book was a mass of inaccuracies and a dastardly attack upon the Church of England. The former accusation was the more important, and the professor devoted years to the proof of it. Unluckily for him, however, the years only revealed more and more clearly the indisputable value of Froude's work in the domain of pure erudition."

Freeman began the tradition of pointing out small errors or typos in Froude's work and making mountains out of them. Since very few people today have the background or the inclination to fact-check twelve volumes of history presented more as an epic than a scholarly treatise, mistakes have been counted monsters, though Froude himself went over all twelve volumes to find only a half dozen substantial errors.

This is not to defend Froude's atrocious handwriting or haphazard proofreading or a certain impatience with minor points, his eye always on the main picture. He could be careless. But whether one agrees or disagrees with Froude the historian, the cultural significance of *The History of England* was profound and needs to be understood. No supporter or detractor seems to have asked the big question of *why The History of England* sold hundreds of thousands of copies, not only in Great Britain but in America—where Froude was a cash cow for "the Scribners."

Essentially, J. A. Froude took himself and his readers on a voyage of discovery—to what we would call their roots. He asked of his prose style only that it communicate clearly—but that clarity was dazzling. With the inherent narrative skill of the novelist, the historian portrayed the English Reformation unfolding panoramically, in all its suffering and sacrifice, its pageantry and purpose. The clearer the style became, volume after volume, the more it seemed to leap from the mind of the author to that of the reader. Its increasing translucency would become the grand hallmark of his nonfiction.

Froude had given his contemporaries a history of the Reformation that needed no apology, a history of real men and women who lived real, flawed, human lives, whose footsteps they followed, and of whom, all in all, they could be proud. And no doubt for many English-speaking people, as for Froude himself, the nemesis of faith—the nagging questions, the inability to answer the unanswerable—was put into a different perspective, as one understood the historical process by which church merged under state. What we have in *The History of England* is perhaps the greatest prose writer of the nineteenth century leading his people to a revitalized perspective on their past; one that allowed them to reevaluate the conflicts of their own time in light of their own history, to rebuff the religious doubts inspired by the Catholic revival with a reaffirmation of the Protestant values that were won at so great a price more than three centuries past, and that led to the independent modern state. No matter how one views the reevaluation of Henry VIII in the first four volumes of Froude's *History,* one must agree with stage manager, critic, and wit William Bodham Donne, who wrote to actress Fanny Kemble while on his way to Devon to meet Froude for the first time: "Tis a very striking book, and written in first rate English, neither Carlylean nor Maccaulyish nor any-ish but his own."

It was no small accomplishment that within eight years of being thrown out of his father's house, and left to fend for himself in a society in which he was barred from the professions, Froude had become an author with a capital *A,* had written the first of many best sellers, and, on his own terms, had gained financial independence.

But there was still Oxford to contend with. On the verge of leaving Wales in 1853, uneasily reconciled with his father, he wrote to an old school friend, wondering, yet again, "Do you think if I am passing through Oxford the Rector would be pleased (or displeased) to see me? Or do you think he would like to hear from me? There are many things I should be glad to say to him, which time must have calmed him sufficiently to enable him to hear. But if you think it would pain him I would not think of it." Silence.

Five years later, after the publication of the third and fourth volumes of the *History,* Froude wrote the new rector of Exeter College a most peculiar letter, given what had passed: "It seems to be desired by my friends at Oxford that I should offer myself to the consideration of the Prime Minister as a candidate for the vacant office of Regius Professor of Modern History." On the surface, a remarkable request, to say the least, since Froude was still excommunicated and many in Oxford were either deeply hostile or suspicious of his notorious past. The operative words here seem to be *prime minister.* The year was 1858 and the Conservatives were in power; Lord Derby, a friend of the Cecil family, had just become prime minister.

Much of Froude's historical research on Elizabeth would center around the Cecil family, and he would have access to the archives of palatial Hatfield House, at the time the abode of James Gascoyne-Cecil, the second Marquis of Salisbury. And there was already a friendship between Anthony and Salisbury's young second wife, formerly Lady Mary Catherine Sackville-West, who was becoming a force in the Conservative party. Even if the Salisbury-Derby connection was not as meaningful as it would become for Froude over the next twenty-five years, there was already enough pressure from high places; the new rector was not able to ignore Froude's letter.

Would the university take "offense" at such an appointment? Froude asked. He assured the rector "that there is no reason to anticipate from me a repetition of the folly which nine years ago led to my leaving Oxford." In fact, "I have long most deeply regretted my conduct. Long ago I made the only expiation in my power in buying up the copyright of the book which gave so just offense." After two editions, the second with his own explanatory preface, Froude refused to allow republication of *The Nemesis of Faith.*

He explained: "I was young when it was written—I was carried away like many others by the excitement of the Continent in 1848. I have been punished by nine years suspension of confidence and I have spent that time in hard labour at Modern History—not as I hope, without effect. I shall direct my Publisher to send you a copy of the third and fourth volume of my History which have just been published. They will I believe make clear the purpose with which they have been written which is nothing more and nothing less than to clear the English Reformation and the father of the Anglican Church from the stains which have been allowed to gather on them."

Obviously, to be considered for a Regius professorship, Froude would first have to be reinstated. He wrote to William Long: "The Rector of Exeter requested me, in the name of the College, to restore myself to Alma Mater, and become again a member of the college. Of course I could only respond to such an overture in one way, so I am again one of that venerable and amiable body."

Yes and no. Something of the old Anthony remained. The debonair tone, the selection of facts—it was *Anthony's* letter to the rector that could be considered a plea for readmission. It was that letter which the rector sent on to the college. It ended: "If I ever return to Oxford it will be with the object of defending the Church of England from all enemies within and without." Did that mean Anthony Froude would sign the Thirty-Nine Articles again? The rector would not allow him to fudge. He would have to avow the Articles *specifically* if he wished to return.

If he no longer "hated" the articles, he still disliked them, saw them as an outdated form, as he put it in his *History.* Their basis was too theoretical, too narrow, for a national church, he would write elsewhere. He would always believe this. If he wanted Oxford, however, he had to subscribe. Not only did he want Oxford, he wanted the Regius professorship of modern history. So it was that the rebel who less than a decade past had his book burned at Exeter wrote: "Understanding that it is desired, before my name can be replaced on the book of Exeter College that I should again place my signature to the 39 articles I beg hereby to express my full readiness to do so."

The rector allowed no dancing on the heads of pins this time. That there was *readiness* in Anthony to sign—"to do so," as he put it—was not enough. He had *actually* to do so! Froude amended the line: "I beg hereby to express my full readiness to do so and declare my assent to the same."

As a result, "My College regretted the rude measure which it had dealt me. The Rector handsomely invited me to return to membership, though my Fellowship was gone. I was afterwards replaced on the books as an Honorary Fellow, which I am still proud to call myself. The London Athenaeum in the same year paid me the distinguished compliment of electing me a member without ballot under the special rule."

All of this perhaps compensated for the fact that his desire to attain the Regius professorship in modern history ended in what could be considered a compromise. The rector allowed him his Oxford, but the professorship went to Liberal Goldwin Smith, who happened to have written a scathing criticism of Froude's work.

Still, on October 19, 1858, Froude had regained his alma mater in time for his eighty-nine-year-old father to see this further reformation in his youngest son. In the last years of the archdeacon's life, father and son found subjects they could talk about, subjects on which they agreed. The archdeacon had himself a large silent knowledge of English church history, and was interested in his son's opinions. He was one of the first to recognize that Anthony was probably right about Henry VIII. He could understand how the popular unfavorable impression of Henry developed, he told Anthony. "The Reformation had been a lay revolt against the clergy. The clergy, Protestant and Catholic, had been allowed to write the history of it, and both had been exasperated against a Government which had forced the spirituality of both persuasions under the control of the State." Anthony was infinitely delighted by his father's understanding.

In his later revealing biography of Benjamin Disraeli, *The Earl of Beaconsfield,* Froude would insist that it was worse than useless to attempt the biography of a man unless you knew, or thought you knew, his inner nature. Biographical methods go in and out of fashion, and one can spend a decade debating what one human can know of another. But one wonders about that mystery of Froude's smile, that sense of vulnerability around the eyes of which his contemporaries spoke. He had overcome the abuses of his childhood, though he was aware that some marks remained for life. He knew physical courage was something he had trained himself to, something that had not come naturally. There was a part of him that would always see himself as he felt his father saw him, particularly during the dark periods of his life. That part would always be the youngest son striving to be worthier of that father. For the archdeacon could offer Anthony concern, a growing respect, even kindness at the end, but never unqualified affection or complete trust.

"Poor Ned Fowler!" the narrator said of Anthony's persona in *Shadows.* "I remember him showing me, with tears in his eyes, the spot in the garden at Darling, where he had listened to the last genuine hearty words his father had ever addressed to him. It was the merest trifle, a flower-bed, where as a little boy, he was driving in a stick to bind up a refractory carnation; but the 'Well done, Ned' (it was the last time he had called him Ned) had rung on the single, soft sweet note among the weary years of discord."

It was little "Tony's" destiny to be the youngest of eight, born at Dartington in the midst of his brilliant mother's decline, to lose her before he knew her, and to have a stern father preoccupied by cares beyond a weak infant who, given his mother's condition, most probably should not have been conceived and was certain to die. One reads in all the archdeacon's letters at one's disposal, to Keble, to Newman, to Hurrell, to William, of his parental concern for his youngest son's character, his education, and his future prospects. He constantly, albeit silently, looked after Anthony. On the old man's death, Anthony as well as William went through many family papers that display this concern and that added to Froude's guilt over the portrait he painted of his father in his fiction. However, among all the remains of the archdeacon's long and venerable life, one cannot help but wonder, could his youngest son, the historian who would become the great biographer of his time, find any conclusive evidence that his father *liked* him?

The Venerable Archdeacon of Totnes died at Dartington Parsonage in his ninetieth year, on February 23, 1859, two months to the day before Anthony's forty-first birthday. His body failed, but his mind remained clear almost to the end. He handled the consequences of his death "as if they were but part of the routine duty of daily life—referring to them precisely as he would to any other matter." He guided himself, as always, by his single, resolute, straightforward determination to do his duty. William wrote to Newman poignantly, recalling time long past when Newman and Hurrell had traveled with the archdeacon: "I think it will interest you to know with what unfailing interest he always referred to your Mediterranean expedition; which the occasional examination of his sketch books should not so much to recall, as to open out into complete and vivid presence." Looking at those sketches, the archdeacon always dwelt with particular pleasure on the share Newman had in them. When he had the time, William planned to send on to Newman those drawings that might be of special interest to him. The sketchbooks William selected are at the Birmingham Oratory today. Even in their neglected state, tattered beauty shines through. They deserve the praise Ruskin once had for them.

And so death finally came to the archdeacon. "He has left all to the eldest son, after the English manner," Clough wrote. "Froude, I believe, received a gift of £6000 some years ago—after the two volumes of his history came out. But by his father's will I am told he has nothing." That was not exactly accurate.

For Froude the most satisfying result of his readmittance to Oxford and the first four volumes of his *History* was that "my father, now growing a very old man, was able to feel before he died that good might come of me after all. The loss of my Fellowship, the abandonment of my profession, which was then a scandal, had irritated and bitterly disappointed him. My worldly prospects had been destroyed and were past recovery. No promotion was to be looked for, for me, on any beaten road of life. All this was gone and could not be recalled. But he saw that I had faculties for which he had ceased to give me credit, that I had perseverance, and that I had even sense and judgement."

The most Froude could reasonably hope for had occurred. "Left in the streets to look for a living under the hoofs of horses," he had escaped being trampled, though he understood that he owed success "more to fortune than to management." To a modern reader the many choices the tall, handsome, articulate rebel had when he left the beaten way seem as remarkable as the newer roads he refused to take. What he did instead was pick himself up by his own bootstraps, marry a most respectable, well-bred woman, make a man of himself, make a living for himself and his family, and restore himself, as much as he legally could, to his society. The greatest reward for his repatriation was that his father, the Venerable Archdeacon of Totnes, "died with the sense that after all I might not prove unworthy of his name."

The perceptions of worth and worthlessness are not conclusions of reasoning, but immediate sensations like those of seeing and hearing.

—J.A.F.

The Perfect Marriage

A little more than a year after his father's death we find Anthony sitting vigil at his wife's sickbed, and writing to another man who valued her dearly, their brother-in-law Charles Kingsley: "When I married Charlotte I little knew how precious a gift God was bestowing upon me. If I have belied in any way the evil promise of my youth, it is to her, to contact with her brave, upright, generous, noble nature that I owe it, and now when every day and hour was teaching me more and more what a treasure she was, when it was my pride to think I was showing myself at last not unworthy of her confidence, it comes to this."

Charlotte, in failing health since the last years in Wales, died the next morning. The twenty-third of April, 1860, which could have marked the celebration of Anthony's forty-second birthday and the simultaneous publication of the fifth and sixth volumes of his *History,* turned into a period of mourning. He would one day, in his biography, divide Carlyle's life into two parts, his first forty years and his life in London. He knew of what he wrote; the only neatness in Froude's own controversial life was how it sliced into sections.

Charlotte's funeral brought Anthony back to the days of his courtship and early marriage, for Charlotte was buried in the churchyard of Charles Kingsley's parsonage at Eversley under the very fir trees she used to admire, on grounds where she and Anthony so often walked. On a nasty spring day, Anthony stood under the firs, surrounded by friends and family, a widower, like his father before him, with three motherless children to tend to: Margaret, ten; Rose Mary, eight; and Grenny, six.

It brought Kingsley back as well—to the days of *Yeast,* when Argemone's coffin was lowered in the ground, her lover's erotic drawings buried with her. Once more Kingsley melded love and death in his peculiar fashion. He had already designed his and Fanny's graves. Their plots in the Eversley churchyard were arranged so that he could view them from the rectory. Morbidly—and erroneously—convinced that Fanny would predecease him, he fed his obsession by going often to the window that overlooked her plot to meditate and mourn his future loss. But "the vacant space by the side of his own proposed grave was soon to have a tenant he little dreamt of," Fanny wrote in her biography of the husband she outlived.

That her favorite sister would be buried next to her husband seemed not to fluster Fanny, who wrote that Kingsley had been more than a brother in some of the most important circumstances of Charlotte's life. Rather than muse by his window, Kingsley would now go out to that "sacred spot" almost every day to commune "in spirit with the dead." Fresh flowers were placed on Charlotte's grave in all seasons, and on Sunday mornings Kingsley himself would lovingly superintend the decorations, placing the cross and wreaths of choice flowers on it with his own hands.

Anthony, after the funeral, had pressing concerns, and was probably remiss in floral arrangements. "Froude has just lost his wife—a heavy loss to him," William Bodham Donne wrote two months later. "She died on the very day that his volumes on Edward and Mary were borne to the world. His household is to be broken up—his children have fortunately some excellent female relatives to care for them, and Froude himself will settle in or near London."

Anthony himself knew what it was to be motherless at an early age and to be left with a remote father and strict aunt. Any qualms he might have had about the children's welfare were dispelled by the fact that they had grown close to Charlotte's sisters during their mother's illness. And one relative had not only been Charlotte's close friend but had been of great help, spending much time with the Froudes: intelligent, empathetic Henrietta Warre. Anthony himself was already leaning on

Henrietta's calm levelheadedness, while he saw to the practical realities of his situation.

During the dreary, wet summer that followed his wife's death, Anthony took a short trip to Ireland to get away from it all, then returned to spend some time with his children and to settle his affairs at Bideford—their second home in Devon. Though the new man Anthony had become resembled his father in many ways, unlike the governor, he was not a landed clergyman, rooted to home, parsonage, stables. He had to make a new life for himself and his family. Professionally, he was at the midpoint of his career, when, then as now, if one can withstand vicissitude, events necessarily move swiftly. He took up temporary lodgings in London, on Clifton Place, close to the archives and libraries he needed for his research. He had pleaded his own health as well as his wife's as the reason for his distance from that city, yet with Charlotte gone, there he was. Almost a reflex action for a literary man—when left to his own devices.

In London, after the death of his father and his wife, we find Anthony very attuned to human suffering, able to care for the sick with a tenderness often remarked upon. That autumn, his close friend, the editor of *Fraser's Magazine,* John Parker Jr., was struck down at forty. Anthony nursed him as he would a brother, it was said; he was at his side constantly, there when he passed.

His older friend and Charlotte's brother-in-law John Ashley Warre was ill as well. When Froude wasn't nursing Parker, he was off at Ramsgate with his stricken friend. He was there often enough to use it, at times, as an address. Anthony was emotionally close to the Warre household on many levels. Not only was he a close friend of John Warre's son and namesake from Warre's *first* marriage, but he was also very close to Henrietta Warre, John Warre's only daughter by his *second* marriage. Charlotte's sister Caroline, Warre's *third* wife, was Henrietta's stepmother. Victorians, too, had expanded nuclear families, though as a result of rampant death rather than divorce.

Henrietta was in her midthirties at the time. Margaret Froude would one day tell biographer Waldo Dunn "that her mother had hoped that ultimately Henrietta might marry Froude and in this hope had died content, knowing that in Henrietta the three motherless children would find a wise and loving second mother." Well, either Charlotte "had" (daughter Margaret) or "would have" (Froude) chosen Henrietta Warre. What we know for certain is that Froude chose her. Henrietta Warre became the love of Anthony's life.

That same autumn, Fanny Kingsley invited her brother-in-law to make the short trip from London to Eversley to see the monument to Charlotte that the Kingsleys had put in place. He'd come down one day, Anthony responded, perhaps when she and Charles were away. He would hold his grief close, just as his father before him. Also, he might have been running a bit shy of his protective sister-in-law, for his life was already taking its new turn.

Kingsley pointed out with alacrity that both John Ashley Warre Sr. and John Parker Jr. had been to Charlotte's funeral, and that within a year the next two funerals were theirs. Parker—"a great soul in a pigmy body," according to Kingsley—had published both Kingsley and Froude. In Froude's obituary of his friend in the February 1861 *Gentleman's Magazine,* he recalled Parker's conviction that the "Press" in the Victorian period had come to have the persuasive power that the "Pulpit" used to have for the public. Parker's recognition of this truth of modern life made him so exaggerate the moral imperative of the press that he believed "he and the heads of the other publishing houses were our virtual spiritual fathers and directors. Such views may appear overstrained, but in him they were at least most real."

The obit appears overstrained as well. Perhaps death demanded a heavier mantle of somber phraseology (though other notices were more lively). Or, perhaps so many deaths so close were weighing Froude down. Then again, having immediately been made the new editor of *Fraser's* by Parker's father, Froude was in the uncomfortable position of impressing the reader with his own high seriousness, at the same time as he dissociated himself from the narrowness latent in his predecessor's taste. "But enough of this,—it is almost laughable to speak of excessive moral sensibility as a fault."

The tone of *Fraser's* was much changed from the uproarious days of the Fraserians under William Maginn in the 1830s, when artist Maclise caricatured that oval table crowded round by hard-drinking literary men, clergymen, and scoundrels: William Thackeray; Count D'Orsay; the renegade Jesuit "Father Prout"; the charismatic preacher Edward Irving; Irving's best friend up from Scotland, young Carlyle; and, among the many others, the older, so talkative Coleridge, who used to irk Carlyle with the spray from his endless monologues.

Though Parker published Kingsley's *Yeast,* he refused *Alton Locke* as the former serialization had infuriated some and cut sales. When Edward Fitzgerald sent Parker his *Rubáiyát,* he told Parker "he might find it dangerous among his divines," and indeed Parker rejected it. Still, under

Parker's editorship, *Fraser's* was liberal within limits and what was beginning to be called Broad Church—a midcentury Anglican development—in its point of view. The Broad Church ascribed to the "latitude" in personal belief that Froude had felt necessary in a national church, in the days when he rationalized in order to take deacon's vows. That thinking had led to the worst mistake he was ever to make, and might be the reason that he never warmed to the Broad Church largesse. Still, Froude's own editorial policy would be quite inclusive (broad, not Broad Church); he would compare his intellectual and political openness to an earlier historical model, to a time during the Reformation when Saint Paul's pulpit accommodated Lutherans, Catholics, and Calvinists on alternating Sundays.

So it was that within a year of Charlotte's death, Froude was living in London, editing *Fraser's* at four hundred pounds per annum, a position he'd hold for the next fourteen years. But at the beginning he was not at all sure he'd continue in this capacity. Anthony had planned a six-volume history. Six volumes were published, the last two the week that Charlotte died, and it was only as a new widower that he began his *Reign of Elizabeth* that would eventually run to six volumes as well. This was a "new epoch" in his *History of England*. It was also a curtain down on the first half of his life.

"There may be persons who having gone so far with me, may not care to accompany me further; others may be interested in the later and brighter period, who may not care to encumber themselves with the earlier volumes."

He needed to travel to research his *Reign of Elizabeth*, and here, timing was with him. The royal archives at Simancas had just been opened, and he thought the government might finance his trip to Spain to see the till-then-secret documents from Philip the Second and his ambassadors to Elizabeth. The government did not come through with a stipend; still, almost immediately after being made editor, Froude left others temporarily in charge, and traveled to Spain with Henrietta Warre's half brother.

Froude's ambiguity about *Fraser's* and his heightened activity in the twenty months following Charlotte's death recall to mind a friend from an old New England family who told me that her family trust had been so constructed that only first spouses and their issue inherited. Their axiom: The first time one marries for family, the second time for love. This is not to disparage Froude's respect and gratitude to Charlotte, who made a man of him in so many ways. But deeply felt, passionate love—

the kind that makes a man like Froude write love poetry in his own magazine—he had not experienced in his first marriage. Charlotte, "sweet Prude," had been a highly nervous, temperamental person, and this had caused conflict. "Together," Anthony entitled the unsigned poem he wrote to Henrietta: "Let my blood speak to thine."

In Spain, open to the warm, soft south wind, breathing in the fragrance of the Mediterranean, "the flowers breaking," Anthony felt life surge. John Warre was an *invaluable* companion as they both drank in the sights and sounds and character of the country. Letters back and forth with Henrietta must have mixed with the spirit of the place. Being physically separated from her for a time was perhaps as meaningful as the return would be. It gave Anthony the promise of the future without embarking on it too soon.

He didn't much care for Madrid, where he had to wait for permission to work at Simancas. The city was "of no interest except for the pictures, which are the finest in the world I suppose." Portrait painting was the height of art for him. He studied the portraits of Philip II and Charles V at every age and condition; this brought him closer to their psychology and character. In Madrid his intention deepened to reconfigure the building blocks of history from their point of view, the Roman Catholic, Roman Empire point of view, after he completed his work on Henry VIII and Elizabeth Rex.

At the royal archives at Simancas, a treasure trove of material awaited him. Through the letters and journals of Philip's ambassadors and envoys to England, and through the many languages and the impossible scrawl of royalty itself, the court of Elizabeth came to life. He felt the value of the documents lay less in the facts they contained than in the insight they gave "into the secret passions and motives of the great actors in European history." The primary material concerning the young Elizabeth's headlong infatuation with Dudley, at the same time as she so astutely kept Philip II (her widowed brother-in-law) on the hook, was so tantalizing that Froude, immersed in so much new material, wrote an essay for *Fraser's* too close to the heat of the moment; it would need later revision. In the Spanish archives, he found flesh and blood restored to the bones of history. In the soft warmth of Spain, Froude found his own heart racing.

At the end of Froude's months there he wrote to his eldest child, who even at ten years of age was becoming his mainstay, his darling Margaret, that "your daddy is on his way back to you at last, and hopes to be at Clifton Place on Wednesday evening." It was a delightful letter meant for

Rose as well, filled with descriptions of his travels, full of fun: "My dear little creatures, I shall be very glad to see you again, and you, I hope will be glad to see me, and won't ask me what I have for you. For fear you should, I think it better to tell you that I have got two little Spanish silver cups to drink chocolate in, and you must settle among yourselves which of you shall have which. The cups are not alike. If you can't manage it otherwise, you had better draw lots." He ended his letter "Good bye, my darlings." His son was not mentioned. Perhaps Grenny was staying with a different aunt.

By the time his first son was born, Anthony and Charlotte had just moved to Devonshire, and Grenny, like his father before him, seems to have had a mother who was in declining health and a father who, deeply committed to his older children, suffered some health problems himself, particularly with his eyes, and most possibly appeared remote. Anthony was quite busy, away often, in London, researching in the records office or abroad. When he was at home he was given to religious observance, decorum, and family prayer. No longer was he bobbing on the deep lakes at midnight, fly-fishing under the moon.

Then when Anthony came back from Spain that June, he was both doing catch-up at *Fraser's* and courting Henrietta. Perhaps he'd have to let the editorship go, he wrote to his friend Mrs. Long, who was enjoying the pleasures of Italy. He told her, "What I chiefly arrived at in Spain was the same passionate liking you describe yourself as having caught for the wandering life." She shouldn't be surprised if he joined her in Italy one day soon. But not alone.

He was noticeably reticent in describing his situation to Mrs. Long: "For—I wonder what you will think of what I am going to tell you. I am going early in the autumn to be married again, to one of Charlotte's dearest friends, whom of all others she would have chosen as her children's mother."

On September 12, in 1861, at Trinity Church, Chelsea, Anthony married Henrietta Elizabeth Warre. He was forty-three, she thirty-six.

The couple did not go to Italy. They took their honeymoon in Wales, the new husband having no compunction sharing the romance of the place with his second wife. He found time to write to Mrs. Long, for he was quite relieved by her and her husband's warm and kind letter in response to his nuptials. They both had known him since Oxford days and were privy to the ins and outs of his "chequered fortune." In Henrietta, he could now confide, he had found a wife more precious than rubies—his comparison. "As Charlotte's dear friend, she will be the tenderest mother to the children, while I shall have in her, I trust and pray, for the remainder of *both* our lives, the sweetest friend, the most affectionate companion, and the soundest and wisest advisor."

It may have been his sweetest friend and wisest advisor who dissuaded him from the euphoric dream of a prolonged honeymoon, of leaving the children with Charlotte's sisters for a longer time, of taking his books and papers with him and, in Florence or Valencia, being free to enjoy with her what he described as "the light-hearted careless irresponsibility only to be had abroad," where one could live without thought for tomorrow. Instead, "I do not know exactly where we shall live," Froude informed Mrs. Long. "There is to be a Modern History Professorship started at Oxford next term, for which I offer myself." He aimed once more for professorship. Once more Oxford was not responsive.

London was where he would live. He, his wife, his three children by Charlotte, and, eventually, his two children by Henrietta. Henrietta Froude, from the beginning, devoted herself not only to her husband, whom she adored, but to his children, who were already dear to her. In the annals of daughters and stepmothers, few relationships stand out as so mutually satisfying. "Momma," his children called Henrietta and meant it. Intelligent, nurturing, empathetic, she devoted herself to them and their interests as well as to their father, voluntarily refusing new associations now that she had her own family to tend.

What Anthony's oft-noted irony covered was a nature that was in private acutely sensitive to slights. Henrietta understood the fluctuation in Anthony's moods and had the ability, through humor and common sense to bring him back to the true proportions of things when he was depressed. The children remembered her saying that for all the brilliant social affairs the couple attended, they missed nothing by staying home, as their father's best conversation was what they heard in the bosom of the family. One suspects that Henrietta had as well a close relationship with her own stepmother, Charlotte's sister Caroline. For when she and Anthony had children of their own, Caroline became "grandmother" to them, not "aunt," as she was to Margaret, Rose, and Grenny.

"Margaret Froude once remarked to me," Waldo Dunn wrote, "'My mother and father were in temperament unsuited to each other. My mother was a nervous, excitable person like me. His marriage with my stepmother was one of those perfect marriages. Through it there came to him perfect peace. With her he enjoyed twelve years of entire happiness, the only entirely happy period of his life.'"

The same year that Anthony remarried, to his great surprise Thomas

Carlyle himself came to his door, expressing a wish to spend more time with him. Anthony was invited to visit 5 Cheyne Row more often and to be Carlyle's companion in his long walks through London. Carlyle was sixty-six years old, and might have even arrived on horseback—his daily relief in all sorts of weather from the ongoing toil of writing his voluminous life of Frederick the Great. Tall, gaunt, ruddy-complected with a full head of hair and a newly grown beard, Scottish Carlyle was still young-looking for his age. "Ten generations of his Annandale ancestors have given him a constitution as hard as granite."

Dyspepsia does not kill, but its pain no doubt contributed to Carlyle's lifelong hypochondria and his growing misanthropy. For years he felt himself an old man, always on the verge of cutting the mortal coil, daily besieged by his bowels and by the enormous stress he felt as he wrote.

His wife, Jane Welsh Carlyle, was six years younger and unfortunately looked the way Carlyle said he felt. Formerly a vivacious, buxom beauty with exciting, if irregular, features, she was by sixty a thin, sadly desiccated shadow of her former self. Photographs of her at the time were "horrid," as Virginia Woolf pointed out. "The eyes are the only parts with warmth and depth in them; the rest is granulated skin tight stretched over a skull." When an old friend from her childhood visited, the friend broke into tears when Carlyle walked into the room after his horseback ride. The contrast between Carlyle's health and Jane's painful state was doubly pathetic to someone who had known her when she was young.

Now that Froude was coming to Cheyne Row often, he usually found Jane in her drawing room, alone, or with those waiting to see the great man. Jane had from the first been fond of him, and he soon became a confidant. She had not lost her sharp tongue or wit, though her pale, drawn, and suffering face came back to Froude in his dreams. When Carlyle entered, he would spew forth in his exaggerated and emphatic way, taking over the conversation and the very air in the room. He "poured out whole Niagaras of scorn and vituperation sometimes for hours together, and she was wearied, as she confessed, of a tale which she had heard so often and in much of which she imperfectly believed.

"Carlyle himself I admired intensely, but it was with admiration too complete for pleasant social relationship. His manner was impatient and overbearing. He denounced everybody and everything, and, though what he said was in my opinion intensely true and right, yet I felt that it would be impossible to live with him on equal terms. One loves those who are not far removed from oneself. He seemed to me a superior order of being, whom one approached with genuine reverence, but could scarcely dare to love."

The youngest son had a lifetime of a father whom he considered, if not intellectually, morally "a superior order of being" who had been "far removed" from him, whom he had learned to approach with reverence, rather than the old fear, but with whom he had never lived on equal terms. It is not surprising that Froude, a busy man, in love with his new wife, accepted in the most brilliant London society, was pleased to keep a respectful distance from the aging, erratic Carlyle and his family secrets, for the Carlyle marriage was obviously a difficult one. Jane's wit often centered on Carlyle's foibles, and he, as difficult as he was to live with, seemed to enjoy these barbs as much as those assembled.

Though Froude himself had not pressed for a closer friendship with Carlyle: "To refuse such hands when they were held out to me I thought would be ungracious and unnecessary. I felt myself highly honoured besides, and I promised myself pleasure and advantage from increased opportunities of quiet conversation with him." For "when alone with a single companion he was delightful, brilliantly entertaining, sympathetic, and even occasionally tolerant of what at other times he would execrate, and full of the widest information about all things and subjects." To really understand Carlyle's effect on all those he influenced in his times, one would have had to hear him talk.

Though the domestic situation on Cheyne Row worried Anthony, he was flattered that Carlyle had chosen him as an intimate. Given his own gifts, he felt himself more honored than he perhaps should have been by Carlyle's increasing attention.

Froude's enemies would one day paint Anthony as an erstwhile Boswell fawning a Great Man. Nothing could be farther from the truth. Anthony Froude in London was a literary lion himself, and a noted historian, involved at the moment with his own life.

He was at the heart of all things literary and political, editor of *Fraser's,* a sought-after author, an astonishingly well-read and learned—if endemically controversial—man. His and Henrietta's dinner parties "were famous for their brilliancy and charm." Froude was a unique combination, a real man of letters who was also a man of the world. He could talk—and did—with anyone from a child to a fisherman to a cabinet minister. He did not suffer fools gladly; when he was bored he was silent, but it showed on his face. Being a bore, he would write, was the one deadly sin. He had a sense of humor, but he didn't take the wild verbal leaps of Carlyle; instead he was known for sardonic wit, subtle enough, one would imagine from his writings, to be aimed in more than one direction, so that the hearer couldn't exactly pinpoint the barb. He was, as Moncure Conway pointed out, "profoundly skeptical of all general subjects," but at the same time, he could be "rather credulous concerning persons." True enough.

With Henrietta by his side among everybody who was anybody, J. A. Froude no longer felt the need to prove his worth. To others. Or to her. She, after all, had married the new man, was in no way connected to the "evil promise" of his youth. He was who he was, said what he said, knew what he knew, and devil take the hindmost. (Devil often did.) It is within the context of a full life that Froude's relationship with Thomas Carlyle has to be seen.

On June 28, 1863, Henrietta, close to forty, gave birth to her first child, a son, Ashley Anthony, named for her deceased father, John Ashley, and her husband, James Anthony. Froude wrote to Elizabeth Gaskell from Salcombe: "Henrietta got through her travail wonderfully well, and now after three months by the sea is stronger and more active than ever. I hardly knew how the little girls would take to the new-comer, but as it turns out they are devoted to him. It was lucky on their account that it was a boy. Another girl would have been far more likely to be an object of jealousy."

Froude was mute on the point of whether or not this new boy became an object of jealousy to his half brother. What was lucky for Margaret and Rose Mary might not have been for him. Grenny had been born on the downward slope of the first marriage, his own mother drug-addicted and in decline, his father saddened. Ashley, by contrast, was the firstborn of Anthony's only entirely happy period. He was soon followed by a sister, Froude's youngest daughter, Mary, known as May, the object of much affection. Family prayers continued, but within the warm bosom of a happy household. Henrietta pictured Anthony on vacation, entertaining the children "dressed as a magician in a peaked cap."

"The Magazine prospers," Froude was able to report after only two years as editor of *Fraser's*: "The circulation now exceeds 3,000 and more copies must be printed." He was "highly complimented by Carlyle last night on the management."

This to Scottish John Skelton, long a contributor to the magazine, one Froude hoped to keep writing for it. More than a decade younger than Froude, Skelton, who used the pen name Shirley, combined wit and psychological perceptivity with political heterodoxy. He had written the

"Things in General" column for the weekly *Edinburgh Guardian* during its five-year existence during the 1850s. In his memoir, *The Table-Talk of Shirley,* Skelton defined that paper as one where "the Dissenters, the rebels, the despised minority" were given the chance of a hearing. Only the Whigs were excluded, and "we took to recommending the incomprehensible heresies of Maurice and the muscular latitudinarianism of Kingsley." His independence of mind by itself would have recommended him to Froude.

They became close friends. In his memoirs, Skelton remembered the first impression he had of the new editor of *Fraser's*: "His presence was striking and impressive,—coal-black eyes, wonderfully lustrous and luminous," full of genius. His hair was coal black, too, though streaked with gray, his massive features strongly lined "and capable of the subtlest play of expression." For himself, Skelton said without any reserve that Froude was the most interesting man he had ever known.

It is illuminating to compare *Fraser's* respectable circulation with that of Thackeray's *Cornhill Magazine,* which paid very high prices when it came to fiction. Again, from his side of the pond, William Bodham Donne kept friend Fanny Kemble abreast in America: "Thackeray's Cornhill Magazine is a thriving concern—selling 95,000 numbers per month. Both his story and Trollope's are very good: but my principal attraction to its orange-tawny cover is the Natural History by G. H. Lewes." Donne praised Lewes's article to Thackeray's daughter, who disagreed, saying everybody told her they knew as much about the subject beforehand: "Whereupon, I answered that 'Everybody was much wiser than I gave them credit for!'"

Fiction was not the strength of *Fraser's* under Froude, nor did he mean it to be. (And he never cared for George Eliot's Lewes.) His was mainly an issue-driven magazine, and by and large reflected a major characteristic of Froude's mind, the ability of encompassing many sides of the same subject. A mixed blessing, but a fine quality in an editor. A letter of acceptance might read: *I don't agree with you, but, then again, why should I?* A letter of rejection would announce his reservations loud and clear.

He could respond with amazing alacrity. One evening Florence Nightingale sent him a paper on pauperism: "Although unable to claim the honour of your acquaintance, I venture . . ."

The same evening Froude wrote to thank her and to discuss the issue: "Most thinking people are beginning to see at last that Political Economy does not solve all social problems. . . ."

"Froude has lost no time," Nightingale wrote to a friend the next morning, having received his answer. "I did not send my paper to him till late last night. Does that mean it is to be in the March Frasers?"

Yes.

Speed was not amiss in a man who was in correspondence with would-be contributors, reading submissions, responding honestly and intelligently, writing his own books and articles, reading widely in the many areas that interested him, traveling widely in Ireland and Spain, working constantly in archives, spending as much time as possible with his growing family.

In his editorial responses, many of Froude's letters to contributors begin "Dear Sir" rather than with a name. Most of his extant letters state month and day and *all* throughout his life exclude year. And his handwriting ranks with the most indecipherable of the period—surpassing the scrawl of royalty. One can understand how the printer could make many a small typographical error because of it during Froude's long career. His hand seemed to be in a constant rush to keep up with his mind, and his mind most often wins the race, while his handwriting is reduced to a squiggle as it finishes second. One imagines he proofread the same way, concentrating on concepts rather than word for word. Frequent infections of the eye may have abetted this tendency. Here Anthony is the exact opposite of Carlyle, who, until palsy in his right hand stopped him, wrote with an absolute precision that belies—or controls—the uncontrollable in his nature. There was never an undotted *i* or an uncrossed *t* or the lack of a hyphen no matter how unsettling the thought. In contrast, no Froude, neither father nor son, found an apostrophe necessary to define possession.

On Easter Monday 1862, when Skelton inquired about submitting his long essay on Robert Browning, who had just returned to London from years in Italy, he expected a quick acceptance, as usual. Froude and Browning were well acquainted. Both had highly developed philosophical minds, were incredibly well read in modern and classical literature, and were able to converse on many levels. And Froude always had a certain respect, mixed with a slight dash of awe and envy, for those men who had the strength of character to rise in the world without the benefit of being to Oxford born.

Browning came from a dissenting family and could not attend. He had a gentle and scholarly father, proud of his son, encouraging, indulging his artistic ambitions. Browning senior was an original subscriber to University College, London, but his brilliant son did not last there a year. Instead, Robert read on his own in his father's extensive library, traveled, wrote, went to visit the middle-aged invalid poet Elizabeth Barrett, known throughout the world, married her secretly, and went off with her for sixteen years in Italy. Not entirely happy years, according to the poet, given his wife's health and her father's refusal to forgive her for marrying. They were instead, he recalled, the only years in which he really *lived*.

After his wife's death, Browning devoted what was left of life to his son. Pen had been raised by a doting mother who called him her "Florentine," insisted on his long blond hair, his Renaissance-ish frocks. Browning cut the twelve-year-old's hair, put him in trousers (too many pins in frocks), and brought him home to make an Englishman of him before it was too late. Which it already was, though Browning, his eyes unblinkingly directed toward Oxford, would soon ask no less than Benjamin Jowett to prepare his son. Pen would never make it to Balliol or Oriel, though he squeezed into Christ Church and spent lots of his father's money, before he went off to Holland to learn to paint, married an American heiress, and settled in Venice.

"I know very little of Browning's poetry: but Browning himself I admire extremely," Anthony answered Skelton. "I have often wished for leisure to read him. I tried *Paracelsus* twenty years ago unsuccessfully, and this, I suppose, has prevented me from exciting myself about him as I ought. By all means let me have your article."

It was a lukewarm response at best.

But then, in the early 1860s, the recently deceased Elizabeth Barrett Browning had a worldwide reputation, while Browning's poems were still considered obscure. When they had secretly married, Wordsworth reportedly quipped, "So Robert Browning and Elizabeth Barrett have run away together. Let's hope they understand each other, nobody else does." In the intervening period, they both strived toward clarity. Robert's best dramatic monologues appeared in the only book he published during his marriage, *Men and Women,* still in print today. But on the publication date, 1855, *The Athenaeum* pronounced it obscure and the edition sold fewer than two hundred copies, a blow to both poets.

Thomas Carlyle had a genuine affection for Browning before and after his marriage and not only because Browning's mother was Scottish. Carlyle was impressed by the breadth and passion of his knowledge and the promise of his youth. No "blockhead" Browning, who always recorded with a fair amount of surprise, as had Froude, that it was Carlyle who sought him out. Carlyle was in his midforties, Browning in his late twenties when they met. Years later, it was to Carlyle that Browning turned after *Men and Women* failed. He handed the Carlyles a copy personally, as he, Elizabeth, and Pen had come to London to be there on publication, sure that the world would find him "much clearer this time."

Carlyle took a year to write to him about the book: "I really knew not what to say, and hesitated always." He loathed giving advice, so would offer instead a few "honest words, rough and ready, from a fellow-pilgrim well-affected to you." After praising Browning's intellect, his "genius if you like," his extraordinary power of expression, his poetic fancy: "What is the shadow side of the Picture then? For in that too I ought to be equally honest. My friend, it is what they call 'unintelligibility!' That is a fact: you are dreadfully difficult to understand; and that is really a sin."

The usually efficient Froude reported on Skelton's Browning essay close to a year after submission, in January 1863: "My dear Skelton,—I am very sorry about Browning. The length has been the difficulty. Were it made up of your own work it should have gone in long ago, without a day's delay. But Browning's verse!" It had intellect, thought, power, grace, the charm in detail which poetry should have, yet with all that, it still, unfortunately, rang "like a bell of lead."

For Skelton's sake alone he would run the essay in the next issue, telling him in quintessential Froudeanese: "No doubt he deserves all you say; yet it will be vain. To this generation Browning is as uninteresting as Shakespeare's Sonnets were to the last century. In making the comparison you see I admit that you might be right."

"It's about time that we began to do justice to Robert Browning," Skelton's critical reevaluation began. Browning was grateful. He had "no doubt" that the article "exercised much influence on the fortunes of my poetry." Soon Queen Victoria, famously widowed herself, invited the poet to tea, discreetly inquiring if she was free to ask the poet about his dead wife. Ironically, *Fraser's* established Robert Browning's reputation, which from then on grew like the proverbial mustard seed.

Froude's editorship coincided with the beginning of the American Civil War, and *Fraser's* closely covered it and the Reconstruction period.

Unlike Carlyle, Froude felt slavery was an evil, but he believed it would take hundreds of years for it to be abolished in America. Like most Englishmen, he favored the Confederacy, as well as believing that once fractured, the Union could not reset itself and heal. But this did not prevent him from publishing abolitionists such as Carlyle's young friend Moncure Conway, a Virginian who came to England with a letter from Emerson. After Moncure graduated from Harvard's School of Theology and before he arrived to stir up audiences throughout England with his pro-North lectures, the Virginian led his father's slaves to freedom in neighboring Washington. Carlyle encouraged Froude to publish Moncure despite the fact that when in print the same articles drove Carlyle to outrage and hyperbole as he and Moncure walked. All these men valued strength of mind and moral conviction. It is striking to read how they could criticize each other's views both by letter and in print and still maintain strong friendships. None were—or sought to be—among sycophants and yes-men. Intelligence and strength of conviction were what impressed them—and what cemented the long relationship between Froude and Carlyle.

Moncure remembered Froude telling him: "Fifty years hence people will look upon the whole emancipation enthusiasm as—like many other enthusiasms—a dream of madness." Yet Froude published John Stuart Mill: "I am not blind to the possibility that it may require a long war to lower the arrogance and tame the aggressive ambition of the slave owners," Mill wrote in the February 1862 *Fraser's*. "War, in a good cause, is not the greatest evil which a nation can suffer."

"Mill would be a good subject for you," Froude wrote to an unnamed contributor during the time the author of *On Liberty* served in Parliament. "I leave you free to take your own line about him, provided you treat him like a gentleman. I myself have a moderate admiration for him— without however liking him compared to Hume, whom he intellectually resembles—except at a prodigious distance. Mill has a strange dash of fanaticism about him which is the secret of his shortcomings, & will perhaps make a shipwreck of him in public life."

After the North won, Moncure was free to write on Reconstruction in *Fraser's* as he pleased, but Froude warned him to remember what the English said from the beginning, that difficulty would come after the war: "So far as we can see, things are going exactly the way we expected. You are compelled to keep up a military government in the South, and that military government increases the feeling which renders it necessary." His "old world people" had their reasons for hesitation and distrust, he told Moncure, using examples from the Reformation, history once more becoming metaphor: "You cannot treat an institution as old as mankind as a crime to be put out by force. . . . You are playing once again on a new stage the old game of Philip the Second and Alva. You cannot be more persuaded of the wickedness of slavery than they were of the wickedness of heresy. The universe does not allow one section of mankind to inflict its view upon another at the point of the sword. If the sword is pressed into service beyond the common sense of mankind, it will kill the man that uses it."

However, when the Union survived, Froude looked toward the United States with growing respect for its accomplishments and changed his point of view. In fact, the States often replaced the Reformation as Froude's metaphor for the future, for how England could expand its boundaries and maintain its culture. Froude's America was based on English values. Free and united she drew closer to England of her own volition, and England should see in her success the brightest example for uniting her own colonies. He could even "hope and believe that a time will come when there will no longer be Englishmen and Americans, but we shall be of one heart and mind, and perhaps one name."

The first two volumes of Froude's *Reign of Elizabeth* (volumes seven and eight of the *History*) were published, allowing Kingsley to begin New Year's 1864 by writing a laudatory review in *Macmillan's Magazine*. In these volumes Froude expressed more openly his *personal* reservations concerning the Roman Catholic faith. Catholicism had long since ceased to be the expression of the true convictions of sensible men on the relation between themselves and heaven: "Credible to the student in the cloister, credible to those whose thoughts were but echoes of tradition, it was not credible any more to men of active and original vigour of understanding. Credible to the uneducated, the eccentric, the imaginative, the superstitious; credible to those who reasoned by sentiment, and made syllogisms of their passions, it was incredible then and evermore to the sane and healthy intelligence which in the long run commands the mind of the world."

Kingsley made an additional leap in his review of Froude's volumes, and named a *living* Roman Catholic as a *manipulator* of credible souls: "Truth, for its own sake, had never been a virtue with the Roman clergy. Father Newman informs us that it need not, and on the whole ought not to be; that cunning is the weapon which Heaven has given to the saints where with to withstand the brute male force of the wicked world which marries and is given in marriage. Whether his notion be doctrinally correct or not, it is at least historically so."

Bad news traveled its winged route and Father Newman received the review posthaste "with a pencil mark calling my attention to page 217."

He didn't ask for an apology from *Macmillan's,* he just wrote, in his most gentle manner, to tell the publisher he had been slandered.

When Newman found out the reviewer was Kingsley he was surprised, and he probably saw Froude behind it. He took advantage of an opportunity that he said might never occur again, not only to rebut Kingsley but the anti–Roman Catholic assumptions underlying Froude's widely read *History of England,* without ever calling attention to the work or Anthony's name.

As the controversy developed, Kingsley replied to Newman's call of slander, Newman replied to Kingsley's reply, a private correspondence was followed by public letters, then by each man publishing pamphlets on the issue. And out of the tangle instigated by three cutting sentences in Kingsley's review of Froude came Newman's seven pamphlets transposed into one of the great autobiographies of the Victorian period: his *Apologia pro Vita Sua.* (In the extremely useful Norton Critical Edition of that work, so well edited by David J. DeLaura, one can revisit the texts of the controversy.)

Froude's general attack, Kingsley's personal attack, Newman's *Apologia* as well, were to some degree propelled by a very human drama going on in the background: Newman's role in converting all of William Froude's family to Roman Catholicism. As a young man, it had been Anthony who came to his married brother William at a time when his life was shattered. Once Anthony was reunited with his father, it became he who bore witness to what his older brother suffered and William who came to Anthony and Henrietta for advice. William's wife converted in the archdeacon's lifetime, but his sons, Hurrell and Eddy, waited until their grandfather passed.

By the time William's son Hurrell was ready for university, Catholics were allowed to matriculate at Oxford. In fact, Newman himself had wished to build an oratory on land he bought there, and return to Oxford as a priest in a new capacity. But that was not to be. The pope, who was suspicious of the peculiar Englishman, contained him at Birmingham—when he was not being sent to Ireland to found a Roman Catholic university there. In Birmingham, Newman established his Oratory of St. Philip Neri, an Italian Renaissance enclave on the long stretch of road that led from the city to the outskirt of Edgbaston (as a youth, J. R. R. Tolkien lived next door). It was perhaps not as dreary a stretch of road as it is today. Newman ran a school for boys, and William's Roman Catholic sons attended it, Newman their confessor.

When William's son Hurrell went on to Oxford, Newman advised him through his mother "not to talk of religion, not to argue, not to attempt to proselytize," but to focus on his studies. If forced to Anglican services, he could hide a cross in his hand. Still, as Newman wrote to Kate, "A Catholic cannot comfortably or profitably go to Oxford. Oxford belongs to the country and the country's religion." Hurrell did not take a degree.

William's younger son, Eddy, had ability in science and before his conversion had helped in his father's laboratory. He surprised William by staying close to him after he became a Roman Catholic and continuing to assist him in his experiments when he was at home. Daughter Elizabeth converted, too, and later became the Countess von Hügel. Only the youngest daughter, Mary, remained in the Church of England—and she was consumptive. The year that Anthony published his first volumes of *Reign of Elizabeth,* the child was near death. "To see a child die slowly before one's eyes seems an incredible trial," Newman commiserated. "William was besides himself," Kate responded. The awful irony of the only Anglican member of his family being struck down by tuberculosis was not lost, even on Mary herself. When the sick child burst a blood vessel in her lung, she knew the end was near. "Pray don't think I'm unhappy about it; for I think I'd rather," she said. "But I'm sorry for Papa."

Papa was inconsolable. "All Monday he was very much overwhelmed," Kate wrote to Newman. "That last terrible half hour, during which he held her in his arms, was always present to his imagination."

Mother had an additional worry: Mary had refused last rites. "As to dear Mary, I cannot be surprised at your being down about her," Newman wrote, but he reassured Kate that Mary was too young to have consciously rejected the grace offered her. "God will love her."

On the heels of Mary's death, sixteen-year-old Eddy suddenly announced to Kate from the Oratory that it would be a waste of William's money to send him on to Oxford, as he was going to become a priest. Newman was Eddy's confessor, but it had been another priest who had encouraged this in Newman's absence, and Newman was upset when he found out—"A soul cannot have two physicians at once." He was quite anxious concerning the pain the boy's announcement would cause his father. He knew of William's increasing isolation, and to lose Eddy as well as Mary in the same year was a dreadful blow. Eddy's "primary duty is to obey you," he wrote to William. "I do not see that he can plead any sense of ecclesiastical duty strong enough to overcome this—yet, just as I think he will go through Oxford (if sent there) as a religious youth keeping his principles, so I expect he will keep to this wish."

Let him take a degree first. Afterward, "my dear William, I think you would be in the position of many a parent . . . who wishes his son to succeed him . . . and he *will* go into a profession or into the army—or who wants his son to marry a certain lady, and he *will* fix his affections on some one else. I do not think you would have any right to complain, *because* Eddy would be a *man*."

It was a skillful argument, for hadn't William himself *insisted* on a profession, *insisted* on the woman of his choice? "When a man is old enough to vow to love for ever a certain woman, I think he is old enough to vow celibacy," Newman continued in a memorable line.

When William was informed that Eddy was going to become a priest, he controlled the great state of excitement and anxiety that seized him, and rather than broaching the subject when his son came home, he first went to speak with the man who would understand his plight.

"Wm is going to Salcombe to see Anthony, who is there, and *that* will do him no good," Kate informed Newman.

But of course it did do him good. By the time their father died in 1859, only the two brothers remained, and they alone had the unique experience of having grown up under the influence of Hurrell and Newman—and to seeing where it all led. They both remembered their dead brother's words, that they would be able to come to their own religious conclusions on the day when Keble and Newman disagreed.

Newman told William that he wasn't the universal skeptic he thought he had become. The assumption that he understood William better than William understood himself led William, who had stayed relatively silent concerning religion in his ongoing correspondence with Newman, to articulate his position. He explained that scientific *probability,* which his brother Hurrell had applied to validate his religious position, had brought him to the opposite conclusion. He was indeed a universal skeptic. He owed Newman an explanation because to remain silent "might have implied sulkiness or cowardice." In fact he would have spoken sooner "if my thoughts were less unready than they are, to shape themselves into words," or, more revealingly, if he could entertain a rational hope that his words would be conveyed to another's mind as they existed in his own. Speaking out was instead "painful from its laboriousness and its hopelessness."

At Salcombe that summer of 1864, at the zenith of his own domestic tragedy, William found in his younger brother someone who would understand his plight, with whom he could talk on this issue without the pain of being hopelessly misunderstood as he was in the bosom of his family. He could express the anxiety and loss, the anger, he felt, convinced his boy was giving up the promise of a rational, useful life and brilliant career, turning his back on home, father, laboratory, and entering a monastery. Of course, Anthony would more than support William's steadfast refusal to become a Roman Catholic, as his wife, children, and Newman wished. In the end, young Eddy changed his mind about entering the priesthood in those days of religious confusion and upheaval. And the priest who led him to his early calling later left the Oratory and became a "sort of" Unitarian—par for the course. Roman Catholic Eddy didn't attempt Oxford, however, though he did become a scientist who worked with his father at the laboratory at Torquay, and became prominent himself in the field of naval science well into the mid-twentieth century.

In witnessing William's agitated/despondent condition in the years leading up to Mary's death and Eddy's call to the priesthood, Anthony did respond in his writings, with a freer, more personal indictment of contemporary Roman Catholicism. Also, our "muscular Christian" Charles Kingsley, privy to William's heartache through Anthony, and certainly to Newman's claim that when a man was old enough to marry, he was old enough as well to choose celibacy, was stimulated to strike out. To Kingsley, celibacy was close to the work of the devil: As he said in *Macmillan's,* "Cunning is the weapon which Heaven has given to the saints where with to withstand the brute male force of the wicked world which marries and is given in marriage."

The impulse for Newman's *Apologia* went beyond a controversy with Kingsley, whom everyone agreed, Newman knocked flat any time the two entered the ring of theological speculation. In 1864 Newman wanted to explain himself.

After the *Apologia* was published, William wrote to him that he and other men of science—such as friend John Tyndall on the train up to London—took great interest in the work while remaining curious to know how Newman stepped so freely from the state of doubt based on empirical probability to a state of absolute certitude that seemed to substitute suddenly for scientific method. Continuing discussions of this point in the correspondence between Newman and William Froude would later lead Newman to inscribe *The Grammar of Ascent:* "To you, my dear William, I dedicate these miscellaneous compositions, old and new, as to a true friend, dear to me in your own person, and in your family, and in the special claim which your brother Hurrell has upon my memory."

Anthony, after reading the *Apologia,* believed it to be, as he told Kingsley, "profoundly interesting, very dignified, and I think establishes what I told you was my own conviction about him, that he was a man of most perfect personal truthfulness." On the other hand, "It more than justifies all the unfavourable things which the world thought of him. No sane person could ever have divined the workings of his mind, or could have interpreted them otherwise than you, in common with so many others, did." He'd review *The Grammar of Ascent* in similar fashion.

Yet Anthony went on to give Kingsley advice he did not heed, and which Newman would not believe Anthony capable of. He told Kingsley to write *Macmillan's:* "That you retain your opinion, so far as it concerns the nature of the absurdities which Catholicism requires men to believe, but that as regards Newman personally you see you were mistaken, concluding with a sentence of frank and unreserved apology for the pain which you have given him."

In fact *both* William and Anthony Froude held the highest respect for Newman as a person, although such respect had never kept Anthony from expressing his views in print. One can't help but wonder what the Froude brothers thought when they came across this line in the *Apologia:* "Since I have been a Catholic, people have sometimes accused me of backwardness in making converts." Backward or not he converted William Froude's wife, his children, and unavoidably become the catalyst that brought his dear friend to loneliness and despair. Anthony considered his brother's determination not to bend and go over to Rome with the rest of his family heroic. For all of William's sense of isolation, he could not make syllogisms of his passions. His was a sane and healthy intellect to which Roman Catholicism was as incredible as the miracles Anthony once read of in the lives of the saints. Still, the religious upheavals of the day had torn his older brother's life asunder.

While working on the next two volumes of his *History,* Anthony decided he would not follow Queen Elizabeth's reign till its end as his subtitle indicated. The high point of it lay in the period leading up to that English triumph of the seas. "It is all action, and I shall use my materials badly if I cannot make it as interesting as a novel." He would close "in a blaze of fireworks, with the Armada."

There were two major reasons for his decision. One was his growing disillusionment with the queen's character, which he had begun by thinking spotless. The *Pall Mall Gazette* captured Froude's ambiguity neatly in its review of the penultimate volumes: "Towards Elizabeth he is a jealous lover, anxious to believe the best of her, but feeling that the best cannot always be satisfactorily believed."

In private Froude had already resolved that ambiguity. He had found letters between Lord Burghley and Lord Walsingham concerning Elizabeth which destroyed "finally the prejudice that still clung to me that, notwithstanding her many faults, she was a woman of ability. Evidently in their opinion she had no ability at all, worth calling by the name."

Froude had come to consider William Cecil and his son Robert, the first Earl of Salisbury, the spirits that informed the Elizabethan age, the wisdom behind all the queen's decisions. Even as noble a line as those who resided at Hatfield House in unbroken succession since Elizabeth's time could not fail to notice that the prominent historian was crediting their forebears with the birth of modern England.

In David Cecil's twentieth-century sketch of his family, *The Cecils of Hatfield House,* he wrote, "I must start with Queen Elizabeth. For though this story is the story of the Cecil family, she knew Hatfield before they did [she was imprisoned there as a young woman] and, if it had not been for her, they might not have come there at all. Indeed, their fate and hers were one. Throughout her long reign, her chief minister was always a Cecil—first William, Lord Burghley, then his son Robert—and each identified himself with her in a way that is true of no other monarch and minister in our history. She herself spoke of William Cecil as 'my spirit.'"

Froude was able to visit Hatfield House and read there as well as at the records office. He was always careful to apply only when necessary and to obtain Lord Salisbury's permission through his young second wife, Froude's friend Lady Mary Sackville-West (grand-aunt to Virginia Woolf's great friend Vita). Lord Salisbury had married her in 1847, when he was fifty-six and she twenty-three. David Cecil recorded that she was a "sharp-witted, ambitious young woman out to cut a figure in the world and not very scrupulous about how she did it. It seems unlikely that she married the elderly Matador for any but worldly reasons, and she was later to acquire a reputation for intrigue and mischief-making." Queen Victoria would not be amused by her vocal upholding of Russia over Turkey (a view shared by Froude) and her meddling in state affairs. It is a shame that Froude felt it necessary to suppress her part of their thirty-year correspondence before he died; it must have told quite an interesting story. To Froude's credit, though he didn't approve of Queen Elizabeth's morality, he did appreciate a sharp-witted, politically ambitious woman only a bit younger than himself, a woman who was and would be an éminence grise to the Conservative party.

On her husband's death, Mary Sackville-West's Oxford-educated, High Church stepson, six years her junior, became the third Marquess of Salisbury. This abstracted, intellectual Salisbury, bearish in form, subtle in thinking, would become the future Conservative prime minister, returning again and again to power up through the early twentieth century. Two years after her old husband died, in 1870, Sackville-West remarried, becoming the wife of another Conservative, the fifteenth Marquess of Derby. Many strands of the party came together through Lady Derby's hands. She did not "entertain," was not the conventional political hostess, disliking display and overindulgence. Instead, she promoted the Tory cause through privileged conversations, tête-à-têtes with like-minded powerful men. Froude relished these high-minded political dialogues. But not even her stepson's nomination could secure Froude the position of Regius professor of modern history at Oxford, when he tried to return to Oxford yet again in 1868.

Carlyle was the other reason for Froude's ending his *History of England* in twelve volumes. The Sage of Chelsea complained of the length of the work and thought him too severe concerning Queen Elizabeth. As he was concluding the series, Froude was in constant contact with the older man. From 1866 on, the relationship between the two became even closer, Froude witnessing Carlyle's treatment of his wife from a new—if sad—perspective.

Froude had been in London when Mrs. Carlyle had a brutal accident returning from a visit to a needy cousin, the details of which she confided in him and he to the second half of the Carlyle biography, *His Life in London*. At the age of sixty-two, Jane, in attempting to hail an omnibus home, was thrown to the curb as she tried to avoid a passing cab. Her right arm was disabled by neuralgia, and she was unable to break her fall. "The sinews of one thigh were sprained and lacerated, and she was brought home in a fly in dreadful pain. She knew that Carlyle would be expecting her and her chief anxiety, she told me, was to get into the house without his knowledge, to spare him agitation. For herself, she could not move. She stopped at the door of Mr. Larken, who lived in the adjoining house, to ask him to help her."

Carlyle heard the commotion, however, and both he and Mr. Larken carried her upstairs to her bed. It was the worst pain she had ever known, and she told Froude she and the doctors attempted to conceal the worst of it from Carlyle.

One side of her face had been severely damaged in the fall, and because of the muscle and nerve damage her jaw dropped and she could not close her mouth. Carlyle disliked an open mouth; it made one look a fool. He himself had a pronounced under jaw; perhaps that was the reason. Jane told Froude that one morning Carlyle walked into her bedroom, leaned against her mantel, and stared at her for a while.

"'Jane,' he said presently, 'ye had better shut your mouth.'"

She tried to tell him that she could not.

"'Jane,' he began again, 'ye'll find yourself in a more compact and pious frame of mind, if ye shut your mouth.' In old-fashioned and, in him, perfectly sincere phraseology, he told her that she ought to be thankful that the accident was no worse.

"'Thankful!' she said to him; 'thankful for what? for having been thrown down in the street when I had gone on an errand of charity? for being disabled, crushed, made to suffer in this way? I am not thankful, and I will not say that I am.' He left her, saying he was sorry to see her so rebellious. We can hardly wonder after this that he had to report sadly to his brother: 'She speaks little to me, and does not accept me as a sick nurse, which, truly, I had never any talent to be.'"

This accident occurred in 1863, just after Anthony and Henrietta moved to their second home in London, 5 Onslow Gardens, in walking distance of Jane and Carlyle. The contrast between what Froude witnessed on their first visit to Cheyne Row as new neighbors and the way Carlyle remembered it must have struck Froude when he read Carlyle's account years later.

"Monday evening, November 23 (as I laboriously make out the date)," Carlyle wrote, "The Froudes, Froude and his wife, the pleasantest, indeed almost the only pleasant, kindly, courteous, sincere couple arrived. (They had come to live near us, and we hoped for a larger share of such evenings, of which, probably this was the first? Alas to me, too surely it was in effect the last!)."

As the Froudes sat with Carlyle, bedridden Jane made the most extraordinary effort, and in retrospect Carlyle fleshed out the scene with all the tone of later regrets, though it is difficult for the reader to discern if Jane made the effort for her husband, as he interpreted it, or for her new neighbors:

"The door from her bedroom went wide open, and my little darling, all radiant in graceful evening dress, followed by a maid with new lights, came gliding in to me, gently stooping, leaning on a fine Malacca cane." Carlyle interpreted Jane's wordless entry, her silence toward him, as actually saying: "Here I am come back to you, dear!"

"Cheerful enough this evening was; my darling sat latterly on the sofa, talking chiefly to Mrs. Froude; the Froudes gone she silently at once withdrew to her bed, saying nothing to me of the state she was in." (Or anything to him, period.)

It would be ten more months of racking pain, mental as well as physical, "before I saw her sit with me again in this drawing-room—in body weak as a child, but again composed into quiet."

Mrs. Carlyle's terrible illnesses and her physical and mental derangements were such that she had to leave London under doctors' supervision for a time. She was so ill, and in such pain and anguish, that she had to be carried down the stairs from her red-wallpapered bedroom at Cheyne Row in a contraption that looked like a coffin and to be placed in a carriage that resembled a hearse to be sent by railroad to a private doctor at St. Leonard's. No one thought she would ever return. Her unusual illness seemed centered in the womb; it affected her mind, and brought her up against her recurring worst fear: insanity. Somehow, after many months and many moves, she found the strength to rouse herself and take her care into her own hands. She rallied. People said she rose from the dead; it did seem a miraculous recovery. It led Carlyle to come to what Jane called a previously nonexistent characteristic—consideration. And in the last eighteen months of her life the couple came to a peace that Carlyle remembered as more forgiving and harmonious than Jane described it to Anthony—in whom she continued to confide.

Still, Mrs. Carlyle was no longer living under the valley of the shadow of Frederick the Great, whose multivolumed life has been considered the final literary accomplishment of the seventy-one-year-old Sage of Chelsea. And she was extremely gratified when at long last Carlyle was acknowledged by their native Scotland. However, she was not up to accompanying Carlyle to the University of Edinburgh, where he was to receive the honor of the rectorship from his alma mater. She was sixty-five at the time and far too nervous to be in a crowded room while Carlyle made his speech, which she advised, quite rightly, he should extemporize.

Froude witnessed both the Carlyles' delight at the rectorship—although it rattled the couple's extremely shaky nerves. Forty-five years previously, Jane's circle had been shocked that she, so sought after, would marry a peasant's son, with no professional future, who was rude and sullen to boot. Nothing is so sweet as victory at home, spiced by the unspoken "I told you so."

"A perfect triumph," John Tyndall telegraphed her from Edinburgh, after Carlyle's stirring speech to the young men of his old university, and Jane became so elated at her husband's success that she fainted. She read the glowing newspaper accounts of Carlyle's victory with élan. Even *Punch* was complimentary. She did meet one naysayer, who when introduced to her remarked: "Oh, you're the wife of the man who believes in the least good for the greatest number." It hardly fazed her. What mattered was that she had nurtured a man whose genius she understood years before he had any public recognition. She had been right in her prophecy of his fame—that last impediment of her own noble mind.

Because he sprained his ankle, Carlyle spent longer than he had planned with his relatives in the Lowlands. On April 21, 1866, shortly before Carlyle's return, and two days before Froude's forty-eighth birthday, Jane planned a small evening party. Froude and Henrietta were invited along with a Professor Tulloch and his wife, who wished to meet with the historian. Geraldine Jewsbury, the fiery redheaded novelist and critic whom Froude had attempted to entertain in his Manchester days, had long since moved to London to be closer to her dear friend. "Mrs. Carlyle, in her own journal, calls Geraldine her *Consuelo,* her chosen comforter," Froude wrote.

That morning Jane was well enough to compose and bring to the post her daily letter to Carlyle. Then she went out in her brougham for her usual afternoon drive around Hyde Park, taking her little dog with her. The brougham was a testament to Carlyle's newfound consideration— he had actually taken the time to buy it for her, something he had spoken of doing for years.

Near Victoria Gate she let the dog out for exercise. But another carriage came along and seemed to swipe him. Without a thought for herself, Jane jumped out of her brougham before it was fully stopped, picked up the poor animal, and brought it back into the carriage.

Was he hurt? the coachman asked, but as other carriages were passing, she seemed not to hear. The dog squeaked, as if Jane had been feeling it for injuries—only a toe was actually injured—and the coachman continued on.

He got no further directions from Mrs. Carlyle and for close to three quarters of an hour drove on. He looked back. Her hands were on her lap, right hand palm up, left hand palm down. She did not sign to him.

So he continued but began to feel a bit uneasy. He looked back again and her hands had not moved. Becoming alarmed, he made for the street entrance and asked a lady to look in. Jane was leaning back in one corner of the carriage, rugs spread over her knees, her eyes closed, her mouth slightly open. The woman said, "I dare not open the door for I am afraid the lady is dead."

Anthony was at home late that day when a servant from Cheyne Row came to tell him something had happened to Mrs. Carlyle and begged him to go immediately to St. George Hospital. "Instinct told me what it must be. I went on the way to Geraldine; she was getting ready for the party and supposed that I had called to take her there. I told her the message which I had received. She flung a cloak around her, and we drove to the hospital together. There, on a bed in a small room, we found Mrs. Carlyle, beautifully dressed, dressed as she always was, in quietly perfect taste. Nothing had been touched. Her bonnet had not been taken off. It was as if she had sate upon the bed after leaving the brougham, and had fallen back upon it asleep. But there was an expression on her face which was not sleep, and which, long as I had known her, resembled nothing which I had ever seen there. The forehead, which had been contracted in life by continued pain, had spread out to its natural breadth, and I saw for the first time how magnificent it was. The brilliant mockery, the sad softness with which the mockery alternated, both were alike gone. The features lay composed in a stern majestic calm. I have seen many faces beautiful in death, but never any so grand as hers. I can write no more of it. I did not then know all her history. I knew only she had suffered, and how heroically she had borne it. Geraldine knew everything. . . . She could not speak. I took her home."

Because of a mix-up, Carlyle received and read with his own eyes the telegram informing the family of Jane's death. There was no Jane to buffer reality; this blow he was forced to take in the face. One cannot overestimate his shock. He never, never, ill as she had been, thought he would survive her. He was older and would go first. He insisted on going home immediately, in order to accompany his wife's bier back to Scotland, where she was laid to rest, as she had requested years before, in her father's grave in her native Haddington. After the burial he returned to Chelsea Row and went into total seclusion. A few weeks later, however, he wanted to see Froude:

"He came down to me into the library in his dressing gown, haggard, as if turned to stone. He had scarcely slept, he said, since the funeral. He could not 'cry.' He was stunned and stupefied. He had never realised the possibility of losing her. He had settled that he would die first, and now she was gone. From this time and onwards, as long as he was in town, I saw him almost daily. He was looking through her papers, her notebooks and journals; and old scenes came mercilessly back to him in vistas of mournful memory. In his long sleepless nights, he recognised too late what she had felt and suffered under his childish irritabilities. His faults rose up in remorseless judgment, and as he had thought too little of them before, so now he exaggerated them to himself in his helpless repentance. For such faults an atonement was due, and to her no atonement could now be made."

It was then that Froude saw Carlyle not only as a prophet in the wilderness but as a suffering soul. He was extremely touched by Carlyle's repentance. It redeemed the part of him that Froude could never accept. Because of how sincerely Carlyle regretted the mistakes he made in his marriage, he became less—using Geraldine Jewsbury's phrase—a sphinx in the living room and more a flawed human with whom one could identify. Froude took on the added responsibilities of Carlyle in his widowerhood, seeing him almost every day. The closer attachment in the late 1860s and early 1870s caused Carlyle's influence on his friend to become more pronounced.

In the same year as Froude's penultimate volumes of the *History* were published, seventy-three-year-old Carlyle—who virtually stopped writing after Jane's death—wrote his last essay on world affairs, "Shooting Niagara: and After?" It was Conservative prime minister Benjamin Disraeli's decision to reverse himself and back the second reform bill extending the franchise that stirred the widower's wrath. Carlyle had not forgiven Disraeli, who as a young man had launched his own career by blasting his party leader, Conservative prime minister Peel, for giving up his opposition to free trade and siding with the Liberals on abolishing the corn laws. Now Disraeli had blatantly reversed himself concerning voting rights—and was skillful enough to gain political capital to boot. Carlyle was furious. Simon Heffer, in *Moral Desperado*—finally a brilliantly balanced analysis of Carlyle's political thought—called the essay Carlyle's masterpiece of reaction. Reactionary it certainly was: "All the great themes of his philosophy are included in it: the regard for strength, the importance of silence, the loathing of democracy, the importance of disciplining a fractious people along military lines, the spuriousness of the contemporary idea of equality, the hope that the aristocracy might stop shooting its game and instead start playing a proper feudal role of active leadership, the hypocrisy of 'nigger philanthropists,' the need to bring back the proper regard for God instead of the phoney regard for the ballot box."

Add to the list Carlyle's rejection of literature as a serious endeavor. Carlyle himself realized early on that he was not a poet—that highest form of art. He wanted to act, to change things, but he could only write about changing the world. Froude pointed out in his biography of Carlyle an important truth often ignored, that perhaps Carlyle considered himself meant for something other, higher, more important than prose, but never found his way. Both Carlyle and Froude came to literature by default. Carlyle had previously rejected studying for the ministry, law, astronomy, mathematics, whereas Froude, once he rejected his deaconship, had no professional options left him. Froude, however, was a born writer, with an insatiable need to communicate. The more he was misunderstood, the more he wrote, the more he attempted to make himself clear. For Carlyle the act of writing itself was a daily torment, for him and for those who were close to him. He was clearly aware of the limits of his vocation as he wrote of men who acted and affected their times: Oliver Cromwell and Frederick the Great.

Gladstone, who headed the Liberal party in an ever-changing society, found time to translate Homer and to write voluminously. Disraeli, that brilliant Conservative politician whom Carlyle abhorred, believed himself one of those leaders of men that Carlyle envisioned. At the same time he was an extremely talented political novelist and social satirist. First and foremost, however, he acted. John Stuart Mill, Dicky Milnes, Bulwer-Lytton, to name a few writers, made their way to Parliament. Carlyle, by temperament rather than inclination, could not enter into the public arena.

The man who once stirred Anthony to become an author came to write: "We of 'Literature' by trade, we shall sink again, I perceive, to the rank of street-fiddling; no higher rank, though with endless increase of sixpences flung into the hat. Of 'Literature,' keep well to windward, my serious friend!"

One has the usual reaction to Carlyle's hyperbole, of not knowing whether to laugh along with him or question his stability. But "Shooting Niagara" could be no laughing matter to Anthony, for Carlyle derided, by inescapable implication, Froude's attempt to write a history of England that could profit his generation. Of writers, Carlyle admitted Shakespeare was the highest genius, divinely gifted—not for his "Fiction," for his "Facts." "To say truth, what I most of all admire are the traces he shows of a talent that could have turned the *History of England* into a kind of *Iliad,* almost perhaps into a kind of *Bible.*" Then he went further: "Innumerable grave Books there are; but for none of us any real *History* of England, intelligible, profitable, or even conceivable . . . !" He wrote this as his best friend J. A. Froude concluded his twelve-volume *History of England.* Brutal criticism indeed.

An Oxford graduate from the latter part of the nineteenth century, and Froude's first biographer, the historian Herbert Paul summarized the *History*'s impact on his generation quite perceptively: "Froude's History, the great work of his life, was completed in 1870. He deliberately chose, after the twelve volumes, to leave Elizabeth at the height of her power, mistress of the seas, with Spain crushed at her feet. As he says himself, in the opening paragraph of his own Conclusion: 'Chess players, when they have brought their game to a point at which the result can be foreseen with certainty, regard their contest as ended, and sweep the pieces from the board.' Froude had accomplished his purpose. He had rewritten the story of the Reformation. He had proved that the Church of England, though in a sense it dated from St. Austin of Canterbury, became under Henry VIII a self-contained institution, independent of Rome and subject to the supremacy of the Crown. Elizabeth altered the form of words in which her father had expressed his ecclesiastical authority; but the substance was in both cases the same. The sovereign was everything. The Bishop of Rome was nothing." Since Elizabeth's reign Anglican "service has been performed in English, and the English Bible has been open to every one who can read." The opponents of the Reformation—as well as those who wish to ignore it—have "never recovered from the crushing onslaught of Froude."

Lytton Strachey wrote that Froude's "grand set-pieces—the execution of Somerset and Mary Queen of Scots, the end of Cranmer, the ruin of the Armada—go off magnificently, and cannot be forgotten; and, apart from these, the extraordinary succession of events assumes, as it flows through his pages, the thrilling lineaments of a great story, upon whose issue the most *blasé* reader is forced to hang entranced." Froude's prose style and his approach to historical character had an influence on the Bloomsbury group, on Strachey himself, and on Virginia Woolf, both of whose forebears were part of the Carlyle-Froude circle, though this is mainly forgotten.

As A. L. Rowse wrote at the end of the twentieth century, "Froude was an historian of genius, who fell into no conventional categories and so has been overlooked when people have gone on and on writing about Macaulay and Carlyle. Froude was a better stylist than either—he got that from Newman—where I find Carlyle's intolerable. He is the last great Victorian awaiting revival, when so many inferior to him have been regurgitated."

In a certain sense *The History of England from the Fall of Wolsey to the Defeat of the Spanish Armada* was indeed "a kind of *Bible*," written by a defrocked clergyman to defend the faith of his fathers from the onslaught of the Tractarians and to give his own generation a track they could follow. It was not only mainly dependent on primary documents, new to its day, but it rendered history dramatically; Froude's history told a story, as Lytton Strachey's would as well. Froude did not believe in the necessity of the Thirty-Nine Articles of Anglican faith, or in the divinity of Christ, or in "incredible" Roman Catholicism. He believed in the spiritual and moral values of England's mighty land-based feudal past over the capitalistic interests of industrialized society. He knew democracy was encroaching and that the ideas of John Stuart Mill and his ilk were to have their day. It might be too late, but perhaps if the aristocracy did stop thinking of their own pleasures, as Carlyle and he advocated, and applied themselves to their old feudal responsibilities to their country and their people, as the Reformation left them free to do, the greatness of "merry old" England would be restored and its values—and its language—would become not only the industrial but the moral lingua franca of the civilized world. Like all good epics through the ages, *History of England* rose to song, though Carlyle did not hear it—a prose epic, if you wish, to the political and moral evolution of its people.

Carlyle had urged Froude to turn from his *History of England* and write on Ireland. The day Anthony first walked into the Carlyles' home in Chelsea in 1849, Carlyle had just returned from Ireland, with notes that at the time he thought he would turn into a book. But that was not to be. Froude knew Ireland well, and now after the death of Jane, when Carlyle lived more and more through his younger friend, Carlyle thought Froude should examine Ireland's political history in order to clarify the botch England and Parliament had made of her most troublesome colony. For Carlyle, Oliver Cromwell and his Ironsides had the right method; what Ireland needed was more Protestantism, not less.

Carlyle had also introduced Anthony to a serious consideration of Knox and Calvin, and the son of the Archdeacon of Totnes, brother of Hurrell, had become increasingly Calvinistic in his thought—whether or not he believed.

Froude was surprised to find himself voted rector of St. Andrews by the students in 1868—he beat out Disraeli by a slim margin—and his address the next year was on Calvinism. Calvinists believed in election, predestination, and, generally, the absolute arbitrary sovereignty of God, he wrote to John Skelton. Yet these men, "not the moderate Liberals and the reasonable prudent people who seem to us most commendable, have had the shaping of the world's destinies. In fact I suppose if there is such a thing as a Personal God at all, this sort of theory is the true one, and most consistent with facts."

Evangelical Calvinism, as he called it, came close to his position. It is interesting, Froudean to the nth degree, that he came to the conclusion that our destiny depended on election rather than our individual selves, in the midst of his happiest years. "I say nothing of what is called technically revelation. I am treating these matters as phenomena of human experience, the lessons of which would be identically the same if no revelation existed," he told the Scottish students.

It would take more than Carlyle's urging for Froude to commence his three-volume *The English in Ireland in the Eighteenth Century.* It would take what it usually took—controversy. A major dust storm came when least expected. Anthony may have had a point about predestination.

It was the summer of 1869, the last two volumes of his *History* were nearing publication, and Froude was relaxing at his vacation home in Southern Ireland with Henrietta, the children, and his visiting friends. His historical researches had not impeded him from writing many essays over the years, and they were widely published, not only in *Fraser's* but in many British and American magazines. He would select, edit, and reprint many of them—as he told Chapman he would do at the beginning of his career. Eventually they would turn into four volumes of *Short Studies on Great Subjects,* widely read and reprinted in his day.

Froude had built up a large audience that he could address as directly and in as relaxed a manner as one might a familiar friend greeted on a summer day. Certainly that sense of warm familiarity and mellow play is illustrated in the first installment of his "A Fortnight in Kerry," an intimate travel memoir that he called "light fare," and which illuminates some of his most joyous days. Ruskin wrote of it and its sequel that it made him feel "that you could have written a better *Modern Painters* than I."

Anthony intended his to be a personal record of Ireland to go beyond political concerns and contribute a little bit "towards setting her condition in a truer light—towards showing how among the dark features there were redeeming traits of singular interest and attractiveness." He cele-brated the beauty of his country home, Derreen, blind to any nuance of condescension, English to Irish.

Derreen was cut off from the world by mountain and ocean. But for the daily post and the croquet wires he "stumbled over on the lawn," Froude and his party seemed completely cut off from the world and its concerns. Of an evening they would wander through the woods along the shore. "The water was like a sheet of pale gold, lighted in the shad-ows by phosphorescent flashes where a seal was chasing a mullet for his supper. Far off we heard the cries of the fishermen as they were laying out their mackerel nets, a heron or two flew screaming out of some large trees beside the boat-house, resentful at the intrusion on their night's rest; and from overhead came a rush of wings and the long wild whistle of the curlew."

One of the women meandering with him was a famous actor and observed that it was like a scene in a play. Though that simile might sound absurd, Froude himself once had the same sensation: "I was going up Channel in a steamer. It was precisely such another warm, breathless, moonlight summer night, save that there was a light mist over the water which prevented us from seeing very clearly objects that were at any distance from us. The watch on the forecastle called out 'A Sail ahead!' We shut off the steam, and passed slowly within a biscuit's throw of an enormous China clipper, with all her canvas set, and every sail drooping flat from the yards. We heard the officers talking on the quarter-deck. The ship's bell struck the hour as we went by. Why the rec-ollection of the familiar sea moonlight of Drury Lane should have rushed over me at such a moment I know not, unless it be that those only who are rarely gifted feel natural beauty with real intensity. With the rest of us our high sensations are at best partly artificial. We make an effort to realize emotions which we imagine that we ought to experience, and are theatrical ourselves."

Natural beauty might transcend one's ability to experience it authen-tically, but not the art of fly-fishing, which Froude evoked with enough gusto to make fly fishers of us all. "Among the marvels of art and nature I know nothing equal to a salmon-fly," he informed his readers, describ-ing the fly as resembling "no insect, winged or unwinged, which the fish can have seen. A shrimp, perhaps, is the most like it, if there are degrees in utter dissimilarity. Yet every river is supposed to have its favourite flies. Size, colour, shape, all are peculiar. Here vain tastes prevail for golden pheasant and blue and crimson paroquet. There the salmon are sober as

Quakers, and will look at nothing but drabs and browns. Nine parts of this are fancy, but there is still a portion of truth in it. Bold hungry fish will take anything in any river, shy fish will undoubtedly rise and splash at a stranger's fly, while they will swallow what is offered them by any one who knows their ways. It may be something in the colour of the water; it may be something in the colour of the banks: experience is too uniform to allow the fact itself to be questioned."

A large salmon eluded Anthony's first throw: an old stager by his color, "no longer ravenous as when fresh from salt water. He was either lazy and misses the fly, or it was not entirely to his mind. He was not touched." Anthony and his companion John Skelton, who in the article is called Jack, drew back to consider. " 'Over him again while he is angry' is the saying in some rivers, and I have known it to answer where the fish feed greedily. But it will not do here; we must give him time; and we turn again to the fly-book."

Finally Jack closed his book and produced a "hook" out of his hat— Froude would not call it a fly—of his own dressing: "It is like a parti-coloured father-long-legs, a thing which only some frantic specimen of orchid ever seriously approached, a creature whose wings were two strips of the fringe of a peacock's tail, whose legs descended from blue jay through red to brown, and terminated in a pair of pink trailers two inches long. Jack had found it to do, and he believed it would do for me. And so it did. I began to throw again six feet above the bush, for a salmon often shifts his ground after rising."

After several unsuccessful throws: "There is a swirl like the wave which arises under the blade of an oar, a sharp sense of hard resistance, a pause, and then a rush for the dear life. The wheel shrieks, the line hisses through the rings, and thirty yards down the pool the great fish springs madly six feet into the air. The hook is firm in his upper jaw; he had not shaken its hold, for the hook had gone into the bone—pretty sub-ject of delight for a reasonable man, an editor of a magazine, and a would-be philosopher, turned fifty! The enjoyments of the unreasoning part of us cannot be defended on grounds of reason, and experience shows that men who are all logic and morals, and have nothing of the animal left in them, are poor creatures after all. Any way, I defy philos-ophy with a twenty-pound salmon fast hooked and a pool right ahead four hundred yards long, and half full of water lilies."

The salmon fought on till he "played his best stroke": "He now sur-rendered like a gentleman. The mean-spirited fish will go to the bottom, bury himself in the weeds, and sulk. Ours set his head towards the sea, and sailed down the length of the pool in the open water without attempting any more plunges. As his strength failed, he turned heavily on his back, and allowed himself to be drawn to the shore. The gaff was in his side and he was ours. He was larger than we had guessed him. Clean run he would have weighed twenty-five pounds. The fresh water had reduced him to twenty-two, but without softening his muscle or touching his strength.

"The fight had tired us all. If middle age does not impair the enjoyment of sport, it makes the appetite for it less voracious, and a little pleases more than a great deal. . . . Anyhow I had had enough of salmon fishing for the day."

Froude informed his audience, with the nonchalance that behooved a vacationing editor: "My space has run out." There was more to tell if his readers maintained an interest. However, if they had had enough of such light fare, why then: "The rest of my pleasant memories shall abide with myself, woven in bright colours in the web of my life . . . my own, and never to be taken from me, let the Future bring what fate it will."

Fate turned out to be quite Calvinistic. The second installment of "A Fortnight in Kerry," published a year later, made his readers privy to what the Future brought: "I trusted that if my friends in Kerry did not approve of all that I said, they would at least recognize my good-will. How great was my surprise to find that I was regarded as an intruder into business which was none of mine, affecting English airs of insolent superiority, and under pretence of patronage turning the county and its inhabitants into ridicule!"

He had "stirred a hornet's nest" in describing "a once notorious character" from "a past generation in Kerry." Rather than using the man's real name, he'd looked over a list of Irish chiefs and decided on "Morty O'Sullivan." The result was: "A dozen living Morty O'Sullivans, and the representative of a dozen more who were dead, clamorously appropriated my description, while they denounced the inaccuracy of its details."

Well, Morty O'Sullivan's legacy was not lost in Kerry, as Froude would illustrate twenty years later, when he encapsulated him in the only novel he wrote since his Oxford days: *The Two Chiefs of Dunboy*. It was either disingenuous to think the name would not give offense to the people of O'Sullivan's region, or perhaps, as was often the case with Froude, he took no notice of the possible consequences of his words. On the other hand, the shock of the reception might well have turned him back to a reassessment of the real Morty O'Sullivan. For he would date his interest in writing an Irish novel to this period.

More damaging, he had said that in Kerry, religion appeared "to mean the knowledge of right and wrong, and to mean little besides." He was blind to the "insolent superiority" of the phraseology, that it could be interpreted as being arrogant. "By 'little besides' I had myself intended to imply that no Fenian sermons were to be heard . . . that no hatred was preached against England or English landlords." Again, the explanation could be disingenuous, but it could also be that he assumed his words would be taken in the mellow spirit in which they were written in this unique period of personal happiness.

They weren't. The local priest "declared in the county papers that he was cut to the heart; that he had suffered many wrongs in his life, but never one that had afflicted him so deeply as the insinuation that his flock learnt nothing from him but the obligations of morality."

"The storm was renewed in America—files were forwarded to me of the *Irish Republic,* in which I was denounced as a representative of the hereditary enemies of Ireland."

He confided to his readers that he hadn't been a visitor to the area, as he'd told them in his essay the previous year, but was actually a tenant of the property he described. He had another season on his lease, at the same time as "it was hinted to me that I should be a brave man if I again ventured into Kerry."

Venture he had. He was a frugal and stubborn man as well as a brave one. And his unintentional slights against the Irish led him to a rather tardy epiphany: "What dark insinuations the writer never dreamt of may be discovered in an unguarded word!"

"When we arrived at our beautiful home a canard reached us that we had been censured, if not denounced, at a neighbouring Catholic chapel. The children of the National School, for whom in past years we had provided an occasional holiday entertainment, had been forbidden, it was whispered, to come near us any more. For a few days—such was the effect of a guilty conscience—we imagined the people were less polite to us. The 'Good evening kindly' of the peasant coming home from his work, the sure sign of genuine good will, seemed less frequent than silence or an inaudible mutter. Fewer old women than usual brought their sore legs to be mended or pitied, fewer family quarrels were brought to us to arbitrate, interminable disputes about 'the grass of a cow,' or the interpretation of a will."

John Skelton remembered that the happiest of Froude's summers were passed with Henrietta at Derreen, and he kept a travel journal during his own visit to the Froudes. The friendliness of the people was such that the coldness Froude subsequently felt must have been more than a figment of his guilty conscience. Skelton pictured the colorful Sundays when people from all over the area came to the Catholic chapel, tethering their donkeys and ponies to the bushes. "One sees young women, who have walked without shoes eight or ten or twelve miles, washing their feet in the running water. (They don't wear shoes in rainy Ireland, on the principle that it is *dryer* to wet their feet only, than their feet *plus* shoes and stockings.) Men and women and children are sitting about everywhere, a profusion of bright reds blazing through the green." When the Mass was over, the congregation left their humble, half-completed chapel and gathered in groups one sees at fairs, "eating, drinking, buying, selling, winding up with a dance on the green. If you are looking on, some pretty, swift-footed Kerry girl will insist on your dancing with her—it is the custom of the country—and you must submit with the best grace you can." The summer after his essay, no one was asking Anthony for a dance.

He had felt at home in Ireland, knew it well from the days of his rebellion to the heydays of his second marriage. He had found in Kerry a bit of paradise, where he could fly-fish, yacht, shoot grouse (sparingly on a rugged mountaintop two thousand feet up), and be with his family. From his point of view he had sincerely meant to reveal to his readers, as he said in the first paragraph of the first installment of his essay, that "when all is said, Ireland is still the most beautiful island in the world, and the Irish themselves, though their temperament is ill-matched with ours, are still among the most interesting of peoples."

The neighborhood people *had* previously come to him for advice. After a long day of shooting he actually *still* bade companions good-bye and walked around the entire side of a mountain to nurse a poor, aged Irishwoman who he knew was left alone. Shades of the squirearchy and the archdeacon. Shades also of the lost values of feudalism that both he and Carlyle regretted. No matter how one sliced it there still remained the "ill-matched temperament" between the English squire and the needy Irish peasant. Though Anthony could write that the Irish accused him of condescension, he never seemed to grasp that the way he as an Englishman viewed the Irish actually *was* condescending. He felt his motives and actions were misunderstood. When he was a frail, motherless boy, brutalized at public school, when his father's thunder soured his relationship with his first love, he felt himself treated unfairly. He found himself in the same situation after the publication of his first travel piece on Kerry. Once more he thought himself rudely dissociated from his surroundings, once more he was in a kind of local disgrace. The

Irish made it clear that he did not fit in. The old feelings came back, they were wind to his kite and probably more important than Carlyle for provoking him to his Irish history.

In the second installment of his essay, wisely not published until he left Kerry for good, gone was the heartfelt, relaxed surety and good humor, returned was the urbane humor laced with Froudean irony, as when the local priest finally realized that Anthony "was no worse than a stupid John Bull."

There was a temporary reconciliation. The Froudes provided a party for the schoolchildren on their lawn. The children "leapt, raced, wrestled, jumped in sacks, climbed greasy poles, and the rest of it—a hundred stout little fellows with as many of their sisters; four out of five of the boys to grow up, thanks to the paternal wisdom of our legislators, into citizens of the United States; the fifth to be a Fenian at home; the girls to be mothers of families on the Ohio or the Missouri, where the Irish race seems intended to close its eventful history and disappear in the American Republic."

If he had to fear for his life that last summer in Derreen, after the second installment of "A Fortnight in Kerry" was published, his risk was doubled. In any case, he was evicted from his tenancy. Lord Landowne gave him a polite excuse; he planned to use his estate. Froude decided against seeking a new tenancy in the same area—a wise decision, he was told. "Driven out of Derreen," is the way he expressed it half humorously to John Skelton.

"I had given mortal offence where I had least thought of offending. I was an instance in my own person of the mistakes which Englishmen seem doomed to make, when they meddle, however lightly, with this singular people." Not for the last time would Anthony Froude stand as such a prime example: "Anthony is very busy with his Irish history," Henrietta wrote to a friend at the end of 1871, "which will *not* exhibit human nature in its most pleasing aspects!"

By the time Froude decided to write on Ireland, an important political development had profound personal implications for him. A law abolishing ecclesiastical disability was passed. By 1870, Froude was able to free himself legally from the bondage of the deacon's orders that he had taken over twenty-five years previously, and which barred him from other professions as well as from any public office. He was one of the first to file a Certificate of Relinquishment and legally to "drop the Rev'd" from his name. Froude was fifty-two at the time, healthy, vigorous, influential, and finally he had regained full citizenship. Should he wish to, or should the opportunity arise, he was free to enter the public arena. The Liberals were in power at the time, but if nothing else, this freedom from the mistake of his youth was a psychological victory. He was not forced to view his society from the sidelines. Now, as he wrote of Ireland, Froude spoke as well of visiting the States, something Carlyle had often pondered but never accomplished. Kingsley had just returned from a successful—and profitable—lecture tour, and Froude was toying with the idea of giving lectures there as well: on the Irish, to explain the English point of view. The very audacity of the plan enthused him.

"I go like an Arab of the desert," he told Skelton before embarking the autumn of 1872. "My hand will be against every man, and therefore every man's hand will be against me. Protestant and Catholic, English, English-Irish, and Celtic—my one hope will be, like St Paul's, to fling in some word or words among them which will set them by the ears among themselves."

Though he was no fool, Anthony Froude was constitutionally driven to where angels feared to tread. Even Carlyle questioned the wisdom of this trip.

Anthony was a well-known, popular author in the States. The Americans read him, valued him as a historian. Without landing on their shores, he had already been made a member of the Massachusetts Historical Society. "The Scribners," as they were then referred to, had already sold over a hundred and fifty thousand copies of *The History of England* by 1872 when Anthony arrived in New York, and would reprint it, along with much of Froude's extensive list, well into the twentieth century. In Manhattan, Froude was immediately made a member of the Lotos Club, the journalists' home away from home. Froude was, as some remarked, a cash cow for the Scribners, who gave him a sumptuous banquet at Delmonico's, attended by *all* the literary lights of the times, and Ralph Waldo Emerson himself traveled to New York to introduce Anthony.

Carlyle had already written to him: "Froude is coming to you in October. You will find him a most clear, friendly, ingenious, solid, and excellent man; and I am very glad to find you among those who are to take care of him when he comes to your new Country. Do your best and wisest towards him, for my sake, withal. He is the valuablest Friend I now have in England, nearly though not quite altogether the one man in talking with whom I can get any real profit or comfort." He seemed unaware of Emerson's and Froude's prior relationship.

In New York, at Delmonico's, in a warm and rather rambling toast, Emerson said that it gave him great pleasure to see his old friend again, and complimented both the substance and style of his *History*. Then he recalled his own visit to Oxford twenty-four years ago. It was there that he met as well Matthew Arnold, Arthur Stanley, Francis Turner Palgrave, and Arthur Clough, who died too young. Froude was one of the best representatives of that generation, exhibiting the culture, power, and moral determination which was indicative of all those young men.

Froude rose to respond. He told his audience that it had been eighteen months ago, at a London breakfast, after talk of a prominent Fenian leader lecturing in the United States on English tyranny and the wrongs of Ireland, that he had said offhandedly, "I think I will go over and give some lectures on the other side." He hadn't spoken with seriousness, but once the idea came to him, it grew rather than receded. Though he was not an Irishman and did not own an acre in Ireland, he had often been in Ireland over the last thirty years. In college he spent vacations wandering in the Irish mountains. In the wilds of Mayo he had once contracted smallpox, and peasants took him into their cottage and treated him with a tenderness that he would never forget. He knew Ireland before the famine and after it. He had been an Irish tenant. "Indeed, I may say I am an evicted tenant. I have been turned out of my holding, and can sympathize with the special wrong of the country, as I was very unwilling to go. But my landlord simply wanted to live in his own house and attend to his duties. If all evictions were as innocent as mine, there would be little to complain of, and when I go back I hope to find some other place in the same county which will suit me as well." The eviction was not as innocent as he led his audience, and perhaps himself, to believe, and Froude would never be a tenant in Ireland again. The rest was accurate.

America surprised Anthony. He found New York to be much more civilized than he had imagined. Among the wealthy there was a lack of vulgarity as well as long predinner prayers. What amazed him most about Americans on this first visit was that after they accumulated wealth, they spent it on the common good. "There is Mr Cornell, who has made all this money, living in a little poky house in a street with a couple of maids, his wife and daughters dressed in the homeliest manner. His name will be remembered for centuries as having spent his wealth in the very best institutions on which a country's prosperity depends. Our people spend their fortunes in buying great landed estates to found and perpetuate their own family. I wonder which name will last the longest, Mr Cornell's or Lord Overstone's?"

And so the affable Anthony began his lectures on the Irish, arranged through the American Literary Bureau. The *New York Sun* described him as "the celebrated historian," tall, well built, engaging: When animated "his eyes sparkle, his large mouth is drawn into a winning smile—the whole face fairly beams with good-nature."

He had five prepared lectures, first to be delivered in New York, Philadelphia, and Boston. Then he was to lecture in the Washington area and on to Chicago. The *New York Times* believed Froude was showing a large section of the American public what they failed to appreciate beforehand, "how honest had been the efforts of the English governors of Ireland to do justice to their peculiarly intractable subjects."

Still, they were critical of Froude's unconscious supposition that he understood the Irish emigrant better than . . . say, the *New York Times:* "We can study the Irish character any day as minutely amid the shanties around Central Park as we could in the mud-cabins of Connaught. This 'land hunger' of the Irish peasant, his shiftlessness, his low ideal of comfort, his ready wit, and his superstitious kind of piety are all so faithfully daguerreotyped at our very doors as to leave nobody who cares to understand the matter any excuse for ignorance."

In New York at the time, Irish Dominican friar Thomas Burke was speaking and fund-raising for Roman Catholic causes. He was not a Fenian or an agitator, but when Burke heard of Froude's lectures, he flamed up in opposition, speaking with eloquence against each of Froude's positions. Froude, who, as he said, had a sincere fondness for the Irish peasant, was against home rule on the historical basis that the Irish hadn't the capacity to rule themselves. For their own good the Irish should accept English rule. What Ireland needed, as Carlyle said, was not less but more Protestantism. This is what he attempted to present in what he considered "rational debate," logically explaining that if Father Burke and his friends would only stop "agitating for a separation from England," they could work together to liberate the peasant through English law. At the same time he attacked Burke's sense of history with his usual caustic wit.

Father Burke answered in fiery rhetoric, which stirred up the smoldering hostilities among the downtrodden Irish. Froude's lectures drew agitators and there was a growing potential for violence. As Froude went from city to city he had to be protected by a special guard. Irish railroad attendants didn't want him on the trains. At each stop his life was threatened, and at any hotel or private house at which he stayed, the Irish maids walked out.

Rumors spread that Froude was a paid agent of the British government. The newspapers were in a turmoil describing the agitation. Finally it was evident that he had to cut his tour short and return home before he did more damage. The threat was even more real than it had been in Derreen. He was on the verge of causing civil uprising and getting himself killed.

He became the source of a year-end caricature in *Harper's Weekly,* which recalled his Boston fiasco. There he was staying with banker George Peabody, when Peabody's servants came in to tell him they'd leave if Froude remained. The long-legged, debonair historian stands at the Peabody dining room table, swooping toward the seated banker and his wife with a rolled proclamation in his hand. The Irish maid points him to the door, where the Irish butler stands ready to usher him out. The Peabodys hide their embarrassed faces in their hands

The caption dryly and ironically captures the historian: "If my object in coming to America was to draw attention to the Irish subject, I may so far be said to have succeeded."

"The American Irish are mad," he wrote Moncure Conway from Syracuse, New York. "Father Burke let out at me. I hit back and got the best of it, for which I am hated more than before. The Catholics grow stronger every day and sooner or later it will come to blows! A war of religions is not impossible."

Sailing home, he wrote his beloved Henrietta a line that could have been an alternate caption to the *Harper's Weekly* caricature: "I do not see great things for Americans; Anglo Saxon power is running to seed."

In Froude's absence, Carlyle wondered occasionally about the advisability of Froude's washing England's "dirty linen" in America. Yet as the dust storm turned murderous—and Froude could have been assassinated there, just as he could have been in Kerry—Carlyle stayed close to the Froude family. He wrote supportive letters to a worried Henrietta insisting on Froude's bravery and veracity, as well he might.

The English in Ireland in the Eighteenth Century was to be the most Carlylean of all Froude's works. The first of the three volumes began: "Had nature meant us to live uncontrolled by any will but our own," we would have been constructed differently. "On the whole, and as a rule, superior strength is the equivalent of superior merit; and when a weaker people are induced or forced to part with their separate existence, and are not treated as subjects, but are admitted freely to share the privileges of the nation in which they are absorbed, they forfeit nothing which they need care to lose, and rather gain than suffer by the exchange."

Froude's new *History* would portray Ireland while completely under English, i.e., Protestant, rule, beginning with the conquest and submission of the people and ending with rebellion and the form of government the English had established.

Margaret and Ashley saved Carlyle's admiring letters concerning the Irish question and were happy to show them to Waldo Dunn, Froude's twentieth-century biographer, who along with Froude's children saw *The English in Ireland* in a positive light. Fenians and Irish home rule advocates did as well: Froude accurately described the English Parliament's mistakes in governing Ireland, at the same time as he stood himself as positive prima facie evidence of what an Englishman thought of the Irish.

The controversy about his views in *The English in Ireland* came as no shock to Froude, as had controversy after the publication of "A Fortnight in Kerry." He knew what he was getting into and he provoked it. His and Carlyle's mutual friend, the historian W. E. H. Lecky, while underlining his respect for Froude's work, blasted the point of view of the three volumes as they were published with clarity and justification, in two long articles in *Macmillan's*. But most criticism, as usual, rolled off Froude's back during these years, when he not only had a loving marriage but was returned to full citizenship as well.

At home with Henrietta and the children, there was a fly in the ointment. Grenny, his son by his first marriage, was now a teenager, difficult, unfocused, and a heavy drinker. Apparently Froude attempted to educate him through lectures and exhortations. Reason was having as little effect on the boy as it had on the Irish in America. Anthony was as powerless in his way as the archdeacon had once been with his repeated threats and beatings. Not only was Grenny more and more out of control, but Froude's daughter Rose Mary, also by his first marriage, was showing signs of tuberculosis, the dreaded family disease. Still, he was very happily married, with two young children, Ashley and May by Henrietta, and his older daughter, Margaret, as close to him as his sister Margaret had once been to his father.

He was fifty-six years of age and more or less free to choose his path. His next historical project might well be Charles V and Philip II, which he had thought of time and again over the years. And, of course, a new historical series by J. A. Froude would ensure his financial future. He saw himself in later life as rather well established and settled. Then, just as the last volume of *The English in Ireland* was completed, on February 12, 1874, with that strange synchronicity common in his life, completely unexpected, completely out of the blue, calamity struck. Henrietta died.

For several weeks past, Carlyle wrote to his brother, Mrs. Froude had been confined with "a kind of Bronchitis," which neither she nor her family considered dangerous, thinking she only needed to stay home and rest. Froude hardly spoke of it in his almost daily visits. In fact Anthony "seemed cheery and happy beyond wont, just about finishing his Book on Ireland." Then on "Thursday night at 8 o'clock she died; all on a sudden;—and has left poor Froude, I dare well believe, drowned in such black deluges of woes as no other man in London."

Twelve years before, Anthony had celebrated his wedding by publishing his poem "Together." Henrietta's hand held in his seemed the one thing he could not live without, his soul's one anchor in life's storm and doubt. He took that hand as the sign "of sweeter days in store." He told her, "I have not much to say," but rather let his blood speak to hers. And he ended as he began, her sweet hand, the one thing he could not live without, his heart's one anchor through storm and doubt. The two of them together.

"You were one of the very few people who Momma really got fond of after she married," Margaret Froude wrote to Henrietta's friend Miss Eliot a month later. "She always used to say that with a husband & children she did not care to make new friends—but she used to except you and one or two others, who she said she liked as much as any of her earlier friends made before she had her husband & children. Our loss seems to get worse every day—for one misses her at every turn. I think she threw herself in the most peculiar way into *every* interest—not only of my father's, but of Rose's and mine, so that nothing seems left for us to do—that we can do without her. The few things I can do for my Father are some comfort, but she was all the world to him. We are hoping to go to a quiet little place in Wales in about a fortnight—away from the recollections of this house, & where we can be *absolutely* alone."

Henrietta's death "was a terrible blow for him, poor fellow," James Fitzjames Stephen reported to Skelton. "You will not expect me to say anything of what has befallen me," Anthony wrote to Skelton in March, before going to Wales. "Rigid silence is my only present resource."

Anthony was not to have his sweetest, wisest friend through *both* their lives. Memories once pleasant now had the power to compound loss—not only at first, but all through the twenty years left him. Henrietta died at forty-nine, around the same age as Charlotte when she passed. Froude's perfect marriage and his happiest years had ended, gone, as they might say in Kerry, like youth, too soon.

Confronting the Labyrinth
of Modern Confusion

*I*mmediately on hearing of Henrietta Froude's death, seventy-nine-year-old Thomas Carlyle arrived at Onslow Gardens. Margaret Froude would never forget that "poor crumpled figure," asking meekly whether it would be possible to see her father. She ushered him in.

Anthony, as his father before him, suffered loss in silence. For the past eight years, however, since Mrs. Carlyle died in 1866, he had been in almost daily contact with Carlyle, for whom the opposite was true. Carlyle's grief at the loss of his wife had been vocal, insatiable, and laced with wrenching guilt. "Woe's me, woe's me!" he cried, lamentation becoming, as he called it, his habitual mood from then on. And Anthony had been drawn—as Jane would have phrased it—into the valley of the shadow of the Carlyles' marriage. And in the most unexpected way.

In June 1871, while Froude was at work on his Irish history, Carlyle had made one of his sudden and rare appearances at Froude's door. His young niece Mary Aitken was by then living with him as his secretary and companion. Carlyle brought with him "a large parcel of papers," which he handed over to Froude.

"He explained, when he saw me surprised, that it was an account of his wife's history, that it was incomplete, that he could himself form no opinion whether it ought to be published or not, that he could do no more to it, and must pass it over to me. He wished never to hear of it again. I must judge. I must publish it, the whole or part—or else destroy it all, if I thought that this would be the wise thing to do. . . . I was to wait only till he was dead, and he was then in constant expectation of his end."

What Carlyle had done in the first years of his widowerhood had been to collect and put in order as many of Jane Welsh Carlyle's letters as possible, letters spanning their five-year courtship and forty-year marriage. He had brought Froude a substantial bulk of them. Carlyle had edited them and supplied them with "notes, commentaries, and introductory explanations of his own." While he had been lamenting her loss to Anthony, he had been silently obsessed with this correspondence, just about the only literary work he'd done since she died.

Carlyle told Anthony unequivocally that Jane's letters and Carlyle's annotation of them were "simply and absolutely" given to him as his own, to do with as he pleased, after Carlyle was gone. Froude was deeply touched by this confidence, realizing at the same time that he had been handed a responsibility not to be "hastily accepted." He'd go through all the papers during the summer, when he, Henrietta, and the children were away on vacation, he told Carlyle. Which he did.

Reading her letters to Carlyle, that summer of 1871, five years after Jane's death, Anthony for the first time fully understood Carlyle's passionate and constant expressions of remorse. The letters revealed that the couple's marriage had been even more dysfunctional than it had appeared on the surface—it had been a living hell. Carlyle excised nothing from the record to spare himself embarrassment or shame. The act of editing had been one of expiation. Froude had previously brought himself to believe that Carlyle's faults were simply the result of an irritable temperament, and though he "extravagantly exaggerated them," they still had saddened Jane's married life. "But I had not known the extent of it; and this action of Carlyle's struck me as something so beautiful, so unexampled in the whole history of literature, that I could but admire it with all my heart."

Carlyle had hoped for some response from Froude over the summer, and let him know he was anxiously awaiting his verdict. The older man seemed unaware that it would take time for the reality of these records to be reconciled with Froude's great respect for him. Froude couldn't tell Carlyle there was nothing to repent of in his relationship with Jane, "for there was much, and more than I had guessed." The question was whether Carlyle, even as penance, should reveal himself in this way. Anthony was free to burn the letters, to tell Carlyle there was no useful purpose in allowing the shadow side of the marriage to be made public after his death. It was, as Froude said, an extraordinary gesture. Men of importance did not go about advertising their veniality. Of course, should the letters be published, Froude would pick and choose for publication, but still, the expressed desire was not to whitewash. The book could not be the usual *Life and Letters* of Victorian times, where the great man is chiseled in pure white marble and is then unveiled, bigger than life, as a blank-eyed statue.

Burning Jane's letters, however, would not ensure privacy. "Mrs. Carlyle had been a voluminous letter-writer, and had never been reticent about her grievances. Other letters of hers would infallibly in time come to light, telling the same story. I should then have done Carlyle's memory irreparable wrong. He had himself been ready with a frank and noble confession, and the world, after its first astonishment, would have felt increased admiration for the man who had the courage to make it. I should have stepped between him and the completion of a purpose which would have washed his reputation clear of the only reproach which could be brought against it." Sooner or later the truth about the marriage would be revealed. The question as Froude saw it was whether it should be told voluntarily by him or maliciously by others later on.

There was a remarkable notebook in the parcel as well. It had been sent to Carlyle by Geraldine Jewsbury, and it contained scattered memories of the stories Jane had told and retold over the years, concerning her girlhood in the market town of Haddington, Scotland, as the privileged only child of a widely respected doctor she adored. The doctor's sudden death when Jane was eighteen devastated her and left her with her mother, a beautiful woman with wonderful taste, extraordinary domestic skill, and a capricious temperament, who fretted over her precocious, highly imaginative daughter. In those days Jane's knowledge of life was garnered through literature, and she dreamed of escaping small-town Scotland to London and a life of literature and ideal love. She would only marry a genius.

Geraldine wrote and the widower read that when Jane finally decided to marry him: "Of course people thought she was making a dreadfully bad match; they only saw the outside of the thing; but she had faith in her own insight. Long afterwards, when the world began to admire her husband, at the time he delivered the 'Lectures on Hero-Worship,' she gave a little half-scornful laugh, and said, 'They tell me things as if they were new that I found out years ago.' She knew the power of help and sympathy that lay in her, and she knew she had strength to stand the struggle and pause before he was recognized. She told me that she resolved that he should never write for money, only when he wished it, when he had a message in his heart to deliver, and she determined that she would make whatever money he gave her answer for all needful purposes. . . . She managed so well that comfort was never absent from her house, and no one looking on could have guessed whether they were rich or poor. . . . No one who in later years saw her lying on the sofa in broken health, and languor, would guess the amount of energetic hard work she had done in her life. She could do everything and anything, from mending the Venetian blinds to making picture-frames or trimming a dress. Her judgment in all literary matters was thoroughly good; she could get to the very core of a thing, and her insight was like witchcraft."

The small notebook was Carlyle's madeleine. On the same page that Geraldine ended, Carlyle wrote, "Few or none of these narratives are correct in details, but there is a certain mythical truth in all or most of them." He didn't stop there. The past welled up; he continued, as if in a trance, penning his own memories of his wife with a lyrical spontaneity free of the stylized, over-the-top hyperbole that often earmarked his style. His "notes" on his wife's life were impressionistic brushstrokes of true feeling, the breathless quality enhanced the sense of loss. Jane was his youth, his Scotland, his past; her sufferings the ghost of his failings that haunted him. A year after he denounced it, the mourning Carlyle consoled himself by creating "Literature."

Anthony was reading a remarkable memoir, perhaps one of Carlyle's finest accomplishments. He realized the worth of the account on all levels, literarily, biographically, psychologically, morally. Carlyle told Froude he could do what he wished with all the papers, but Anthony also found a note in the parcel prohibiting publication of the reminiscence of Jane.

Such ambiguity was not unique in the period. Robert Browning at the end of his life faced the same problems with the letters between himself and Elizabeth Barrett during their fourteen-month courtship. These letters, though filled with a passionate love the Carlyles never fully approved, also revealed secrets, particularly of Elizabeth Barrett's father's unbalanced denial of any of his adult children's right to marry, and of how she and Browning had to plot her escape from Wimpole Street in order to marry secretly. There was in them as well a certain amount of gossip concerning contemporaries. Still, the letters were personally significant, and they told an unparalleled love story, even more extraordinary because it was true. Browning could not find it in himself to destroy the 573 letters, and he certainly would not entertain the thought of publishing them. Unable to decide, he simply handed the letters to his son to deal with. Carlyle didn't have a son, but he did have Froude.

As anxious as Carlyle had been for an answer, Anthony said little till he returned to London, in the fall of 1871, when he could talk everything over with Carlyle personally. "I told him that, so far as I could then form an opinion, I thought that the letters *might* be published," provided Carlyle lifted the prohibition concerning the "reminiscence" of his wife. In fact, before publishing the letters, Carlyle's *The Reminiscence of Jane Welsh Carlyle* should be published to show the public "what his feeling had really been, and what she had really been." The public might be "hard" not only on Carlyle but on Jane if they were introduced to the marriage through "the sharp censures of Mrs. Carlyle's pen." Let the public first read the moving testimony of Carlyle's affection, which gives as well a sparkling portrait of his wife. "To this Carlyle instantly assented." In fact, he might have forgotten "that any prohibition had been attached, but I required, and I received, a direct permission to print."

Still, Froude was handling dynamite. Carlyle himself suggested that nothing be published, if anything was to be published, till twenty years after his death. "Though I was considerably younger than he was, I could not calculate on living twenty years, and the letters, if published at all, were to be published by me." Carlyle halved the time; nothing was to be published before the early 1880s. "There were many allusions in the letters to people and things, anecdotes, criticisms, observations, written in the confidence of private correspondence which ought not to be printed within so short a time. I mentioned some of these, which he directed me to omit. On these conditions I accepted the charge, but still only hypothetically. It had been entrusted to me alone, and I wished for further advice."

Carlyle told him he could consult John Forster, Froude's age, a good friend to both the Carlyles, and one of the early admirers of Jane when she arrived in London. Not only was Forster an editor as was Froude, but he was also the biographer of contemporaries, such as his close friend

Charles Dickens and Walter Savage Landor, among others. Forster read the material and kept his mouth shut, did not say one word about the contents to Froude. He might have been surprised that as close as he had been to Jane, she had kept from him much of her story. Forster's silence itself was also strong indication of the problems the marriage presented a biographer. "He merely said that he would talk to Carlyle himself, and would tell him that he must make my position perfectly clear in his will or trouble would certainly arise about it." *Merely?* Forster offered Froude the best—and some of the only intelligent—advice he was ever to get concerning the papers. Two years later, Carlyle included his gift of his wife's papers to Froude in his will.

About the same time Froude had returned from his truncated lecture tour in the States, he was completing *The English in Ireland,* when, in the closing months of 1873, without a word of warning, a large delivery was made to Onslow Gardens. Carlyle had sent his friend all of his and the rest of his wife's private papers, journals, and correspondence, a collection of more than ten thousand letters.

"Being a person of most methodical habits, he had preserved every letter which he had ever received of not entirely trifling import. His mother, his wife, his brothers, and many of his friends had kept as carefully every letter from himself. The most remarkable of his contemporaries had been among his correspondents—English, French, Italian, German, and American. Goethe had recognised his genius, and had written to him often, advising and encouraging. His own and Mrs. Carlyle's journals were records of their most secret thoughts. All these Mr. Carlyle, scarcely remembering what they contained, but with characteristic fearlessness, gave me leave to use as I might please."

Early in his professional life, in a review essay of Emerson's "Representative Men," Froude had written that his contemporaries had no histories or biographies that gave them the path trodden by real men. His history of the English Reformation set out to relieve half of those lacunae. Little could Anthony conceive that a quarter of a century later he would be handed all the personal papers of the man he considered to be the greatest genius of his time, the prophet he was sure would influence future ages. *Should* he supply his generation with a biography tracking the real path trodden by the real Carlyle? That was more problematical.

"Take them," Carlyle said the day in 1873 when he presented his private papers to Froude, "and do what you can with them. All I can say to you is, Burn freely. If you have any affection for me, the more you burn the better."

"I burnt nothing."

Carlyle waited to die. However, his "expectation of an early end was perhaps suggested by the wish for it," Froude recounted. "He could no longer write. His hand was disabled by palsy. His temperament did not suit with dictation, and he was impatient of an existence which he could not longer turn to any useful purpose. He lingered on, however, year after year."

In earlier years Carlyle complained daily of the painful dyspepsia that plagued him, along with any kind of noise or day-to-day concern—all domestic obligations were whisked away for him by Jane. Since she died his complaints were of her loss and his complicity in her unhappy life.

So things stood on the day when Carlyle, approaching eighty and still alive despite himself, appeared at Froude's door to sit by his grieving friend, himself so suddenly a widower. Anthony, after listening to the old man's lamentations for the last eight years, had just lost his own, much younger wife, whom he had loved wholeheartedly, always appreciated, never abused, the mother of their young children. That day, in unrelieved gloom, Froude and Carlyle sat silently together at Onslow Gardens. In the same house, in closets and under lock and key, was Carlyle's burgeoning memorial to the wife he had treated so poorly.

All Froude wished for was silence and seclusion, to leave London as soon as possible, to get to North Wales to be alone with his children and his grief. And from Wales, he wrote to daughter Margaret (she was away on family business), "I was very miserable yesterday, feeling as if I could never recover heart and spirits again, and dreading the length of years which might lie before me, before I could have my discharge from service. I am better today."

Useful work was the only salvation. But as Froude wrote to Skelton, he was "unable just now to attend to the Magazine work." Carlyle, who had previously convinced Froude to bring on William Allingham as subeditor, now urged him to leave *Fraser's* and to make Allingham editor, which, in his period of mourning, he did. He would later blame Carlyle for this decision. One wonders if besides wishing to get Allingham paying work, Carlyle also wished Froude to have more time to devote to his papers—and to him.

Froude might be in possession of most of Carlyle's papers, but in Wales, he concentrated on a different issue, England's treatment of her colonies. In the months after Anthony legally divested himself of his deacon's orders in 1870, he had entered the public arena in a more forceful way. He wrote two essays in *Fraser's:* "England and Her Colonies" and

"The Colonies Once More," in which he laid out his colonial views with a conviction that bordered on the visionary.

Under Gladstone and the Liberals there were constant discussions about loosening colonial ties to Australia, New Zealand, Canada, and the Cape. England protected her colonies militarily, but the colonies were not producing enough revenue. That the colonies were seen in economic terms as a drag on the economy appalled Froude. For they were "other Englands," having the ability to extend English blood and English values far beyond the small island that was the motherland. They could be as well a solution to the problem of the industrial cities that were crowded with poor, degraded, and downcast souls who needed land to live on and cultivate, needed somewhere to go to grow and realize their potential. As it was, in the last twenty-five years nearly four million English, Irish, and Scots had emigrated to the United States, "the one great power whose interests and whose pretensions compete with our own." British emigration had made the United States stronger and the English empire weaker. Yet the politicians told the people in words, or by their apathy, "that the direction of our emigration is of not the slightest consequence to us."

These politicians were only interested in British emigrants' going wherever they could to make enough money to consume as many English products as possible. They didn't care about them staying English, they cared about them buying English. They even argued that the colonies were a burden to the motherland and should be set adrift, the sooner the better. Froude considered this an unprecedented argument historically. Dropping the Reformation as his basis of comparison, he looked toward the United States. The States had recently spent hundreds of millions of dollars and half a million lives to preserve their national unity, and here England was careless of the value of her citizens as they sought to better themselves through immigration to her own colonies.

In the England of old, the first duty of an English citizen was to his country, and his country was bound to care for and preserve him in return. "What change has passed over us, that allegiance can now be shifted at pleasure like a suit of clothes?" The answer of course was that capitalism and industrialism were turning England from the land-based society it had been since feudal days. For Froude the fate of the English colonies should not be a question of political party. Everyone in England had a stake in their success. Of greater concern was the fate of the English workingman. "Let broad bridges be established into other Englands, and they may exchange brighter homes and brighter prospects for their children for a life which is no life in the foul alleys of London and Glasgow; while by relieving the pressure at home they may end the war between masters and men, and solve the problems of labour which trade unions can only embitter."

England could not save the millions of Irish who had immigrated to the States to find better lives for themselves as Americans. "Are we to wait till our own artisans, discovering the hopelessness of the struggle with capital, and exasperated by hunger and neglect, follow in millions also the Irish example, carry their industry where the Irish have carried theirs, and with them the hearts and hopes and sympathies of three-quarters of the English nation?" And if Mr. Gladstone and the Liberals, in power at the time, were indifferent to this plea, Froude would appeal to Mr. Disraeli.

In "The Colonies Once More" he was even more outspoken. Was Parliament, that house of rich men, going to allow its citizens to do what the Irish had done, be absorbed into the United States? "The attachment of a people to their country depends upon the sense in which it is really and truly their home. . . . And the idea of home is inseparably connected with the possession or permanent occupation of land. Where a man's property is in money, a slip of paper will now transfer it to any part of the world to which he pleases to send it. Where it is in the skill of his hands there is another hemisphere now open to him, where employers speaking his own language are eager to secure his services. Land alone he cannot take with him. The fortunes of the possessors of the soil of any country are bound up in the fortunes of the country to which they belong, and thus those nations have always been the most stable in which the land is most widely divided, or where the largest number of people have a personal concern in it."

In yet another instance of the synchronicity particular to Froude's life, a few days after Henrietta's death, the Conservative Disraeli administration did come into power again and Froude's friend Lord Carnarvon, who as colonial minister had confederated Canada five years previously, was reinstated. So was Froude's other good friend Lord Derby. Added to that, Mary Sackville-West, now Lady Derby, had the power through her tête-à-têtes to bring her Salisbury stepson into the administration. Salisbury deplored Disraeli, but Lady Derby managed to broker their shaking of hands and negotiate the coalition by which Salisbury served with Disraeli, a man he would soon learn not to hate. The Conservatives had a true second chance to conserve England's values. The building blocks of history seemed to be stacking up to Froude's way. If there was anything that could hold his interest after the death of his wife, it was the direction of the English colonies now that Gladstone was out of office.

From Wales he wrote to Margaret that he had done a rough draft of a paper on colonial policy that he sent on to Lord Carnarvon. Such useful work made him "feel generally less entirely unhopeful." Years before as he poured out his convictions in *The Nemesis of Faith,* he planned to emigrate to Tasmania, but that was not to be. Now in his crisis of grief, his heart turned once more to the "other Englands," and he thought to find solace in finally visiting the Pacific colonies and seeing things there for himself. The long voyage itself was appealing, for nothing was ever as therapeutic for Froude than being on the seas.

In the letter Froude sent to Lord Carnarvon along with his paper on the colonies, he told his friend he had just completed *The English in Ireland* and was thinking of a trip to Australia and New Zealand to see for himself if a possibility existed of drawing the Australasian colonies "closer to us and giving permanence to the relations which exist." Carnarvon, obviously impressed by Froude's paper, replied with an alternative suggestion. He wondered if Anthony would first visit South Africa and give the government an assessment that would help them to understand the state of affairs there. "The Chancellor of the Exchequer, Lord Derby, and Mr Disraeli considered that such a mission would be well worth the expenditure."

It would be a secret diplomatic mission; no one was to know Froude's trip was on behalf of his government, to sound out the possibility of confederating the South African states, somewhat the way Carnarvon had confederated Canada. He was to report back on the Dutch in the Orange Free States, on the diamond fields, on the suppression of a native uprising in Natal, as well. Froude, who had *written* with passionate conviction on the importance of the colonies, was asked to *do* something that could affect colonial policy.

The opportunity came at exactly the right moment. Only work kept Anthony's mind off a grief that he revealed in short stabs of sentences in his long letters to Margaret. Margaret was in her twenties and would see to the younger children after they spent the summer in Wales with their father. In those long months, Froude scrambled to find reading matter to enliven Ashley's and May's time. He read to them from *Don Quixote* and *Pilgrim's Progress* until the passages appropriate for their age seemed to be running out. His older son, "our poor Grenfell," as Anthony referred to Grenny, was on an alcoholic downward spiral, and as usual out of the picture. "You remind me most justly that it is useless to preach to him or to threaten him," Anthony admitted to Margaret a few years later. "He cannot resist temptation." Whereas he was killing himself, poor Rose Mary was showing advanced signs of the family disease, but that did not stop Froude from going.

Henrietta's death, Grenny's debauchery, and Rose Mary's health, as well as the uncertainties of the long voyage to South Africa, brought his emotions to the surface in an extraordinary letter he wrote to Carlyle from North Wales on July 10, 1874, and which deserves to be read in its entirety:

My dear Mr Carlyle

The hot weather has come but we hear nothing of you. In three weeks we leave this place to return to London to prepare for my departure. I have taken my passage in a steamer which leaves Dartmouth on the 23rd of August. I am uncertain now whether you will come here, or whether I can even press it when the time is so short. I do not know whether I shall find you on my arrival still in Cheyne Row. The risks of life increase in a long journey like that which I have before me—I should like to hear something of your plans that I may see you again before I go. You must give me directions about the sacred letters and Papers which you have trusted to my charge—whether you wish them to be returned to your custody during my absence . . . or whether they shall be locked up in a sealed parcel in Onslow Gardens, with instructions in case I never come back, to be placed in such hands as you shall desire.

If God so orders it, I will fulfil the trust which you have committed to me with such powers as I have. No greater evidence of confidence was ever given by one man to another—and in receiving it from you I am receiving it from one to whom no words of mine will ever convey the obligation which I feel—from one too whose writings I am certain have yet to do their work and form a new starting point for the spiritual hopes of mankind. To me, you & only you have appeared to see your way in the labyrinth of modern confusion—you have made it possible for me still to believe in truths & righteousness and the spiritual significance of life while creeds & systems have been falling to pieces.—as more & more our inherited formulas are seen to be incredible; so more & more the English speaking world will turn to you for light. Centuries hence perhaps the meaning of your presence here will only be fully recognized. My own self, whatever it be worth, was falling to wreck when I first came to know you. Since that time in whatever I have done or written I have endeavoured to keep you before my eyes and at each step I have asked myself whether it was such as you would approve. What you have been to me you have been to thousands of others. Now when I am about to part with you on this long & uncertain journey I feel compelled to tell you in words which hitherto however imperfectly & unwortherly I have tried to shew you silently. This journey itself is virtually yours. It is only an attempt to give form to ideas which I have so often heard you express. I hope we may both live till I can relate my experience to you, and witness, I trust, some effect produced which you will recognize as good. The thought of you will still be with me wherever I go to encourage guide & govern me.

Lord Carnarvon is very anxious, but I see he feels himself powerless till public opinion [for Confederation] *can be roused. May you be among us when I come back—if I do come back—to help me to rouse it.*

Let your niece write to me & tell me your intended movements.

> *Ever dear Mr Carlyle*
> *Affectionately yours*
> *J. A. Froude*

Carlyle's papers remained at Onslow Gardens and on August 23, 1874, Froude sailed to South Africa aboard the *Walmer Castle.* Yachtsman, fisherman, Devonshire man, sailor that he was, the sea restored him. Two weeks out, he noted that the stars were changing, the pole star under the horizon. "Already a new heaven; in a few days there will be a new earth. The sea is no longer violet, but brilliantly transparent bluish green. It is spring this side of the line. At the Cape I shall find the almonds coming into flower."

On board he talked to as many colonists as he could, an essential part of his fact-finding mission. "I hear much of the Cape Dutch. The English colonists seem not to like them." He began a friendship with a fellow passenger from Devon, Henry Lushington Phillips, returning to his position in Natal: "The judge and I talk and smoke, and gradually the condition of the colony comes out. Coloured men do not serve on juries in Natal, and the result is what might be expected. He once himself tried a white man who had murdered a Kafir, and was caught red-handed. The jury brought a verdict of not guilty, and the audience in the court cheered. The judge said he could hardly speak for shame. I do not yet make out the Boers, who are described as lazy, indifferent to progress or money-making, thinking little of politics, and only resenting English interference with them; yet most people to whom I talk seem to agree that in the Orange Free State the natives are better managed than any other part of Africa."

After a month at sea, the Cape was sighted: "Running into Table Bay. The mountain magnificent, 4000 feet high, and hanging over the town." He used a peculiar image to describe their cliffs: "So sheer that a revolver would send a bullet from the edge of the precipice into the principal street."

The pier was crowded with a mélange of peoples: Chinese, Hottentots, lounging Yankees, not to mention professors from the college intent on meeting Froude. So many different costumes: peaked straw hats with enormously wide brims; turbans; headdresses with handkerchiefs of all colors, the brightest most in favor; and in the middle of it all, colonial bobbies, looking just as English policemen did at home, along with English hansoms and four-wheelers. All and all "the strange and the familiar in wonderful and absurd combination."

On disembarking he tried to avoid the professors. They came to the hotel right after him, a reminder that he was a famous author and would be sought out through his journey not only by professors but by the press. He gave daughter Margaret his satiric account of meeting the leader of the opposition at the Cape and the future colonial prime minister, the owner of the *Argus* newspaper, Saul Solomon, whose name he spied over a store and to whom he introduced himself. In "Leaves from a South African Journal," he described Solomon as the size of Tom Thumb. To Margaret he wrote he was a dwarf about four feet tall with a big head, and that in ideas he was "a diminutive John Mill, about as like him and in the same relation to him as the Cape Colony is to England. But these are the people to whom the control of this country is made over, and who perhaps manage it for the present better than we should do." (Some years later, he would regard Saul Solomon a great man.)

The Disraeli administration was counting on Froude for a firsthand account of the South African situation. There were two major issues on which they sought his advice, and that affected the issue of confederation. The first was the Langalibalele disturbance in Natal: Two large tribes had been savagely destroyed by the colonial forces. The head of one, Chief Langalibalele, had been accused of gun-running and treason, tried, and imprisoned. Froude considered that the whole proceeding appeared to be both arbitrary and violent, and he wanted to discern the truth. There was outrage in England over Langalibalele's imprisonment.

He asked Solomon what could be said in defense of the government in this instance. Solomon offered nothing, and instead strongly opposed what had been done. At the same time he was cautious and would not promise to help convince the Cape Parliament to release Langalibalele, should the imperial government desire it. He seemed to understand the political friction between the two Parliaments more clearly than Froude, who had just arrived.

Froude visited three of Langalibalele's sons in prison. He found the young chiefs perfect gentlemen, mannered, dignified, and self-possessed. Prison uniforms could not conceal superior breeding. The youngest brother was silent; the eldest spoke in a full voice and with authority when he deigned to speak at all. It was the middle brother who did most of the talking. Froude described him as looking like an Italian, with a handsome forehead, dark eyes, and a mouth that though "coarse was finer than [that of] most tribesmen." And it probably added to his credibility when "I observed that his nails and the last joints of his fingers were almost white."

The brothers told Froude that their guns had been honestly purchased through their work at the diamond fields, that they never dreamed of any rebellion. "My own impression was that they were speaking truth so far they knew it. My interpreter, who was not prejudiced in their favour, said that if they had been lying he would have detected it in a moment."

Froude eventually advised the government along the lines of the more liberal Saul Solomon: that an injustice had been committed and one would hope to avoid such in the future, but like Solomon, Froude thought that to try to undo the present injustice would cause even greater problems among the colonists of the Cape. However, Carnarvon's first concern was not the Cape colonists but the English at home, incensed by the injustice, and he released Langalibalele, the first of his race to have been imprisoned at Robben Island, where Nelson Mandela would later spend so many years.

The second issue was the diamond fields: "The facts are briefly these. The Diamond Fields lay within the territory which had been occupied by the Boers since 1854. In the treaties by which we made the two Free States independent, we promised to leave them for the future to settle their differences with the natives without interference on our side. The most important of these treaties we had actually renewed in 1869. In 1870 the diamonds were discovered. A claim was put in for the diamond district by a native chief, and directly contrary to our engagement, we took the chief's side in the quarrel. We settled the dispute in his favour; we took possession in his name; we then induced him to make it over to us, and to justify ourselves we have heaped charges of foul dealing on the unhappy Free State Governments."

Froude believed that if England had only left the diamond fields alone, the influx of British population of its own would have brought both provinces back. "By our stupid interference we have exasperated the entire Dutch population," both in and out of the colony, and have jeopardized the possibility of confederation, because of the preponderance of the Dutch. He became more and more convinced that "the Imperial Government should confine itself to the Table Mountain Peninsula [the Cape], fortify the two harbours, and hold it as a naval and military station, leaving the rest of the country to itself."

Diamond and gold mines had nothing to do with Froude's colonial policies. They were but another indication of the materialistic values of his time, this industrialized greed, this self-expression—each man for himself—he saw all around him, this "democracy" based on the belief that all men were equal, no matter what their values, education, abilities. Work, not democracy, made men free, Carlyle proclaimed time and again, sometimes calmly, sometimes blasting the blockheads. Now Anthony's own Carlylean ideas took on political form. Rich, fertile land was what the poor and the workers needed. Enough land to become home to those who were crowded into unhealthy, overrun, industrialized cities with no way of improving their lot except through immigration to America. Let them immigrate to other Englands instead.

Throughout his trip, he attempted to contain curiosity about what brought him to South Africa, but of course rumors abounded. At a public dinner in his honor at Kimberley at the heart of the diamond fields, he told his Dutch audience: "I have been for many years occupied in studying what the English people were in the past. I wished to study the English of the future. I knew what we had been, I wished to know what we were to be." What he hoped was that the Dutch and the English then living side by side in South Africa might be confederated into one.

Speaking at the capital of the Dutch Orange Free State, he told the suspicious Dutchmen that the only true colonists were those who were cultivating the soil. There were fifteen thousand homesteads occupied by Dutch families, broken up into a few acres each, and he wished with his whole heart that there were fifteen hundred thousand of them. Those adventurers who were swarming to South Africa looking for Transvaal prosperity in the gold and diamond fields were "Not the men who in the English and Dutch fleets dyed the English Channel with the blood of the Spaniards of the Armada." Back to Reformation days yet again, he evoked those "hardy yeomanry and peasantry and fishermen" who once fought not for mercenary gain, but for home and fireside.

"Enclose your wilderness," he exhorted the Dutch with visionary zeal, "plough, dig, and drain, and sow and plant; for every homestead now standing make a thousand." Simplify down to the necessities of life, to a level that would tempt the European peasant to become a settler. "Breed up a hardy population whose home shall be South Africa, and whose hopes shall be centered there. Then you may hope to see your own Confederate flag floating over Cape Town. Then with pride and pleasure we shall pass over to your hands the trust which there will no longer be need for us to discharge."

"We?" Was he speaking for the English government? Was he giving the Cape to Holland? Was he carried way beyond political considerations by his own historical vision?

This address was severely criticized from many points of view, and not only by those who wished to defeat Lord Carnarvon's attempts at confederation, but also by those in favor of confederation who heard in Froude's words encouragement for the Dutch to oppose confederation and follow their own political objectives. The truth was, Anthony was saying what he believed with reckless abandon, as usual without weighing the effects his words might have, indication enough that his political career might be short-lived. The gist of what he was attempting to do was to pave the way to confederation in South Africa, a confederation that would bind together the interests of the English and Dutch farming colonists and allow those colonies to grow. At the age of fifty-six, he would drive over sixteen thousands miles of rutted South African roads, by mule, by murderously bumpy mail cart, and by African bearer. Stretches of such drives he confided in his journal were often "as rough as Browning's poetry." It was worth it, for he was on a mission. The historian told his audience at Port Elizabeth, there was little one man could do, but if there was any ambition left in him, it was to contribute something, even if it was a single thread to the golden cord that might bind the colonies to Great Britain.

Native populations were always a secondary concern. His opinion was that the Dutch, with their tougher policies toward the Africans, did better than the English in that regard.

And so he headed home, having enthused some, confused some, outraged others. He returned to England by February 1875. Having taken their own impressions of Froude's South African policy, the Liberals asked him to stand for Parliament for Glasgow and Aberdeen Universities. His clerical disqualification removed, not only was he now free to run, but that particular seat was more or less guaranteed to the Liberal candidate. Carlyle was extremely keen on his entering Parliament and more than encouraged him. Here was his chance to effect change through his disciple. But Froude was Froude. Though he was not of either party, he could not stand as a Liberal. Disraeli himself wished him to stand, for no Conservative could be elected there, and he could have used Froude's support. In fact Disraeli offered not to put up a Conservative to oppose Froude. Lord Carnarvon as well made an attempt to convince him. It was he who had spoken with Disraeli about the plan to ease his election. Disraeli and Carnarvon aside, not even Carlyle could make Froude change his mind.

Froude's earlier biographers recount that when his butler was asked about Froude's political party, he answered, "Mr. Froude was a conservative when liberals were in power and always a liberal when conservatives were in power." And it is true that at a time when Disraeli's government was in office, Froude wrote an essay, "Political Parties," for which the inscription under the title was "A curse on both your houses." Still for all Froude's talk of independence, his heart was with the Conservatives—which he equated with the conserving of English values. And there was no way he would ever attach "Liberal" to his name.

He hinted (in parentheses) to Mary Sackville-West, Lady Derby: "I said no. (I would stand on the Conservative side, if on any.) I was neither Conservative nor Liberal *per se,* but would not oppose Mr. Disraeli. So there this matter lies, unless your people have as good an opinion of me as the others, and want a candidate of my lax description." Subtlety aside, he had made his bid to run as a Conservative.

A discreet disclaimer followed: "But indeed I have no wish to go into Parliament. I am too old to begin a Parliamentary life, and infinitely prefer making myself of use to the Conservative side in some other way." He was at Lord Carnarvon's service if he wished him to go on with colonial affairs. "I came home from the Cape to be of use to him."

Lord Carnarvon did have use for him. After receiving Froude's detailed report of his mission, he hoped to bring together a conference on the *possibility* of confederation. The plan would be to "*indicate* Federation . . . but not *urge* it." One had to be careful of stepping on the toes of the newly formed colonial government of the Cape. Sir Henry Barkly, then the crown-appointed governor of the Cape colony, though he was suspicious of Froude and the motives of Carnarvon, would act as chairman, and Froude would return to South Africa as Lord Carnarvon's and Her Majesty's representative to advocate a conference of the colonies and the states to consider native affairs.

Though the Conservatives did not ask Froude to stand for Parliament, as Froude so broadly hinted to Lady Derby, either she or Carnarvon must have brought up to him the possibility of his serving in another way—as a future governor of the Cape colony. It was a possibility that made daughter Margaret more nervous than usual, as her father mulled over the likelihood of such a move, along with its ten-thousand-pound stipend. In New York, at Delmonico's, Waldo Emerson had recalled Froude's brilliant Oxford generation; Anthony himself was probably one of the last of those for whom religious doubts had led to legal disability. There he stood, just past his mid-fifties, having had for the first time in his adult life the opportunity of accepting public office should it be offered.

Barkly, if he hadn't already gotten wind of the rumor of Froude's replacing him, was seasoned enough to intuit danger, and it goes a long way to understanding Barkly's personal resistance to Froude, which began with the icy reception he gave him when Froude returned to the Cape that spring of 1875, on a new—and official—mission, scant months after his departure.

Lord Carnarvon had been too quick, sending a dispatch to Barkly outlining a conference to include the Cape, the Orange Free State, the Transvaal, Griqualand West, and Natal on the question of confederation. He requested Barkly to both publish it at once, and to do what he could to advance it. He was also to discuss the issue with Froude when he arrived in his capacity of commissioner of Her Majesty's government. Forewarned, Barkly had time to do the opposite. He did not publish the dispatch, he *did* have the motion for a conference quickly rejected by the Cape Parliament, and then ended the session. The Cape officials would not be told what to do by the imperial government.

So when Froude arrived in South Africa for the second time, the idea of holding the conference was already dead in the water. Froude disembarked at the Cape on June 21, 1875, to read about it—and himself— in Saul Solomon's *Cape Argus*. He could make speeches about confederation all through South Africa, on his own, if he wished: "But he can do so only as an Agitator; and we are very certain that nothing could be more abhorrent to his refined and cultured nature than the mere mention of such a role as that."

Solomon misjudged the taller man. Froude was invited to talk at a commercial exchange dinner a few days after his arrival, but was also warned by the Cape prime minister, Charles Molteno, that he must not disclose anything that wasn't generally already known concerning the rejected conference.

In his long after-dinner talk, Froude informed his audience—to appreciative laughter—that he had been told by the highest authority that since he came with an official position, he was not entitled to communicate with the people of South Africa upon any political subject. He imagined that warning might be true and that his position was to a certain degree ambiguous. But he reasoned differently. Since the idea of the conference had fallen through already, "I shall be nothing now but myself as long as I am in the Colony."

Being himself, he would say exactly what he wanted to say, all through South Africa, the *Cape Argus* reprinting his words. Froude was not reading from prepared speeches, he was speaking his own mind, regardless of the audience and the powers that be. When Lord Tennyson once asked Carlyle why he had chosen Froude to be his biographer, Carlyle answered, "Because of his reticence," and repeated the same to his young niece. No better proof of either the Sage of Chelsea's sense of humor or of his lack of interest in the psychological workings of his closest friend. Froude had exceptionally good manners (as did his children), but he was constitutionally incapable of intellectual reticence. Look at his early novels, look at his tour in America, witness, as Carlyle did, the effect of his speeches through South Africa. This lack of intellectual reticence contributed much to the best and the worst of his writings and to his short, if delightfully unorthodox, political career.

What he did on this second trip to South Africa might prove that the passages of *Don Quixote* that he read and reread to his motherless young children when they were in deep mourning in Wales must have included the Don's fight with the windmills. "The first battle is over," he wrote to Margaret. "After a series of intrigues to keep me silent, which would be very amusing in a novel, I addressed a large audience on Saturday night. My speech has brought almost all Cape Town to see the real character of these proceedings."

Colonial Governor Barkly was fiercely hostile and held himself aloof from the antics of this revolutionary firebrand. It would take weeks for Froude to hear from the colonial office at home, so he was not in an easy position, but he decided on his own to go on to Port Elizabeth, where he had more friends. "If ever I allowed myself to fancy being a Colonial

Governor, make yourself easy," he wrote to Margaret. "The experience of colonial politics is quite enough for me, and to have the remains of my life given to such work, and such society is not what I will have"— but he added a disclaimer—"if I can help it."

It was an important disclaimer, for the people loved him. The idea of confederation appealed to the colonists, land over diamonds appealed to the farmers, and perhaps even more appealing was Her Majesty's representative speaking his mind. Froude was greeted by enormous audiences as he traveled through South Africa. In the western provinces at every town the people came out to meet him. They constructed triumphal arches in the streets, they lined the roads, shouting for Lord Carnarvon and Mr. Froude. The gentry carried him through the province in grand carriages. Farmers, forty and fifty at a time, waited for him at the crossroad to shake his hand, read him addresses, and require him to assure them that Lord Carnarvon meant what he said. When he did, they shouted and shouted till the very valleys rang with their voices. Approaching Port Elizabeth, he informed Margaret, "I am treated everywhere like a Prince." (Or a conqueror, such as he'd portray in *Caesar; a Sketch*.)

He was quite aware he was guiding a popular movement, in a strange country, against the established government. "Any serious mistake would ruin me, yet it will be a miracle if I escape mistakes."

Governor Barkly had passed through Worcester a day before Froude arrived, and at first thought the triumphal arch had been erected for him. "When he heard it was for me, I am told that he was rather impatient. They refused to take him in at the best hotel, too, because I was expected, and only let him sleep there on condition of his going away the first thing in the morning. I am sorry about it all. I liked Sir Henry very well, and I wish he could have seen his way to fall in with Lord Carnarvon's views."

Needless to say, reports of traffic jams caused by Froude's arrival at towns, triumphant arches, and of Carnarvon's appointee openly defying Barkly in his name would not be greatly appreciated by the colonial minister. "I have been, and still am, engaged in a desperate battle in which I shall win, but like the Fairy Princess in the *Arabian Nights* shall most likely be burnt up in the process. I entirely expect that the Ministry will make the sacrifice of me the price of giving way."

The man who did not trust democracy found that he had stirred the people to an extent that a conference on confederation would occur (in London the following year). "I shall be blamed as injudicious, but if I had not been injudicious Lord Carnarvon might have waited for his Conference. Indeed I am well sick of it all. The ministerial papers are like mud volcanoes in eruption and I am daily pasted with mud, till I have to ask myself whether it is really I that have to appear in such a figure."

Back at Cape Town in October, just before the new parliamentary session commenced, the officials set up such a cry about Froude's speechmaking that he thought it best to stay quiet. "They pretend that they can't govern the Colony for me."

Formal complaints were sent back to London, and the colonial parliament would be "chiefly occupied with me and my doings, the Ministers complaining of me as a firebrand, my supporters exulting in me for the same reason, while the outside of my misdeeds is to have told the people that Lord Carnarvon's objects were nothing in the world but to ask their advice in matters where they are concerned and he must act, and that he does not wish to do anything to displease them, and that it has not been very courteous to slap him in the face for doing so."

Froude returned to England by the end of 1875. "If anybody had told me two years ago that I should be leading an agitation within Cape Colony, I should have thought my informant delirious," he wrote Skelton that Christmas. "And though the world cannot yet understand what has happened, I have picked the one Diamond out of the rubbish-heap, and brought it home with me." A conference on South African affairs would open in London in August 1876 and keep him constantly busy.

Froude's most solid accomplishment was his insistence that the Dutch had been cheated when England reclaimed the diamond fields. After much negotiation, "On 13 July 1876 an agreement was reached whereby Great Britain retained the Diamond Fields, while the Free State, in addition to a small rectification of frontier, received financial compensation." And President Brand came to England to represent the Free State at the conference.

But since Charles Molteno did not appear and neither the Cape nor the Transvaal sent representatives, the conference was doomed to failure. Confederation would not occur. Configuring the building blocks of history from this perspective, Waldo Dunn posited "Most of the agony and bloodshed between 1876 and 1910 could have been avoided if the counsels of Carnarvon and Froude had been followed." Disraeli, on the other hand, complained that all Froude had accomplished was to cost England money.

*　　*　　*

149

"Oh, that I was editing *Fraser* again and writing a new book!" he wrote to Margaret from South Africa. "If I am dragged deeper into the political mud pond, I shall never have a pleasant moment again."

He had become even more reminiscent of his father during these two African voyages. On the first trip, he was so overwhelmed, finally, by talk of colonial issues day and night that he wrote Margaret he had decided (after careful consideration, naturally) to spend the money necessary to buy artist supplies and to begin sketching again. He sketched local scenes during his second voyage as well. And he would publish his own sketches to illustrate his later travel books.

When he returned home the first time he found his dearest friend and brother-in-law had been laid to rest beside Charlotte. Kingsley was gone. He and Fanny had both been desperately ill in different rooms, and Kingsley died convinced she led the way. But despite all odds, Fanny recovered.

During Froude's second voyage, Margaret wrote to say her cousin, Kingsley's daughter, who was to become the writer Lucas Malet, and who would address sexual concerns in her novels as daringly as her father before her, said that she could see farther than Carlyle. Froude replied, she might indeed, but she should let others find it out. "I don't doubt she is very clever." She had more of her father's qualities than the rest of his children. "I never questioned Charles's gifts or the generosity and goodness of his disposition. But genius for its full development requires self-forgetfulness, and though he was the most unselfish of living men, he was one of the most self-conscious. But who cares to recollect his faults? I shall never look upon his like again."

In the same letter, he apologized for forgetting Margaret's birthday. He ought to have remembered. "How well I recollect your birth and babyhood at Plas Gwynant." Perhaps he was trying not to think of Rose, whose birth there had been so easy that Froude wished her a life as free of pain. But when he left for Africa this second time, Rose was in the advanced stages of consumption. He must have known he would never look upon her like again.

From Mossel Bay on July 25 he wrote, "I can hardly bring myself to think about home, for fear I should break down. I need hardening rather than softening for my present occupation." And a month and a day later he wrote to Margaret from Pietermaritzburg: "A few words are all I can send you in answer to your sad letter. You and I can settle down where we please, as you say, 'for both are gone to whom climate mattered' [Henrietta, now Rose]. And so we will when this work is done and you will get fresh interests, and I, so long as I can work, may perhaps, with your companionship and the two little ones, look forward to a grey and sad tranquillity."

In Froude's muted twilight reaction to Rose's death, one remembers the archdeacon, surprising his congregation when he appeared to hold services on the Sunday his favorite daughter was at home on her bier.

For all of the controversy that was so much a part of his destiny, Froude returned from South Africa as established in his society as his father had been before him, and putting great hope in the Conservative administration. "When you came into power in 1874," he wrote to Lady Derby, "I dreamed of a revival of real Conservatism which under wiser guiding might and would have lasted to the end of the century."

By 1878 he wrote to Skelton: "A 'Tory'! I don't know what I am. Nobody rejoiced more than I when the Tories came in, or wished them longer life. But they seem to me to be no wiser than their predecessors. . . . . But what am I? And what do I know? I have lived long enough to distrust my own judgment beyond that of most reasonable men. . . . And yet I hated the Crimean War, and I saw every one (a few years ago) come round to my old opinion."

The Liberals returned to power in 1880 and it was "gone,—gone for ever. The old England of order and rational government is past and will not return." Lord Derby himself went over and joined Gladstone's cabinet. Rumors of it abounded beforehand, and Froude wrote Lady Derby that he had been quite sulky as he imagined Lord D. delivering himself over to the enemy. "But what right have I to say anything when I am going this evening to dine with Chamberlain? I like Chamberlain. He knows his mind. There is no dust in his eyes, and he throws no dust in the eyes of others."

In the shifting building blocks of politics, Joseph Chamberlain would later become a Conservative and serve under Lady Derby's stepson, Salisbury, who hated war as much as Froude. In the twentieth century, Salisbury rarely referred to the Boer War by name. "Joe's war," he called it.

In 1874, on his way to South Africa, Froude had hopes of putting political form to his and Carlyle's ideas. "To me, you & only you," he wrote to Carlyle, "have appeared to see your way in the labyrinth of modern confusion—you have made it possible for me still to believe in truths & righteousness and the spiritual significance of life." That spiritual significance in the modern world involved ruminating and attempting to affect the great national concerns of the day. Froude felt he had done some good in South Africa. And when he returned, there was Carlyle awaiting him. He had already promised to take on the burden of Carlyle's papers as a sacred duty to his mentor. In the next decade, it would make the controversy he stirred up early in his life in Oxford, later in Ireland, the United States, and South Africa, seem like romps in a park on a spring day.

The forms of objects, whether persons or things, depend on light and shade. What in one aspect is dark and forbidding, in another is engaging and attractive.

—J.A.F.

The Hero as Biographer

*A*fter South Africa, after the conference on confederation in London in 1876, Froude found himself without his editorship of *Fraser's* and unable to begin a new historical series. He was seeing Carlyle almost daily when both were in town, and he was pledged to Mrs. Carlyle's papers. At first there was not to be any biography of the Sage of Chelsea other than Carlyle's own editing and annotating of his wife's letters—that should be stressed. It was left up to Froude to decide as well whether or not to give these letters and Carlyle's memorial to the world. John Ruskin urged his friend not to be distracted by "old love affairs" and to go on with his research concerning Charles V. But Anthony felt the weight of his responsibility and did not heed Ruskin's oft-repeated advice.

While he sorted through papers he also wrote in the late 1870s a reevaluation of Thomas à Becket from what could be called a radical Protestant point of view; a brilliantly lucid short biography of *John Bunyan* that allowed him to explore the evangelical dissenting position that more and more attracted him; and *Caesar; a Sketch,* weightier than its subtitle, which gave him a chance to parody Gladstone in the guise of that ancient orator Cicero. The better the speaker, the more devious the politician, according to both Froude and Carlyle.

In December 1876, the scientist John Tyndall, friend to Anthony and his brother William, brought a beautiful and high-placed Russian woman to meet Carlyle, a woman of strong autocratic beliefs and keen intellect, Madame Olga Novikoff. Froude might have met her on the same occasion at Cheyne Row. She was thirty-six years old, a sister-in-law of a Russian ambassador, wife of a Russian general, and godchild of the empress.

Tyndall had previously introduced her to both Gladstone and Disraeli—at the same function. Gladstone grew to admire her so greatly that rumors abounded. After he delivered a stirring speech at the St. James's Hall Conference on the Eastern Question, highlighting the corruption of the Ottoman Empire and describing the atrocities the Turks had carried out against the Bulgarians, he was late to an important dinner. He kept half the ambassadors in London waiting, unable to sit at table until he arrived. "I am very sorry," he explained breezily, "but I have not even had time to dress for dinner. You see I have just been taking Madame Novikoff home." Many were more infuriated by his excuse than the cause of it. The Turkish newspapers took it up as an example of Gladstone's championing the Russian cause. He was using Madame Novikoff, they declared, as a Russian agent to overthrow Prime Minister Disraeli. The English press considered that Gladstone had brought Madame Novikoff not only back to her hotel but into the arena of public life and public concern. *Vanity Fair* hinted at an illicit affair, that the nature of these relations would eventually be "more explicitly revealed."

If Froude and Gladstone had one thing in common, it was their appreciation of Madame Olga Novikoff. She originally spent her winters in London advancing the cause of the unification of the Greek Orthodox faith with the "Old Catholics." However, her emphasis changed dramatically in 1876 when her brother, the dashing Nicholas Kiréeff, after completing his own military service, was sent to Belgrade by the Russian Slavonic Committee to offer humanitarian aid through the Red Cross. When Kiréeff experienced the devastation of Serbian villages by the Turkish armies, he, without telling his family, volunteered for the Serbian army under the name Hadji Ghiray. Immediately he was given command of a catch-as-catch-can brigade that went to the front. The European newspapers gave accounts of this mysterious Hadji Ghiray, and Madame Novikoff—at Marienbad—was intrigued by the romantic figure, described as being of great height and "extraordinary beauty of features," who fought at the front leading his irregular troops. His men had no problem making him out; he led them dressed completely in white. It was no wonder he became the first Russian volunteer killed in Serbia— though it took three shots to down him and a fourth to stop his cry of "Forward! Forward!" His death did more "to affect the course of history in Eastern Europe" than policies, dispatches, and speeches, according to Madame Novikoff's biographer, the innovative, socially concerned, proto–new journalist, W. T. Stead. It also changed the direction of his sister's life, when she read the news that hit all the papers: "Hadji Ghiray is killed. It is Nicholas Kiréeff." At first she could not believe her eyes.

From then on Madame Novikoff became an outspoken political advocate of Pan-Slavism and the Russian cause against the Turks, and she attempted to explain Russia's position to the English during her annual winters in London, where she held court at her quarters at Claridge's Hotel. Her "Letters of O.K." were printed in *The Northern Echo* and *The Pall Mall Gazette,* both under W. T. Stead's editorship, as well as in *The Times, The Observer,* and *Fraser's,* among others. Her use of her maiden initials O.K.—Olga Kiréeff—was probably an homage to her fallen brother. Her salon was frequented by diplomats, politicians, clergy, authors—most of the men of importance of her day. Froude visited Claridge's constantly, and he and Olga became lifelong friends.

It was Froude who encouraged Novikoff to turn her "Letters of O.K." into books in order to further explain her people's position to the English. So, during the years Froude was involved with the Carlyle papers, he wrote prefaces to O.K.'s *Russia and England* and *Is Russia Wrong?* Novikoff's English style was so strong and straightforward that it would be easy to overstate his influence on it. However, as W. T. Stead, as well as Gladstone and Froude himself remarked, she had astonishing facility in her second tongue. She was, indeed, a first-rate writer in English who was able to turn complex political issues into strong and unambiguous points of view. Disraeli came to calling her, with his usual wit, "The Member of Parliament from Russia."

Froude's private letters to O.K. brim with political advice that show how keen, if increasingly jaundiced, his understanding of complex political issues had become in the years after he returned from South Africa. After all, if he was not meant to be a colonial governor or a Liberal MP, he was still privy to what went on in the corridors of power through cabinet members Carnarvon, Derby, and that éminence grise Lady Derby—all of whom, as Froude himself did, sided with Russia, while Disraeli and most of England sided with Turkey on the Eastern Question. The general belief then was that should Russia invade Constantinople, she would pose a threat to colonial India.

England was indeed in a bellicose mood in the late 1870s, exemplified by what was called the Jingo party. *Jingoism* itself was coined from the chorus of a contemporary dance hall song:

> *We don't want to fight*
> *But by Jingo if we do,*
> *We've got the ships, we've got the men,*
> *We've got the money too.*
> *We've fought the Bear before,*
> *And if we're Britons true,*
> *The Russians shall not have Constantinople.*

The bellicose mood would disappear as it rose, Froude predicted to O.K., in the way children go from one preoccupation to another. But it was dangerous. Froude encouraged Carlyle to write to the newspapers in an attempt to stem the warmongering. On May 5, 1877, Carlyle complied. Disraeli, "our miraculous Premier," he told *The Times,* intended "to send the English Fleet to the Baltic or do something else that would make Russia declare war against England." He went further: "These things I write not on hearsay, but on accurate knowledge."

Carlyle must have been out of his mind, an atypically angry Froude informed Margaret. Yes, Anthony had convinced him to write, but certainly not to betray what was going on in the Cabinet. He predicted, both to Margaret and to Olga Novikoff, that he would be blamed for the leak about the government's intentions—not only by the public but by Carlyle himself. "It was cruelly thoughtless of Carlyle." However, "I daresay the letter actually did prevent mischief from being done." Such an embarrassing blunder did not turn Anthony from his duty.

Anthony knew Carlyle had handed him Mrs. Carlyle's papers because he would have been the person Jane selected. She trusted him, confided in him, liked him from the day he came to Cheyne Row with his cousin. "Did you ever notice Mr Froude's eyes," she once asked Moncure Conway. "At times," she went on, "his eyes appear to me like those of some wild but gentle animal." Of course Carlyle had a very close relationship with his younger friend, but first and foremost his guilt over his treatment of his wife and his attempt to honor her after she died was the impetus for handing Froude the letters and journals. Anthony took on a duty that would not profit him financially as a new historical series would have, and would, as he could see from the beginning of his perusal of the materials, cause controversy when they were published.

The unease Anthony had originally felt in growing closer to Carlyle once he moved to London had always something to do with the strains in the Carlyles' marriage and his wishing not to come too close to that domestic situation. However, a decade later, when Carlyle handed him Jane's letters and asked his advice on what to do with them, Anthony spent a summer reading unpublished material that documented a relationship that was tragic in scope, the situation so much worse than he had imagined—though he had, of course, heard rumors. In those days, Henrietta at his side, he read—and read.

The Jane Welsh Carlyle whom Anthony knew was a woman in her fifties and sixties who had long since said good-bye to the romantic girl she once was. She so clearly saw the ironies of her life that they expressed themselves overtly in the cutting edge of her wit and her ridicule of the cant of others. But the young Jeannie Welsh, as Mrs. Carlyle herself insisted, was indeed a different person. As she grew older, Mrs. Carlyle grew more and more aware of who she had once been and she delighted in those memories.

Geraldine Jewsbury had recorded many of them in a small notebook she sent to Carlyle and which inspired his own *Reminiscence:* how little Jeannie Welsh wrestled a fierce turkey cock blocking her path to school, crossed on a dare over Haddington's high bridge, bloodied the nose of a bully. She wanted to be a boy. Why wasn't she? In Scotland boys and girls took algebra and mathematics together, but then at eight, the boys went on to Latin, not the girls. So this was the difference between the sexes, the little girl opined. She begged her father for a tutor in Latin, but her mother was against it. Grace was what Grace Welsh wanted for her daughter. Social skills, gentility. A daughter should be her mother's companion. Learn a little music, a bit of French, how to sew an elegant stitch, appropriate accomplishments that would lead to a good—perhaps a brilliant—marriage.

Jane's father differed from his wife. He wanted his only child and heir to be educated. Education was something no one could ever take away from a person. Wealth could disappear, land could, as the doctor's birthplace, Craigenputtock, had been taken for a time, but not an education. Though Dr. Welsh was clearly the head of the household, Grace was against having her overly precocious daughter encouraged in such heavy erudition. How often Jane told Geraldine the story of that night after dinner when she hid herself under the heavy crimson tablecloth. Her parents were talking about her education, having their usual difference of opinion, this time on the subject of Jane's learning Latin. (By then, Jane was secretly studying it with the aid of a school friend.) She waited for a pause in the conversation and then took a risk, speaking out from under her parents' legs, her voice small and breathless: "*Penne,* a pen, *pennae,* of a pen . . ." She declined the Latin noun. Her parents were speechless; she scrambled out from under the cloth and ran into her father's arms. "I want to learn Latin. Please let me be a boy!" Her father smothered his exceptional child in kisses and got her the best Latin tutor in town.

That was how Edward Irving entered her life. Irving was to become a most famous charismatic preacher in the early part of the nineteenth century, and Froude as a young boy had heard him preach in London. He had never forgotten the strong impression he made. Now he read of the eighteen-year-old Edward, the same giant of a man, close to six feet five, with long black hair and ruddily masculine good looks. The only discernible flaw in his singular vision was a perennial squint in one eye. Edward had completed university (which began for Scottish boys by the age of fourteen) and was teaching and directing a school while he studied for the ministry. He wore a flowing cape, and in his splendid voice recited poetry as well as scripture.

He was delighted by the renowned doctor's intelligence, his charming wife's gentility, and by his young charge. He tutored before school hours, and at times Jane would still be sleepily in her nightclothes when he arrived before dawn. He'd sweep her up in his arms and bring her to the windows in the drawing room that faced the back gardens of her pretty home and would point out the stars and constellations to her before the sun rose. Edward, between the ages of eighteen and twenty, and Jane, between the ages of nine and eleven, developed a deep affection for one another. For Jane, there was nothing her tutor did not know. Edward was amazed and delighted by Jane with her precocious ways, her clever tongue, her Gypsy looks. In good weather they could be seen walking the roads and roaming the meadows together. But after two years Edward left for a better position in Kirkcaldy, and Jane continued her education with another prominent scholar, James Brown.

They didn't meet again until 1817 when Jane was sixteen. By then, it was quite obvious that little Jeannie Welsh wasn't going to be a boy. When the respected doctor's daughter walked down the street, dressed with the simple elegance, the unerring sense of style she inherited from her mother, the townspeople said, There goes the Rose of Haddington. In fact, with her buxom beauty and high spirits she was playfully and rather scornfully dismissive of her many suitors. For if she married at all, it would have to be to a "genius." And by now, though her father warned her of the dangers of her popularity, her mother once more had her say in her education and sent Jane to finishing school in Edinburgh. Edward was there, preparing to take his vows and go off to Glasgow as a minister's assistant. She was sixteen and he twenty-five.

For the past five years Edward had been promised to a minister's eldest daughter, Isabella Martin, whom he had tutored right after he left Haddington. Being rather obliquely engaged allowed Edward, an expansive man who got along easily with women, a certain freedom. What harm could there be in seeing his former pupil Jeannie Welsh? Edward was a virile, loving man, with a glint in his good eye. Before they consciously admitted it, Edward and Jane fell in love, and kept it a deep secret. The world of books and romance Jane lived in, combined with the constant adoration she received from family, friends, and admirers, set her imagination on fire. She would marry Edward, but only after he received the Martins' permission to break his engagement. In Scotland, Froude wrote, that was the way things were done. And Jane, beyond her romantic vision, was Scottish to the bone.

Edward was by then so deeply in love with Jane that he would have married her whether or not the Martins released him honorably from his engagement. But when the Martins refused, it was Jane who told him he must fulfill his duty to the woman he did not love. She and Edward would share something more exalted and nobler than his marriage to a silly wife. It would all be just like Jean-Jacques Rousseau's *Julie: Or, The New Héloïse,* an epistolary novel about two secret lovers from a small town—a poor brilliant tutor and his student Julie, the beautiful, talented only child of a rich family. The fictional couple, so like them, would not be allowed to marry, but eventually they shared something so much finer—platonic love. Jane sent the book for Edward to read, but he returned the epistolary novel, telling her he received consolation only from Jane's words, not from what he called Rousseau's letters. "That fatal book!" is what Jane would soon call it.

Condemned by Jane to Rousseau's concept of romantic friendship, Edward introduced her to his best friend, Thomas Carlyle. He had been too jealous to bring men friends to her before then, since the day he introduced her to a friend of his in Edinburgh and she paid more attention to him, causing Edward to erupt and Jane to leave the room. Now he praised both Jane and her beautiful mother to Thomas, without a hint of the shattered romance. Jane was simply Edward's dear former pupil, whose education still concerned him. She was a brilliant girl stuck in a small town; her father was the great love of her life. His recent sudden death—from typhoid caught while attending a dying woman—had been a great tragedy. She could not bear to mention his name and wore perpetual black in his memory. And so the two walked the fourteen miles from Edinburgh to Haddington. Sunshine and shadow. Thomas, a violent-tempered mason/farmer's son, was as glum, withdrawn, and awkward socially as Edward, a violent-tempered tanner's son, was outgoing, loving, and graceful.

On daily visits to the Welshes in Haddington—Carlyle had never seen such a pretty and tasteful house—Edward drew out his shy and gloomy friend. Carlyle—that's what Jane would call him, once she learned how to spell his name. Carlyle—or Mr. Carlyle or Mr C., never Thomas, even through their long marriage—talked of the Germans, of Goethe and Schiller, as if he were speaking of a new world. How he reminded her of her father. Here was another man of genius who was impressed by her intellectual potential, who wanted to teach her, who told her she must study German. Carlyle even promised her a reading list.

For Carlyle, women existed on a separate planet. The higher they soared above his head, the more pleasure he took in bowing, submitting, at least inwardly, to their ideal presence. He considered himself the dark son of the earth; he called Jane his sun. He had none of Edward's ease with the fair sex—and knew it. Jane—so brilliant, beautiful, so devoted to her father's memory—captured his imagination, the place in his constitution where women lived. He could swear she held his hand a moment longer than necessary when they parted. He wrote to her with a sweaty palm.

She knew from that first encounter that professionless Carlyle, from a peasant family, was a genius—even more of a genius than Edward. Both of them would be famous, she predicted (correctly)—and both of them told her she put too much stock in fame.

But love Carlyle as a husband? Never, never, she told him. "I will be to you a true, a constant, a devoted *friend*—but not a Mistress—a Sister—but not a Wife." Her devotions were filial; she insisted she had never known passion. In many ways, that suited Carlyle just fine.

Meanwhile Edward and Jane still hoped, for Edward was not married yet, and if he couldn't find a secure living, he might have to go to

Jamaica for a position. At the last moment, however, he was given a trial to preach for a few weeks at the modest Scottish chapel in London at Hattan Gardens. What would have happened to Edward Irving had he been five feet tall? writer William Hazlitt would soon wonder. Instead, he was a towering giant of a man, Christlike in appearance, with a spellbinding oratorical style, and with a burning belief in the message of Jesus at a time when belief was crumbling all around. George Canning stood up in Parliament one day as a bill for increased compensation for Church of England clergy was being discussed and said he had just experienced the most eloquent sermon he ever heard given in a humble chapel by a poorly paid minister of the Scottish church.

This inflamed the imagination of the rich and powerful. Fashionable England flocked to hear Edward Irving preach. Lytton Strachey's grandaunt Julia was already there in the forefront of enthusiasm for the young man. The papers would soon be calling the charismatic orator "the Spanish Adonis." Though in Glasgow his congregation was suspicious of his expressive oratory, and his way of laying on hands and God-blessing those he met in the streets, Edward was not too overdone for London. For a moment fame did what it was famed for doing—gave Edward hopes of reclaiming what he could not have without it. Perhaps he could now marry Jane. But in actuality it gave him a ministry and money enough to fulfill the pledge to Isabella Martin he had avoided for over ten years. And two years later he spent the long weekend before his wedding day in Haddington with Jane, preaching there that Sunday.

"I am almost out of my wits with joy—I think, in my life, I was never so glad before," Jane wrote to Carlyle on the heels of Edward's wedding day, October 13, 1823, with an élan unique in her letters. She was not dissembling. "You and I are going to London! You and I! We are to live a whole summer beside each other, and beside the One whom next to each other we love most." That "One" was the newly married Irving, who, on the weekend before his marriage, invited Jane and Carlyle to stay with him and his new wife in London. "We are to see magnificence of Art as we have never seen, and to get acquainted with such excellence of Man and Woman as we have never known—in short, we are to lead, for three months, the happiest, happiest life that my imagination hath ever conceived—In the same house for months!" And she continued, "Tell me how he gets on with a wife." Carlyle was traveling with the couple for part of their wedding trip. "It must be very laughable."

Of Edward Irving and Jane's attachment Froude would eventually write: "I should not unveil a story so sacred in itself, and in which the public have no concern, merely to amuse their curiosity; but Mrs. Carlyle's character was profoundly affected by this early disappointment, and cannot be understood without a knowledge of it. Carlyle himself, though acquainted generally with the circumstances, never realised completely the intensity of the feeling which had been crushed." But Froude did. These letters brought him in intimate contact with the Jane Welsh who Mrs. Carlyle swore was a completely different person. And it gave him insight into Edward Irving as well.

The married One did not invite the woman he loved to live with him and his pimply wife in Rousseau-like bliss in London. He invited only Carlyle: "Scotland breeds men, but England rears them!" was the way he put it. Tortured by his undiminished love of Jane, he confessed his passion to his wife and the two of them knelt together and prayed for his healing. He wrote to Jane that perhaps the year after next he would be ready to receive her. But Jane realized it would never be. As she phrased it, she had done his wife too great a favor. Then she had a nervous collapse, more severe than her breakdown after her father's death. It was only then that she told her frightened mother of her and Edward's love. It hadn't been Thomas Carlyle, as her mother feared, but the man her mother trusted. *Edward* had caused her child such secret distress.

Can you imagine, Jane wrote to Carlyle, that people are saying she was dreadfully disappointed at Edward's marriage and that he had used her ill? "Was there ever any thing so insufferable?" She, jilted? Why, it was she who convinced Edward to go through with his marriage.

What should idle tongues matter to her? responded the oblivious Carlyle. What mattered was the absolute honesty that existed between himself and Jane.

"How comes it that I have such a Friend as you?" Jane at times wondered out loud to Carlyle. "That I deceive you without seeking to deceive you? I am so different from the idea in your mind! stript of the veil of poetry which your imagination spread around me I am so undeserving of your love!"

Carlyle in these early days encouraged her literary ambitions; he wanted to collaborate with her on an epistolary novel and a book of translations. But she eventually burned her four unfinished novels and her finished play along with her drawings and paintings. Without her father's love (she often melded her love of her father with her secret love of Edward) she hadn't the same motivation. "I am 'alone,' and no one loves me better for my industry." If only she had Carlyle's genius melded to her ambition, she wrote him. "Oh for your head."

If only she could love Carlyle as she should. Why wasn't she his sister? If only she could "love those I have, when I have not those I love."

It was an extremely tortuous and complex five-year courtship that was revealed to Froude in those letters. Jane and Carlyle rarely met, and when they did, they often ended up having fights that frightened Jane's mother, who saw with her own eyes Carlyle's violent nature. This uncontrollable temper—which he'd apologize for after the fact—upset Grace even more than his peasant background and lack of profession.

After Edward Irving married and when Carlyle was with him in London, Jane made a conscious deception, calling their married friend "the Ass," "the Orator," "the Stupendous Ass," in letter after letter ridiculing him to Carlyle at the same time as she dug for information. It was only after Jane began a correspondence with the older woman who was a confidante of Irving's in London—Mrs. Dorothea Benson Montagu, the literary hostess whom both Irving and Carlyle called "the Noble Lady"—that the truth came out. It was Jane who asked Carlyle if the Noble Lady would write to her, though Froude attributed the first move to the older woman.

Mrs. Montagu was quite aware that Jane desired to hear of Irving through this new correspondence, but as sophisticated as she was, and as intimate with Irving, she had no idea that Jane and Edward's love had been kept a secret from Carlyle. In fact, when Mrs. Montagu told Carlyle she feared Jane's heart was still in England with Irving, Carlyle thought she was under a delusion about Jane's "secret history." It was this threat of exposure through Mrs. Montagu that suddenly convinced Jane that she was "engaged" to Carlyle and would marry him. She was bent on proving to Mrs. Montagu—and to herself—that her love of Edward was in the past. However, Mrs. Montagu, who had been married twice, insisted that there could be no engagement without truth between the couple. She would not promise to keep the secret, even though Jane told her that her own mother thought it better if she did. The fear of exposure by Mrs. Montagu led to the remarkable letter Jane wrote to Carlyle: "I have deceived you, 'I' whose truth and frankness you have so often praised have deceived my bosom friend!" She had told him that she did not care for Edward Irving, took pains in fact to make him believe it. "It was false." She couldn't even take credit for honesty now. It was Mrs. Montagu who motivated her, and she enclosed the Noble Lady's letter.

She had so cleverly dissembled that no reader of her letters—including Froude—could have unearthed the depth of her true feelings without the words she now confessed to Carlyle: "I loved him—must I say it—'once' passionately loved him—"

Carlyle's response was no less astounding. Both of these gifted people, whom Froude so admired for pooh-poohing cant, had extremely limited access to their authentic feelings. Carlyle had as great a desire to ignore his emotions as Jane hers, but he answered with true tenderness—and perhaps some relief. She did not know the world outside of Haddington. There were many men she would one day meet who were more worthy than either himself or Edward. As for her loving Edward and deceiving him about it: "You exaggerate this matter greatly; it is an evil, but it may be borne; we must bear it 'together;' what else can we do? Much of the annoyance it occasions to me proceeds from selfish sources, of a poor enough description; this is unworthy of our notice."

Then Carlyle proceeded to be as truthful to Jane as she had been to him, issuing his one and only warning: "I can no longer love," he responded. "Think of it, Jane! I can never make you happy. Leave me, then! Why should I destroy you?"

His inability to love apparently made itself evident after disappointment in first love: one Margaret Gordon, another of Edward Irving's adoring students. The conveniently engaged man of the cloth introduced her to Carlyle. Margaret rejected him, and afterward went on a platonic road trip with Edward. The carriage wheels rolled, leaving young Carlyle standing in its dust. It was then that Carlyle's dyspepsia worsened. It was one thing to die romantically of a broken heart, he would write in his semiautobiographical *Sartor Resartus*. Quite another, like the book's Germanic hero, Teufelsdrockh ("Devil's shit" in plain English), to live with churned bowels and ghastly indigestion. His "stomach" was never the same.

When the married Jane was once complimented on her husband's fidelity, she replied that it would have been different were it not for Mr. Carlyle's stomach. And when Carlyle became enchanted by Lady Harriet Ashburton, prostrating himself to her the way he had once bowed before the distant and haughty Jeannie Welsh, Carlyle could not understand his wife's jealousy. After all, he told her blithely, she knew he did not love women the way other men did. If not before, certainly after Margaret Gordon, Carlyle could no longer love.

In fact, while Carlyle was more or less courting Jane by post, he left London for a while attempting a cure for his problem through Mrs. Montagu's friend Dr. Badams. Plied with castor oil and mercury and whatever else could by chance purge the tormenting fire of his dyspepsia, this man who had little confidence in his body was in constant contact with his excrement. No wonder he called himself the man of earth, of dirt; the woman he wrote to lived on a different planet than he—the sun. It was not a lack of romantic love that Carlyle was warning Jane about. Mrs. Welsh understood the meaning of Carlyle's inability to love and developed a new caprice after reading the letter: "Now *sighs* and looks terribly cross, at the last allusion to you."

Through these letters and journals, Anthony Froude, the victim of a brutal childhood and an early cowardice he considered constitutional, who had surpassed the mistakes of his youth and had educated himself into both a cultivated and physically active British manhood, who had two marriages and fathered five children, was finding out that the man he revered above all others was impotent.

Carlyle had told him there was a secret about him that no one knew and which made a real biography impossible, and Froude believed his mentor expected he'd come to it as he read through his papers. The impotence was shocking enough, and slight reverberations of Carlyle's failing echo through all four volumes of the biography. But Froude wasn't sure that impotence was the whole secret, especially as he came to realize that it was an open secret to some in the Carlyle circle. There was something concerning his mentor's condition that was even more troubling, something Froude did come across, something he believed must never be revealed—at least through anything he wrote. He felt it his duty to keep it out of the public view forever—and in a certain sense, he has been successful to this day. It was epitomized for him in lines from Jane's journal, and underscored when Anthony witnessed Carlyle's distraught reaction to reading there: "The chief interest of to-day expressed by blue marks on my wrists." Followed by: "Oh! My mother! nobody sees what I am suffering now."

The day after that journal entry, Froude saw that Jane went to Hempstead with Geraldine Jewsbury: "I asked Miss Jewsbury if she recollected anything about it: She remembered it only too well. The marks were made by personal violence. Geraldine did not acquit her friend in all this. She admitted she could be extremely provoking. She said to me that Carlyle was the nobler of the two. Her veneration for her teacher never flagged in spite of it all."

This he wrote in pencil, in a private journal, years later in Cuba. Even though Carlyle considered sections of Geraldine's novels phallic worship—he used the word—she stuck to her opinion that Carlyle's violence was an aberration due to his impotency. She would also later confide in

Froude how she had seen Carlyle's fingerprints embedded on Jane's skin.

Carlyle came from the Lowlands, and the Carlyle clan was known for its violent temper. Before Carlyle started school, his mother bade him not to fight with other boys. It should not be taken as overprotection, any more than her asking her son to write to her the day after his wedding night should be. The old peasant woman, who knew the fields, may not have named her oldest and favorite son's impotence, but she understood it with the underlying psychic connection between the two that allowed Froude to call her—rightly—the love of Carlyle's life. In terms of her making Tom promise he would not fight when he went off to school, Margaret Carlyle was probably more worried by *his* tendency toward violence than that of his schoolmates, as later she was worried about whether or not he'd "heft" to his "gang" on his wedding night. The complexity of the violence in Carlyle's nature was not lost on Froude. He would give lip service to Jane's diary entry as the "only" example of physical violence, but his obsession about keeping it out of print indicates that he knew more.

Young Tom, the pride of his family, was his mother's first child. However, Carlyle was preceded by a half brother from James Carlyle's earlier marriage. That son lived with his grandfather after the death of his mother, but he did come to visit his father and his stepfamily.

Carlyle's earliest recollection, at little more than two years old, was of throwing his little brown stool at his half brother in such "a mad passion of rage" that the stool broke. Immediately after, Carlyle told Anthony, he felt "for the first time the united pangs of loss and remorse." There he was, Carlyle in miniature, right from the first pages of what was to become Froude's monumental biography—a biography that was never decided on beforehand as a whole. It developed in stages.

English law allowed for the annulment of unconsummated marriages, and both the Carlyles knew Jane had the right to leave. Carlyle could not make love to her, could not give her the children she wished for, any more than after marriage he could give her companionship or, at least, include her in his intellectual life as she had believed he would. She confronted him, while he was writing on Cromwell, with the fact that she had almost left him for another. He told her it was up to her whether or not she left, and he had been so busy at the time he might not have noticed. Who knows if he was that unaffected or if he was passively striking back at her, though the obliqueness of his response reminds one of his bland acceptance of her confession that she and Edward had kept their passionate love a secret from him. In either case, the psychological barrenness of Jane Welsh Carlyle's life, given who she was and how she once naively aspired, was indeed the stuff of tragedy.

Froude's shock—or perhaps *indignation* is a better word—was that a man in Carlyle's position held a woman to this life of barrenness. It offended his manhood. Froude was not so far from Charles Kingsley, who mocked Newman's celibacy with his remark that cunning had been Heaven's weapon to give the saints the ability to withstand the brute male force of marriage. For a married man not to be able to satisfy his wife sexually, to have brute male force only when it came to restraining her physically, to take no responsibility except to tell her she was free to go if she wished, was unthinkable. So was denying a woman what Froude would consider her destiny of motherhood, and leaving her through forty years of marriage more and more alone, as she faced her own demons. This physical violence toward Mrs. Carlyle was the secret that had to be kept—and with the help of those who would rather not see, Froude has kept it.

When Jane was thinking of running away with another man, Giuseppe Mazzini, Italian patriot and Jane's best buddy, wrote urging her to think of her parents in heaven and desist. Geraldine Jewsbury told Froude that afterward Jane was thinking of killing herself by slipping off a ship should she have made a certain trip to Scotland—but she never made that voyage. Froude knew who the man was but never revealed the name, thinking it would just cause more controversy. But any time he alluded to the possibility of Jane's leaving her husband, he wrote of Mrs. Carlyle's decision whether or not "to marry." That is rather a quaint way of referring to whether or not one would commit adultery, but that was just it. It wouldn't be adultery, according to Froude's logic, for Jane and Carlyle weren't really married. If there is one slightly "Victorian" tendency in the biography, it is Froude's protective shielding of Mrs. Carlyle from any aspersion on her name. She knew who she was talking to when she confided in Anthony Froude.

Jane had, during some of the worst days of their marriage, accused Carlyle of writing not to her but to his biographers in the letters he sent her, filled with local color and with little hint of trouble at home. Carlyle was quite sensitive to that criticism, according to Froude. It may have been one reason Carlyle decided at first to look at his own life exclusively through his *wife's* letters. It was only after Carlyle realized that others besides himself were waiting for him to die before they published *their* reminiscences that Carlyle decided, if a biography was inevitable, if he was not to be allowed to be interred with his bones as he said he wished, then at least Froude should write it.

Froude's son Ashley became a teenager during these Carlyle-soaked years. And his memory of them is a pastiche, blending decades of his and his father's mixed emotions. Ashley told Waldo Dunn that he and his sisters, particularly his older sister Margaret, knew his father was to take charge of Carlyle's papers and write his biography, and that such matters were being constantly discussed when his father and Carlyle were together: "It had a very depressing effect on my father, who told me that he was to be made Carlyle's 'whipping boy.' My sister and I thought it hard that Carlyle would not expiate his sins while he was alive, instead of leaving the task to be performed vicariously by my father. The effect of the whole affair on my sisters and me was that we hated the name of Carlyle and everything connected with him. The conclusion that I came to was that Carlyle's remorse was genuine and that the history of his married life gave ample grounds for it; that if it was not genuine, he was an arrant humbug, and this, much as I disliked him, I could not believe. I could never understand the veneration, respect, and affection with which my father regarded his memory, but this was the ignorance of extreme youth."

Underneath the levels of sophistication, sarcasm, stoicism, and overly polished manners that made the mature Anthony so difficult for the casual acquaintance to fathom, one has to ask if the burden of Carlyle's expectations actually caused the once whipped and bullied Anthony to consider himself whipping boy again.

Froude soon found out that like all deepest, darkest secrets, Carlyle's "constitution was known to several contemporaries, that in fact his unconsummated marriage was an open secret. Perhaps it was discovered by the physicians who attended in Mrs. Carlyle's illness." John Ruskin found out about it through one of her doctors; so did Froude's most notorious disciple, Frank Harris, through another doctor. Harris, born in Galway in 1856 of an Irish father and Welsh mother, was known for his tall tales, and he became widely discredited even when he told the truth.

The Frank Harris who arrived in London seeking his fortune with a letter of introduction to Froude from Carlyle, however, was late-Victorian Frank Harris, a young man in his twenties being introduced to a world that was passing. "How I Met Froude and Won a Place in London" is a chapter from his infamous autobiography, *My Life and Loves*. He portrayed himself in London as intently studying Froude's essays, which were collected in the four volumes of *Short Studies on Great Subjects*, forcing himself "every day to write one or two sentences as carefully as possible" in imitation of Froude. Through this study, which, he maintained in his autobiography, lasted for some years, he gained mastery over "the structure of our English speech."

One sees Froude's influence in both style and psychological astuteness through Harris's revealing sketches of Carlyle and Browning, as well as in his biography of friend Oscar Wilde, which is today proving to be more prescient than previously supposed. All this after he immigrated to America and became early-twentieth-century Frank Harris. Harris then provided the bridge between male spiritual autobiography in the nineteenth century, of which Froude's *Nemesis of Faith* is a prime example, and male autobiography of the twentieth century. In *My Life and Loves* the sexual quest moved to center stage and the penis penetrated mainstream prose.

At their first meeting Harris told Froude that Carlyle had been his hero since the days when as a teenager Harris had been "a cowboy in western America."

A cowboy! repeated Froude, as if amazed.

Harris went on to say it had been Carlyle's advice that sent him for four years to German universities, and that he had finished his schooling with a year in Athens.

How interesting, the skeptical Froude replied, evidently, according to Harris, not understanding that adventures come to the adventurous.

Froude apparently did understand that tall tales come from the young and the ambitious (not to mention, in Froude's view, the Irish). Harris's preposterous exaggerations did not dissuade the older man from launching his career in London by introducing him to the prestigious *Fortnightly Review:* "You will perhaps be as much puzzled by him as I am, still as an Editor you would be sorry to miss the chance of encouraging a person who may turn out something exceptional and thereby [I] send him to you."

Oscar Wilde quipped: "Frank Harris has been to all the great houses of England—once!" But Anthony Froude, a literary lion in his time, had a hand in Harris's destiny. And in those early years, Harris brought a keen eye to Froude's circle.

In *My Life and Loves,* Harris told two stories about the Carlyles' marriage that he said came to him from their friend Dr. Richard Quain. Sir Richard attended Jane during her menopause. Quain was convinced one of Jane's illnesses was gynecological and finally insisted that he examine her. The first time she agreed, she reneged by locking her bedroom door rather than preparing for the examination, and Quain left 5 Cheyne Row in a huff. The second time, a month later, she lay down for the exam with a scarf covering her face. Quain found this modesty so exaggerated in a middle-aged married woman that he rather abruptly pulled her lower on the bed and raised her skirts—to find as he examined her that she was an intact virgin. Jane's response to his astonishment: "What did you expect?"

Quain's curiosity was piqued, and through Jane's illness he plied her with questions. He supposedly told Harris that Jane described her wedding night (culminating a day of no kisses) with Carlyle lying there next to her "jiggling, jiggling." One imagines Carlyle was trying to arouse himself, but Jane, married without the least idea of the physiognomy of sex, burst out giggling. She'd never heard of anything so absurd about a wedding night. Carlyle left the bed in a fury, muttering, "Women." Not only Froude's suggestion about confiding in her physicians, but Jane's later shame and hiding from Dr. Quain, writing to a confidante (the wife of yet another of her physicians) that she was mortified by the things she said to him while she was ill, substantiates the basic truth of Harris's account. It was also Quain who saw to it on John Forster's and Froude's urgings that the usual autopsy was not performed on Jane after she died suddenly in her carriage. It would have been more than Carlyle could bear, his friends argued. Such an autopsy would have substantiated that she died a virgin.

Carlyle's sexuality? Who knows what would be the earliest sexual experience of a provincial boy of unusual genius and no social skills, who was sent on the long walk to the University of Edinburgh at the accustomed age of fourteen to find lodgings, and to live on his own for the five months a year he was not needed back on the farm. What a contrast in type to the young English gentleman entering Oxford for the first time, the shopkeepers and loose ladies salivating. Edinburgh was a big, sinful city, particularly to a boy from Ecclefechan, whose town was the size of its name. Not only was Carlyle a hayseed but he was essentially a loner; he might, in fact, have been protected by his suspicious and rather condescending nature. He would always idealize his loving mother—and his intractable, violent father. No one in England would come up to them in virtue, and perhaps this unresolved narcissism of Carlyle's, this myth he carried through his life of the all-virtuous, omniscient parents, isolated and protected him as a teenager. On the other hand, Carlyle lived at a time when moral responsibility began in dreams, too. He could easily find guilt in any unclean thought or action.

For Carlyle, women lived on a different planet, as he wrote in his unfinished first novel, and he approached them romantically on the level of fantasy. Froude found this overidealization in Carlyle's later letters to the immensely brilliant, immensely fat Lady Harriet Baring, later Lady Harriet Ashburton. This aristocrat, the queen of London society, made Carlyle, rather exotic in his peasant background, her pet philosopher after he became famous, entertaining him—or, more accurately, he entertaining her—at Bath House in London and at her many country homes, leaving Jane even more alone. She had all of Jane's intellect and wit, plus power and influence in the wider world. In his Cuban journal Froude portrayed Carlyle's letters to Lady Ashburton as "masses" of extravagant homage to the "great lady" as ecstatic as Don Quixote to Dulcinea. The letters were "of course the purest Gloriana worship, the homage of the slave to his imperious mistress." One sees the same slavelike devotion, a delight in debasement—Dreck to sun—in Carlyle's early letters to Jane, during the time that Jane was extremely disdainful of his advances. And throughout the stormy marriage, for all Carlyle's temper, not only Froude but other frequenters of Cheyne Row witnessed how Carlyle enjoyed Jane's mocking him in public, as was her witty wont. Perhaps it is not so shocking that politically Carlyle saw nothing wrong with slavery. In his sexual fantasies, women were masters and he was taken care of, bowing to the lash of their tongues with obvious delight.

Homosexuality was not a word invented in Carlyle's lifetime, but one has to wonder if that was part of the secret he believed no one could know. One suspects that the homoerotic impulse in Carlyle was on the level of deep same-sex friendships, stirring feelings that, whether expressed or not, had to be repressed. A revealing letter John Sterling wrote to Carlyle appeared in *John Sterling*—Carlyle's only biography of a contemporary. Dying before his time of the dreaded tuberculosis, Sterling sent a poignant farewell, including the curious line "With regard to You and Me I cannot begin to write; having nothing for it but to keep shut the lid of those secrets with all the iron weights that are in my power." What secrets are these that do not go gently into that dark night, secrets a dying man reassures his dear friend he will keep the lid on with all his remaining strength? Biographer Carlyle does not explain the reference—neither does he delete it. Had Carlyle, with his peculiar temperament, his idealization of his devout peasant parents, and his own streak of Calvinistic severity, been aroused by homoerotic yearning in dreams or in reality, had he acted on such impulses in any way, the guilt attached may have, in the long run, contributed to the severity of his impotence.

It was in December 1880, only three months preceding the old man's death, that Carlyle brought up the letters and memorials of Jane that he had collected and annotated. During a carriage ride he asked Froude what he had finally decided to do with them. "He knew what my own feeling had originally been—that the intended collection of those 'Letters' was the most heroic act of his life; that they ought to be published, and the 'Memoir' published along with them. He had then been evidently pleased. He left it all to me."

But since Anthony's first reaction almost a decade previously, things had changed. First of all, Carlyle had decided that since a biography of him was inevitable, Froude should write it, and the year before suddenly urged him to begin immediately, while he was alive. So Froude had already incorporated excerpts from many of Jane's letters during the long five-year courtship and the early marriage. There was no need to publish those revealing letters separately.

Froude had also made an exciting discovery as he went through thousands of pages of the Carlyles' letters and intimate journals. Carlyle had written not only his reminiscence of his wife, but there were other unpublished memoirs that captured the essence of time past and had profound emotional, literary, and biographical value. The prose was breathless, lyrical, at times mannered, at times eccentric, at times notes to himself, for he was often simply thinking aloud. It was all vintage Carlyle, much closer to his letters, to the man himself, than to much of his other writings. Carlyle had been quite conscious of the hyperbolic nature of his style, which he knew to be a stumbling block. He told Froude he realized the style could be mistaken for affectation, "but it was a natural growth." It originated in the Annandale farmhouse of his youth. The humor was from his mother, the form from his father's unique phraseology. Still, he often wished he could write his essays and books with the naturalness with which he wrote his letters. Froude recognized that particular naturalness in the memoirs he discovered among the papers. In them he believed Carlyle had become his own Boswell.

There was a remembrance of Edward Irving, written immediately after Carlyle had finished writing of Jane. When Froude pointed out the manuscript to him, the old man, whose mind stayed sharp till the end, had no memory of writing it, so "peculiar" had his state been after Jane's death. It was in a sense semiautomatic writing. Carlyle then went on, perhaps part of the same trance, to write of Jane's early admirer and his benefactor (whose help he begrudged), Lord welco. And he penned shorter sketches of Southey and Wordsworth. Froude found, as well, a half-century-old notebook in which Carlyle wrote a touching tribute to his father in lieu of returning to Scotland to attend James Carlyle's burial. "I thought them extremely beautiful. I thought they gave the most favourable picture of Carlyle himself which could possibly be conveyed. I thought they ought to be published as they stood in a separate volume. I proposed it to him and he readily assented."

There was even talk of Carlyle's editing these memoirs himself, but he proved emotionally not up to that task. It was agreed that these reminiscences of James Carlyle, Edward Irving, Lord Jeffrey, Southey, and Wordsworth were to be published as soon after his death as possible, when there was likely to be a stir. In fact, by the December of the carriage ride, they were already in galleys.

Earlier, there had been an international clamor on Carlyle's eightieth birthday. Newspapermen from the Continent and America were constantly coming to his door in hopes of an interview. And his eighty-fifth birthday had occasioned feature articles in England and abroad. The older he got, the more of a legend he became, though he was no longer writing. He tried to avoid all the hoopla (except the congratulations of Bismarck). As he told Froude, "They call me a great man now, but not one believes what I have told them." To have new work published on the heels of the great man's death would be good timing. Both men were practical and professional enough to know it. But Froude was not planning to publish *The Reminiscence of Jane Welsh Carlyle* along with the other memoirs. It was very intimate in nature, and Froude had already incorporated significant portions from it into his biography of Carlyle's first forty years.

One pictures the two in that carriage, at the end of 1880. Carlyle had aged significantly in recent months; there were no more long walks culminating in taking the omnibus home, the conductor pointing out the great man and his companion. Carlyle spoke to Froude "exactly in the tone which I had feared: in the old melancholy, heart-broken way which I knew so well." What did Froude intend to do with the memorial to his wife? He knew it had not been set in galleys, so the question was quite pointed.

"I had not the courage to tell him that I had changed my mind. Indeed, I had not changed my mind so far as the right and wrong were concerned. I had been merely cowardly. I told him that the 'Letters' should be published and the 'Memoir' also. He seemed at once relieved and easy." So it was that three short months before Carlyle passed, *The Reminiscence of Jane Welsh Carlyle* was added to the other memoirs. It meant the addition of a second volume to contain it—along with an appendix consisting of the short memoirs of Wordsworth and Southey. On March 5, 1881, a month to the day after Carlyle passed, the two-volume set of *Reminiscences* by Thomas Carlyle, edited by James Anthony Froude, was published. No dust storm this. A winter blizzard.

"It was very painful to me to read the *Reminiscences* which Froude has printed," niece Mary Aitken wrote to Charles Eliot Norton at Harvard. "My Uncle often said his memory would be safe in Froude's hands, for whether he wrote a good book or a bad one he would always be so gentlemanly and so 'reticent.'"

Carlyle had brought his niece Mary Aitken from Scotland to Cheyne Row a few years after Jane's death, when the slight, dark-haired Mary was only twenty. The "little girl" or "little woman" was how Carlyle and Froude and even John Ruskin endearingly referred to her. She lifted the gloom of the house, Carlyle wrote. Her mother was Carlyle's most intellectual and willful favorite sister, and her father, a prosperous Dumfries housepainter and decorator by trade, who was also an amateur artist. Carlyle was suspicious of James Aitken when he courted his sister. But when he saw the copy he had painted of a Ruysdael over their fireplace, he was astonished—verisimilitude being to Carlyle the height of art. Mary came to London hoping to fulfill the unrealized artistic ambitions of her parents and to become a writer herself.

Carlyle had ostensibly stopped writing after his wife's death, and this was underscored by a palsy affecting his right hand. Mary was not only her widower uncle's companion but his amanuensis as he went through his papers, dictating prefaces to his wife's letters, which Mary copied and which Carlyle later sent to Froude.

We can paint our own picture of Carlyle, two years after his wife's death, in his armchair at Cheyne Row dictating to his little niece. He is preparing a preface to a letter his wife sent to Mary's mother *forty-three years before,* when Mary's mother, nicknamed "Craw Jean" because of her crow black hair and eyes, was only twelve years old.

When Jane first met her, she took to the bright child, telling Carlyle, "Such a child ought to be educated," and she generously brought little Craw Jean to live with the Carlyles during the first years of their marriage, both in Edinburgh and then Craigenputtock. Jane's motherly instincts would always be in tandem with her desire to teach. But James Carlyle wanted Craw Jean to help at home, so she returned to the farmhouse to be raised a "peasant" girl, as Carlyle phrased it, though she turned herself into a superior woman.

As one pictures Carlyle in his armchair dictating in 1868—perhaps, as they often did, they were sharing the same light—one can almost feel Mary lifting her uncle's spirits by her presence. As part of his preface to Jane's letter to Mary's mother, he described Craw Jean and her husband, ending, "Parents they, too, of my bright little niece, Mary C. Aitken, who copies for me, and helps me all she can in this my final operation in the world."

Froude had already blended this passage into the biography of Carlyle's first forty years, at a time when he thought he would not publish Jane's letters and Carlyle's annotations of them separately.

Dictation didn't suit Carlyle, Froude tells us, and after he finished annotating his wife's letters, not only did he give up "Literature"—except, as we have seen, for the occasional outraged letter to the *Times*—but he more or less gave up dictating responses to personal letters as well. He told his friends he would still be pleased to hear from them, should they accept a one-way correspondence. It was then that the correspondence between niece Mary and Harvard professor Charles Eliot Norton took on a life of its own.

Norton, a well traveled Yankee from an old New England family, had first met Mary and her uncle in 1869, on a trip to England three years after Jane Carlyle's death. Carlyle had determined to leave parts of his personal library to America, and Norton's introduction to Cheyne Row was in connection with securing them for Harvard, where, indeed, the collection remains to this day. Like Mary herself, he knew Carlyle as an old man, his fame secured, his writing days behind him. At first Mary transcribed Carlyle's letters to Norton, but after Carlyle gave up answering his letters, except for calling out a greeting or two, Mary became the correspondent. The "little girl" had a combination of bright intelligence, a desire to learn, and an innocence that was quite endearing to older men such as Norton.

She described a visit to Darwin and his family: "Probably you know Mr Darwin? I was hardly ever so much surprised as when I saw him; he looks such a fine good Patriarch, and has such a gentle voice it seems strange that he should be the founder of so revolting a faith."

On the early novels of Henry James that Norton sent over to her as they appeared (he was fond of sending her such gifts): "He takes nice

American country girls and contrasts them with the most odious type of European worldly wise ladies as if there were not nice country girls in the old world and no scheming worldly wise women in the new. It is not fair!"

In certain respects Mary remained for a long time a nice Scottish country girl. And Norton had his own American innocence in the Jamesian mode; at least friend John Ruskin would accuse him of not understanding the shadow side: "Your entirely happy and unselfish life puts you out of touch in judging of those mixed characters—Carlyle or Froude or me!"

Norton met Froude the same year he met Mary, at a dinner Virginia Woolf's father, Leslie Stephen, gave, and disliked him immediately. The impression remained. Four years later, in London again: "After lunch went to see Carlyle and found Froude and Allingham with him. I have never taken to Froude, and his late performance in America is not calculated to raise one's opinion of him. His face exhibits the cynical insincerity of his disposition. Carlyle is fond of him, and assures me I should like him better, if I knew him better. . . . He, doubtless, has his good qualities which Carlyle sees, and Carlyle is not insensible to the flattery of being accepted as a master by a man of Froude's capacity."

Froude almost won the New Englander over during a long walk through Kensington Gardens: "We grew amicable as we walked, and he talked much and well of his American experiences. How much he conceals it is hard to say; but he said nothing but pleasant things to me."

A clue to Norton's visceral dislike of Froude can be gleaned from Norton's much younger brother-in-law, Arthur Sedgwick, who remembered the professor speaking highly of J. L. Motley, the historian and diplomat, excepting that Motley wasn't entirely simple. At first Sedgwick thought that a strange criticism of a man of the world, but throughout Norton's life: "His critic's eyes were fixed on simplicity as a final test of character." It was a test Anthony Froude was born to flunk.

Mary tried to change Norton's opinion. While Froude was in South Africa, Carlyle sorely missed him. "I don't think any one quite fills up Mr Froude's place," she wrote. On Froude's return, there was rejoicing. "Mr Froude, a favorite disciple (& very justly so I think) has got back from the Cape and comes to walk with him two or three times a week and is a great resource. He is most kind and tender and good to my Uncle."

When the constant care of her uncle overcame her, at the end of 1877, she needed a month's holiday away from him as she was ill and close to breaking down. Froude took her along with his children on his yacht bound for Ireland. She told Norton, "The Froudes were very kind and pleasant companions; the journey very pleasant in its way; but I think one grows weary of the long hours of idleness; at least I did and the continually running from side to side when the yacht was sailing to avoid the waves did not answer well for reading. But the rest and sea air did me far more good than the visit home which was pleasanter."

Mary's relationship with Froude could not have been more cordial—up until the last years of Carlyle's life. Then, after her uncle died, Mary became furious over the publication of *Reminiscences*. She received plenty of encouragement at home, for she had been married to her first cousin Alexander Carlyle two years earlier. Alexander was the son and namesake of Carlyle's hard-drinking brother who had farmed Craigenputtock during the Carlyles' stay there before the farm failed, and who had later immigrated to Canada. Carlyle considered him his most naturally intelligent sibling—which is saying a lot, since brother John became a doctor and a translator of Dante, as was Norton, who published Dante in prose. Alexander died in Canada; in his last moments his mind wandered back to Ecclefechan, wondering if young Tom had returned from university. This very much moved his oldest brother. Alexander Jr., better educated than his father, a graduate of the University of Toronto and a secondary-school teacher there, came to London in July 1879 and quite suddenly, the very next month, married his first cousin Mary and joined his new wife on Cheyne Row.

Mary—even before she became Mrs. Carlyle—had begun to urge her uncle, perhaps with Canadian encouragement, that the papers he had given Froude to do with as he wished should be returned to the family after he had finished with them. Carlyle throughout his long marriage had been shielded from the unpleasantness that arises in daily life. He sent his wife to argue his taxes and to figure out how to keep the neighbor's noisy cock from crowing, dogs from barking. Added to Carlyle's natural propensity to avoid such confrontation, he was now an old man who certainly did not want unpleasantness to arise between those who tended to his needs. Carlyle told Mary that he had mentioned this change of plans to Froude. She urged him to make it crystal clear, but Carlyle did not burden Froude further. The return of the papers that his niece was demanding must have been a warning signal to the old man. For it was only on the heels of her marriage, and with Alex moving into Cheyne Row, that Carlyle asked Froude to begin the biography immediately, while he was still alive.

It was also only after the marriage that Froude remembered hearing that the papers were to be returned, Carlyle dropping the news in a casual way. He was thankful he hadn't obeyed Carlyle's earlier request—to burn as much as he could. The new Mrs. Carlyle persisted in reminding Froude of the change of plans—to a point of irritation: "I would sooner replace everything in your hands at once and let you do the editing yourself, as you easily could do, if I am not to be left to work at my leisure and to bear the responsibility." In 1880, with Carlyle still alive, Froude was issuing a threat, not a promise, and Mary backed off.

Alexander probably had something to do with turning the nice Scottish country girl he married into a determined woman. But time was more persuasive. Mary was no longer twenty. Fourteen years previously, she had given over her youth to the care of her famous uncle and to dreams of her own literary life. She was now at an age to experience the results of youthful decisions.

Carlyle was not a mean man, but he was a frugal one. Though very generous in his silent charities, as Froude informs us, he kept his household under careful control. "My uncle always drew his own cheques." He painfully regretted and sought penance for his treatment of his wife after she was gone, but not in a way that made him aware of the worth of women's work. Carlyle's sincere gratitude to Mary hit a blind spot when it came to financial considerations. He bequeathed Mary, that "dear little soul," all of "Five Hundred Pounds for the loving care, and unwearied patience and helpfulness she has shown to me in these my last solitary and infirm years." No one thought it fair.

"I was sorry for her," Margaret Froude told Waldo Dunn almost half a century later. "It seemed hard that she should have worked for so many years and yet should only share equally with all the many other nephews and nieces, as by Carlyle's will it was arranged. I remember speaking to her often of what seemed to me an injustice."

Froude's two-volume edition of the *Reminiscences* did more than cause a stir. Froude considered that Carlyle was writing his own biography through these memoirs, but Carlyle's uncensored comments on people, some still alive, caused a public uproar. Many respectable people apparently were not amused when Carlyle remembered that to Cheyne Row, "Charles Lamb and his sister came daily once or oftener; a very sorry pair of phenomena. Insuperable proclivity to gin in poor old Lamb. His talk contemptibly small, indicating wondrous ignorance and shallowness, even when it was serious and good-mannered, which it seldom was, usually ill-mannered (to a degree), screwed into frosty artificialities, ghastly make-believe of wit; in fact, more like 'diluted insanity.'" And the plaintive tone of Carlyle's regrets about his wife—the "Ah, me! Ah, me!" aspect—seemed below the great man's dignity.

How could the man Carlyle trusted publish such material? some questioned as they and others rushed to buy the book. The criticism did not intimidate Froude. In the biography he didn't suppress similar scathing and characteristic passages—including Lamb again—though Froude informed his readers there were aspects of Lamb's life unknown to Carlyle.

Mary wrote to Norton that the *Reminiscences* were no more a portrait of her uncle than the "hideous" silhouettes published in it were likenesses of his father and mother. Norton, to his credit, saw the brilliance of the work and replied that there was little he regretted reading; he only wished the audience had been confined to the few who could properly understand Carlyle's meaning. "It is one of the most human of books; as sincere and serious a record of life as exists anywhere."

There he and Froude agreed. "It is Carlyle himself—the same Carlyle precisely that I have known for thirty years; and it seemed to me that my duty was to represent him (or let him represent himself) as near the truth as possible. To me in no one of his writings does he appear under a more beautiful aspect; and so, I am still convinced, will all mankind eventually think." Froude wrote this to John Skelton, who had vetted Carlyle's Scottish vernacular for the edition, telling him, "I am more surprised that I should have been at the reception."

But to many in literary London, it had been sacrilege for Froude to have published these unguarded and spontaneous outpourings—a breach of trust. It exhibited the old shiftiness and allowed new talk of the old scandals. It brought back memories of the younger man who published *The Nemesis of Faith* for his father the archdeacon and his Oxford fellows to read, who got thrown out of Oxford, dropped the "Reverend" from his name, and caused a dust storm in the newspapers.

These earlier issues had in fact been raised anew only a few years previously by Froude's archenemy, E. A. Freeman. When Froude serialized the book-length "Life and Times of Thomas Becket" in *The Nineteenth Century,* Freeman wrote a ninety-eight-page review essay attacking the author's character to a point that was libelous. For decades, Anthony had endured the anonymous censure of *The Saturday Review,* often the work of Freeman. This time, Anthony felt the necessity of response, and in April 1879, in nineteen pages of *The Nineteenth Century,* he wrote "A Few Words on Mr. Freeman."

For Freeman had accused Anthony of "stabs in the dark" at his long dead brother Hurrell, and for the most ludicrous of reasons: Anthony had *not* mentioned Hurrell Froude's name specifically while criticizing the Oxford Movement for turning Thomas Becket, the murdered Archbishop of Canterbury who upheld church over his king, into a saint. Hurrell's *Becket,* published in his *Remains,* was in diametric opposition to the interpretation offered by Anthony. It was "unbrotherly," Freeman said, not to pick Hurrell out by name. Here he hit a nerve. For Anthony had found a way throughout his writing career of differing from Hurrell's interpretations of history without *directly* confronting him. Freeman had committed a "gross impertinence" that could not be ignored:

"How can Mr. Freeman know my motive for not speaking of my brother in connexion with Becket, that he should venture upon ground so sensitive?" The natural kindness Freeman referred to "would have been more violated if I had specified my brother as a person with whose opinions on the subject I was compelled to differ."

Instead, Froude had mentioned generally that Becket's "rehabilitation" was one of the first things the Oxford Movement had attempted. He had purposely left out the fact that Newman and Keble accomplished this by publishing Hurrell's work on Becket in his *Remains*. For the first time Anthony gave his view of the *Remains* that his father, brother William, and John Keble told him time and again to read for edification during his rebellious youth: Hurrell Froude's journals and writings were brought out by the leaders of the Tractarian movement after Hurrell's death as a party manifesto. "And for my own part, I consider the publication of the *Remains* the greatest injury ever done to my brother's memory."

Had Anthony written anonymous articles attacking his brother, they would have been stabs in the dark and Freeman could have used that expression. As it was "I look back upon my brother as on the whole the most remarkable man I have ever met in my life." Of Anthony's personal feelings for Hurrell, he could not speak. "I am ashamed to have been compelled, by what I can describe only as an inexcusable insult, to say what I have said."

Freeman had spoken of Froude as being his *victim*. "The word exactly expressed my condition. Victims are generally innocent and helpless. I know myself to be guiltless of nine-tenths of the crimes against me." Freeman had gone beyond the office of reviewer. "He has used the occasion for an invective upon my whole literary life, and even my personal character and history; he has described me as dishonest, careless of the truth, destitute of every reputable quality save facility in writing which I turn to a bad purpose."

Totnes. A contemporary view of the town.

John Henry Newman.
He, along with John Keble
and Hurrell Froude, founded
the Oxford Movement.

John Keble.
Hurrell Froude's tutor and friend.

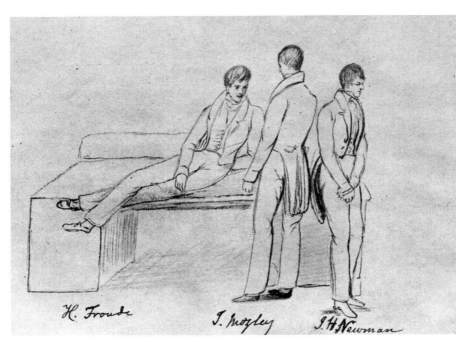

Hurrell Froude, Thomas Mozley, and John Henry Newman.
The only image of Hurrell Froude as an adult

"Leghorn." A drawing by Archdeacon R. H. Froude
during the 1833 Mediterranean trip he took with son Hurrell
and John Henry Newman, hoping that Hurrell's health would improve.

Harriet Bush.
Anthony's first love.

J. A. Froude. The young rebel
sent Carlyle this carte de visite.

Charles and Fanny Kingsley
at Eversely. This couple supported
Anthony after he gave up
his deaconship and left Oxford.
He married Fanny's sister,
whom he met during this period.

"He Is Not Dead but Sleepeth."
One of Charles Kingsley's
erotic drawings of himself
and Fanny merging sexual
and spiritual desire.

F. Max Müller. The great Sanskrit scholar
and philologist who became a lifelong friend
of Froude.

William Froude. Anthony's silent brother
who mediated between him and his father.

Olga Novikoff in court dress *(left)* and Mary Sackville-West, Lady Derby *(right)*.
Two of the intellectual, politically engaged, and influential women
who were Anthony's close and steadfast friends.

"Who Shall Rule?" *Harper's Bazaar*'s 1872 cartoon depicting Froude
being shown the door in Boston by irate Irish servants.

Jane Welsh at age twenty-five *(left)* and Edward Irving preaching *(right)*.
Anthony learned of the secret, early love affair between Jane
and Carlyle's best friend in letters that Carlyle asked him to read and edit.

Geraldine Jewsbury *(seated)*
with Jane Welsh Carlyle. Geraldine
was Jane's devoted friend and comforter.

Jane Carlyle during her last years. "The worst," Carlyle wrote of this picture. Only after she died did he see and repent for his complicity in her shattered life.

E. A. Freeman. Anthony Froude's critic from hell.

"CRITICS."

(Who have not exactly "failed in literature and art.")—See Mr. D.'s New Work.

Mr. G-D-S-T-NE. "Hm!—Flippant!"   Mr. D-S-R-L-I. "Ha!—Prosy!"

Gladstone *(left)* and Disraeli *(right)*. The opposing Liberal and Conservative prime ministers criticize each other's literary accomplishments in this *Punch* cartoon.

Carlyle with his niece Mary Aitken. Mary Aitken entered her uncle's household after his wife's death and became his companion and secretary.

Mary Aitken and Alexander Carlyle in 1879, when the first cousins met, married, and attempted to wrest their uncle's papers from Froude's control.

"Sir George Grey's House." Anthony drew scenes from his travels, as did the archdeacon. Like father, like son.

His relinquishing of his deaconship forty years previously was brought up by Freeman as an example of what he called Anthony's "fanatical hatred" for the Church of England, at the same time reminding his readers that "hatred" was the worst of human passions. There Froude agreed with him: "Mr. Freeman must be presumed to be incapable of such a passion, or I might have inferred that he had written this passage under the influence of it."

Froude went on to explain that he had never left the English church, only the deaconship that was the condition for tenure of an Oxford fellowship thirty-four years before. "I gave up my profession with the loss of my existing means of maintenance and with the sacrifice of my future prospects." Was it likely, he asked, that "I should have selected instead to make my way across country on the back of literature, where besides the natural difficulties, the anonymous reviewer is waiting to trip the unhappy rider at every fence," if it were not from conviction and a need to be honest? "Is it fair, is it tolerable, that Mr Freeman and the *Saturday Reviewer* should avail themself of that prejudice to point to my deacon's orders as if they were an ink-blot and a mark of shame?" Literary criticism did little credit to itself when it condescended to such unworthy expedients.

"After thirty years of severe and I believe honest labour, I will not suffer a picture to be drawn of me in such colours that Mr. Freeman has been pleased to use without entering my own protest with such emphasis as I can command."

However, Froude made a mistake it behooves authors to avoid. He *quoted* his critic's slurs against his character. If readers' eyes had, by chance, glossed over Freeman's endless invective, Froude offered a thumbnail sketch of it in a much more lively style: Freeman said that an "inborn incurable twist" made it impossible for Froude to make an accurate statement about any matter. Anthony repeated that sentence before asking if that "incurable twist" existed instead in Freeman himself. "If I were to argue from his own language as he has argued from mine, I should suppose him influenced by 'fanatical hatred' of me."

Froude had replied to his "tormentor" in a "crushing" article, Lytton Strachey wrote. Anthony's article indeed ran rings around Freeman and was widely appreciated at the time; its vivid language, as well as its essential truth, made it memorable. Still, as late as 1879, thirty years after the *Nemesis*, his early life had come to light and been rehashed yet again—and on the pages of two prominent journals. Freeman had written that an inborn quality, an "incurable twist" made it impossible for Froude to tell the truth about anything. In case once wasn't enough, Froude quoted that accusation word for word. Just as Gladstone, with rather touching innocence, announced to the assembled diplomats that he had kept them standing, stomachs growling, because he escorted Madame Olga Novikoff back to Claridge's, Froude stood up for himself against libelous criticism and won the battle for his reputation in a way that left him open to losing the war.

With the publication of *Reminiscences* two years after the exchange, Norton now had the armature for his instinctive dislike of Froude and wrote to Mary that he felt the same as she about the man: "More than once I spoke to your uncle, with even more freedom, perhaps, than was altogether becoming, of my mistrust of Mr. Froude. He used to assure me that if I knew him better I should think better of him."

The editors of the *Times* took Froude's side: All the world knew Carlyle had strong prejudices and allowed for them. "The man possessed a crotchety, imperious, whimsical way of looking at things and persons. People are not misled by these little extravagances." As for the attacks on Froude, the *Times* phrased it memorably, as if ushering in new times: "In these days of multitudinous criticism a thick skin is the most valuable commodity that one can have. It is perhaps more essential to ambition than genius or industry."

Whatever anger or sense of injustice Mary felt, she turned it not toward her dead uncle, who was becoming more and more her hero as literary saint, but toward Froude, who had such authority over his affairs. Froude had been convinced by Moncure Conway that Harper & Brothers would pay an immense sum for the American edition of *Reminiscences,* and Froude then promised the entire American proceeds to Mary.

But once it was apparent Carlyle was not up to doing his own editing, and perhaps writing an introduction to *Reminiscences,* Harper and Brothers appeared less interested, and Froude published with Scribner as usual. Harper, not to be outdone, published an edition as well, but only a hundred pounds came in at first from America. "I therefore decided in my own mind that Mary Carlyle should share the profits of the English edition." Froude wanted to give her half what Longman paid for the first English edition and all future profits from America. Of course there were now two volumes rather than one. The memoir of Jane was Carlyle's behest to Froude and had to be acknowledged as such. He determined it to be a third of the publication. Still, of the original 750 pounds he wanted to give Mary 450. It was 50 pounds short of what Carlyle had left her. "I thought that she might feel scruples in taking so much, so I added that she had well deserved it by her long service to her uncle in copying his manuscripts. I was surprised and disturbed to find that she was greatly disappointed; that either I had not expressed myself clearly, or that she had entirely misunderstood me; that she demanded the whole profits both England and American and refused to take less."

Though he explained her mistake to her, she didn't accept it, and went to her lawyers. "I was very unwilling that there should be a dispute between me and her uncle's niece on the subject of money. I thought that perhaps I might not have spoken clearly enough. The English sale was rapid, and the £750 rose in a week to £1800." Froude made his calculations and, simply put, decided he would accept three hundred pounds in total for his edition of *Reminiscences*—a token of the fact that the memoir of Jane was Carlyle's gift to him. All future proceeds from England and America would go to Mary.

Mary's lawyers wrote that if Froude had forgotten the letter of his promise, he had certainly fulfilled the spirit of it. A grateful Mary sent Froude a copy of that letter and then came to see him. She told him he was being much too generous, and he told her he accepted her version of what occurred and that when they had discussed the matter, he must have somehow misled her through carelessness of expression. She agreed that her uncle specifically bequeathed him her aunt's memoir. and Froude thought the entire unsavory situation was agreeably settled.

One can only surmise that Alexander Carlyle was not pleased. Suddenly, "Mary Carlyle sent me word through her solicitors that she would receive *nothing* from me. It appeared that she thought she had a *right* to the money, and would not therefore take it as a favor. One of the solicitors hinted to me that perhaps she might take it from him, and I at once placed £1500 in his hands to be held in trust for her."

Froude, exhausted and in ill health, sailed to Norway soon after *Reminiscences* was published, returning the manuscript of the first volume of them to Mary before he left. She hadn't even asked for it yet. But he needed a break from it all. He, too, had been in constant contact with Carlyle in his slow decline, offering him the kindness remarked upon by Carlyle himself, Mary, Ruskin, and others. He had completed part of his decade-long responsibility. *Reminiscences* was seeing the light of day; the biography of the first forty years was ready to be published the next year. He would wait till after that to publish Jane's letters, giving the public a longer time to digest some of the explosive issues apparent in the Carlyles' marriage. He had no doubt that the stir about *Reminiscences* would die down and its merits would prevail for future generations to glean. Meanwhile, he needed the type of rest he found at sea.

When he returned, he sent to Mary the original notebook that contained *The Reminiscence of Jane Welsh Carlyle*. In Carlyle's handwriting, at the end of it, was her uncle's original injunction against publishing it, a prohibition Carlyle had long since revoked. Froude had simply sent it along—the rather careless noblesse oblige of an innocent gentleman who was yet to fathom the depths of Mary's animosity. He did not understand that he needed to protect himself.

Not only had Carlyle changed his mind about publishing, but the will suggested that this notebook was Froude's to keep. However, Froude wanted done with it all, to give everything back as soon as he could and get on with his life. He was slow in realizing that he would never go back to the life he once led.

It didn't take Mary two days to turn the matter public. She wrote to both the *Times* and the *Daily Telegraph* on May 5, 1881, three months to the day of her uncle's death. After quoting her uncle's 1866 prohibition against publishing his memoir of his wife, and Froude's explanation in the introduction to *Reminiscences* that Carlyle had canceled the prohibition orally, she stated that she was not aware of that and "was astounded when I learned by chance that it was in print."

In fact, while her uncle lived, Mary *was* kept to the side of his affairs. Only Carlyle's death brought her to center stage. There is an anecdote appended to Mrs. Ireland's biography of Jane Welsh Carlyle of a gravedigger at Haddington describing the old man's visits to his wife's grave. He would leave his niece at the gate, enter, take off his hat, and kneel on the ground, sobbing. Then he would rise, return to the gate, and collect his niece.

The balance of power had changed. Mary Aitken Carlyle no longer stood by the gate, and Froude was forced to reply in public. The next day he explained that Carlyle had given him complete "discretionary authority" in this matter in his Will. "I did not seek this charge. I did not like it. Mrs. Carlyle will remember that two years ago I offered to surrender it into her hands."

Indeed Mary remembered and immediately responded in the *Times* that she now wished to accept that offer. She wanted Froude to hand over all her uncle's papers to three of Carlyle's friends who would substitute for the two executors who died before her uncle—Carlyle's brother John and friend John Forster. They would judge what was fit to be published. She said this would make all of Carlyle's family happy.

However, Carlyle's living siblings—outside of Mary's mother—and their children maintained faith in Froude as the man Carlyle had chosen, and wrote that to him.

Froude replied in the *Times* that he was the sole judge of what should or shouldn't be published. "Neither Mrs. Alexander Carlyle, nor any one else has a right to call in question the discretion which Mr. Carlyle left with me alone." The memoir was published. The letters would be published. "I decline to allow any person or persons, whether friends of Mr. Carlyle or not, to be associated with me in the discharge of a trust which belongs exclusively to myself."

A strong reply was needed and he had given it. Controversy had once more led him to resolve. Then, in anger and offended self-righteousness, he went too far: "The remaining papers, which I was directed to return to Mrs. Alexander Carlyle as soon as I had done with them, I will restore at once to any responsible person whom she will empower to receive them from me." While Carlyle lived, such an intention might have been considered a threat. Now Froude had stupidly made a public promise.

He had spent a good decade on the papers, yet he rashly said he would return them before *The First Forty Years* was published. Then there were Jane's letters that he told Carlyle he would publish, and which he planned, at the time, would substitute for a biography of the London years. Froude's good friend and coexecutor, Virginia Woolf's uncle, Sir James Fitzjames Stephen, respected high court judge, literary man, and codifier of laws in India, made it clear that neither Froude nor he had the legal right to return papers until Carlyle's wishes were fulfilled, even if they wanted to. But that was window dressing, for when a representative showed up on Froude's doorstep the next day to collect the papers, Froude retracted the offer. He had gone back on his very hasty word and all London knew it. "An inborn 'incurable twist,'" Freeman had written, "made it impossible for Mr. Froude to make an accurate statement about any matter."

Anthony's responsibility to Carlyle had taken on a new life, and he was caught in the middle of an ugly controversy that was not going to die out. On both sides were injured parties. Neither Mary nor Anthony thought they were being dealt with fairly. Both had wounded feelings and shattered expectations. Both thought they deserved better from the other. Then there was Carlyle's will, which was ungenerous to the woman who had served him well; Carlyle's verbal communications with Froude that should have been written out; and, of course, money, property, and literary rights. Mary could not consciously blame her uncle for any of the resulting confusion, for she deified him after his death. All her resentment—and perhaps jealousy—of Froude's authority in her uncle's affairs turned quickly into hate. Froude became more and more conscious that Carlyle had not protected him in these matters, and he grew angry at him and angry at himself. What biographer would have accepted the task under such terms—especially after papers that were given to him freely suddenly had strings attached. He came to wonder why he had been so deferential. He always knew he was handling dynamite. Why hadn't he protected himself? Why—and here the old self-pity creeps in—hadn't *Carlyle* protected him? Why had he accepted the burden of keeping Carlyle's secret?

But accept he had. As it turned out, he did not have to await the publication of *Thomas Carlyle: A History of the First Forty Years of His Life* in 1882 to see his reputation in tatters. The publication of *Reminiscences* the year before had already brought him close to the element of Greek tragedy he found in the Carlyles' marriage: "Men think to mend their condition by a change of circumstances. They might as well hope to escape from their shadows."

Froude was convinced that Carlyle sought *repentance* for his treatment of his wife. Carlyle's niece more than disagreed. It was *reticence* her uncle expected from Froude, whether he wrote a good biography or a bad one. Froude recounted in the biography how stunned and stupefied Carlyle had been after Jane's death. How his faults rose up in front of his eyes and he knew atonement was necessary. Carlyle in his grief compared his feelings with those of Samuel Johnson when he sought penance for his treatment of his father at the Uttoxeter market. He made this comparison to Froude, not once, but many times. He felt something similar was required of him if he could find a way.

This penance of Samuel Johnson's was no fanciful literary allusion. It was both meaningful and specific to Carlyle and Froude. If there was one person, one man of letters, who could be said to have been a role model for Carlyle—he'd call it a hero—from the beginning of his career onward, it was Samuel Johnson. How Carlyle enjoyed retelling that story of destitute Johnson during his one precious year at Oxford. His shoes were so worn out that one night, a classmate, taking pity, took them, leaving a new pair in their place outside his room. When Johnson found them there in the morning he threw them away in anger. Better barefooted than beggared. Carlyle gloried in such pride.

Johnson, in the eighteenth century, came to London as poor and professionless as Carlyle in the nineteenth and had also to depend on journalism for his daily bread. Johnson had to write, first to stay alive, but second, to tell "the *Truth* that was in him." What a problem to accomplish both in this world. "To Johnson Life was a Prison, to be endured with heroic faith." The same was true for Carlyle.

This is not to say Carlyle would have been less constantly hypochondriacal had he not a precedent in the partially deaf, half-blind, physically unwieldy Johnson's melancholy, or been less impatient of "cant" and the "Blockheads" had he not appropriated those words from Johnson (and run with them), or less proud and steadfast in his prejudices. But he admired good John, in his words worshipped him as a hero throughout his life, though Johnson had been born in what Carlyle considered the most decadent of centuries. "I have always considered him to be, by nature, one of our great English souls. A strong and noble man; so much left undeveloped in him to the last: in a kindlier element what might he not have been—poet, priest, sovereign ruler!" So much was left undeveloped in Carlyle as well.

Johnson was the only Englishman Carlyle chose in his London lecture on "The Hero as Man of Letters," part of the series on hero worship he gave in 1840 that initiated much wider recognition leading to the fame his wife knew he would achieve. And long before Froude's editorship, Carlyle wrote a book-length review, "Boswell's Life of Johnson" for *Fraser's,* which Froude tells us was well received and brought him a certain amount of early recognition. In it Carlyle related in detail Johnson's penance at the Uttoxeter market, quoting Johnson's letter to his hostess—in Boswell's biography—begging her pardon for leaving abruptly one morning. Conscience compelled him:

"Fifty years ago, Madam, on this day, I committed a breach of filial piety. My father had been in the habit of attending Uttoxeter market, and opening a stall there for the sale of his Books. Confined by indisposition [the old man was close to death], he desired me, that day, to go and attend the stall in his place. My pride prevented me; I gave my father a refusal.—And now today I have been at Uttoxeter; I went into the market at the time of business, uncovered my head, and stood with it bare, for an hour, on the spot where my father's stall used to stand. In contrition I stood, and I hope the penance was expiatory."

For Carlyle, "The picture of Samuel Johnson standing bareheaded in the market there, is one of the grandest and saddest we can paint. Repentance! Repentance! he proclaims, as with passionate sobs: but only to the ear of Heaven . . . the earthly ear and heart, that should have heard it, are now closed, unresponsive forever."

Repentance! Repentance! For the rest of his life, Froude tells us, Carlyle never passed the spot near the Serpentine where Jane died without taking off his hat and bowing to her memory as did Johnson at Uttoxeter.

"'Oh!'" Carlyle cried again and again, in Froude's presence, "'if I could but see her once more, were it but for five minutes, to let her know that I always loved her through all that. She never did know it, never.' If he could but see her again! His heart seemed breaking as he said it, and through these weeks and months he was often mournfully reverting to the subject."

Carlyle *himself* might have been reticent, to use a much more fitting word for choosing Froude as his biographer, one which might have appeared too grandiose to utter to his niece—or to Tennyson when he asked. Again we look to his essay "Boswell's Life of Johnson": "How comes it that in England we have simply one good Biography, this *Boswell's Johnson*?" Carlyle questioned. He answered that Boswell had the heart and eye to discern wisdom and the skill to re-create it. Toward Johnson, Boswell's "feeling was not Sycophancy, which is the lowest, but Reverence, which is the highest of human feelings."

Froude had shown the highest of human feelings for Carlyle since their first meeting. Reverence is what Froude had for his mentor, a pious regard. Perhaps to see a man of Froude's stature, so respectful in his dealing with someone on his own level, was peculiar. Son Ashley never understood it—even Norton remarked it. But then they weren't Oxford circa 1840. Froude was of the generation that Carlyle affected most viscerally. And though others—Matt Arnold, Arthur Clough—went on to different paths, Froude remained true to Carlylean spiritual values; Carlyle remained his hero as spiritual guide.

At the death of Henrietta and his impending travels to South Africa, Froude put that reverence in words, reverence that he had previously shown by his actions and writings. He wrote that Carlyle had saved him from spiritual and moral wreckage in his years of religious doubts, was the only man to see his way in the "labyrinth of modern confusion." If appreciation was fading for the Sage of Chelsea in his own day, Froude felt future generations would look to Carlyle for light, and later centuries would fully recognize why he had been put on the earth.

Carlyle had responded that Froude's letter left a great impression on him. "Deducting from it all the immense exaggeration of your kindness to me, I accept and will for ever remember it with a sacred thankfulness full of blessed sorrow and something better than joy." If Carlyle smarted from his wife's gibe that his letters to her were written for his biographers, it is doubtful that he would take the responsibility of acknowledging that Samuel Johnson was again his prototype when he chose Froude. One wonders if he had even the most fleeting thought that perhaps the "only good Biography" in the English language might be followed by a second. What he must have known for sure was a variant of what he told Mary and Tennyson. Whether Froude wrote a good book or a bad book, Carlyle knew it would be reverent.

And that's the rub. Secrets or no secrets, Froude was convinced through his close association with Carlyle—not to mention Carlyle's own actions after his wife's death—that Carlyle did not want his life, as seen through Jane's letters and his explanatory notes, to be whitewashed like most "mealy mouthed" English biography, or to be excised into meaningless cant as the letters would have been had the relatives got to them before Froude published. A biographer's true reverence differed from sycophancy, in the same way as intellectual integrity differed from unctuous cant, or a plainly dressed man differed from a dandy. Carlyle delivered his papers to one of the few left who had sympathetic understanding of his positions, and who had done what he never could, actually acted on them in South Africa and even on his Quixotic American tour—this after he wound up the most Carlylean of his works, the three-volume *The English in Ireland in the Eighteenth Century*. Carlyle left himself in the hands of the man he most respected. And he fearlessly, if at times pathetically, revealed himself to Froude in what he said and what he wrote about his marriage. If Froude's son Ashley's memories are accurate, Carlyle constantly talked of it all. As a result of this intimacy, Froude the biographer was in a position to be damned if he did or damned if he didn't tell the truth.

In *Thomas Carlyle: A History of the First Forty Years of His Life*, Froude responded to this dilemma by at times breaking into the narrative flow of the letters and journals in order to give his own shrewd overview of the situation in the guise of a Greek chorus. He must have felt somewhat like Cassandra—or Mrs. Montagu—witnessing a tragedy he saw unfolding but could not prevent.

One sees this in the first volume of the biography, as the possibility of marriage loomed, and Carlyle wished to take up farming on Jane's father's desolate property outside of Dumfries. Froude quoted Jane's letter telling Carlyle she could never live in godforsaken Craigenputtock.

Only someone madly in love could make such a sacrifice. "But I am not *in love* with you; that is to say, my love for you is not a passion which overclouds my judgment and absorbs all my regards for myself and others. It is a simple, honest, serene affection, made up of admiration and sympathy, and better perhaps to found domestic enjoyment on than any other. In short, it is a love which *influences,* does not *make,* the destiny of a life."

Carlyle replied, "Without deep sacrifices on both sides, the possibility of our union is an empty dream." He wanted them to unite their resources, but the wealth and the rank that he mentioned as well as what he called the judgment, patience, and prudence were all on her side. He would expect all of this willing sacrifice from "a generous spirit, one whose happiness depended on seeing me happy."

"The functions of a biographer are like the functions of a Greek chorus, occasionally at important moments to throw in some moral remarks which seem to fit the situation," Froude commented. "The chorus after such a letter would remark, perhaps on the subtle forms of self-deception to which the human heart is liable, of the momentous nature of marriage, and how men and women plunge heedlessly into the net, thinking only of the satisfaction of their own immediate wishes. Self sacrifice it might say was a noble thing. But a sacrifice which one person might properly make, the other might have no reasonable right to ask or to allow. It would conclude, however, that the issues of human acts are in the hands of the gods, and would hope for the best in fear and trembling."

Carlyle expected his wife to be "content and happy in assisting him in the development of his own destiny; and this was selfishness—selfishness of a rare and elevated kind, but selfishness still; and it followed him throughout his married life." The "chorus" was not only prescient but apparently had experienced passionate love, for it was quite aware that Carlyle's attitude indicated that "he admired Miss Welsh; he loved her in a certain sense; but, like her, he was not *in love.*"

Both compared the anticipation of their forthcoming marriage to an execution, but marry they finally did. Two days after the ceremony, Carlyle wrote the letter he promised his concerned mother, telling her he remained sullen, "sick with sleeplessness, quite nervous, bilious, splenetic and all the rest of it." Froude did not quote further. No mother could have been kinder than Jane, Carlyle continued. The good soul had already ordered him a bed to be made and placed in an adjoining room.

He left unpublished as well, Carlyle's letter to his mother four weeks later: "I am by no means 'come to' as you would say, or get 'hefted to my new gang.'" He couldn't pull his weight, too sick to survive without drugs for his stomach. "Give me time, I say still, give me time."

Froude remained convinced that Carlyle had not married knowing he was impotent. Indeed, Mrs. Montagu had augmented the magical power inherent in the very institution of matrimony, often telling Carlyle that a man of his talents needed, must have, a dutiful "Wife." Or as Carlyle underscored the concept to Jane: *"The Man should bear rule in the house and not the Woman.* This is an eternal axiom, the Law of Nature." Carlyle, hardly a sexual sophisticate himself, might still have hoped. His and Jane's shared belief that marriage would change them allowed Jane to write that if Carlyle could not love Jane Welsh, he certainly would be able to love "Mrs. Carlyle."

When the news circulated that Froude was to be Carlyle's biographer, Geraldine Jewsbury came to Froude to tell him something he should know. The marriage was not satisfactory and the whole explanation was that "Carlyle was one of those persons who ought never to have married." Froude knew by then that there was some sort of mystery concerning the marriage, but had assumed that the unique couple with their lofty literary goals had decided not to have children. "Miss Jewsbury entirely dispelled this supposition. She said that Mrs Carlyle never forgave the injury which she believed herself to have received." Not having experienced the wine of life—Geraldine's image quoted in the biography—was only part of it. Jane had very much desired children.

On Geraldine's deathbed she repeated all this to Froude, with many specific examples, he wrote in his Cuban journal: "I will mention one, as it shows that Carlyle did not know when he married what his constitution was. The morning after his wedding-day he tore to pieces the flower-garden at Comely Bank in a fit of ungovernable fury."

It was important for Froude to believe Carlyle still hoped to consummate his marriage. Without that glimmer, the man in Froude—and one is tempted to add the Englishman in Froude—would not have been able to forgive Carlyle the marriage despite Carlyle's heartfelt expiation. Everything Froude had striven for in adulthood made such treatment of a wife unthinkable.

Froude's charge was to keep such secrets and still write a truthful biography. He felt himself honor-bound to suppress certain things that would have allowed the reader to understand everything else that he did tell. For example, how does a reliable biographer describe a wedding night that he knows ended with flower beds torn up and second beds ordered? Froude's solution was to follow the newlyweds from their small wedding at Templand on October 17, 1826, on to Comely Bank and their new home in Edinburgh, but not to cross the threshold with them.

"Regrets and speculations on the might-have-beens of life are proverbially vain. Nor is it certain that there is anything to regret. The married life of Carlyle and Jane Welsh was not happy in the roseate sense of happiness." They were like two diamonds whose facets chafed one against the other without ever wearing down to surfaces that harmoniously corresponded.

When Carlyle doubted, it was she who spurred him on. But Carlyle didn't find marriage to offer "the miraculous transformation of nature which he had promised himself. He remained lonely and dyspeptic, possessed by thoughts and convictions which struggled in him for utterance, and which could be fused and cast into form only (as I have heard him say) when his whole mind was like a furnace at white heat." He needed this woman by his side to bear what Froude called his outbreaks of dyspeptic humor, this woman who would "shield him from the petty troubles of a poor man's life—from vexations which would have irritated him to madness—by her own incessant toil." This woman who would become "a victim" to the completion of Carlyle's life work. Jane would most probably have lived a more pleasant life with one of the many suitors of her own class. "Carlyle might have gone through it successfully with his mother or a sister to look after him."

Though the Carlyles would not live happy lives, their lives would be "grandly beautiful" for "neither of them probably under other conditions would have risen as high in excellence as in fact they each achieved; and the main question is not how happy men and women have been in the world, but what they have made of themselves."

The Victorian reader, who was unaware of the secrets being kept, might understandably be taken aback by this bleak picture of the marriage given by Carlyle's closest and most trusted friend. Then veering from prophetic chorus to personal remembrance, Froude topped it off with flair: "I well remember the bright assenting laugh with which Mrs Carlyle once responded to some words of mine when the propriety was being discussed of relaxing the marriage laws. I had said that the true way to look at marriage was as a discipline of character."

If a biographer is allowed a tragic flaw, Froude's was that he kept Carlyle's secrets—the *fact* of the impotence and the *extent* of the violent dysfunction in the marriage. Froude realized it himself in the long run. In holding back what he felt he must, he revealed even more than perhaps he realized. The reader was given expiation without clear explanation of why it was needed. From that vantage point, Froude did not appear to be a very loyal friend.

After the first year of their marriage spent in Edinburgh, Froude followed the couple to the dreaded Craigenputtock, where Jane had previously told Carlyle she would not live a month with an angel. They'd spend six years there: Froude described Craigenputtock "as the dreariest spot in all the British dominions." Even today it is difficult to find the remote hilltop from nearby Dumfries. Froude was not exaggerating about its being more than a mile from the nearest cottage, of the elevation being such to stunt the trees and limit the garden's produce to the hardiest vegetables. "The house is gaunt and hungry-looking. It stands with the scanty fields attached as an island in a sea of morass. The landscape is unredeemed either by grace or grandeur, mere undulating hills of grass and heather, with peat bogs in the hollows between them."

Carlyle thought that this change of scene would enable him to fling off his shadow. "But, his shadow remained sticking to him; and the poor place where he had cast his lot had as usual to bear the blame of his disappointment."

These are the years when Carlyle sat in his study writing *Sartor Resartus* and Jane learned to make cheese and bread, using work as a means of maintaining sanity. Froude so expertly handled the documents that one discovers for oneself Carlyle's growing disenchantment and boredom with Craigenputtock even before Froude assumes the role of Greek chorus once more and narrates the disaffection. He ends the biography not at the conclusion of their six years there, but after their first year in London.

The words of Carlyle to his mother after his unconsummated marriage were still in Froude's head—if not on the page—when he wrote that Carlyle's first letters from London suggest him tolerably "hefted" to his new life, but the salutary effects of change wore off in a few weeks, and in Carlyle's diary entries, which Froude quoted at length, he exhibited a despondency greater than that at Craigenputtock.

Froude may have chosen to include the first year in London, not only to round out the forty years but in order to narrate Edward Irving's death through Carlyle's letters, as part of the closure to those years. Irving was so much part and parcel of them. His early promise and too much early fame had turned the orator fanatical. He believed God spoke through his parishioners, and he allowed the chaotic jumping up and the jumbled "speaking in tongues" during his services whenever God seized one of the faithful. Jane, on seeing him again in London, once cried all the way home from his house, after she and her husband witnessed his deterioration and Carlyle earnestly exhorted him to give up these new beliefs. Irving was excommunicated from his church, started another—the Catholic Apostolic Church—and half-mad and tubercular, he died in Scotland, where he had traveled to preach. He went there, a disease-wracked forty-two-year-old man, on horseback through the rain, convinced God would not let him die; death was punishment for sin. Jane once remarked that there would have been no speaking in tongues if she had married Irving.

"Irving was dead, and with it closed the last chapter of Jane Welsh's early romance. Much might be said of the effect of it both on Irving and on her. The characters of neither of them escaped unscathed by the passionate love which had once existed between them. But all that is gone, and concerns the world no longer."

Carlyle had handed him no instructions other than to tell the truth, shadows and all, Froude felt it necessary to underscore as he ended the first half of *Thomas Carlyle:* "The Annandale peasant boy was to be the wonder of the London world. He had wrought himself into a personality which all were to be compelled to admire, and in whom a few recognised, like Goethe, the advent of a new moral force the effects of which it was impossible to predict."

What one *could* readily predict was the response to the biography: "I cannot imagine how any unprejudiced person whose opinion is of any value could do other than see through Froude's artful, malicious and sometimes almost imbecile comments on the text," Mary Aitken Carlyle wrote to Norton. "He is a villain and has an utter disregard of truth. He makes it appear that my Aunt left wealth and fortune to ally herself with poverty and squalor, becoming a mere drudge." He blamed her uncle for making her live at Craigenputtock without saying that her mother lived only fourteen miles away in the exact same conditions. As for her aunt's ill health: Well, the Welshes were a sickly lot, and "her Aunt had lived longer than any of her cousins."

But Mary was in her late teens when her aunt passed away, and received most of her ideas through her own mother who, though Jane had tutored her as a child, grew impatient of her older, barb-witted, constantly ill sister-in-law later on. When Jane once interrupted a much-needed rest in Scotland to return to London because Carlyle suddenly wrote that he was returning, only to arrive in the heat and find Carlyle had changed his mind, Mary's mother was unsympathetic. She asked with annoyance why Jane should have gone back just because of a careless word of her husband's. *She* wouldn't have.

Jane replied, Well, had she been Mrs. Aitken, she might not have, either.

After the scandal produced by Froude's publication of *Reminiscences,* reinforced and compounded by his biography of Carlyle's first forty years, there was something heroic in Froude's actually publishing *The Letters and Memorials of Jane Welsh Carlyle*—even if controversy once more stiffened his resolve. These three volumes would appear in 1883. He wrote to Olga Novikoff that Mrs Carlyle's letters would be published on, of all ominous days, April Fools'! He could not guess how the book would be received. He thought it would depend on the first reviews. This was simply wishful thinking.

Two weeks after publication of the letters he wrote to her: "There has been the same excitement as there was two years ago, and the same outcry against my unfortunate self. People will not look at Carlyle's will and see that this special task was bequeathed to me. They will not see that Carlyle's collection of these letters as an act of atonement for offences which, at least, were half imaginary was the noblest action of his own noble life. Hereafter it will be seen in its true light, and he will be honoured and loved for it. As to me, I am under the blackest of clouds, and shall probably be left there."

It is commonplace to assume that what upset Victorian sensibility was a prudishness that an open-minded contemporary reader would not share. But the portrait of the marriage that emerges in Carlyle's *Letters and Memorials of Jane Welsh Carlyle,* as first presented to the public, albeit in Froude's edited version—half the size of what Carlyle left him—was quite shocking, and remains so. It went way beyond the issue of impotence, which, at least, had been hinted at in the biography. Carlyle's obliviousness to his wife's every need is close to monstrous, at the same time as Jane's willing acceptance of her role gives a portrait of constant victimization that appears excruciatingly neurotic. There is no glimpse of the underlying problem of impotence, childlessness, violence.

The Carlyles hardly ever vacationed together. The nature of their relationship was such that they had to spend a lot of time apart. Jane was often left alone in London in the summer to see to the entire housecleaning needed in those days. Froude tells us the truth of middle-class life in that period: All the occupants of the house left during these top-to-bottom cleanings, carpet removals, mattress debugging, painting—

and returned only when the work was done. Elizabeth Barrett secretly married Browning sooner than she had planned after her father suddenly called for one of these housecleaning evacuations from London.

Jane stayed at home and oversaw it all, always believing only she could direct workmen and maids in a way to assure Carlyle's comfort on Cheyne Row. At times she wrote of pitching a tent in the back garden where she could escape the paint fumes. Thieves got in one summer, and she let Carlyle know that she now kept a rifle in her bedroom for protection. No reaction from Carlyle.

Then there were less dramatic, if exceedingly lonely summers: "London heat!" Jane wrote to her dear Scottish friend Mrs. Russell in 1858. "Nobody knows what that is till having tried it; so breathless, and sickening and oppressive as no other heat I ever experienced is!" At the time Carlyle was collapsing under the strain of writing *Frederick the Great,* his biliousness increasing with the heat. He was wild to get away but as usual couldn't decide where to go: "Living beside him has been like living the life of a weathercock, in a high wind, blowing from all points at once!— sensibility superadded!"

He took Jane from one vacation possibility to another: "The imaginary houses, in different parts of the kingdom, in which I have had to look round me on bare walls, and apply my fancy with the strength I have (about equal to my canary's, which, every now and then, drops off the perch on its back, and has to be lifted up), would have driven me crazy, I think, if one day I hadn't got desperate, and burst out crying. Until a woman cries men never think she can be suffering. Bless their blockheadism! However, when I cried and declared I was not strong enough for all that any more, Mr. C. opened his eyes to the fact, so far as to decide that, for the present, he would go to his sister's [the Gill, in Scotland], and let me choose my own course after. And to the Gill he went last Wednesday night, and since then I have been resting, and already feel better for the rest, even without 'change of air.'"

Usually when she wrote even to her closest friends, whatever real pain she was experiencing was phrased with such sharp humor as to delight, and though it was all honest, it was all somehow also a disguise. The sense of humorous strife that visitors to Cheyne Row reported was present in that poor heat-fatigued canary tumbling backward off its perch. Compare it with the letter she had written three days previously to her husband at the Gill in Dumfries:

"Don't let your enjoyment of 'the country' be disturbed by thoughts of me still 'in town.' I won't stay here longer than I find it good for me.

But what I feel to need at present is, above all things human and divine, rest from 'mental worry;' and nowhere is there such fair outlook of that for me as just at home under the present conditions. 'The cares of bread' have been too heavy for me lately; and the influx of 'cousins' most wearing; and to see you constantly discontented, and as much so with me, apparently, as with all other things, when I have neither the strength and spirits to bear up against your discontent, nor the obtuseness to be indifferent to it—that has done me more harm than you have the least notion of. You have not the least notion what a killing thought it is to have put into one's heart, gnawing there day and night, that one ought to be dead, since one can no longer make the same exertions as formerly; that one was taken 'for better,' not by any means 'for worse;' and, in fact, that the only feasible and dignified thing that remains for one to do is to just die, and be done with it."

Carlyle annotated the letter: "Cares of bread" was friend Mazzini's Italo-English that Jane enjoyed parodying and which became part of what has come to be known as the Carlyles' coterie talk, the expressions they had for joint impressions. The "cousins" are named. Then, that he put it in her heart that she should just die and be done with it: "Alas! alas! sinner that I am!" Carlyle footnoted.

These letters and journals reveal a private hell. Their literary and biographical value is great and established Jane Welsh Carlyle as one of the premier letter writers of the nineteenth century. However, on first viewing, without an understanding of the entire situation, one would have to be quite an aesthete to glory in the craft of the baby carriage over the howls of pain from the baby. Even though Froude had carefully edited Carlyle's memorial to his wife, at times with sections melded for economy, clarity, and narrative flow, the letters he published, all from the London years, reveal Carlyle's incredible insensitivity and Jane's neurotic need to supply his every domestic comfort. They were and still are profoundly disturbing. Froude had hoped to lessen the effect by preceding them with Carlyle's lyrical *Reminiscence* of his wife, but that was not enough. It hadn't been what he called his "cowardice" that made Froude hesitate to publish *The Letters and Memorials of Jane Welsh Carlyle*. It had been mature enough editorial judgment to ponder the possible ramifications of public exposure.

As explosive as Jane's edited letters and journals were, they could not have waited for a later time. Had they been returned to Carlyle's family, they would have been burned or mutilated without a second thought. Mary died in 1895, which left Alexander in control of his uncle's literary property. He quickly remarried, and kept a strict accounting of what Carlyle's work brought in.

In a letter to Norton he bemoaned that Froude had published so much of one of Carlyle's journals, that it would be useless to destroy what remained, in a tone that assumed the unalienable right course would have been such destruction. In fact, Froude's publications, by what they revealed, made further destruction dangerous. So why not profit by publishing more letters, more complete texts of letters, while at the same time pointing out any criticism of Froude one could find as the justification for these further publications? It was an onslaught on Froude's typos and melded passages, a weird game of unconsciously substantiating Froude's point of view by underscoring his lacunae—not to mention blasting his reputation in extremely biased introductions to every volume of new letters to be printed. This went on long after Froude's death.

Alexander wrote Norton an extremely careful, respectful letter in the early twentieth century leading up to the fact that though he knew Norton would disapprove, he was going to publish the letters his uncle and aunt wrote to each other before they were married—letters Froude had not published separately—as a two-volume set entitled *The Love Letters of Jane Welsh and Thomas Carlyle.* By then the Brownings' son, Pen, had published his parents' truly extraordinary love letters, and perhaps that success gave Alexander a clue. This packaging of their fate was a great travesty to the lives the Carlyles really lived, and was exactly what his uncle had tried to avoid when he handed his papers to Froude. Love letters? If Jane knew, she would either have screamed out loud or hooted.

Even if Jane's letters could have waited to be published at a later time, Carlyle's intent—atonement—and his state of mind—guilt and regret, sinner that he was—would also have been defused. Contemporary biographers and students of Carlyle do not list Carlyle's annotated letters and memorials of his wife as his last work on this earth. One of the most remarkable and poignant aspects of Carlyle's career—that he had spent the end of his writing life arranging the letters of his wife and annotating them in a way that was both a biography and an atonement for his treatment of her—has simply faded away, or, occasionally, been paid lip service. The heart of the matter has disappeared. Carlyle had not asked Froude to present the world with a scholarly variorum edition of Jane's letters, transcribing them word for word with copious notes. Just the opposite. Froude was given the responsibility of editing the material in a way that it could be brought together for public consumption and at the same time present a truthful account of the marriage.

One might imagine that by the twenty-first century, Froude would be given some credit for his work. Contemporary biographers of Carlyle recognize his worth in passing, but not the academy. The ongoing scholarly edition of *The Collected Letters of Thomas and Jane Welsh Carlyle,* the Duke-Edinburgh edition, has been publishing the couples' letters in chronological order for over thirty-five years, supported by two universities, top professors in two countries, graduate students, assistants, copiers, fax machines, etc. The texts produced are admirable, and slow-going. The editors have reached the letters the Carlyles wrote in the mid-1850s; they are not yet up to publishing the correspondence from the 1860s, when Froude himself arrived in London. Perhaps that is why Froude's name is mentioned generally only in reference to an occasional error in transcription or to compare a passage of his to one edited by Alexander Carlyle.

To Norton, Mary Carlyle expressed the wish that her uncle's letters could be brought together someday without Froude's name: "If I were printing my Uncle's letters, I should try never to mention him at all." So far, she is close to getting her way. Perhaps there might be some future recognition of this man who went through most all of the same papers with a pen and a magnifying glass, one man alone in his own home, with daughter Margaret occasionally acting as assistant. He not only wrote one of the best biographies in English but is responsible for the survival of so much primary material that allows the true story of the lives led by Jane Welsh and Thomas Carlyle to be told.

Froude deserves credit for single-handedly preserving the memory of Jane Welsh Carlyle until a time when it would be possible to recognize her as one of the literary lights of her era, through the unmatched vitality and talent of those letters. Before Charlotte Brontë's name was revealed, many thought the author of her novels was Jane. The ironic sensibility is similar, indeed. But it was Jane's choice to give up thoughts of her own literary fame to support a greater genius—"Oh, for your head." Later she would advise, Never marry a genius. She found herself screaming out loud when one young friend announced her decision to wed, and cried hysterically when she received that news from another. She paid a great price for idealistic youthful decisions, and one wonders what she'd have to say about the ironies involved in the history of her posthumous fame—or about women admitted to universities, women having careers, women and men having "women's studies." Most particularly, her response to a wife's letters being included in a great man's variorum edition.

When we look at her today, Jane Welsh Carlyle could be considered the prototype for the bohemian woman behind the male artist that existed as a suitable role for women of singular ability up until—and perhaps through—the 1960s: the woman sacrificing all to cater to the genius in the house. Jane Carlyle came to realize the irony of her situation, how her youthful, book-centered idealism and stubborn nature marched her right to her fate. Yet with further Scottish resolve, since she made her bed, she insisted on lying in it. Housework became an antidote for depression, as well as for showing literary London the no-nonsense approach of a good Scottish wife. It was useful work. It was indeed taken to an extreme, and Carlyle, who came from a peasant family in which women worked without being thanked for the effort, drew no distinctions between them and Jane, as Froude noted.

Anthony found Carlyle's treatment of his wife unthinkable, at the same time as he believed Carlyle's act of attrition—his collecting and annotating of his wife's letters—"so beautiful," that for years he struggled with the question of whether to publish what Carlyle had purposely preserved. As he told John Ruskin, those letters had hung around his neck "like a bag of shot" for twelve years.

With their publication he believed he had finally fulfilled his promise to Carlyle. He had given the world *Reminiscences*. Without Froude's advice, some of Carlyle's best late work might never have seen the light of day. Then he published *Thomas Carlyle: A History of the First Forty Years of His Life*, a biography that made much use of Carlyle's own letters and journals. In publishing *The Letters and Memorials of Jane Welsh Carlyle*, he thought he had in effect presented what amounted to the second half of Carlyle's biography, giving the public a way of looking at the great man's life in London up through his wife's death and his completion of *Frederick the Great*.

They say that Froude's publications culminated in the chimneys of literary London giving out an abundance of smoke, as prominent people burned their own papers. In terms of Froude's own life, he watched former friends cross the street rather than greet him. His reputation suffered enormous damage. Charles Eliot Norton became Jamesian to the hilt, calling Froude "that Continental liar." Froude was as unwelcome in some circles as he had been after the publication of *The Nemesis of Faith*—only now, a man in his sixties, this new lack of "respectability" did not amuse, but plagued him. At the same time, his health was failing and his spirits were depressed. He thought of perhaps adding some personal recollections of Carlyle's life in London in order to round off his duty, without a full-scale biography of the second half of his mentor's life. He played with that idea, hesitated.

Carlyle was no longer beside him—walking, riding, bellyaching. A few years before the old man's death Froude wrote to Olga Novikoff with wry amusement: "Carlyle ate some strawberries last week; they disagreed with him, and he told us solemnly that he was dying. We represented that things need not be so serious, and were told indignantly that we knew nothing about the matter. He is well again now, better perhaps than he was before, but we have to be cautious how we tell him so."

Human nature condemns us not to appreciate the other fully, until that person (along with all annoying, albeit humorous, traits and inconvenient needs) is gone. It is the stuff of tragedy and of memorial services. Spirit is fully in the round only after the flesh departs. Froude was now free to see not only the man, not only his effect on his own life and values, but in his absence to reflect more fully on his future influence—on his immortality. This was not just any man of importance in his times. This was one of the few men of his century that Froude believed would be remembered a hundred years hence. He couldn't let it go. Controversy was always the wind that flew his kite, he had told John Skelton. It would always make him strive to be clearer in his next book. He had a mission to complete his mentor's life, to make others feel what he really meant about Carlyle's humanity and his importance. To write a second half of the monumental biography was not his way of justifying *himself* to his times. He believed it his duty to re-create the man who held the keys to the future. He knew it would take all his strength to accomplish it, he told Olga Novikoff. And when he did, the world would see that he wasn't wanting in love and admiration for Carlyle, no matter what else they thought. He would paint "a sort of Rembrandt portrait" and attempt to make others feel as he did, that Carlyle was *"intensely lovable."*

One might assume that in presenting Carlyle as intensely lovable, Froude would turn to the conventional tradition of praise and deletion. Or, given Froude's despondency, ill health, and sense of injustice, that this second part would have an aura of self-justification. Instead, as a biographer, as an artist, really, he soared above his own ego as he wrote. To him, the Carlyle who had suffered over his treatment of his wife was lovable, tenderhearted, virtuous. But of course, shade all human intention chiaroscuro.

The difference between the first and second halves of the biography of Thomas Carlyle is in the degree of freedom Froude allowed himself.

In the first half, Froude is under obligation, second chair to the documents themselves. One does not feel this restraint in *Thomas Carlyle: His Life in London.* Froude is no longer a Greek chorus. Instead he is the fluency of the story, his personal knowledge seamlessly combining with documents.

The style is remarkable, not that Froude ever believed in style for its own sake. "I have never thought about style at any time in my life," he wrote when asked to contribute to *The Art of Authorship* in the 1890s. "I have tried merely to express what I had to say with as much simplicity and as little affectation as I could command. When I have been tempted into exaggeration, I have checked myself with imagining what some one whose judgement I respected would say if I used such language in speaking or writing to him; and this was usually sufficient. As a rule, when I go over what I have written, I find myself striking out superfluous epithets, reducing superlatives into positives, bringing subjunctive moods into indicative, and in most instances passing my pen through every passage which had seemed, while I was writing it, to be particularly fine. If you sincerely desire to write nothing but what you really know or think, and to say that as clearly and as briefly as you can, style will come as a matter of course. Ornament for ornament's sake is always to be avoided. There is a rhythm in prose as well as in verse, but you must trust your ear for that. This is very vague and inadequate, but it is all that I can give you."

Froude's prose is as fresh today as when it was written, prose as clean and clear and deep as the mountain lakes he loved to fly-fish. One is prepared, to some extent, for its contemporary verve through the works of Lytton Strachey, Virginia Woolf, and even Frank Harris at his best, when they, too, handled other people's lives. Froude was the common link; they all read him; they all grew in their method. When one first comes to *Thomas Carlyle: His Life in London,* it is difficult to believe it was written by a man who was hounded by his enemies, disappointed in himself, and, as Dunn pointed out, physically exhausted. The brighter side of Froude's selfless dedication to Carlyle was that in *His Life in London,* his own powers as artist and historian found their full range.

Before writing, Froude took to the sea again, yachted to Norway to fly-fish his way back to balance. The years of his dedication to Carlyle and the criticism of his work had aged him. He was now habitually insomniac, and try as he might, as irrational as he knew it to be, he could not escape Mary Carlyle, who haunted him through many a nightmarish night, little woman transposed to small demon. With his usual desire to end things once and for all, he had more than wanted a law court to decide whether he or Mary Carlyle had authority over Carlyle's literary remains. Again, the good sense of James Fitzjames Stephen and others prevailed, and this was settled out of court, for Mary soon learned Froude was legally within his rights under Carlyle's will. What was at issue was his integrity, his good name. No law court could restore the damage among those who considered him a false friend to the great man.

He had told Carlyle he'd treat Mary as his own daughter. What he offered, she took as hers by right, not his to give. He could understand her dissatisfaction with him for not painting her uncle the pure white she wished for, but he was unnerved by the extent of her hate and bile. He returned to London, as if shipwrecked on his own island, and wrote. One would never suspect the inner turmoil, given the results.

One of the most remarkable aspects of *Thomas Carlyle: His Life in London* is how Froude achieved the impression he aimed at without sacrificing his point of view, how clearly Froude's reverence, one could say his tenderness, for Carlyle shines through as he articulates Carlyle's life work. There is nothing doctrinaire or strident, but instead a seamless narration to the heart of the matter. What he told John Ruskin bears underscoring; he was free at last to draw the picture of his mentor from his own point of view—he was no longer second chair to the documents he presented.

He had absolutely no need to proselytize, to exaggerate Carlyle's virtues, to obscure his flaws, or to defend himself. It is Carlyle himself who comes center stage—not only the outer facts but what Carlyle would call the inner man.

By the end of February 1884 Froude was hard at work completing the life, convinced people would then at least know how much he thought— and *still did* think—of Carlyle. Carlyle would be, of all those worthies of his times, one of the few to be remembered a century later—and he was as good as he was great.

For Froude this hardly meant obscuring the unpleasant. He wrote a chapter on "The Effects of a Literary Life upon the Character." There were no emendations in his view of the Carlyle marriage, for he had been a witness. And despite Carlyle's sterling character and "pure" life, devoid of personal ambition, the very heights to which he rose and the awe in which his disciples held him—people bowing to his superiority—deprived him of what Froude considered the healthy criticism that even the best and wisest among us need. For his admirers his defects were at most a by-product of his sensitivity. His peculiarities could amuse them, for they visited and left. For his wife it was quite different.

Carlyle was kinder to Jane after her long illness. He gave her free command of her money, and he even finally bought her her own brougham so that she could take her drives more easily. Still his temper could erupt into long episodes of biliousness at any noise or any minor irritation—real or imaginary—making her feel at times she was the keeper of a madhouse. For most of the fifteen years he was in the throes of his multivolume *Frederick the Great* he worked away in his specially constructed soundproof study at the top of the house. Still, his agony reverberated on Cheyne Row, where Jane, who had walked in the valley of the shadow of *Cromwell,* would walk in the valley of the shadow of the Prussian warrior king almost to the very end of her life.

For both Carlyle and Froude, biography was "the only history":

"To say that the characters of men cannot be thus completely known, that their inner nature is beyond our reach, that the dramatic portraiture of things is only possible to poetry, is to say that history ought not to be written, for the inner nature of the persons of whom it speaks is the essential thing about them; and, in fact, the historian assumes that he does know it, for his work without it is pointless and colourless. And yet to penetrate really into the hearts and souls of men, to give each his due, to represent him as he appeared at his best, to himself and not to his enemies, to sympathize in the collision of principles with each party in turn; to feel as they felt, to think as they thought, and to reproduce the various beliefs, the acquirements, the intellectual atmosphere of another age, is a task which requires gifts as great or greater than those of the greatest dramatists; for all is required which is required of the dramatist, with the obligation to truth of ascertained fact beside."

Froude considered it Carlyle's special gift, though it certainly was Froude's as well—a rare double gift, as Froude described it: the very fetter of facts from which all biography stems infused by narrative power so that the lived life emerges.

Though *Frederick the Great* does not inspire the contemporary reader, Froude saw it as living literature, and he also noticed the similarities between the biographer and his subject. The Prussian king's bursts of passion, his wild words in relation to his wife—and sometimes things "worse than words"—followed by immediate regret and revulsion, must have sadly reminded Mrs. Carlyle of similar episodes on Cheyne Row, he wrote.

Empathetic identification was, and is, as necessary to the biographer as it is to the novelist and the poet. Just as Frederick was part of Carlyle's psyche, each of the Carlyles was part of Froude's. Froude had come to Carlyle as a young man, had even been in the audience for one of his lectures on hero worship. Perhaps he heard with his own ears that only "a *reverent* man (which so unspeakably few are)" could have found his way to Samuel Johnson as Boswell had and could worship him as a real, God-made superior. In the same way, Froude worshipped Carlyle as a sage, a prophet.

Up close he would see Carlyle's human feet, clay as are ours. But there was a part of Carlyle that was immortal, a part that was the truth teller, who if he hadn't led mankind out of the desert of contemporary spiritual obliqueness, in the future, after democracy had its day, still would. Carlyle had predicted that the hero might come from out of the people. There Froude found him, son of Lowlands Scottish peasants— a peasant himself. And when Froude used *peasant* rather than *laborer* or *farmer,* he used the word just as Disraeli did—to indicate an older England and the values of the feudal past. His reverence for Carlyle was the set piece of his spiritual identity and the cornerstone of his maturity.

He could well empathize with Jane's emotional barrenness and her sense of victimization, as well. Charles Eliot Norton, of all people, inadvertently pointed it out. He accused Froude of not omitting enough from his edition of *Reminiscences*—as Carlyle had requested—and then blasted him for excluding a passage he said Froude excised as a result of his carelessness. In Norton's edition of *Reminiscences,* he restored it. It dealt with Jane's mother's sending her tomboy daughter at the age of eight or nine to board with a retired military man and his wife, an ex-governess, who were supposedly able to educate a young lady by teaching her genteel manners. In the unpublished passage Carlyle had written:

"In this place, with a Miss Something, a friend and playmate of like age, she was fixed down, for a good few months, and suffered, she and the companion manifold disgust, even hardships, even want of proper food; wholly without complaining (too proud and loyal for that); till it was, by some accident, found out, and instantly put an end to. This was the little cup of bitter; which, I suppose, sweetened into new sweetness all the other happy years of her home."

Far from Froude's omission being an oversight, it was, in fact, both intentional and revealing. Froude had been a victim of abuse when a child himself, both through Hurrell at home and being sent too young to Westminster, and he could imagine—if he dared to—what the silent Jane might have suffered under the ex-military man and his wife, what "manifold disgust, even hardship" was perpetrated on two hungry little girls. Jane's stoic acceptance of abusive treatment stems from her earliest days. It was no little cup of bitter to Froude—he saw to what it led.

He called Jane a victim in the biography, and Mrs. Carlyle brought him back to his childhood. To his own victimization. To the days when the motherless child was made fun of by his siblings, lectured to by his stern father, and sent to Westminster to live among bullies older than he, who burnt his flesh with cigars as he slept and turned his life into a living hell. Carlyle had picked not only a biographer who knew him well, but a biographer particularly able to empathize with his wife.

Froude would continue to insist, as we will see in his later biography of Disraeli, *The Earl of Beaconsfield,* that a good biographer like a good novelist has to empathize in order to breathe life into personality. Facts are the science of biography, the "fetter" of what can be known inductively and can be put in order. But delineation of character is the art of biography. George Eliot was once asked how in *Middlemarch* she was able to portray a bean counter such as the scholar Casaubon (modeled after Froude's old friend Mark Pattison). She replied that she *was* Casaubon. The biographer, too, finds a part of himself or herself in the subject. The building blocks are the primary records, the letters, the journals, the documents of the time. No one knew more thoroughly than Froude that the building blocks of history were facts that from one point of view could illuminate the worth of the English Reformation, from another the valor of the Holy Roman Empire and Charles V. They are everything in themselves, but like that proverbial tree falling in the forest, they need a human presence to give them voice.

Both the Carlyles were part of Froude. For all the conflicts in his own nature, he had that double gift of factual understanding and narrative power, and ultimately could stand apart from his own subjectivity—the distance of the artist from his easel—to create a most telling psychological portrait. Froude's *Carlyle* is, arguably, the most significant pre-Freudian biography in the English language.

Froude ended his fourth volume where his first volume began, in the Ecclefechan of Carlyle's birth, and where Carlyle insisted on being buried, rather than at the Poets' Corner of Westminster Abbey. He had begun his monumental work looking in on the Carlyles' destiny as a Greek chorus might on a drama it could not affect. He concluded in his own voice: "We traveled by the mail train. We arrived at Ecclefechan on a cold dreary February morning; such a morning as he himself describes when he laid his mother in the same grave where he was now to rest. Snow had fallen, and road and field were wrapped in a white winding sheet."

Froude was accompanied by the scientist John Tyndall and historian William Lecky, and they first walked the two miles to Mainhill, to the small farmhouse where Carlyle spent his boyhood along with his seven younger siblings. Froude had been there before. He found the house enlarged since his last visit, though the old part where Carlyle had grown up was the same—a kitchen and two bedrooms, as well as the old alcoves that still contained more beds. The new family were of the same station in life as the Carlyles had been, the father a shrewd and industrious farmer, the wife a good housewife who made cheese in the dairy from the cows she milked. "Again there were eight children, the elder sons at school in the village, the little ones running about barefoot as Carlyle had done, the girls with their brooms and dusters, and one little fellow not strong enough for farm work, but believed to have gifts, and designed, by-and-by, for college. It was the old scene over again, the same stage, the same play, with new players."

At the churchyard on that dreary, chilly, wet, gray day they found a crowd of hundreds gathered, not out of feeling but out of curiosity. Boys and girls in bright colors climbed the churchyard walls in droves. There was no clergyman and in the Scottish tradition, no ceremony. In a letter to John Ruskin, Froude commented that one man who'd come from Edinburgh said in a condescending way that the university's giving Carlyle the rectorship had been a great honor to Carlyle. "I told him that a thousand years hence only two Scots would be known to mankind; Knox and Carlyle—on which he left me, I suppose thinking me mad."

To his readers he confided he couldn't help but compare the ragged scene at the grave with the thousands that would have paid mournful tribute to Carlyle had he accepted Dean Stanley's offer to be buried at Westminster Abbey: "I half-regretted the resolution which had made the Abbey impossible. Melancholy, indeed, was the impression left upon me by that final leave-taking of my honoured master. The kirkyard was peopled with ghosts. All round me were headstones, with the names of the good old villagers of whom I had heard so many stories from him . . . woven into the life which was now over, and which it was to fall to myself to describe. But the graves were soiled with half-thawed sleet, the newspaper correspondents were busy with their pencils, the people were pressing and pushing as the coffin was lowered down. Not in this way, I thought for a moment, ought Scotland to have laid her best and greatest in his solemn sleeping-place. But it was for a moment only. It was as he had himself desired."

And so Froude's duty to his mentor ended with a dirge. In the future, Froude predicted, Scotland would raise a monument over such a son's grave. But instead the kirk and churchyard have a forlorn aspect. The only monuments are the iron gate surrounding the small patch, unkempt and graceless, where Carlyle and his family are interred, and three rather perfunctory plaques affixed to the gate that name all the family members. Farm fields spread beyond, and on the day at the end of the twentieth century when I went to pay respects, on those flat fields behind Carlyle's old headstone an empty tractor stood, silhouetted against the low sky, the bleakness Froude described endemic.

You do not alienate men by allowing them opportunities of improving their condition, and a slack chain is less easily broken than a tight one.

—J.A.F.

The Unstrung Bow

*H*e always signed himself "J. A. Froude," the anonymous initials leading one to the family name. But he was Anthony, all right, and he couldn't escape the implications. When we first met him he was sitting at the Exeter high table, staring at ashes. Then he was thirty with a life ahead of him that would open up in a most particular way, allowing him a host of new opportunities, quite advanced ways to approach the world he knew was changing rapidly and irreversibly. He was the rebel of the moment, and *The Nemesis of Faith* remains a historical marker of his generation's spiritual angst. As it turned out, he was not meant for the new ways of Germany or Manchester. And he was no Red once he met that tall, heady, self-involved Grenfell sister who became his first wife. He had been a callow youth, an ungrateful son. He spent his maturity using his genius to link him in some new way to his fathers—and to his own father, the archdeacon, first while he lived, and then in memory of what had been.

In fact, when we come upon Anthony in 1884, sitting in his study at Onslow Gardens, reading over the shipping news, it would appear that only his sixty-six years separated him from the youth he had once been. The entire structure of his own reformation lay in ashes around him. He had nothing to return to after the publication of the Carlyle biography. Henrietta was gone. Because of Carlyle's insistence, he had given up the editorship of *Fraser's*. So there were no deadlines to be met, no plethora of authors to correspond with, no monthly readers to keep him company through a bad patch. Finally, because of his work on Carlyle, there was no historical series to continue. He was too physically exhausted, too spent, to think he could ever now explore the Reformation from the Charles V–Holy Roman Empire point of view. He told Olga Novikoff, he told Ruskin, he might be through with writing forever. Then what was he to do? he wondered out loud to Ruskin. Die of *ennui*?—he underscored the word. He was not Carlyle, to whom writing was a constant, almost physical agony—who created in a passion of white heat that drove everyone around him to distraction. He was a man who had from his earliest years found in literature the structure for his passions, always the desire to encompass his universe, always the desire to be clear this time, to make himself understood. And always the desire to earn his daily bread on his own—rather content his father had the good judgment to thrust him from the moorings of the family to find his sea legs for himself. After all, it was for his own good.

He had to wonder how anyone would doubt his motives, when he had dedicated a good fourteen years to his mentor's care and his mentor's papers. He was a best-selling historian—people read and continued to buy *History of England*. He could have named his terms for a new historical series. He knew right from the beginning that he was making a financial sacrifice when he accepted the burden of Carlyle's papers, though he hadn't reckoned on money, time, spirit, flowing out to lawyers—all sorts of expenses due to Mary Carlyle's opposition. He also realized he would be sacrificing some of the comforts his age and position warranted, as controversy would inevitably follow publication. But he thought the clamor would die down as quickly as it rose when people came to value the heroic nature of Carlyle's repentance. He had no idea, it had simply not crossed his mind, that he was to lose his good name, that the respectability he had spent his maturity reestablishing would be demolished. Sixty-six years old and he was back where he had started at Oxford. Only now there was no future to redeem him.

"I am listless and hopeless," he wrote to Ruskin. He perhaps pushed aside the shipping news to write this letter. What the modern world taught people by the end of 1884 was to stick to their own interests, albeit in an enlightened manner, and do what the society approved. For that they were understood and praised. Veer from the established wisdom, and take the consequences. He was mainly hopeless about himself. "For I see all through my life that when I have ever done what my reason and conscience tell me to be right—I have done it always in the wrong way, or what seems to be the wrong way, by the effects produced."

It had been his nature to look toward a human authority as his traditional beliefs receded. Before Carlyle he had been drawn to Newman. In "The Oxford Counter-Reformation," which he wrote three years previously in 1881 as Ashley entered Oxford, he described days when he and his school friends heard Newman preach at St. Mary's. *Credo in Newmannum* became the cry of their generation. For hundreds of young men it became the genuine symbol of faith.

Some, after Newman went over to Rome, learned not to put their faith in one man, even as a symbol. It was a form of hero worship. But Carlyle had already turned the worship of the superior man into a virtue. *Credo in Carlyle?* Anthony knew the man himself too well not to see the contradictions. He confided in Ruskin that Carlyle's belief in natural supernaturalism—of seeing what was everlasting in the natural world—was no metaphor. Carlyle had actual moments of clairvoyance when the world appeared spectral to him. When he could look at a man and see beyond flesh. Moments when the very crowded streets of London were a horde of ghosts in a dance of death. Who would wish to be seen stripped of his skin that way, before the inevitable day arrived? he asked Ruskin. It was enough we all die. Yes, Carlyle was limited, and at times frightening, but for Anthony the message resounded: Carlyle spoke the truth.

Anthony said that a biographer must know his subject through and through. But who could ever really understand Anthony? In his own time, even his friends were aware of the paradoxes of his nature. His emotional reactions were often at variance with his intellectual positions. Carlyle was all passion, he wrote to Ruskin. And that passion ran out of control in him at every turn. Still, his *strength* was moral determination, to do the right thing, to speak only the truth—the absolute truth—with a complete vision of it unparalleled in his day. That, despite and beyond the eruptions of his temper, the passion that had no boundaries. It was the truth in Carlyle that Anthony followed.

Yet, his biography completed, his reputation ruined, he had hints from Ruskin, who had given up the Slade professorship of art at Oxford owing to precarious mental health, that Ruskin might go over to Rome. Froude told Ruskin should he do so, it would help to "drown the plank on which

I try to float." When Anthony had married Henrietta so many years before, he wrote a poem imploring her "thrice blessed hand" to hold him fast: "Let me not go beneath the floods at last, So near the better land." Now he wrote to Ruskin, "We live by faith and the faith of one supports the faith of another. I have held on and mean to hold on to what Carlyle believed." If Ruskin, another of the dwindling number who believed what Carlyle believed, changed his allegiances, it would puncture the life raft Carlyle provided Anthony, and heave him into the turbulent sea of doubt all round him (to paraphrase friend Matt's most famous poem). "All the confidence I have in you will go to weaken my own convictions." So the man who once was thrown out of Oxford for denying Christ's divinity looked to men to buoy him.

Son Ashley wondered why Froude needed to revere a great man, given his own powers. Even Norton commented on it. Froude had always had ambivalent feelings toward Carlyle. He could not love him, he learned to love him, he could not love him yet again. Let's say as he said of the Carlyles' feelings for one another: He was not *in love* with his mentor, not blinded to the errant nature that made life at Cheyne Row so difficult that at times it literally *was* the madhouse Jane described. For certainly, even if the "kernel" contained the truth, as Anthony would soon ponder, he could not separate kernel from one of the forms it took. For Froude that form was Carlyle. There had to be some man, some great man, to float what he believed. Carlyle was dead; Ruskin with his erratic mood swings had longer periods of madness. Froude was on rough seas, as he continued to hold on to the truth that was in his mentor.

This exaggerated reverence remains a paradox. Psychologically, the metaphor of staying afloat might have related to an incident he would soon recall both in a letter to Ruskin and in an unpublished autobiography of his own first forty years, the stress of the Carlyle controversy rekindling his past. Once, his oldest brother threw him overboard to teach him to swim, which it did not. It would have been better had Hurrell offered a hand. At the age of twenty, Anthony complained to Mark Pattison that if he lived to be a hundred, he would still be considered and treated as youngest son by his family. On an emotional level, he remained to some degree the baby brother. From his earliest years he had to look up to those who loomed above him: Everybody in his household. His sisters who teased him. His tough aunt. His father, his brother Hurrell, Newman, and then later in his life Carlyle and even Ruskin, who was chronologically the same age. It was a reflex. On an emotional level he admired his superiors—though few youngest children have a Hurrell Froude or a John Henry Newman or a Carlyle to emulate. That was part of his destiny. The complexity was that this emotional need was in no way reflected in his intellectual development. Excepting certain incidents in his callow youth that he regretted, not only did Froude think for himself but he took full responsibility. Signed his name. His views might change, but they were his while he held them. No admiration of Newman could alter his opinion of Newman's *Lives of the English Saints*. No admiration for Hurrell kept him from his history of the Protestant Reformation. No belief in Carlyle would allow him to write anything that did not respect the records on which the biography was based—at the same time as he attributed that integrity not to himself as much as to his mentor.

The truth that Carlyle represented to Froude by 1884 was directly connected to the political concerns of the nation. It became Froude, more than Carlyle, once deacon's orders no longer kept him to one side of his society, who was able to act, to make his attempt to change things. On that playing field, it was Carlyle who had lived through Anthony. Froude had long since settled his religious concerns; religion for him was living a life of integrity and duty, and attending the church of his fathers. He faced the modern predicament: In what does one have faith when one no longer believes in a personal God?

Religion had become a matter of opinion, not a certainty. Men's beliefs no longer exercised a pervasive influence on their behavior. That serious side of the English nature needed some other object to contemplate and act upon so that "we remember we have souls and use them." He himself had found that object. Modern people had national concerns to look after, national risks to run. Through serious contemplation of national responsibilities, "our thoughts and anxieties are enlarged." What kept men's souls from rusting in the modern world were the serious issues of state, of nationality. And for Anthony, no single political issue was more important than how England was to regard her colonies. Ten years previously, in 1874, in an emotional letter he informed Carlyle that he was going to South Africa in the hopes of spreading Carlyle's ideas. But intellectually, it was Froude, particularly in the years after Carlyle's death, who would bring home to his people the importance of England's colonies—no matter that as he expressed his own ideas, he maintained the habit of looking up.

"I have a sort of notion," he ended his letter to Ruskin, "of getting a Cabin in an Australian Steamer, and sailing round the globe."

It was a notion that always buoyed him in times of trouble. Forty-five years previously, both he and Arthur Clough dreamed of emigrating. While still undergraduates they had come to the conclusion they had no business to be gentlemen, that they should work with their hands—"etc"—as Froude put it. But rather than going off to New Zealand to become farmers, Clough wrote his poem "The Bothie of Tober-na Vuolich" and "constructed a hero who should be the double of himself, married him to a Highland lassie, and sent them off instead." And Froude—not only didn't he go to farm, he later lost that teaching position in Tasmania because of the scandal of *Nemesis* in 1849.

Then, after the trauma of Henrietta's sudden, unexpected death in 1874, he was planning to head to those colonies once more to see things for himself when he was waylaid by the Conservative government and sent to South Africa.

He felt that should he go there now, all he could do was flit by like a ghost. Only one element made the idea less spectral. Ashley had just graduated Oxford. Perhaps he would take his son to see new worlds, just as his father so long ago went with Hurrell and Newman to find hope in warmer climes.

Ashley had been his father's constant companion since boyhood, always finding him a most trustworthy guide. "This applied equally to catching my first fish, to accompanying him on walks or in omnibuses with Mr Carlyle, and later when staying in country houses or when travelling abroad." Anthony never seemed to be consciously instructing his children, but they relied on that feeling they had of his "immensely superior knowledge to which one had only to refer for the immediate solution of a difficulty." Outside of the failed attempts to impede his older son's alcoholism and degeneration, their father rarely gave advice.

When his son by Charlotte was in his early twenties, Anthony, returned from South Africa, wrote to Max Müller at Oxford: "I cannot tell what to expect about Grenny. He seems to be very like what he always was—but his cousins think that he is conscious of the risk which he will run by any more folly and that at least he will try to mend himself."

By then, Max Müller had been happily married for years to Charlotte Froude's niece Georgie Grenfell, after a rough courtship during which Froude offered his support to the often separated couple. Three months after Grenny's birth, Anthony managed to squeeze in to one of those early letters that "the baby flourishes and looks as well and as handsome as his absurd resemblance to *me* will let him." One suspects the physical resemblance between father and son did not diminish as Grenny and his debauchery grew.

"My own Christmas is sad enough," Anthony wrote to John Ruskin at the end of 1879, the same year in which he began the Carlyle biography. He had recently secured Grenny a respectable position in South Africa as an official's private secretary. It was another solution that did not take. A telegram arrived informing him briefly of his son's death scant months before his twenty-sixth birthday. Sadness, frustration, anger, resignation, as well as the shadow of his own father's harsh disappointment, are all reflected in his curt: "The post when it comes will tell me whether he has drunk himself to death, or shot himself to death. It is one or the other."

That news had rounded out a disastrous year in which he lost as well brother William, who died of dysentery while in South Africa, a trip he made for his health. William Froude, the great naval architect, inventor, and engineer was gone. The nation remembered him as one of the greatest masters of applied mathematics in modern times, whose investigations on wave resistance, oscillations of ships, and the bilge keel led to designs adapted by every British warship. His was a military funeral with full honors. Anthony mourned him, remembering the trials of his life, emphasizing to Olga Novikoff the family pressures on him to go over to Rome, and his brother's steadfast refusal. William's death left Anthony, the frail child who was not expected to live, the sole survivor—and eventually, the longest lived of his sisters and brothers. It left him more alone.

In that same *annus horribilus,* E. A. Freeman, who had hounded Anthony for over twenty years, accused him in the pages of *The Saturday Review* of stabs in the dark at his brother Hurrell. Now, five years after the exchange that followed, there Anthony was, rather aimlessly perusing shipping advertisements. Freeman, on the other hand—the irony must have rankled—was comfortably perched at high table, having just been named the new Regius Professor of Modern History at Oxford.

Ah well, as Froude put it to Olga Novikoff when her son was dangerously ill. "Be stoic if nothing else will serve."

Stoic he might have been, but his pain since Henrietta's death was not lost on his children. Three remained. Margaret, his oldest child from his first marriage. And from his second, son Ashley, followed by most modern May.

One vivid glimpse we have of Anthony's relationship with his children by Henrietta comes from the American writer Bret Harte, who after his literary success became an American consul in Germany. He regularly summered in England, in Devonshire, where he was Froude's neighbor at Salcombe from 1878 on. "Froude—dear old noble fellow—is splendid. I love him more than I ever did in America," Harte wrote home. "There are only a few literary men like him but they are kings." Froude was Tennyson's friend, and was anxious to introduce Harte to the literary lions in a way to make his entrée among them a success.

Harte, author of "The Outcasts of Poker Flat," brought an American eye to Froude's children when he first met them. May was only ten years old at the time. She reported to grown sister Margaret a conversation she heard between Harte and her father and commented that she feared Mr. Harte inclined to be *skeptical*: "Doesn't this exceed any English story of the precocity of American children?"

Ashley, then fourteen, acted like a younger boy but talked with the verbal facility of a man: "His manners are perfect—yet he is perfectly simple and boylike. The culture and breeding of these English children is something tremendous. But sometimes—and here comes one of my buts—there's always a suggestion of some repression—some discipline that I don't like." The *"respect"* Froude's children showed him, this deference to their elders, "is something fine—and *depressing*."

One suspects that the repression Harte sensed was the children's desire and need to please their widower father, who often appeared so sad under his smile. They well knew that for him, vulgarity was the eighth deadly sin. It was the hallmark of democracy, which sought to level the playing field between the educated and the illiterate and erroneously equated equality with freedom.

"Let me be quite clear," Froude would soon qualify; he found little vulgarity in the United States: "Vulgarity lies in manners unsuited to the condition of life to which you belong. A lady is vulgar when she has the manners of a kitchen maid, the kitchen maid is vulgar when she affects the manner of a lady. Neither is vulgar so long as she is contented to be herself."

Froude was not raising kitchen maids. Manners, being who you are—what you were born to be—were essential to him. His children were highly intelligent, sensitive souls, born to upper-middle-class breeding. The sons were sent to public school, the daughters were educated at home. They loved their father, had an empathetic understanding of his needs, and—poor Grenny and negative attention aside—they did not want to disappoint him. They were all motherless, after all. The paternal chain was golden, but, as Froude wrote about the colonies, a slack chain was more difficult to cut than a tight one.

What a moment it must have been for Froude when Ashley went off to Oxford in 1881, as his grandfather, father, uncles, cousins before him. Anthony did not counsel Ashley with thunderous threats, nor did he send him those weekly homilies on conduct that he had received from his own father. He had just one word of advice: "It would be better not to play whist for more than sixpenny points, unless the conditions were exceptional."

When Anthony was young he had believed it had been the age difference that separated him from his own remote father. Ashley was forty-five years younger than Anthony, yet with this younger and only remaining son Froude had established bonds not only of affection but friendship. It must have been of solace to him to have reared Ashley in a way that fostered the type of intimacy that once existed between the archdeacon and his adored oldest son, Hurrell. Still, he had failed Pascoe Grenfell, his son by Charlotte.

Sitting in his study he saw and circled an advertisement in the *Times*. The *Australasian* would be sailing in a few days. It would carry 170 emigrants to the colonies. There was also room for 30 passengers. With a spontaneity that brought him closer to the vigor of his youth, he booked for two. On December 6, 1884, a scant two months after *Thomas Carlyle: His Life in London* was published, Froude and Ashley went off to see the world. The voyage was all about renewal. The *Australasian* would take them to South Africa, and on to Australia. Then to New Zealand and an American ship to the Sandwich Islands, Hawaii, and San Francisco.

Anthony would look at America through new eyes, beginning in a joyful visit to San Francisco, then on to New York by train and carriage, stopping in Salt Lake City, Denver, Chicago, and Buffalo before catching a bad cold and sailing on the Cunard line, crossing the pond in record time: six days and twelve hours to Cork. Then twelve more hours to Liverpool. None other than Mr. Cunard himself was on board, clocking and quietly enjoying the success. New York to Liverpool in one week. The times were changing.

Froude was not. He came on deck with his son, his pocket edition of the classics, his drawing supplies, and his journal. An ocean voyage always had the power to restore him. Though he spoke of age in that journal, as he voyaged, his impressive physical elasticity returned and he seemed to grow young. That daily journal would become the basis of the book he was not intending to write, a book that would not stem from any controversy, one that grew naturally from edifying calm gained far away from newspapers and critics and the unending storm caused by his biography of Carlyle. Weeks at sea with Ashley with dinner at the captain's table, and quiet reading from his pocket editions of the classics, brought him peace of mind. On the high seas he was having a complete reprieve from the world's noise in those days when on shipboard one could literally escape from every interference and burrow into one's thoughts. He would plunge into the issue that was closest to his heart, his vision of the colonies and their importance to the future of his country. From it would come *Oceana, or England and Her Colonies,* one of his most celebrated works, which surprised him by its unexpected popular appeal and the new perspective it brought to many, given that he remained persona non grata at home.

He took the word *Oceana* from Sir James Harrington's seventeenth-century Utopian vision of a perfect commonwealth that was reserved for the English-speaking people. The seas were the law that allowed Venice to grow, but, as Harrington wrote, the growth of Oceana would give the law to the seas. *Oceana* was Froude's finding his way back to himself and to a restored vision of the "merry England" of the past, after the damage caused by his work on Carlyle. It revealed a natural familiarity, and along with it a certain zestful hopefulness, that hadn't been felt since those long summer days in Kerry.

Being on this trip with Ashley gave him the type of private satisfaction that went beyond Mary Carlyle and the slings and arrows of *The Saturday Review.* He was even able to swat back at that journal (and by extension Professor Freeman), comparing the annoying bite of criticism at home to that of the blackest flies and mosquitoes he found in Australia: poisonous at first, but then vermin of all kind usually leave the healthy alone.

Sighting Table Bay for the third time in his life, Froude felt the same thrill he had ten years before for the natural beauty of its sheer cliffs—despite its expanded harbor. But the mood was broken when he disembarked at Cape Town to find himself circled by journalists. Frank Harris had published a private conversation he had with Froude in England right before he embarked, and it had been republished in the *Argus.* At first he was irritated. There should be laws about people printing private conversations. But then it amused him in his wry fashion. They were his thoughts, after all, whether or not he had meant them for public consumption.

He found at Cape Town, as he suspected, that "the history of Ireland is repeating itself—as if Ireland was not enough." The English had been unfair to the Dutch, both in territorial disputes and in their championing the "coloured races" over the Boers. Parliament was to blame for a policy that alternated between severity and indulgence then back to severity again. There was no persistence, no keeping to one system—"a process which drives nations mad as it drives children."

On shipboard once more he washed away the squalor of Cape Town politics by reading Pindar. "Great souls," Pindar whispered in his ear, "dwell only with what is good, and do not stop to quarrel with its opposite." Anthony attempted to do just that, to rise above the fray by not defending his actions. Still, as Pindar predicted: "The back biting tongue waits upon illustrious actions, soiling what is bright and beautiful, and giving honour to the low."

Only the classics brought Anthony comfort. In "The Oxford Counter-Reformation" he seemed to be critical when he spoke of Oxford's not giving the students of his day access to modern literature. But here he was less than four years later finding only in the Greeks moral consolation. He had been the boy who could memorize hundreds of lines of Homer and recite them at Dartington Parsonage for a shilling. He had been the elfin young man who entertained Geraldine Jewsbury and her friends in bygone Manchester days with his spontaneous translations of classics pulled at random from anyone's library. Now he was on shipboard, sitting on deck, reading his pocket classics. He must have appeared an old-fashioned gentleman, indeed, as the world grew smaller and the nineteenth century peaked.

He was rereading Sophocles and Homer when New Year's Eve turned his shipmates sybaritic. He watched one of the women emigrants, "a Moenad with flashing eyes, and long, black, snaky hair," plunge her way through the celebrants, distributing liquor from her flask as she squeezed past. Her songs weren't hymns of praise, her brow wasn't wreathed with righteousness. "The dame herself, though in Corybantian frenzy, was redolent of Billingsgate. From Pindar to Mrs. X. was a long road in the progress of the species; but she did what she could, poor woman, to celebrate the occasion."

Eighteen eighty-five arrived to the ringing of ship bells, the clanking of pots and pans, and the choral songs of colonial emigrants. "Here is the New Year," Froude said to himself. "May I and those belonging to me pass through it without sin." And when the noise was over, he slept as he hadn't for months, not waking until late New Year's morning.

On the voyage he had time to muse about the nature of truth. He decided that the apple fell by gravity whether or not Newton ever watched it. Truth was the kernel, legend the outer shell that wrapped around it. "In a long voyage where we can do nothing but read and reflect, such thoughts come like shadows upon water when it is untouched by the breeze. The air ruffles it again and they are gone." And on a long voyage as well one observes one's fellow man. Seabirds followed the ship, and the English aboard spent their time shooting as many as possible from the deck. Froude didn't suppose that this constant shooting came exclusively from a love of killing; the motives must be more complex, as he didn't believe ordinary men were devils. Still, wild animals never kill for the sport of it. In fact, "Man is the only one to whom the torture and death of his fellow-creatures is amusing in itself."

He considered war a result of lazy politicians, having none of Carlyle's blood urge or cry for universal military discipline, à la Prussia. For Anthony, most all disputes could be adjusted through negotiation and hard work. His suggestion was that instead of sending young men to fight battles against those they considered—in the nineteenth century as well—"the evil enemy," the foreign office send their own men to duel the foreign officers of the offending nation, and let that settle the usually trivial dispute. Of course, then there would be no war at all, for these gentlemen would save their own skins.

The salutary effects of being out of touch with everything and everybody, being on the wine dark sea with his son and his classics and his conversations with as many immigrants to the colonies as possible, far, far away from the Carlyle controversies, was evident when they sighted Australia. He packed away his books and journal and got ready to disembark. From the Cape to Australia was six thousand miles, a quarter of the globe. Altogether Froude and Ashley had spent six weeks aboard the *Australasian,* catered to by the attentive captain and crew. "I hope I was properly grateful for so blessed a relief."

Human imagination had produced nothing as grand as *Oedipus at Colonus,* he opined, but then again, he was soon to find himself among the Australians, who stemmed from the same race. There wasn't going to be a Sophocles among them, he knew that. Still, "If progress was not a dream, who could say what future of intellectual greatness might not yet lie before a people whose national life was still in its infancy?" Youth was promise. He saw this in his son, and in his own vision of England's Pacific colonies.

Adelaide lived up to his expectations. "We were 12,000 miles from England; yet we were in England still, and England at its best." But Melbourne surpassed all expectations. At his hotel he found a message from Sir Henry and Lady Lock inviting him to stay at Government House, where he was treated as an honored guest. As a young man he had dreamed of going to the colonies and working with his hands; as an old man he had to travel to Australia to find himself a respected gentleman once more.

He described the wonders of the parks and gardens that his hosts brought him and Ashley to see. One party followed another; it was English life redux. "All was the same—dress, manners, talk, appearance. Sensible men and pretty women, all intelligent and agreeable. I could not help asking myself what, after all, is the meaning of uniting the colonies more closely to ourselves. They are closely united; they are ourselves." Those with whom he mingled spoke the language exactly as it was spoken at home. This pleased him on one level, but on another he found it too imitative. A new country needs its own accent—its stamp of originality. "Original force and vigour always tend to make a form for themselves, after their own likeness."

At a dinner not long after debarking he had a moment of synchronicity. For with great pleasure he met Edward Irving's son Martin, long a professor, and now the gray-haired rector of Melbourne University. It had been fifty years since Edward Irving passed. In the Carlyle letters, Anthony had come across Irving's pride in his newborn son. How the giant of a man, on vacation with his wife, the Stracheys, and Carlyle, walked the beach with his baby boy in his big hands. Carlyle wrote to Jane Welsh how absurd it all was, Irving gushing and cooing over a baby, giving him a bath himself. Actually conferring with his wife about whether the water was too warm, too cold. Such incredible nonsense, unheard of in a grown man.

Martin had been educated at Balliol, and distinguished himself. But the Oxford fellowship that he should have attained as a matter of course was denied him because he would not separate himself from his father's Catholic Apostolic Church—founded after the Scottish Church divested Edward. Froude said that he wrote of Edward Irving not for his own sake, but because of his role in the life of Jane Welsh Carlyle. Yet he was obviously fascinated by the charismatic preacher, whom he had once heard preach. Meeting Edward Irving's son was a true pleasure. Martin was as handsome as his father, with the same open countenance, but he was also more calm and quiet. Irving's almost demonic enthusiasms were turned into more rational and practical energies.

The leaders of Melbourne went out of their way both for the Froudes and Lord Elphinstone, a witty fifty-year-old Scottish nobleman, who went on part of the journey with his friend. "We delight in Lord Elphinstone," Anthony wrote to Margaret. "He will go with us to Sydney, where, alas, he joins the Admiral of the Station, and the squadron, and we shall see him no more."

Not only were they all given free railway passes, but to spare Froude, who called himself an old man, the fatigue of normal travel, a special train was provided with blue satin seats and all the luxuries of a drawing-room car—not to mention a cabinet member as guide. There were carriages at the stations, rooms at the best hotels—for free. "We were to look on ourselves as guests of the colony."

Froude was not one to appreciate the whirlwind of sightseeing that his hosts provided him in Melbourne while the luxurious travel arrangements were being completed. He was the type of tourist that couldn't look at too much in one day. He liked to concentrate on one thing at a time. Otherwise everything blurred together: "A day spent in walking from room to room, from books to paintings, from paintings to sculpture, from sculpture to crystals and minerals and stuffed birds and beasts, leaves me bewildered." But of course his hosts were trying to show him everything their new country had to offer.

The tour of Victoria proper took weeks, champagne and grapes and all the best people waiting for them at each stop. It was as if Froude had found the path back to the respect he had before the Carlyle-soaked years—and then some. The party finally returned to Melbourne, and before Froude left for Sydney, the mayor hosted a farewell entertainment for him at the town hall. Anthony thanked them all for their kindness, governor, ministers, the people. He told the crowded assembly that their hospitality made him feel as if he must be a person of some importance and that when he went back to London he'd feel like Cinderella coming home from the ball. Still, if his account of the colonies gave England in the smallest degree a clearer understanding of what the colonies were doing, "I shall be content for myself to sweep the ashes again, and I will ask no fairy godmother for any further present."

The Cinderella metaphor was as apt as it was wry, though he didn't have to return home in order to taste ashes once more. In Sydney he made the mistake of reading an English paper that came his way. He had purposely avoided all newspapers, particularly English ones, while he traveled. Disgusted, he threw down the stray *Pall Mall Gazette*. Carlyle was accused of worshipping aristocrats and wealth. Froude was called the "slipshod Nemesis." He took it as a classical allusion related to his laying bare Carlyle's weaknesses. He felt an immediate vexation but rationalized that this was the price he had to pay for telling the truth, as far as he knew it, the way one must in the biography of a great man. He had told himself from the beginning that he could not be troubled by contemporary reaction. Sounding rather like Pindar, he gave himself some advice: "You are to consider the wise, and in the long run the opinion of the wise will be the opinion of the multitude."

He refused the cutting edge of the insult. Calling Froude the slipshod Nemesis was an obvious jab at careless editing and, more damaging, his past transgressions as author of *The Nemesis of Faith*. But he had more important issues to tend to than talking himself out of a bad mood due to the recurring Carlyle controversy. A second incident of synchronicity occurred at the end of his stay in Melbourne. For it was there he received news of the British defeat, the fall of Khartoum, and the death of General Gordon.

He blamed the parliamentary system, whereby a vote in the House of Commons could incapacitate the ministers from following rational policy, and which, he said, drove them from one insanity to another. Politicians were men given two eyes only to blind one—either the left or the right depending on party. "A wise man keeps both his eyes, belongs to no party, and can see things as they are." After the Khartoum massacre, the colonists unanimously laid the blame on the Liberal government. It was Gladstone who consistently wondered about the importance of the colonies to the motherland. He was personally responsible, more than any other, "for the helpless condition into which the executive administration of the English Empire seems to have fallen."

Before he left Victoria, Froude gave a talk to the gentlemen of the Melbourne club, an inspired talk. He told the Australians that Carlyle believed England enchanted, under a spell for the last fifty years. "According to him England's business, if she understood it, was to gather her colonies close to her and spread her people where they could breathe again, and send the stream of life back into her loaded veins. Instead of doing this, she had been feeding herself on cant and fine phrases and delusive promises of unexampled prosperity."

It was an illusory prosperity in which England became a great workhouse while its green and pleasant land became soiled by the soot of steam engines, then became overrun by burgeoning factory towns that turned "our flowery lanes" into brick, church spires into smoky chimneys. The English people were becoming a nation of slaves, slaves "to mechanical drudgery and cozening trade." The England Carlyle looked forward to was "an England with the soul in her awake once more—no longer a small island, but an ocean empire, where her millions and tens of millions would be spread over their broad inheritance, each leading wholesome and happy lives on their own fields, and by their own firesides, hardened into men by the sun of Australia or the frosts of Canada—free human beings."

These views were received enthusiastically, though Froude said he had of course translated them into practical concerns, toning down the metaphorical parts. This translation from Carlylean ideals to practical action was pure Froude. Happy lives and free human beings were hardly Carlyle's rhetoric. As far as "other Englands," one can almost hear Carlyle caution Froude, as he did when reading the first chapters of Froude's history years before, to tone down John Bull. And it is difficult to imagine Carlyle being less enthusiastic about "other Prussias."

Do we understand clearly what makes a nation great? Froude questioned. Not its material but its spiritual growth. The assumption that once all men have the vote and political liberty is secured virtue will follow is erroneous. That was why Aristotle knew democracies were always short-lived. For virtue resided not in having a vote, but in binding duty and obligation to the common wellness.

However, it was obvious to Froude that modern man, once having been emancipated from human authority, had no intention of replacing the chains on his limbs. He wanted to attend to his own interests. What does that mean in a democracy? Getting as much money as he can and as much pleasure as the money will buy for him, while losing the older and sterner moral training along the way. The soul dies out of him—why, he forgets he ever had one. "Hitherto this has been the history of every democratic experiment in the world." Still, if the flaws of democracy and a party system are evident, solutions are much more difficult to prescribe, Froude admitted.

"But enough of this." The disaster at Khartoum underlined his essential belief. Froude had argued long for England to understand that the worth of her Pacific colonies was not to be measured in gold. These colonies were bound to England through common race, history, interests, and values. The real test of the strength of this allegiance, he had often opined, would come when England was at war. Only then would England find out if the colonies would volunteer to rally round the motherland in her time of need. It was nothing that could be *forced*. It had to come freely out of the very roots that bound them.

Khartoum fell while the colonial parliament was in recess and the premier was absent. The attorney general, Mr. Dalley, took it on himself to offer England the aid of a regiment of 700 soldiers. Froude, of course, approved of what for him was this heroic decisiveness: "No great thing has ever been done in this world by a man who is afraid of responsibility."

Others such as Sir Henry Parkes, the ex-premier, disagreed. He was against offering this aid that Froude championed. It was quite understandable. As Froude himself said, the Egyptian affair was a war of England's own seeking and it had left his country without a friend in Europe. And by then, England had withdrawn her own troops from the colonies, and had charged colonists with the cost of their own defense. Though an English fleet was still in colonial waters, the English government expected the colonists to fit out their own ships. Even though Parkes's opinion was in the minority, if England persisted in undervaluing her colonies, that view might become the majority.

Sir Henry Parkes greeted Froude at the Sydney train station with an offer to stay at his home, but he realized that Froude might want to stay in Sydney itself. Froude was equally polite. He told his readers: "I desired to observe impartially the movements of opinion, and I hesitated to put myself directly in the hands of anyone who was taking a decided part."

In town, he refused the lodgings Sir Henry engaged for him and Ashley. The "modest price" of fifteen pounds a week might be modest in Sydney, where wages were twice as high as in England, but not for Froude, whose frugality would have done his father proud. To the Australian Club in the city center he went, Ashley following in a cab with their suitcases—cost, five shillings. Not the splendor nor the service of Melbourne, but comfortable. Froude slept well, only to awake to one of the casualties of the pennywise traveler: Mosquitoes got through the net and he was bitten all over his face and hands the way "a young author is bitten by the critics on his first appearance in print." The simile of the bitten young author suggests that the real meaning of "slipshod Nemesis" was not lost on him.

Though the Sydney mosquito was "the most venomous of his whole detested race," and left what developed into an open wound on the back of his right hand, which took a month to heal, such misfortune did not convince our traveler to leave his inexpensive lodgings. "Happily, again like the critic, he chiefly torments the new-comers. I was inoculated that night and suffered no more afterwards."

He forgot mosquito bites in the club reading room as all waited to see if the offer to send troops to aid England in the Sudan was accepted. The suspense was heightened because certain telegraph wires were down. He remarked a fact of modern life, that a breakdown far away could affect the entire world.

One of Froude's major beliefs had just been confirmed by the colonists' having offered to aid England in time of war. But what if England refused the help? That would be the coldest rejection, an underscoring of the indifference the English government had for the colonies, proof of the ongoing separatist policy. But if England accepted the hand held out to it, it had the power to draw the nation together. Instead of division, it could be "a turning-point in the relation between the colonies and the mother country."

When the wires in Persia were reassembled, word came that the offer was not only accepted but warmly appreciated by the whole English nation. The enthusiasm in Australia was irresistible. Froude wrote that to share the battlefield, as part of a British army, at once was a distinction as well as a guarantee of the colonists' future position as British subjects. It might be only a contingent of seven hundred men to be sent to the Sudan, but within a few years Australia would number ten million men, an inexhaustible source. The present gesture was a practical demonstration in favor of imperial unity. He saw in it a reawakening of the old English character.

In Sydney, at a lavish dinner party, he caught another glimmer of that character in an eighty-year-old clergyman whom he described as beautiful and who obviously reminded him of the archdeacon. The old man told him he had read all of Anthony's books—and he deeply disapproved of much in them. But at the same time he had formed a certain kind of regard for the author. When Anthony left the party, the old clergyman followed him into the hall, came up to him, and gave him a blessing. "Few gifts have ever been bestowed on me in this world which I have valued more."

As Anthony aged, the character that he so admired told on him as well. Not only his frugality reminds one of his father, who once threatened to withdraw him from Oxford if he continued to spend and run into debt. He also now wore old clothes just as the archdeacon before him, though as Ashley emphasized they were well tailored. And in his travels, since a decade past—when he added up expenditures in South Africa and wrote to Margaret he had decided it would not be an extravagance to buy sketching material—he like his father before him drew scenes from the lands he was passing through with a similar, if not as vibrant, talent. He published four of the sketches in *Oceana*.

In a sense Froude still ached to be the dutiful son. At the same time he was more than a dutiful father; he was a loving one on whom Ashley could depend. Right before leaving New Zealand, they were staying with Sir George Gray on Gray's own island. Sir George had once been the governor of Cape Town, and according to Froude "a Radical of the Radicals," on the side of the oppressed. Now late in life he lived on his own island with a dwindled staff of seven servants. It was very difficult to find proper "help"—as the Americans called it—in the Pacific colonies. When Froude's friend Maria Rye organized the emigration of destitute gentlewomen to the Pacific colonies, to find there meaningful work as teachers, secretaries, and nurses, she found that they were considered redundant—what the colonists needed were good English servants.

Sir George along with his remaining servants were "alike republicans," yet they had what Froude called an unconsciously feudal relationship, seeming to feel they belonged to one another for life. They were respectful of Sir George in all ways at the same time as they were frank and open and even contradicted him when necessary, face-to-face, man to man. Sir George's small island with its feudal associations was a Froudean paradise in miniature.

One day, he and Ashley decided to go out on a small boat, just the two of them and the boatman. The calm weather turned wild and they were caught in a sudden squall. They could anchor and ride it out or head back to the mainland. Both had their risks, so Froude decided on a third option, quite daring: to take a chance and head to the nearest island. Seaman that he was, Froude steered Ashley and the boatman safely to land. Once on the island, they were sheltered at a remote farmhouse. "Our good landlady charged me and my son four shillings each for two suppers, two breakfasts and two faultless beds." He felt that hardly covered their stay (not that he offered more). The boatman was entertained as a friend and paid nothing.

Halfway back to Sir George's island the next day, on the small boat that had miraculously survived the storm, Froude and Ashley came upon a steamer. It had been sent out to look for them by a concerned Sir George, who had assumed the worst when they hadn't returned. Upon reaching Sir George, Froude realized that the man had been more uneasy than his consideration for his guests would allow him to express. Now, those were good manners.

Throughout his travels Froude emphasized his avoidance of the crueler side of nature. It was enough that we cannot avoid irrational forces, without touring to seek them out. Yet his last drawing in New Zealand,

"A Maori Banquet Hall," presented a dark, nightmarish vision through a grove of giant Pohutukawa trees. Their massive trunks stood like the columns of a temple while the roots twisted and coiled in the earth like slithering pythons, and their branches, replete with moving bands of parasites, eerily twisted and interwove, creating something akin to a horrible Druid grove. It was under that twisted canopy that the Maori pirates once held their feasts, Froude wrote. There they brought their prisoners, killed them, butchered them, cooked them. It was in this forest of the night that "I could fancy that I saw the smoking fires, the hideous preparations, the dusky groups of savage warriors. I could hear the shrieks of the victims echoing through the hollows of the forest." In his *History*, Froude never had problems describing a grisly scene, a burning at the stake. Something about these early-nineteenth-century Maori pirates was familiar to him, and not only did he draw that ghastly grove, but he and Ashley picked up artifacts, stone knives, chisels, ax heads, "forgotten when all was over and the island was left to desolation."

The visit to the Pacific colonies was almost over. Froude wrote to Margaret that everywhere they went Ashley won "golden opinions." Lady Lock offered Froude the highest compliments on his son's manners. Father had certainly given son the advantage of getting to know the best people, had certainly opened doors, should Ashley decide on the colonial career that eluded Anthony and that could not sustain Grenny.

No matter what the future held, most important, Anthony and his son had months of close companionship. A high point was the baths of New Zealand's Pink Terrace. Colorful, strong Maori women guided them there. To Froude's relief, he found, once they arrived, that men, not women, guides would superintend their baths in this crystalline eighth wonder of the world. Lord Elphinstone, soon to depart, declined and left father and son to their pleasure. Froude and Ashley disrobed, hung their clothes from a Ti-bush, and plunged into the waters after their guide. Naked and jubilant in the perfect purity of the falls, they swam about in the ninety-five-degree water. Then, they lay on their backs and floated for a good ten minutes in what Anthony called exquisite enjoyment.

"I, for one, when I was dressed again, could have fancied myself back in the old days when I did not know that I had a body, and could run up hill as lightly as down."

Aboard an American ship with its ghastly food, father and son headed to San Francisco. When the ship stopped at the Sandwich Islands, Froude did not go to see the volcano: "It was merely an instrument of destruc-

tion, and the irrational forces of nature in violent action I feel distressing."
As distressing were the second generation of colonists he found back on
the ship. They were not their pioneering fathers. They were young, mon-
eyed, and leisured. Froude didn't like any of them; they were con-
ceited, ignorant, underbred. He contrasted their manners with those of
the few English youths aboard. Though of the same social class, they
might have been another order of human beings. (Ashley, of course,
being one of the other order.)

At Honolulu he wandered about studying the people and their cus-
toms, wondering at the homogenizing effect of "our Anglo-American
character," which was spreading over the world. The natural and picturesque were everywhere exchanged for what was commonplace and
materially useful. Those who could convert to this worship of the material, democracy would feed and house along the newest lines. It would
set people to improving their condition by making money, gaining
practical knowledge, and enjoying themselves in tea gardens and music
halls. Those who could not or stubbornly would not be converted to
materialistic ends would be swept away. He was one of the uncon-
verted and might have felt outmoded. In any case, in this transition from
the Pacific colonies to the United States, his mood darkened.

It was only on April 20 as Ashley and Froude entered the bay of San
Francisco, three days short of Anthony's sixty-seventh birthday, that his
spirits again rose. A city that had fifty years ago been a sleepy Spanish village had become by the spring of 1885 one of the preeminent cities of the
world. The life and energy Anthony felt on disembarking at San Francisco was even greater than that in Melbourne and Sydney. He heard it
immediately in the decisive ring of the pilot's voice when he boarded.
Then there were the great ocean liners with the Stars and Stripes flying,
the enormous ferries rushing by, "black with passengers" piled deck upon
deck. Looking farther he could see the lines of houses along the shore,
stretching far beyond the town itself. "All spoke of the pulsations of a
great national existence, which were beating to its farthest extremity."
That was what revived him. The youthful optimism that would make
Oceana so lively, and at times thrilling, had returned. Froude was feeling
the pulse of a great nation.

Previously he had seen the eastern states, but California was new to
him, the land of romance replete with gold fields and cornfields, fir trees
and grizzly bears, diggers and hidalgos, "heathen Chinese" and Yankee
millionaires. "It was with a sort of youthful excitement that I found
myself landed at *Frisco.*"

He'd been told that money poured in rivers in Frisco, but that turned out to be a myth. He had expected the high prices of New York or Sydney and now found that even the luxuries of the biggest and far from the worst hotel, The Palace, in which he and Ashley shared a spacious suite, were incredibly reasonable. The fixed meals were served in the great dining room, and the time allotted for them was ample. Or he and Ashley could order "from the cart," with as large a choice and as good quality as at the Palais Royal—that is if one didn't care about the price. Even staying with the fixed menu was sumptuous—which one assumes they did, as the bill came to three and a half dollars each, or as he translated it, fifteen shillings a day. "Nowhere in Europe, nowhere else in America, can one be lodged and provided for on such a scale and on such terms—and this was California."

With paeans of praise to the produce and prices of California, Froude toured the Golden City. The English tourists considered the Chinese quarter a principal tourist attraction, going there at night with police guard. He didn't go, but would have if he knew any of the Chinese themselves who could show him something other than the usual. "But I did not care to go among human beings as if they were wild beasts, and stare at opium orgies and gambling-hells." Other parties went and returned delighted. One wonders if Ashley went among them; after all, he was young, and perhaps had more curiosity and excitement about the exotic underside of this city of contrasts.

Journalists crowded around Froude as usual, and his impressions were constantly in the press. Though Americans were good to strangers and thankfully did not insist on taking him to see geological artifacts till he was blurry, the reporters often told him he *must* go to the Yosemite Valley, *must* see the big trees. He'd seen big trees in New Zealand!—even drawn them in all their tangled menace. And he always avoided going on purpose to tourist sights. "I can admire beautiful objects when they come upon me in a natural order of things, but I cannot command the proper emotions when I go deliberately in search of them." He grew so impatient with the constant advice to see big trees that he told the reporters, "I would rather go a thousand miles to talk to one sensible man, than walk to the end of the street for the finest view in America."

It was reported the very next morning, and cost him dear. From then on he was fair game. One gentleman after another came up to him: Sir, encouraged by words of yours which I have just read, I venture to introduce myself. . . .

The joke was on him. The question remained: Was the stranger the sensible man, or was he sensible who spoke to reporters without factoring in the consequences?

He realized of course that his impressions of California were the result of a brief stay. Life was like a tapestry. The outside only, not the side with the loose threads, was meant to be seen. He was describing immediate impressions, and he had appreciated it all, the young city and the young wine, not to mention the only really good oranges he had tasted in years. California might be even better than Victoria or New South Wales for the poor man, he thought, for not only are the necessities cheaper, but the luxuries as well. "If one had to live one's life over again, one might do worse than make one's home there." He was sorry to leave.

Off he went, via the Pacific Railroad to New York. It was a weeklong trip with a stop in Utah. He was curious about the Mormons and quite indignant at their polygamy. He gave one old man evil looks till he realized the women surrounding him were his daughters. Stops at Denver and Chicago did not impress him any more than the cross-country landscape. Outside of the Rocky Mountains there was nothing grand to his view "except the indomitable energy of the Americans themselves."

He arrived in Buffalo, New York, after months of world travel and after the sunshine, good wine, and warmth of California. The sixty-seven-year-old man looked at Lake Erie and at first thought a gale was blowing, given the direction of the breaking waves. "But I found the breakers were breakers of ice—huge hills of ice driven in upon the shallows and piled one upon the other." The frigid conditions determined direction. He did not find it "essential" to go on to Canada. "If I went at all, it might be at a more convenient season, when colonial federation had become—if it ever is to become—a question of practical politics."

On to New York. He had to qualify his opinion about the lack of visual grandeur when he arrived and saw that new wonder, the Brooklyn suspension bridge. Construction had just begun when he was last there. To him the Brooklyn Bridge appeared more admirable than Niagara Falls. "The view from the center is superb; New York itself with its spires and domes, and palaces; Brooklyn opposite, aspiring to rival it." Then the long reaches of the estuary, and the great bay into which it flowed, "flanked and framed by the New Jersey Hills." He was fascinated at the sight of it all. As beautiful as the picture was from the bridge itself, he found it dissolving, and from behind it rose for him "the vision of the New York that is to be." He prophesied that as long as civilization and commerce last, New York and San Francisco were the two outlets "which nature has made and man cannot change, through which the trade of America must issue eastward and westward."

But more than anything else, what the northern states had produced were men. He knew of no finer men anywhere. Still, "Let the Britisher take heart." The Australian, the New Zealander, the Californian, had as much of the "merry England" of hearty earlier days in them as these sober, earnest northeasterners, whom, in 1885, he saw remaining Puritans at the bottom of their hearts, "though in modern shape."

What Froude had recognized at a time when many in England felt the colonies simply a burden was the energy and renewal that the immigrant brought to the new land. He was a visionary when it came to what the English, Scottish, and Irish immigration to Australia, New Zealand, Canada, and the United States could mean for their adopted countries and the motherland. *Oceana* would have a profound effect on opinion at home, allowing many to see the colonies in a new light. Just as in *History of England* he gave his people a pride in their roots, in *Oceana* Froude gave them hope for a *new* spiritual center—in serious thought and moral concern about their nation. "In the colonies only we can safely multiply, and the people, I think, are awakening to know it."

If people hadn't focused on the value of confederation before *Oceana,* they did after it. And for Froude, Americans were still "the English reproduced in a new sphere." More than twenty years previously, using the past as prologue, Froude had been certain that the Civil War could not be won by the North. He had more than changed his perspective in the light of what had been accomplished. Now he wrote that if the union had been dissolved it would have resulted in rival states. Democracy would have turned into "military despotisms, standing armies, intrigues, and quarrels, and wars on wars." The Americans had understood this and hadn't let it happen.

Froude was no believer in democracy—as if he needed to tell his readers that. It was not a form of government, historically, that could last. Still, it was clear that at present the people who voted were sovereign and told the government what to do. The States were a generation ahead of England in the growth of that form of government. What the Americans had proved through the Civil War was that whatever its limitations, "democracy does not mean disunion." In fact, Froude now looked to the United States of America as a metaphor for the United States of Oceana: "The problem of how to combine a number of self-governed communities into a single commonwealth, which now lies before Englishmen who desire to see a federation of the empire, has been solved, and solved completely, in the American Union. The bond, which at the Declaration of Independence, was looser than that which now connects Australia and England, became strengthened by time and custom." The attempt to break it apart had been successfully thwarted. As a result the American republic was and would remain indissoluble. It was up to the British people to tell their government that it was not to further weaken the bonds that held the empire together. The "United British Empire" could be based on the American experience.

The Americans had settled the matter for themselves. "Can we settle it for ours? It is *the* question for us." The future depended on it: for "we are one—though the bond be but a spiritual one."

Nationality had become the modern spiritual center, as well as the modern concern, and in the colonies it provided Froude with a hope for the future and a sense of spiritual awakening. These young Englands were a further development of the values implicit in the English Reformation. And there was only one way to achieve this, through the will of the people. It could not be forced or dictated. It needed, of all things, democracy in order to flourish. To be British might indeed still be religion enough—if it meant a voluntary striving toward a renewal of love of the land, duty over ease, a reawakening to moral values, which like gravity *existed* whether or not Newton watched that apple fall—or whether or not Carlyle could control his temper.

By not going to Canada, Froude had lost the chance to visit Our Western Home, the first stop for English pauper children sent to Canada from the streets of industrialized England. From there they were disbursed to willing families. The originator and champion of such childhood emigration was Froude's friend and Chelsea neighbor the English feminist Maria S. Rye, who created Our Western Home and personally escorted the emigrating children there.

Miss Rye was a High Church Anglican who had the deep evangelical leanings Froude had come to respect. She was also a model for the type of "intolerance" that Froude occasionally championed: "Tolerance means at bottom that no one knows anything about the matter, and that one opinion is as good as another." However, she hadn't the worldly air of other intimate friends of Froude's such as Lady Derby and Olga Novikoff.

Miss Rye, stern, zealous, and name-dropping, knew she was right. She would not minister to Roman Catholic paupers, and this was perhaps a bit of luck for those popish "gutter children," as she called them, who at least for all their misery were not uprooted from the only life they knew and submitted to the stern matriarchy, scant diet, and religious observances of Our Western Home, before being placed with a rural family more or less indentured, in a foreign land.

Many intellectuals championed Miss Rye's work, Froude foremost among them. He had prepared a paper on the subject of childhood emigration for Lord Carnarvon when he returned from South Africa a decade previously. His was an adaptation of Miss Rye's plan, an apprenticeship system to begin for children at the age of thirteen or fourteen, when the grammatical part of their education was completed. Though his friends in high places promised him everything, they ended up wasting reams of paper informing Froude that nothing of the sort could or should be tried. Even though Miss Rye and her circle of women proved it had been done by providing so many destitute children with homes in Canada, government officials could only answer, "Impossible."

Froude persisted. Miss Rye maintained a center in England, as well— the Peckham Home—to which pauper children could apply. Froude was on the board of Peckham Home, and Rye herself was patronized by Lord Salisbury as well as supported by Lord Derby. From 1878 on, the Home's annual report carried an endorsement from Anthony imploring the state to resume its old character and be some sort of constable for helpless children. Let these children be drafted to where their services were needed. Settlers would be "delighted" to receive, clothe, and feed the children, on the lines of the old apprenticeship. If the apprenticeship system was out of favor, some other system could easily be invented. In the grips of his idealized vision, he wrote, "A continued stream of young, well-taught, unspoilt English natures would be the most precious gift which the colonies could receive from us." It might seem that to have such a utopian idea (and such sudden faith in the charitable nature of fallen humankind), one also bore the responsibility of seeing how such concepts worked in actuality. The greatest problem with such ideals was what happened when they were actualized.

Froude really ought to have gone to Canada, where eventually thousands of the teeming poor of English cities, paupers and "orphans" (often illegitimate offspring), were sent to be raised in rural communities, some lucky to be adopted by Canadian parents, others fated to hard lives on cold farms. There were no follow-ups to the placements, and when Andrew Doyle was sent to investigate, he quoted a shrewd and intelligent sixteen-year-old girl who told him: "'Doption, sir, is when folks get a girl to work without wages." That remark was often quoted by those who opposed Miss Rye's childhood emigration, a movement that lasted on into the mid-twentieth century.

Perhaps had he been younger, weather or not, Anthony would have waited till he could press on to Canada. But Froude did not have to see a result of his ideas in order to believe in them—as many of his critics noted. At the end of his voyage he remained in the grips of his ideal, his Oceana, a combination of a deep, authentic love of England and of renewed hope in his country's political and moral destiny.

That summer back in England: "I am writing my Colonial Notes: a book which I shall call *Oceana*," he told John Skelton. "I am in the extraordinary position of having to speak nothing but well of everything and everybody. Having nobody to abuse, I am like trying to fly a kite without wind." It turned out to be a good way to fly. *Oceana, or England and Her Colonies* found a large audience; over 75,000 copies sold quickly—and kept on selling edition after edition—renewing and enlarging interest in the fate of the colonies. "I do not know whether it is a good sign or a bad one, but I like it better than anything which I have hitherto written."

It must have been impossible for many British colonists and many Americans from the Golden Gate to the Brooklyn Bridge not to be charmed when a man of Froude's stature came to their country from an old, established one, and rather than looking down his very English nose at them had nothing but enthusiasm for new ways. "Sons cannot always be the exact copies of their fathers, and their fathers are a little too ready to mistake differences for inferiority."

The very élan, the joy of *Oceana* is reflected in Froude's deeply felt patriotism. It is a particular spiritual identification and belief in empire as seen by one who had been educated in the Oxford of the 1830s and 1840s, who heard John Henry Newman preach at St. Mary's, and who eventually found his spiritual hero in Thomas Carlyle. Froude could not be an exact copy of his father. But he was refashioning the world of his father for his times. The life raft he attempted to hold on to even more tightly once Henrietta's hand slipped away might be Carlyle, but the sea on which Anthony Froude floated was the moral destiny of the English-speaking peoples.

Home from the ball, in time for Queen Victoria's 1886 Golden Jubilee with its congratulatory Colonial and Indian Exhibition in South Kensington, Froude, like Cinderella, swept ashes yet again. That year he turned sixty-eight, and April certainly was the cruelest month. During it Prime Minister Gladstone proposed the first home rule bill for Ireland. Froude was appalled both by Gladstone's proposal and the ensuing riots. Whereas the Pacific colonies' relations with England could only be maintained by the use of a slack chain and a democratic majority, Ireland conversely needed to be ruled—ruled wisely and well, something Parliament had not been able to accomplish. Gladstone's majority in this case was "mad."

In the House of Commons, Gladstone wickedly quoted from Froude to support home rule. "I think when I refer to the mere name of that distinguished man, it shows that I am not seeking to avail myself unduly of the evidence of a witness who has prejudged the case in my favor." For Mr. Froude's opinion was that the right course for the British government in the eighteenth century would have been "to drop the Irish Parliament—that is, never to have summoned it." No one therefore could say that Mr. Froude, "who proposes such an extinction of representative institutions in Ireland, and the substitution of what he meant to be a benevolent absolutism, is a man prepossessed of the policy we recommend."

Gladstone then read from Froude's second volume of *The English in Ireland in the Eighteenth Century,* which was as good a summary as any of the mistakes the English made in Ireland. One can imagine the unsurpassed orator hitting the rhythmic cadence of the repetitions, as Froude listed all the mistakes the English had made. *Had* the English resided on their Irish estates, taught their unwilling tenants that the rule of England meant the rule of justice, *had* colonies of Scots and Englishmen been scattered over the land, *had* the Irish been able to learn by their example the advantages of industry and energy, *had* the English conquerors been beneficent masters who *would* have put down wrongdoing, *would* have erected schools for their children, treated them as human beings and helped them to live in decency, the Irish were not so different from other humans that in time their prejudices would have given way.

Gladstone's reading did nothing to improve Froude's spirits. There was no love lost between the two men, though they dined together occasionally, and Froude often went to hear Gladstone speak. Six years previously, in *Caesar; a Sketch,* he had parodied Gladstone, who, prime minister once more, most liberally returned the favor. Froude wrote to Olga Novikoff: "Gladstone, I have always told you, dislikes me as much as so great a man can dislike an insignificant one. And I, on my side, am conscious of an antipathy of which I could find the grounds if I looked for them." He wouldn't have had to look far.

Quoting Froude on Ireland in the House of Commons to make his own point was clever enough, but Froude's fellow Oxfordian went much further. A voracious reader with a Victorian sensibility, he considered, like so many others, Froude's *Carlyle* a dastardly betrayal of his closest friend, and he prefaced his reading in the House of Commons with a cuttingly ironic personal attack. Perhaps Mr. Froude was biased about Ireland; "on that he gave no opinion." But he certainly was "a man of truth and honour." For when Mr. Froude saw what he believed to be an injustice he would not "allow his heart and his conscience to tamper with the principles involved in exposing it." How many "Hear! Hear!"s were heard at that? one wonders.

Froude had been openly ridiculed in Parliament. Perhaps it was no worse than friend Tennyson saying Froude sold his master out for thirty pieces of silver, or Mary Carlyle and Charles Eliot Norton renewing their attack, albeit without Gladstone's Oxford sense of irony. The storm of controversy kept on raging.

A witness to Froude's despondency that April was John Churton Collins, who called on him with the hopes he would champion a plan for having Oxford admit English literature into the curriculum, to be studied alongside Greek and Roman literature. Collins, rather full of himself, a professor and editor then in his forties, born a year before *The Nemesis of Faith* was published, must have been surprised to find Froude unenthusiastic. After all, he had read "The Oxford Counter-Reformation," in which Froude seemed quite critical that in the Oxford of his day, English literature, as well as literature in other modern languages, had not been studied—if indeed they were known at all. But even if Froude could nowadays find any comfort in modern literature (he couldn't), to correct this lapse was more complicated than pointing it out. In the real world, allowing English literature such status would cause, perhaps, more damage than it cured in a society hell-bent on progress. "My tendency is to dislike changes, and I allow for it."

So Collins did not find the natural ally he had expected, and the conversation ranged. Collins told Froude of his own difficulties as a writer, of how he often struggled for a day just to craft three or four sentences.

Self-consciousness! Froude replied, this exaggerated emphasis on style. The younger man should remember, it will all perish, so why torture oneself taking such elaborate pains? "That is how I comfort myself. We ought to remember it is not one man in a million who is a force in literature—who will live and whose work really matters one way or another."

He spoke so sadly and bitterly of human life. Collins saw a man whose energy and spirits had been greatly impaired by time, experience, and hard work. That fine memory of Froude's seemed weak and sluggish. Still, Collins saw great kindness, apparent sympathy, and what he called real humanity, but it was mixed in with that mysterious something so many others commented on. Something that belonged wholly to a corner of his nature that wasn't even partially revealed. Quoting Theocritus, Collins pinpointed that ubiquitous quality: "Far off he seemed though very near at hand."

Froude had a protracted laugh, a silly laugh, Collins called it, which was an indication of a certain weakness of character, along with a limp handshake. He didn't come to the door with him when he left as—hmm—"Carlyle, Browning, and Swinburne always did," but rang for a servant, and "I left him bustling aimlessly about some papers."

Judging by Froude's nervous laugh and his bustling, he would rather have had a less loquacious visitor. Collins had gotten him on a bad day, as were many in 1886. Short weeks before his sixty-eighth birthday, on April 10, he had written of his despondency to John Ruskin: "But Oh Dear: I shall be well pleased when my time comes to be out of it all. I know as well as you can tell me that nothing which I have ever done has the slightest value and it is too late for me now to learn what you call my proper work. . . . I am so dim and doubtful that I don't know whether I shall ever write any thing more at all."

Perhaps Froude felt freer to express his own depression to a man who could understand mental pain, and who might even benefit by knowing he was not alone. But more than that, with his close friends, as with his children, he, who could seem so far away yet near at hand to the bystander, had not the slightest reserve about revealing himself and his feelings. He had a gift for intimacy, and those within his own circle were quite aware of the long despondency that was sapping him physically as well as mentally.

He delayed sending Ruskin *Oceana,* hesitant for that connoisseur of the fine arts who praised the archdeacon's sketchbooks to see the "bits" of his own drawings he had included in it. "My back is sore from the much beating of the last four years." *Oceana* had become so popular and so well spoken of, and this was so novel for Froude that he wondered what he had done to deserve it.

He did indeed *suffer.* His youngest child, daughter Mary Caroline, called May, now in her early twenties, was often his companion that spring. She "adored" Ruskin: "May observed that it was . . . the most charming visit which she had ever paid in her life. It was like opening out of a new world to her." Froude apparently thought Ruskin was a good influence on his flighty daughter, who seemed to lack self-respect—he might have meant appropriate manners—on certain high-society occasions. (After all, he had only Margaret, his serious-minded firstborn, with whom to compare May.) In any case, the vivacious May convinced her father to escort her to the balls of the season, which succeeded in getting him out into society, though he complained about it and was more than ready to return to Salcombe with her and the rest of his family in June—the month, it turned out, that the first home rule bill was defeated. Among all the fashionable lords and ladies, Alfred, Lord Tennyson, too, sailed into the Salcombe Estuary that summer, but Froude made a point not to see him.

By the spring of the first home rule bill, when Gladstone derided his honor, Froude realized with certainty that he would not be allowed past the Carlyle controversy. His reputation was indeed inalterably damaged. The papers Froude had returned much too quickly to Mary Carlyle were now in the hands of Charles Eliot Norton. And in the same year, Norton published an edition of Carlyle's early letters, with an appendix of severe criticism of Froude, including the charge that he had disregarded Carlyle's instructions to suppress certain papers. Froude had had enough. He found himself once more writing to the *Times*. He had not *chosen* to write about Carlyle, it had been chosen for him. Moreover, he undertook his duty to Carlyle with the understanding that there were no prohibitions as to what he should write. This would be his last explanation, he told the *Times*. "I have been treated with an unfairness to which it would be hard to find a parallel." He was not going either to write or read another word on the subject that had tormented and perplexed him, cutting such a large swath from his life.

He had attempted to bear everything in silence, the silence of a gentleman of integrity who would not deign to defend himself, particularly in open combat with Carlyle's niece. Unfortunately, he had been too much the gentleman. He had greeted with anger that turned into a rather wry amazement the fact that after all the talk about his misprints in *Reminiscences*, Mary Carlyle would not return the manuscripts to him so that he could correct his errors of transcription in the next edition. Instead she sent the manuscripts on to Norton at Harvard, and Norton would not even allow Froude the list of errors he was compiling.

That certainly should have warned Anthony. Yet in face of such determined obstruction, Froude, who still held the legal rights to the *Reminiscences,* made the copyright over to Mary Carlyle, having been assured by her that in the new edition of Carlyle's *Reminiscences* Norton was preparing, the mistakes "(if there were any)" would be corrected silently. He had done his duty to Carlyle. The *Reminiscences,* for all the harm the original publication had done Froude, belonged to the world. All he now wanted to do was get on with his life. He was shocked when Norton published an article remembering Carlyle in which he included a list of misprints from Froude's edition. The list was long, and here are a few examples culled from it:

> *Froude.*—"My darling rolled it all over upon me, and not one straw about it."
> *Carlyle.*—"My Darling rolled it all over upon me, cared not one straw about it."
> *Froude.*—"Chapman (hard-fisted cautious bibliographer)."
> *Carlyle.*—"Chapman (hard-fisted, cautious Bibliopole)."
> *Froude.*—"What joys can surround every well-ordered human heart."
> *Carlyle.*—"What joys can surround every well-ordered human hearth."

The pettiness of it all is memorable for Ruskin's response to his "darling" Charles: "How many wiser folk than I go mad for good and all—or bad and all?" he asked, and answered: Walter Scott, in his pride; Edward Irving, in his faith; and Carlyle because of his neighbor's noisy poultry. "You had better by the way gone crazy for a month yourself than written that niggling and naggling article on Froude's misprints."

Froude could not believe that a gentleman, a man of honor, would have published such a list had Mary Carlyle told Norton of Froude's and her agreement concerning the copyright and the silent correction of any typos or mistakes in transcription. That disbelief recalls Moncure Conway's observation that Froude was skeptical about humankind generally at the same time as he could be credulous when it came to individuals. Froude asked John Ruskin to apprise the Harvard professor of the truth of the matter. Ruskin did so, sending on to Norton Froude's letter. All to no avail.

The last time Anthony had so shot himself in the foot was when at the age of twenty, he copied his father's harsh letter concerning his character and sent it on to Harriet Bush's father. The similarity was not lost on him. The depression and self-loathing that accompanied the loss of Harriet so long ago returned. One can train oneself into manhood, but as he, and his beloved Greeks, well knew, the force of irrationality never loses its ability to thunder arbitrarily. For close to a half century he was able to avoid chaos and panic, just as he avoided touring horrors. And certainly, his passive reaction to Mary Carlyle and Norton was his way of supplicating reason. He might just as well have still been the weak schoolboy with a hernia, for all the good it did trying to make nice with bullies. He was a victim once more, and it triggered the feelings that in youth had overwhelmed him, and were overwhelming him again.

Ruskin assumed he did not know Thirlmere, in the Lake District.

"Do I not?" he answered. "There is no spot in the wide world so strangely bound up with my early life." It was there on a reading party that he and Harriet fell in love. "I thought & think it—perhaps from associations—the most lovely of the lakes."

Yet now he linked the memory of his desperation over losing Harriet to his present situation. His work had not the slightest value, and he had an urge to follow it into the oblivion that befitted it.

"That blue pool!" he concluded, feeling again the suicidal despondency of his youth. What if he had ended it all after he lost his first love forever? With his luck: "If I had jumped into it as I longed to do what a fiery witch would have laid hold of me!" Fifty years after the fact he once more saw himself through his father's eyes—doing everything wrong, especially when he thought he was doing right. His earliest traumas became part of his present anguish.

His reputation inalterably damaged, he could not stop himself from ruminating on the cause: Carlyle's marriage and how he handled it with truth rather than fantasy. Only then did he confide Carlyle's impotence to Ruskin. He didn't know how the revelation would strike him; Ruskin might not think much or anything of it. But for Froude: "I had a weight on my back which I was not strong enough to bear."

Ruskin responded that he knew the marriage was unconsummated. By the bye, so had Ruskin's been. On his wedding night his wife disrobed and Ruskin was horrified. The white marble of Venus de Milo and her sisters in stone had not prepared the art connoisseur for pubic hair. He was convinced—and for a while had his wife convinced—that there was something terribly wrong with her. Perhaps Jane had the same defect. Ruskin blamed Jane, a woman who had defiantly stood by him during the scandal of Ruskin's botched marriage.

"I did not know that you knew it. But it was not wholly as you suppose," Froude corrected. "The fault was in him (according to Geraldine) and *irremediable*."

Returning all the papers to Mary and signing over the copyright of *Reminiscences* was irremediable as well. He gave Mary credit for motives better than avarice or pride. He understood she had wanted to suppress the domestic side of her uncle's life and knew Froude did not intend to do that. As a result, her motive was now what Froude called passionate resentment. Perhaps were he less of a gentleman or more inclined to look into the mouths of volcanos, he might have called it hate.

The great world-weariness and sadness that Collins reported was abundantly present. By the end of 1886 Froude felt it necessary to do something very much out of character. He printed a pamphlet in his own defense for private circulation. He asked his coexecutor, the highly respected Sir James Fitzjames Stephen, to give a full account of the situation. It is perhaps as futile to go over century-old legal matters as it is old love affairs. What is interesting in Stephen's account is the lengths he and Froude had gone to give Mary Carlyle her due. For the returning of the papers to Mary was based on Mary's report of a verbal gift made by her uncle to her, and Stephen made it clear that whether accurately reported or not, such a verbal gift was *not* legally binding. He and Froude returned the papers of their own volition. At the end of the pamphlet Froude once more vowed to say no more of the sordid situation "which from the first had been anxious and now had become detestable."

It was a despondent, world-weary man who boarded the mail steamer *Moselle* during Christmas week 1886, exactly two years after a more hopeful embarkation with Ashley (who was now at the beginning of his career as a naval official). That year marked another death as well, one that brought together the two strands in Froude's life, and kept him longer than he wished from the sea. Caroline Grenfell Warre, Froude's first wife's sister and second wife's stepmother, died in her early seventies. He was often by her bedside that year and then spent months attending to her affairs. "My sister-in-law is gone," he wrote. Caroline's life had been singular: He pointed out her generous instincts and what he called her emotional talent, which had at its center passionate self-assertion and a never-forgotten self. He wondered sadly what part of her could possibly be immortal if that persistent self was now melted away. His description of Caroline's high-minded self-absorption weirdly echoed Kingsley's fictionalized description of Charlotte in *Yeast*. It was almost as if the years hadn't passed—at least when the Grenfell sisters' character was remembered. Ashley was present at Caroline's death and signed the death certificate *grandson*. Had Margaret signed it, it would have been as niece. Froude himself felt in that Grenfell death the sense of loss from both directions.

But now he was free to leave England with hope for a good night's sleep at sea and a healthier winter in warmer climes. The only positive thing during these years had been the unexpected success, increasing popularity, and influence of *Oceana*. It inspired Froude—encouraged by his publishers—to head for colonies that Gladstone's home rule and "election virus" was infecting, England's possessions in the West Indies. On this trip he was all alone.

A certain tone was set right from the beginning of this voyage, when a missionary on board kept his lips closed every time he saw Froude. The only time he talked to him, it was at Anthony's expense, and came out of nowhere: "I wonder, sir, whether you ever read the remarks upon you in the newspapers. If all the attacks upon your writings which I've seen were collected together they would make an interesting volume." He had delivered his soul, as Froude put it, and relapsed into silence.

Sleep was not coming easily this time around. One thing he never lost, however, in the worst storm or drenching—his sea legs. Should a toss of the ship make him slide downstairs, he picked himself up. While others lay in torment in their cabins, the old salt made his way to dinner—and ate heartily, albeit more or less alone.

In the West Indies, various mail steamers would carry him to Dominica, Granada, Jamaica, Trinidad, Barbados, Haiti, and, because he wished to see the fruits of Philip II and Charles V, Cuba. But on this voyage, which became *The English in the West Indies,* there were no delegations to meet him. He arrived at ports alone and at times had no fixed place to stay, choosing a hotel at random, or sending letters of introduction to officials who might house him. The decay of the plantations and the diminished white presence blended with his mood—all his towers were being abolished. His observations were at times contradictory, his view of native life superficial. "Froudacity" was the word coined for his impressions. And from the Froudacious tone and provoking observations of the book, one would never know that in private Froude was trying with less and less success to escape his own shadow.

It could not be pleasant, the second time he had to disembark at Bridgetown, to read the local paper declaring that his arrival was the last straw that might break the colony's back. "I know not why I should be thought likely to add anything to the load of Barbadian afflictions." His political views had the effect among many in the West Indies that his biography of Carlyle had at home.

On a subsequent steamer he met a despondent Jamaican planter who told him it was too late for the imperial government to mend matters in Jamaica—meaning the return to prosperity through landed white proprietors: "The blacks were increasing so fast, and the white influence was diminishing so fast, that Jamaica in a few years would be another Hayti." But Anthony could not accept all this on face value, because he had always discounted the natural anger of a man who saw his fortune slipping from him. He himself never listened to anyone who was in that frame of mind. "Even when a cause is lost utterly, and no rational hope remains, I would still go down, if it had to be so, with my spirit unbroken and my face to the enemy."

Froude was by then certainly the most famous and most eloquent proponent of imperial federation. Everyone already knew that he believed the American colonies were lost to England only through expecting taxation without representation, and that had New England been treated the way he advocated treating Australia, New Zealand, and Canada—through bonds built of mutual interest and blood, not force and political heavy-handedness—the States would still be part of the British empire. After the American Civil War he had grown more and more to respect American power and ingenuity. Later, in his biography of Disraeli, he admitted that his earlier support of disunion echoed that of many of his countrymen who realized the potential political power and advantage on the world stage of a united America.

Now he saw that the downtrodden of England, Ireland, Scotland, and Wales immigrated there by the thousands and found new and productive lives. Why shouldn't his own people emigrate in the same way from the small island that could not sustain them all to British colonies and create "new Englands" all through the world? As portrayed in *Oceana,* with resounding vitality and a deep love of country, it was visionary. Agree with him or not, one had to admire that ideal vision of "merry England," which he believed was merely sleeping and could in time be woken from enchantment. The colonies were not to be judged by the consideration of markets and commerce, but in the value of human souls, freed from the slums of England to the health of farmlands where they and their families could grow. Whereas Froude's temperament was uniquely suited for what he found, and wanted to find, in the Pacific colonies and the United States, no amount of reading—and he did read up—prepared him for a similar approach to colonies in which the colored races couldn't be of secondary concern.

But now Gladstone had stirred the pot. Home rule for Ireland, why not home rule for the West Indies? Why not complete desertion of England's duty? Cane sugar was victim to beet sugar, the plantations were in dire straits, the English were leaving in droves, and the Negroes were to be allowed votes, as if votes would make them free. Instead, without proper government, they would return to wars and savagery. And this, too, would be the fault of Parliament and politicians. They didn't send the best men over to govern. They sent men from good families who needed money without regard to their qualifications. Should they start to do a good job, it was time to relocate them to another colony. Froude went to the West Indies with the same ideas he had about the Pacific colonies, and with added animosity to Gladstone, whom he now felt free to denounce by name in his prose—as an orator, false prophet, spoiler.

In *Oceana* little time was spent on the condition of native populations, and that was just as well. Froude was best served when he left those issues alone, for there was nothing forward-looking in his views. The best that could be said is that he was disinterested, not messianic or jingoistic. He compared England's treatment of her native populations with America's ruthless destruction of the red man, and that for him was enough said. He did not believe he was carrying the white man's burden to indigenous populations. He was striving for the moral health, the wellness of his nation through his translation of Carlyle. He had very little to say about India; he saw South Africa and Ireland going to ruin.

Today, many of the natives of the colonized countries of the nineteenth century have become emigrants. Froude had no idea that the kernel of his truth would later be reflected in diversity throughout the Western world. The youth, the hope, the vigor, the restorative power of emigration, morally as well as economically, are as valid today as when he encapsulated them for his people in *Oceana*—but they wear new clothes.

It was the immigration of English to English colonies and to the United States that was at the heart of Froude's vision. On indigenous populations his quick eye was hardly as keen. On first glance he told the readers of *Oceana* that the present-day Maori men of New Zealand did nothing more than loll around in mud baths. Only later, when he was back at the same village, and spent more time, would he see that they actually did work.

The Chinese, on the other hand, in the Pacific colonies and on the ship that took him to San Francisco two years previously, were always industrious, quiet, patient. They never gave trouble. In fact if the prejudices against them could only be got over, they would be useful in a thousand ways. "But one never knows exactly what is inside a Chinaman. His face has no change of expression."

And when he previously stayed in New South Wales with the governor and his wife, Lady Augustus Loftus—whose stately manner (i.e., her snobbery) made her less than popular—he described a conversation over breakfast.

Lady Augustus, who had very beautiful gardens, told Froude and company that one of her favorite Chinese gardeners was leaving.

Was he dissatisfied? Froude asked.

Not at all.

What then?

His uncle had arrived in the colony. He must be with his uncle. If his uncle could be taken into the governor's service he would stay; if not he must go.

They all laughed. It seemed so odd to them that a Chinese man should have an uncle, or, if he had, should know it and be proud of pretension.

But why was it so odd?

"On thinking it over, I concluded that it was an admission that a Chinaman was a human being. Dogs and horses have sires and dams, but they have no uncles. An uncle is a peculiarly human relationship. And the heathen Chinee had thus unconsciously proved that he had a soul, and was a man and a brother—a man and a brother—in spite of the Yankees who admit the nigger to be their fellow-citizen, but will not admit the Chinaman."

So it went in the nineteenth century.

Another example was a drawing of Lord Elphinstone's that Froude published in *Oceana*. The Maoris did not allow their pictures to be drawn, but Lord Elphinstone had sketched Anthony and Ashley as father and son walked past a grass hut at Ohinemutu, while an old woman was at work.

She was very uneasy when she realized Elphinstone was drawing her. She called to some of her people who were digging potatoes, but they took no notice and she went back to cleaning her fish until she finally looked at Elphinstone, then at Froude and Ashley, and gave a loud and long howl. Elphinstone puffed at his cigar as if he hadn't heard her, simply glancing at her reactions with increasing interest, and kept drawing.

She howled again, stepping toward him in a threatening way with flashing eyes and violent gestures. The angrier she grew, the more picturesque she became and the more deliberately Elphinstone studied her. She picked up a stick and shook it, but Elphinstone simply drew that gesture. His composure was too much for her. She went for him in a fury, got close to his face, and raised her arm to strike. "With the most entire imperturbability he did not move a muscle, but smoked on and drew so calmly as if he had been drawing a tree or a rock. Her features were convulsed with rage. His indifference paralysed her, perhaps frightened her. There is a mesmerism in absolute coolness which is too strong for excited nerves. She dropped her stick, turned sullenly round, and hid herself in her cabin."

Anthony's reaction was "Poor old woman!" He admired Elphinstone's cool at the same time as he felt sorry for her. Genuinely so. Native women were human beings to Froude, and he had toward them the ingrained chivalry he felt for the sex, as well as an eye for their beauty. When offered the tourist attraction that appealed so to foreign male visitors, a view of native dancing that for a larger fee included sexual acts, he refused it—and not out of frugality, but moral disdain. He had an innate respect for women whether they were primitives or some of the most intelligent and powerful women of their times, an interesting aspect of his character.

All the above were side glances of native life in *Oceana*. In *The English in the West Indies* the freed Negro population by necessity came to the forefront of the work, and he was not forgiving of the black man. Froude believed black men were naturally inferior to white men, just as Celts were inferior to Saxons, but with good government, they could be educated and trained to the service class in which they could lead useful, productive lives. He often equated the Negroes of the West Indies with the Irish, as unfit to rule. He envisioned what most of his fellows had deemed impossible: the return of the white race to these fertile islands to farm, to build, to govern. And despite his erudition, he seemed out of touch with the complicated realities of the situation, before and after England abolished slavery in 1833.

Perhaps being introduced to what he called "cocktail" blurred his vision, though it was the necessary curative for West Indies languor. He was introduced to cocktail on disembarking for the first time in Barbados on January 12, 1887, and he made closer acquaintance as he traveled. "It is a compound of rum, sugar, lime juice, angostura bitters, and what else I know not, frisked with effervescence by a stick, highly agreeable and effective for its purpose."

In the heat of the day, cocktail over, he would sit on his balcony while it was too hot to go out and watch the people, thick as bees, swarm by. He rarely saw a white face, but what he did see from his hotel was good humor and self-satisfaction written over each and every black face. To Froude all natives appeared happy at first glance, and therefore he believed all the natives were happy—not to mention lucky. These islands of the West Indies were a paradise for "them"—warm weather, fruit from trees, yams they grew.

In the West Indies, Froude appeared more like the typical tourist on the grand tour than he had in *Oceana,* more the caricature of the Brit, nose in air, taking first impressions as ultimate truth about the foreigners seen from hotel windows and carriages.

If only Froude had been as open to fresh impressions of the people of the West Indies as he was to the mango he also experienced for the first time: "The mango is the size and shape of a swan's egg, of a ruddy yellow colour when ripe, and in flavour like an exceptionally good apricot, with a very slight intimation of resin. The stone is disproportionately large. The flesh adheres to it, and one abandons as hopeless the attempt to eat mangoes with clean lips and fingers. The epicures insist that they should be eaten only in a bath."

The women of the West Indies were the singular bright spot for Froude. He had a decent, manly admiration of their straight and graceful forms, the way they walked with such dignity. It was mainly they whom he saw from his steamers, balancing eighty to a hundred pounds of coal each in baskets on their heads as they proceeded to unload their burden, and then return to gather another. They seemed to fly along, laughing and talking as if they didn't know the meaning of weariness. "If black suffrage is to be the rule in Jamaica, I would take it away from the men and would give it to the superior sex."

Eventually, watching how hard the West Indian women worked allowed his English sense of chivalry to get the best of him. In Jamaica he was the guest of a banker botanist and his lady, "one of the old island aristocracy." They owned the estate Cherry Garden, which thirty years previously belonged to George William Gordon, the son of a female slave and white man who had risen to prominence by his own hard work and who had been the leader of opposition to the colonial government.

After Colonel Eyre violently quelled the Morant uprising in 1868 by ruthlessly killing over four hundred blacks, he had Gordon executed as well.

Edward John Eyre had been an explorer as well as a colonial administrator in Australia and New Zealand, and had served in Jamaica for two years. When John Stuart Mill, Goldwin Smith, and Sir James Fitzjames Stephen, among others, attempted to have Eyre tried for murder for the way he had handled the uprising, Carlyle set up a committee in his defense that included Ruskin, Tennyson, Kingsley, Darwin, T. H. Huxley. Froude at the time was editor of *Fraser's* and sided with neither.

Though he later said it was "cowardice" not to have signed Carlyle's petition, Froude never came to Eyre's defense, then or later. And what Froude called "cowardice" was often what others might call mature judgment. The execution of Gordon was violent and unjust, and Froude had empathy for him.

There were aspects of the Eyre affair that would have bothered him beyond his abhorrence of needless violence. One was that Eyre was an example of a man who was doing a good job as colonial administrator in a part of the world he understood—he sympathized with the Aborigines, for example—who was foolishly sent to another. In Jamaica, Eyre spent too much time in his estate at Flamstead, entertaining the upper crust and removed from the turmoil in Kingston below. Many thought he came down to earth too late. In any case, Eyre was not tried as Mill would have had it, though he was ruined.

Returning to his hosts who now owned Gordon's estate at the end of his tour of the islands, Froude detrained at Kingston, seven miles away, thinking he'd have a delightful drive back before sunset. "But alas! for human expectations." He hired a buggy driven by a decent-looking man, though his horse looked hungry and miserable, and off they went. It was market day, and after a few miles, "the road was thronged as before with women plodding along with their baskets on their heads, a single male on a donkey to each detachment of them, carrying nothing, like an officer with a company of soldiers."

Perhaps had Ashley or Lord Elphinstone been along, Anthony could have expressed what must have been pent-up anger and frustration, and had done with it. Instead, he found himself confronting his driver and appealing to him man to man.

Wasn't the driver ashamed to see these women working so cruelly, while their lords and masters leisurely rode along amusing themselves by doing nothing?

The response was a laugh. "Ah, massa," he said, with his tongue in cheek, "women do women's work, men do men's work—all right."

And what was man's work?

"Look at they women, massa—how they laugh—how happy they be."

Froude did not let the poor man avoid the issue. He continued to prod him until the driver got as excited as Froude had become and the argument grew heated and angry. They got so completely caught up in this verbal brawl that they forgot the rickety horse, who wandered off in the wrong direction only to get stuck in "a deep sandy flat" that was overgrown with bush and from which labyrinthine lanes extended in many different directions. Where were they? Neither of them knew. That's where their quarrel landed them.

By then it was dark. They saw a light through some trees and Froude sent the driver to inquire. They were directed one way, then another, each way the wrong way. Froude attempted to use the stars as compass, but still, they needed further directions. Again they were led astray. They had to climb a steep hill, and the poor horse was so exhausted that the driver began flogging him to make him move on. It was excessive, and Froude realized the driver was taking his own anger out on the beast. Froude tried to get him to stop. When he couldn't through reason, he grabbed him there on the cart and the two ended up in a physical fight. Froude, despite his age, prevailed. By the time the driver was restrained, it was too dark to see at all, and Froude got out of the buggy and walked, leaving the driver to follow behind him and cool off. The walk momentarily calmed Froude as well. For it was a beautiful night, like "the gloaming of a June night in England." It wouldn't be the worst thing to camp out. But on they plodded. More directions, more of an upward climb.

"Vainly I repented . . . what had I to do with black women, or white either for that matter?"

Eventually they came to a trench the horse could not breach, so Froude arbitrarily picked a different road, by now prepared to bivouac till morning and go on with his argument. Instead, this road led to a field and finally lights glimmered, dogs barked, and they reached Cherry Garden to find the entire household alarmed at his absence.

Froude realized it would be unfair to stint the driver of his fare, because he had only himself to blame for the loss of direction. As it turned out, the driver was quite an honest fellow after all. "In the disturbance of my mind I left a rather valuable umbrella in his buggy. He discovered it after he had gone, and had grace enough to see that it was returned to me." (Shades of English proprieties, E. M. Forster style.)

His hosts were very amused when Froude related his misadventure, "to address homilies to the black people on the treatment of their wives not being the fashion in these parts." He wrote of the incident simply as a joke on himself as he left the West Indies for Cuba.

For his readers, he presented another joke on himself during his passage to Cuba. He had previously acknowledged his disinclination to view horrors, but it was really not a good basis for refusing to see the future for himself, in this case what was happening at the construction of the "Darien [Panama] canal." It was all ugliness, prostitution, corruption, murder, and rotting corpses. No need to see it. His mind was made up through reports that he heard about this new materialistic cathedral of the future.

On the steamer to Cuba, the rumor was that prostitutes were aboard— "Spanish ladies on their way to the demonic gaieties at Darien, but they did not show." Such whispers must have given Froude ample opportunity to expound to his shipboard friends on the evils of progress as exemplified by the construction of the canal he had refused to see. Before disembarking, he chose a hotel in Havana at random and then lowered himself into the dinghy that would take him to shore. No sooner was he seated "when the fair damsels bound for Darien, who had been concealed all this time in their cabin, slipped down the ladder and took their places at my side." The view of Froude on the dinghy surrounded by prostitutes was quite entertaining to his new acquaintances, who remained on board and watched the entire proceedings from the deck. Froude found it funny, too. This was the persona he offered his readers throughout *The English in the West Indies*—the proper old English gentleman abroad.

However, under the jovial mask lay the despondency that he could not shake, and it is ever-present in the private journal he wrote at the time, and reveals a much different story. Waldo Dunn, who championed Froude in the twentieth century, attempting to rescue his reputation from the Furies that attended it, thought it best, in the matter of *The English in the West Indies,* to say very little. Instead, he skirted around the book in a very helpful way, by publishing without any editorial comment private entries from Froude's journal of this voyage, that Ashley and Margaret allowed him to see and use. Without their trust in Dunn, it would have otherwise gone to the grave with them, in accordance with their father's expressed wishes.

The journal clearly shows us that Froude, like his beloved Oedipus, could not escape his fate: "The Carlyle worry comes back on me at night sometimes," he wrote on shipboard at the end of February 1887. "What, in the name of truth ought I have done? It was a tragedy, as truly and as terribly as Oedipus; nor was the character altogether unlike. His character, when he was himself, was noble and generous; but he had absolutely no control over himself. He was wayward and violent, and perhaps at bottom believed himself a peculiar man who had a dispensation to have things his own way. Also, his head was turned by Lady Ashburton, to Mrs. Carlyle's further trouble. Was I to hide all this when he himself had prepared his own indictment? Was I to make a heroic poem of it chequered with comedy?"

He knew he should get the subject out of his mind, but found it not easy to do. He would land in Cuba the next day. It preyed on his mind that he had heard nothing from home. He wondered if Mary Carlyle was at work again, and his children were not wanting to tell him. Correct. In Cuba, Froude saw an advertisement for the edition of *Reminiscences* that Norton was publishing, and he was "Foolish enough to have a bad night about it."

He questioned why he should vex himself because he had infuriated certain people. Had he known earlier that Carlyle, who had given him his papers with no restrictions, would later request they be returned to those who could vilify him, he would have had nothing to do with the project. No one would place himself in such a position. "I have been illused in being given a strange responsibility, and in being left unprotected in the use which I made of it." Carlyle should have known his own mind. "If he trusted me at all, he ought to have trusted me altogether."

Again, no mail from home. "I am surprised that the Carlyle business hangs heavy on me and spoils all."

Froude felt he had to protect himself and his family in some way. He had to lay everything out—the whole affair—openly. Get down in writing his exact position as well as the exact circumstances surrounding the matter. Not for the newspapers, or in a pamphlet prepared for private circulation, as he had previously done, but for himself or his children to have and to use—if it really became necessary.

To do this, he needed what eluded him, peace and quiet. The hotel in Havana turned out to be a resort for vacationing Americans. To his readers, he confided in jovial tones, that as dear as Americans were to him and as welcome as the sweet sound of their voices in most places, he hadn't come to Havana to hear them. As the nights passed, these Americans, who individually he was sure were charming, collectively were driving him to distraction. He attributed his inability to sleep to their Yankee twangs through the night. Their singing at the piano was what mixed wildly with his broken dreams, not visions of Norton or Mary Carlyle. Bad dreams had returned with a vengeance: "In youth and strength one can defy the foul fiend and bid him do his worst; in age one finds it wiser to get out of the way." That "foul fiend" is as close as he came in *The English in the West Indies* to admitting he was in the grasp of his own blue devils.

He did find respite seven miles from Havana, in a secluded hotel on the sea at Vedado with its natural beauty and quiet. There from his window he could watch the sea wash the coral rocks. He could take walks in wild terrain as if there were no city at all within reach. He could go where he pleased without fearing questions or interference. Walking alone, he saw blacks and whites living and working peacefully side by side.

In the beauty and peace of Vedado, as if he were on a retreat, he wrote a complete account of his association with what he called the Carlyle business. Ashley and Margaret found it after his death, along with a copy of Carlyle's will and a few business papers in a dispatch box. It was published along with Froude's privately published pamphlet by his children, in 1903, when the attacks on their dead father continued in both Alexander Carlyle's edition of *New Letters of Thomas Carlyle* and his edition of *New Letters and Memorials of Jane Welsh Carlyle*. In the latter Sir James Crichton-Browne wrote an introduction that was as gratuitous a *personal* attack on Froude's character as there has ever been of a man a decade dead, who could no longer bleed when stabbed.

Sir Crichton-Browne blamed Carlyle's entire posthumous decline in reputation on Froude. "Whatever he touched he twisted and transmogrified. . . . It would have been well for all concerned had his Carlyle manuscripts been burnt" as *The Nemesis of Faith* had been at Oxford. He brought up *Shadows of the Clouds,* as well, to illustrate Froude's tendency to stray from the truth. He accused Froude of mutilating Jane Carlyle's letters, at the same time as he, perhaps unconsciously, illustrated what would have happened to Jane's papers if Carlyle's relatives had gotten to the material first: "Had Mrs. Carlyle's correspondence as a whole to be edited *de novo* a very different method of dealing with it from that adopted would have been followed, but Froude's indiscretions have made complete candour necessary."

After this posthumous attack, Margaret and Ashley published their father's short Cuban journal and the once privately published pamphlet—all and all eighty pages in a slender volume. Then the outraged Alexander and Crichton-Browne published a 182-page response with a title that might have had a dead man spinning in his grave: *The Nemesis of Froude.* There would be no letup in the defiling of Froude's memory in the twentieth century. And it must be understood that no author ever paid such a high price for his or her typos.

Quoting from Froude's account, I have called it the Cuban journal. The title it was published under, *My Relations with Carlyle,* makes it sound as if it were some well-thought-out essay written in Anthony's study in a logical frame of mind. It came, instead, out of personal despair and was written at Vedado, Cuba, in pencil, from March 12 to March 15, 1887, a little more than a month before Froude's sixty-ninth birthday. Much of the information in it corresponds with what Froude had written both in the biography of Carlyle and in letters to his friends. Yet from it we can glean more readily not only his intimacy with Mrs. Carlyle but his identification with her victimization.

Jane's pale, drawn, suffering face haunted him in his dreams, he wrote. At first he set it down to her ill health and rationalized that perhaps to be married to such a great man was its own reward. But then as she confided more in him, he was more distressed than interested to hear the bitter things she told him. "I felt that I could never live with such a man. Nothing would do but the most absolute submission to him of your whole being, and then you would do only indifferently."

Perhaps it was this projection of her situation onto his present state that led him to reveal something one doesn't find elsewhere: Carlyle left his wife believing in nothing. "On the spiritual side of things her mind was a perfect blank; she looked into her own heart and into the world beyond her, and it was all void and desert; there was no word of consolation, no word of hope."

She must have had tremendous confidence in Froude to reveal something we do not find so directly stated elsewhere—this total loss of faith. Though always ironic in her wit, she certainly had faith before she married, particularly in the years in which she was passionately in love with Edward Irving, the most stirring of preachers. Froude confided Jane's spiritual void to his Cuban journal at the moment when he was feeling the full impact of Carlyle's effect on his own peace of mind. He had to wonder if the living truth the prophet encapsulated was small consolation for what had been lost.

On that boat to Cuba, he had written in his diary something that strikes a similar chord. In a pithy paragraph Froude listed what his connection with Carlyle cost him: "My own prospects as a young man. Later gave up *Fraser* because Carlyle wanted it for Allingham, and my work on Charles V so as to be free to write Carlyle's biography; then the ten years of worry before the book was finished, and the worry for the rest of my life."

That passage for a long time struck me as indicative of a return to the self-pity of Anthony's boyhood—his looking outside himself rather than taking personal responsibility, no matter how dire the circumstances. There is no doubt that all the boyhood emotions he thought he had thrown off when he married returned in this crisis. On the other hand, Froude was looking over his life from the vantage point of a man close to the end of it. And what Froude observed was true. From the time he picked up and read Carlyle he altered his life. Jane lived with spiritual blankness on Cheyne Row. Yet Froude, from the distance of Onslow Gardens, had been able to accept Carlyle's faults and still look up to him as a guide. By the time Froude traveled to Cuba, Jane's loss of faith became a correlative of his own mental despondency. He worried about his own ability to hold on to himself now that his duty to Carlyle resulted in the loss of what he spent his own manhood reclaiming, his good name.

Writing in his diary on his way to Cuba, he had clung fast to his belief that once he was dead the world would thank him for his biography of Carlyle. And at Vedado, in his penciled account: "My book, if it is still to be condemned at present, will be of use hereafter." He meant "a hundred years hence," when people better appreciated Carlyle's importance. But the biography would do nothing but damage to J. A. Froude in his own lifetime.

On his tour of the West Indies, Froude came as close as he ever would to Jane's state of mind. Cocktail might have soothed his nerves, but it seemed not to dull the edge of what might well have been his own tragedy. His flaw was the opposite of hubris, actually. He hated his *self* in that sense and often said so. His best friends, Max Müller and John Skelton, men who knew him through the years, both commented on the feminine in the nature of this literary man who fly-fished and shot and yachted with the best of them. His physical resilience was remarkable throughout his life. Yet, there was that vulnerability about him that no one could pin down. It was the sense of some deep inaccessible hurt, which along with his looks and intellect attracted some of the most talented women of his time. Men saw more the irony and shifts of perspective that guarded it, and many did not trust him. Women saw that this was a man who was alone in the world, a man who never had a mother.

At the bottom of his darkest hours, he actually *did* take responsibility for his actions: "I have made many blunders—the worst and greatest that when I knew what the circumstances were I did not at once decline to have anything to do with them. I was misled by a too confiding admiration of Carlyle's own heroism. It was unwise of me, and I regret my impudence too late."

No one does what he consciously knows to be wrong without having a specific object in doing it. "If any one will suggest what unworthy motive I can have had, he may perhaps assist me in discovering it. I cannot discover it myself." He hadn't gone into things blindly. From the beginning he knew that what Carlyle asked him to do had dangers. He anticipated that it was not unlikely that Carlyle's relations might resent him, "but Carlyle had selected me apparently because I was not a relation and would be free from influences of a private kind." What he hadn't anticipated was Mary Carlyle's attacking him in the newspapers, friends calling him Judas, Gladstone mocking him in the House of Commons. "I was not prepared for attacks on my character as a gentleman and a man of honour."

He acquitted Carlyle of any devious intentions. "He was incapable of treachery, least of all to me. But faith has not been kept with me. I see it now—I saw it before, but I was unwilling to worry him—that I ought to have insisted on receiving from him in writing his own distinct directions. If they were not satisfactory to me I could then have declined to go on."

Of course he should have insisted on written instructions; that would have been the advice of any father to any son. But he had not attended to his own self-interest in the modern way. It was as if he had pledged loyalty to his liege lord. He had been not only a fool, but an old fool. It comes out clearly in his Cuban journal. At his age, he wondered whatever was going to repair him. At Vedado, he had too many self-inflicted wounds to wax philosophical, too much pain. By maintaining his stance as a gentleman, rarely answering his critics, and allowing Mary Carlyle full range, he had lost his reputation without a fight. It was exactly that loss of honor that unstrung him as if he were some modern-day Ulysses.

That was the title he wanted for his West Indian book—*The Bow of Ulysses*. From the beginning his metaphor was based on Ulysses' returning home to find his land in disorder, his bow unstrung, and the suitors at his gate. The bow of Ulysses had to be restrung, the land restored. His publishers, however, intervened. After all, Gladstone was quoting *The English in Ireland* in the House—no publicity is bad publicity. *The English in Ireland* still sold. The best-selling *Oceana* had the clear subtitle *England*

and Her Colonies. Hence, after much back-and-forth, *The English in the West Indies* was born. Subtitle: *The Bow of Ulysses.*

Long bow! Sir Crichton-Browne corrected in the twentieth century. The correct subtitle would have been *The Long Bow of Ulysses.* Couldn't the scoundrel get anything right?

No surprise that there was a substantial uproar—as well as sales—on publication. Many West Indian writers responded in defense of their civilization and their worth. One of the books, *Froudacity: West Indian Fables by James Anthony Froude,* accurately described Froude's quick and incorrect assessment of different island peoples as one, as well as coining *Froudacity,* the phrase for all of Anthony's wilder plunges.

Yet it is the subtitle of another book of criticism, *Mr. Froude's Negrophobia,* that best describes Froude in the West Indies: *Don Quixote as a Cook's Tourist.* It could not be said better.

What Froude attempted had less to do with the West Indies per se than with countering Gladstone and home rule. Increasingly he considered that the two-party system cared less about protecting the nation from outside enemies and more about each party's defeating the other in some eternal civil war. The possession of a vote never improved the character of any human being and never would. He said of the black race what he said of the Irish—they had suffered enough under England: "They have been sacrificed to slavery; are they to be sacrificed again to a dream or a doctrine?" That doctrine was what he called a new Athanasian Creed with its own priests and prophets. He parodied it in *The English in the West Indies* as Radical Articles of Faith:

Whosoever will be saved, before all things it is necessary that he hold the Radical faith.

And the Radical faith is this: all men are equal, and the voice of one is as the voice of another.

And whereas one man is wise and another foolish, and one is upright and another crooked, yet in this suffrage none is greater or less than another. The vote is equal, the dignity co-eternal.

Truth is one and right is one; yet right is right because the majority so declare it, and justice is justice because the majority so declare it.

And if the majority affirm one thing to-day, that is right; and if the majority affirm the opposite to-morrow, that is right.

Because the will of the majority is the ground of right and there is no other, etc., etc., etc.

This is the Radical faith, which, except every man do keep whole, and undefiled, he is a Tory and an enemy of the State, and without doubt shall perish everlastingly.

By the time he was at sea returning to London at the end of March, he admitted to his journal that he had not the spirit he had when he journeyed two years before. He hadn't replicated the solace that his trip to Oceana with Ashley had brought him. On that voyage he thought he had gotten clear of the shadow of the Carlyle controversy that had been with him so long. "Now it is back again."

Would he be able to shake off despondency, particularly since his mistakes had rekindled the self-pity of his boyhood and brought him even closer to the victimization he empathized with in Jane Carlyle? He wrote that the more distant he got from the position he was placed in, the more unfair and unjust it appeared to him.

Still, he was not one to trust despondency. After all, he was a man, not a boy. "I will shake it off definitely when I get home."

The World According to the Muslim, the Irishman, and the Hebrew Conjurer

When he returned from the West Indies, Anthony's health failed. Eye trouble plagued him. While writing the Carlyle biography dark, sooty spots swirled. Only after its completion, his brain, as he phrased it, entered a more quiet state, and his eyesight cleared. But now these floating black spots that curtailed his reading had returned. After he published *The English in the West Indies* he vowed yet again never to undertake another book. In fact, he didn't think he could if he wanted to. For he was sure his eyes were giving out, and he did not want to go blind before he died. He was determined to save what remained of his vision.

"It has been hard to feel that I was to end my life under a shadow," he wrote at the time. He listed only two supporters of his biography of Carlyle, Lord Derby and then, finally, Ruskin. No—he stopped himself to make another exception. "Jenny Lind though she was nearly dying at the time of cancer held up all through with generous and stern approval."

Except for the three of them he felt as if he were tied to a stake for inso-lent boys to throw dead rats at him. He *must* have committed some "Strange Sin" to have come to this.

His right eyelid was a source of bedevilment and would eventually have to be cauterized time and again. It was the most unpleasant process, this burning out of the inside of his eyelid with an electric wire. "We are told that we ought to console ourselves with thinking how many other poor wretches have worse to bear. It does not console me a bit. Why should it?"

He seemed to have inherited Carlyle's stomach, along with his papers, if not the ability to complain of it daily. His doctors called it a gas-tric condition at the time. Sleep had turned into tossing and turning. His despondency over his lost reputation and his stomach pains kept him awake. When sleep did come, it brought with it bad dreams. But even these concerns paled when he developed a condition similar to—and at least as painful as—shingles.

Bret Harte wrote to cheer the patient, professing some envy of Froude's condition. It was apparently not enough for his friend to be a sweet and gracious cynic, a fascinating historian, a perfect master of style, and the idol of British imperialism. He had to go further and develop a rare condition that perplexed the doctors. Now even dispassionate sci-ence regarded him with admiration. Harte could imagine Froude's doc-tor writing a prescription for J.A.F., a gentleman of independent means, literary taste, not to mention a great traveler, who was rumored as well to be a special correspondent of the *Daily Telegraph*. His pulse was nor-mal, but it rose to 125 on the mention of the name *Gladstone*, with accompanying symptoms of irritation and skin eruptions.

As ill as Anthony was at the age of seventy, it was then that he wrote his first novel in forty years. *The Two Chiefs of Dunboy* was a third-person narration with a defining subtitle: *An Irish Romance of the Last Century*. It took place in his beloved southern Ireland, which he had celebrated in "A Fortnight in Kerry" and which got him in so much trouble with the Irish almost twenty years previously. The action occurs in the mid-eighteenth century, when the conditions in Ireland were those he related in the passages from *The English in Ireland* that Gladstone read out in Par-liament. Harte took Froude's blood pressure well.

Froude said he had been thinking about writing such a novel for fifteen years, which dates it back to the completion of *The English in Ireland* and the death of Henrietta. No doubt, Froude's more and more vocal criti-cism of Gladstone impelled him. Also his voyage to the West Indies impressed upon him what he considered mistakes similar to those made in Ireland. Both Ireland and the West Indies needed to be led well and to accept wise leadership. Instead, English rule was a farce, Parliament in constant vacillation. Another impetus to trying his hand at a novel after so many years might have been Benjamin Disraeli, whose novel *Lothair* Froude greatly admired. It was written after a hiatus of thirty years.

Disraeli himself had asked Froude to review *Lothair,* when it appeared in 1870, but the subject matter made Froude wise enough to decline. Freeman might later accuse him of "stabbing" his brother Hurrell, but Anthony was not about to publish his admiration of a novel in which a cardinal, based on Nicholas Wiseman, attempted to make a huge display of converting a young man who was to become a fabulously wealthy aristocrat. The cardinal and his party ostensibly kidnap the feverish, confused English youth in Rome, and almost succeed in converting him to Roman Catholicism and making a media event of it. This along with all the associated Oxford Movement issues, not to mention that Disraeli, as always, based his novels on actual people and events, was too much wind even for Froude's kite. He sent the book on to Skelton and told him when he read it, he'd understand his decision not to review.

But one main impetus for Froude's actually writing the novel must have been his eyesight. A historian, a biographer is at the mercy of primary documents, faded scripts and heavy tomes that must be scrutinized. A novel is not inordinately dependent on other people's scrawl. In fact a novel, an epic, a poem, even late memoirs such as his friends Max Müller and John Skelton would write, can be accomplished under strict doctor's orders to rest tired eyes. One wonders, however, if the many times "Colonel Goring" is called " Colonel Gordon" in *The Two Chiefs of Dunboy* is more of an unconscious slip linking Jamaica to Ireland than simply misprints overlooked by an author having trouble with his eyes. For a second main impetus inspiring this late novel and the short biography of Benjamin Disraeli that came after it was Froude's looking within himself at the age of seventy, twelve years before the end of his century, to question what his countrymen had made of the modern English nation, which began with Henry VIII and had arrived at empire.

Froude still held with Carlyle on Ireland; in fact he, too, believed that Cromwell and his Ironsides, who had in the mid-seventeenth century almost completely subdued Ireland through the slaughter of so many Irish troops and civilians, would in the long run have provided the country with the moral stability it lacked. More Protestantism, not less, was needed there.

A decade previously he'd written quite a fine, short biography, *John Bunyan,* for the English Men of Letters series. It is as good an introduction to that evangelical Protestant and his times as one finds. Yet again, the roots of interest stemmed from childhood censure. In "The Oxford Counter-Reformation" he recalled that all forms of dissent were a crime at his home. His father was too solid a man to be carried off his feet. His brother Hurrell parodied the evangelicals he found among the Church of England clergy as silly fellows who turned up the whites of their eyes and said, "Lawd." No copy of *Pilgrim's Progress* was allowed at Dartington Parsonage.

He was more than sorry that he hadn't access to *Pilgrim's Progress* until he was a grown-up. This was the book he read to his children while in mourning in Salcombe after Henrietta's death. For theoretical speculations about the church and the sacraments went into his head, but never to his heart. "I fancy, perhaps idly, that I might have escaped some trials and some misfortunes if my spiritual imagination had been allowed food which would have agreed with it."

Now he grouped Calvinists, Huguenots, Puritans, together as the "fighting Protestants." Without them, he came to believe, the Pope and Philip II would have crushed the Reformation. Erasmus—on whom he also wrote—saw issues more logically, but "Intellect fights no battle, Reason is no match for Superstition, and one emotion can only be conquered by another."

He said it had been Carlyle who brought him to an understanding of Knox and Calvin, and a few years after Jane's death, Froude had written a long essay on Calvinism. It came out of that lecture he delivered at St. Andrews after the Scottish students surprised him by enthusiastically electing him rector. In 1871, he published it in *Short Studies on Great Subjects.* He told his readers as he told the students, that in a high transcendental sense he believed Calvinism to be true. Free will was an illusion. Man had no hand in determining his own fate. He took this as an observable fact; he wasn't handling it in the theological sense. "All is as it is ordered to be." There was no lilt in the voice for this *Qué sera sera.*

Perhaps fiction was the only form left in which one could champion Cromwellian Ireland by 1888. *The Two Chiefs of Dunboy* presented the clash between two strong characters. The expatriate Irishman is the historical Morty O'Sullivan (not the generic one of his "A Fortnight in Kerry"), who became a military officer in France and who Froude thought might actually have fought with the Pretender. His opposite is the English colonial administrator of O'Sullivan's native Kerry, Colonel

Goring. Goring commands a colony of dissenting Protestant workers, and his sense of duty makes him attempt to uphold the letter of the law in lawless Ireland. He clashes not only with Morty O'Sullivan, who believes him the cause of his family's ruin, but with his own government, which has adopted dishonest policies that will eventually force Goring's honest Cromwellian Protestant dissenters to leave their well-run copper mines. They had asked only for a school and a church of their own persuasion and were told on the highest authority they could establish them if they lied concerning their use. The government would turn a blind eye.

In many ways Froude's third-person narration in *The Two Chiefs of Dunboy* is effective and is a progression in his talent as a novelist, yet at the same time it points out a limitation to this talent, which he imposed upon himself. He was a man who could understand many points of view, yet either consciously or unconsciously he seemed almost stubbornly averse to seeing things through the eyes of or entering into the consciousness of one of the two chiefs of Dunboy—Irish O'Sullivan.

The novel begins in eighteenth-century France, where we see how the Irish prosper once they leave Ireland, and see, too, that English tariffs have purposely ruined the Irish woolen trade. As a result the Irish almost of necessity smuggle woolens into France and liquor out of it, while government officials are expected to look the other way. But rather than have the first fifty pages or so narrated through the mind or sensibility of the daring, brave, and bitter O'Sullivan, one of the two protagonists of the novel, Froude overuses dialogue. Having one character occasionally tell another he is long-winded does not make certain passages less restrictive in emotional impact. As the plot develops, dialogue flows naturally, helping to build the suspense, but it is a drag on the beginning of the book. The situation is presented more or less through Protestant Colonel Goring's eyes, though the author is quite aware that the rigidness of Goring's moral values will impede him in the long run. But one does not feel a psychological constraint in drawing his readers or himself close to this character. Goring seems less distant, if more severe.

Morty O'Sullivan at times portrays Froude's point of view—the old Froudean device of having criticism come from the criticized. An example is O'Sullivan's portrayal of Goring and his Protestant workers: O'Sullivan, secretly back in Kerry, pushes his books from him and leans back in his carved oak chair to tell us that Cromwell's Ironsides if nothing else were real men. They might have been bigots and heretics, but they lived for a cause, they believed in what they called their God. There were ten Irishmen for every one of them, but according to Morty O'Sullivan, that extraordinary Irish Catholic, Cromwell's ruthless massacre of his people was the result of a fair fight. Those who came after Cromwell were inferior men. In fact, these now hinted they wished to put Goring with his staunch Cromwellian ways out of commission for doing a good job. O'Sullivan's people were lucky there were no other post-Cromwellian Gorings to send to Ireland.

The most memorable passage in the book occurs the only time we do see Ireland directly through O'Sullivan's eyes. It was inspired by Froude's love of Kerry. Those summers at Derreen with Henrietta had been his happiest days. John Skelton remembered it all, including the time during one visit when the two friends came upon a *rath*, an old abandoned underground dwelling. Skelton pictured Froude on his hands and knees opening it up, only to fall in. "The great historian disappeared from our gaze into the bowels of the earth, and reappeared—heavens! if all the mud that the *Saturday Review* has cast at him had *stuck*, he could not have presented a more appalling spectacle."

The year before Carlyle's death Froude was once more tempted back to the Kenmare river, and wrote Skelton he had half decided to go there: "If a Paddy shoots me—well, it will be dying in harness, and I, for my part, shouldn't so much care." That was a line worthy of Colonel Goring. Then, the very year he wrote *The Two Chiefs of Dunboy*, Anthony was offered another chance of vacationing there. Memories of his happiness with Henrietta did what the threat of assassination hadn't—made him literally fear a return to what had been. Instead, Froude drew unusually close to O'Sullivan as the Irishman mused, walking along the shore Froude had known through so many years. The tide was out and O'Sullivan passed a boat high and dry on the beach, men clearing her bottom of shell and weed. A small boy who would one day become chief of the O'Sullivans watched the men scrub with childish interest when he was not chasing crabs along the wet sand. Then an almost cinematic sweep and a prose that emulates ebb and flow:

"For how many ages had the bay and the rocks, and the mountains, looked exactly the same as they were looking then? How many generations had played their part on the same stage, eager and impassioned as if it had been created only for them! the half-naked fishermen of forgotten centuries who had earned a scanty living there; the monks from the Skelligs who had come in on high days in their coracles to say mass for them, baptize the children or bury the dead; the Celtic chief with saffron shirt and battle axe, driven from the richer lands by Norman or Saxon invaders, and keeping hold in this remote spot on his ragged independence; the Scandinavian pirates, the overflow of the Northern Fiords, looking for new soil where they could take root. These had all played their brief parts there and were gone, and as many more would follow in the cycles of the years that were to come, yet the scene itself was unchanged and would not change. The same soil had fed those that were departed, and would feed the others that were to be. The same landscape had affected their imaginations with its beauty or awed them with its splendours; and each alike had yielded to the same delusion that the valley was theirs and was inseparably connected with themselves and their fortunes."

Equally memorable is Froude's portrayal of Dublin with all its light-hearted society and intrigues. The Muslim Achmet with his peculiar English has become a darling of the society because of the Turkish baths he has established. Basing his account on "Personal Sketches of Sir Joseph Barrington," Froude really had a good time portraying the scene in which members of the Irish Parliament have a riotous night of hard drinking at Achmet's baths that leads them to almost drown in said waters. As Achmet rushes to save them his accent abruptly changes. No Muslim he, Achmet is really one Patrick Joyce. All this while Biddy, the Irishwoman he loves but who cannot marry a Turk, secretly watches from the gallery. "Ah, ye false thief!" she screams. "And ye tould me it was a circumcised haythen that ye were, and ye'd the Sultan for your godfather, and if I married ye, I'd be a Princess at worst. It is tear your eyes out, I will, when I can catch ye, ye desaving villain." Froude doesn't use dialect often, but when he does, he has an ear.

Then the drunk parliamentarians form a mock court to try the Muslim manqué with the chief justice presiding. There is reason for pardon: "It was remembered that his baths and his rooms would be none the worse because he was Patrick Joyce, and not the Sultan's barber." He is sentenced to down a pint of brandy without flinching to prove he is a Christian. Other penalties are imagined. "Henry Flood, who liked to show off his acquaintance with the East, proposed that Achmet, in Turkish costume, should ride a donkey through the streets with his face to the tail, and Pat Joyce pinned, in large letters, on his back. Hely Hutchinson suggested that the adventure should be entered in the Journals of the House of Commons, as a lesson against further grants in aid." Eventually the court agrees on the verdict of guilty, with good intentions, and they all sign a round robin to Biddy, recommending mercy for Pat

Joyce on the grounds he is a decent lad with a good Irish name and she had previously professed that was exactly what she had wanted to make of her Turk. Even the earnest Colonel Goring is too diverted by the evening to be able to moralize over it. Ditto the earnest Froude. "Ireland's fortunes might be committed to a singular set of legislators, but Goring had never met with more entertaining companions."

Ultimately, however, both Goring and O'Sullivan meet their fate—both through the treachery of the same man. Goring's earnest attempt to stymie smugglers, collect the taxes he is supposed to, and to uphold law and order brings him to ruin. His colony of honest dissenters, who have manned the copper mines so well, realize they cannot practice their religion openly, and immigrate—where else?—to the United States.

Goring's young cousin Fitzherbert visits the colony before the sober Protestants disperse. He has heard much of the dissenters, and has Froude's childhood idea that modern nonconformists are fanatical and not always honest, though they are in a sense too absurd to be dangerous. Yet at Dunboy he finds an earnest set of people with convictions that turn them into strong, resolute men of powerful character. He previously thought such phrases as their "taking counsel with God," and talking about "God's purpose for them," were downright silly (as had Hurrell Froude). He finds they've had real meaning and that plain men—farmers, seamen, mechanics—have an inflexibility of purpose and indifference to personal gain that make them exceptions to every other kind of human being he has previously encountered. No wonder the English government doesn't want them to succeed. "If Cromwell left Ireland covered over with such communities as yours, which I suppose he did, the Viceroys, and Peers, and Bishops, who were set to govern with the modern commercial code, would have had an uneasy time of it."

"There was something in the Calvinist creed that made them what they were," Froude wrote to Skelton. Like the early Christians, the Calvinists abhorred lies and they'd have nothing to do with false idols. Knox embodied this and Froude thought Knox right. Of course it had all gone to squash in the present day, though it remained in the English nature in different forms. Recently two English sailors had refused to kiss a mandarin's toe in China, even on pain of death, though the kissing was a formality: "Yet one feels it was better for the poor men to die than do so."

Froude couldn't tell whether or not he should publish his novel. It was off his regular line of work, he said, and he wasn't able to judge its merits, whether it was good or bad or a dead failure. He hoped he hadn't stepped on anyone's corns this time, he told Skelton, adding that "You alone of all my friends have been able hitherto to differ from me without flying into a passion!" Not that he cared what most people say. "The pleasure to me is in the writing of the book." And with that he sent the novel off to both Skelton and Lord Derby. One wonders what they thought about Cromwell and his Ironsides being stubbornly offered as a solution for Ireland's contemporary problems. Both said they were amused by the novel and thought others might be as well. Froude took that as good news. He wrote to Skelton in the spring of 1889 from his home, "The Moult," in Salcombe: "I wanted comfort, for I have been out of condition all spring—ever since Christmas indeed; and when one can't sleep, and lies tumbling about all night, the Devil has one at advantage."

He had felt better while writing his Irish story. But it took a lot out of him. He said he had to draw upon his capital to finish it. Afterward, he seemed to break down altogether, though there was nothing more definite the matter with him other than feeling an all-around general failure. Sometimes he was well enough. At other times his tongue was like a strip of yellow blanket. He had a constant pain in his side and unexplained aches that suggested disagreeable possibilities. By August, "*Gastric Catarrh* as they call it hangs over me ready to enter in again and take possession if I think about anything." He gave up another sail to Norway with Lord Ducie, afraid of spoiling his friend's enjoyment.

He describes himself at Salcombe crawling about in the garden in front of his big house on the hill, of not sailing himself but being taken out in a sailboat. Really radical for such an old salt. "I have the sense, quite new to me, of being used up mind and body. I can think about nothing."

His notable physical resiliency returned by the end of 1889. Rather miraculously, he felt better than he had in years. In November he left his retreat at Salcombe for London and his usual round of things, though he had vowed to go to no more dinners.

He didn't know if he would have gone back at all to the city except for the fact that he had been requested to write a short biography of Benjamin Disraeli, who had died short months after Carlyle. *The Earl of Beaconsfield* was to appear in the Prime Minister series, and Froude decided to accept the commission. Disraeli's brother Ralph promised to help him, as did the Duke of Rutland. And Lord Rothschild was helpful as well. The project would give him an opportunity of saying many of the things he wished to about "modern Liberalism and the universal disintegration which Lord Beaconsfield saw *clearer than any one*." He entirely disagreed with Disraeli's policy toward Russia and his upholding of the Turks, as well as his "Peace with Honour, and all that." But he believed

Disraeli understood the social and political condition of England more clearly than anyone else, even more clearly than Carlyle.

At the end of the biography of Carlyle's *Life in London,* Froude wrote that Carlyle's "dislike for Disraeli was perhaps aggravated by his dislike of Jews. He had a true Teutonic aversion for that unfortunate race."

One day when Anthony and Carlyle were walking, Carlyle stopped opposite Rothschild's great house at Hyde Park Corner and looked at it for a while. Then he said: "I do not mean that I want King John back again, but if you ask me which mode of treating these people to have been the nearest to the will of the Almighty about them—to build them palaces like that, or to take the pincers for them, I declare for the pincers."

Then Carlyle imagined himself King John, with the Baron Rothschild on the bench before him. "Now, sir, the State requires some of those millions you have heaped together with your financing work.

"You won't?

"Very well"—and he gave a twist with his wrist—"Now will you?"

And then another twist, until Rothschild gave up the millions.

The incident is presented without comment, but in the biography of Disraeli, Froude is quite succinct: "Carlyle detested Jews."

The Earl of Beaconsfield begins awkwardly; the first two pages are a long quote from Carlyle against Disraeli, that "superlative Hebrew conjuror spell-binding all the great lords, great parties, great interests of England." The reader can easily get caught up in and confused by the unusual language so unlike Froude's. But by the third page things fall into place. Seven years after Disraeli's passage of the Reform Bill, which precipitated Carlyle's reactionary "Shooting Niagara," even Carlyle had some small pleasure in Disraeli's accession to power in 1874. "He was even anxious that I should myself accept a proposal of a seat in Parliament which had been made to me, as a *quasi* follower of Disraeli."

Not only that, Carlyle had actually been touched with some compunction when the prime minister offered him honors, knighthood, pension, as the supreme man of letters, offering them in terms more exalted than Carlyle could possibly have imagined. Carlyle did not accept. (The only official honor Carlyle ever accepted was the Prussian Order of Merit.) "But he was affected by the recognition that of all English ministers the Hebrew conjuror should have been the only one who had acknowledged his services to his country." It was a typical trait of Disraeli's as Froude portrayed him, and it exemplified Froude's political shrewdness as well. He never hated and he never held grudges. He gave the devil his due. Even in his novels, good and bad happens, and good and bad men and women go to the same dinner parties and balls.

Both Carlyle and Froude looked beyond themselves for the hero to worship; Disraeli found the Carlylean Great Man in himself—and that made all the difference. The underlying reason why Froude wrote this short and quite fascinating character study was that he saw in Disraeli the very characteristics he did not find in himself. And he had the humility to admire, not detest, a man who had the very strengths he felt he lacked. The Hebrew more than the Calvinist, Disraeli more than Carlyle, reflected Froude's political hopes for England.

All Froude's biographies are of those whose lives and ideas in one way or another affected his own. In Disraeli he found an objective correlative that seemed to lift him out of himself and contribute to his return to health. Here was an extraordinary man who had none of the advantages of birth that Froude had, who as a brave-hearted and incorrigible boy confronted many of the same bullies, not because of any inherent weakness in character or physique, for he would have been their leader had he not been born a Jew. Yet rather than succumbing to the self-hatred and cowardice that Froude saw in his own youth and that had come back to haunt him after the Carlyle controversy, Disraeli had from the beginning—and never lost—his strong and confident sense of self. Hero worship was in the air. Well, young Ben was going to be the hero.

His father, Isaac Disraeli, was a well-known writer of scholarly habit. Byron was a great admirer of his *Curiosities of Literature*. And his work *Genius of Judaism* was influential as well. Froude studied it carefully. When Benjamin Disraeli's grandfather died and Isaac came into his inheritance, he converted with his family to the Church of England. He did it so that his children could enter English life and succeed in the world. He himself was not worldly. Benjamin Disraeli was ten at the time and accepted Christianity as the natural flowering of Judaism. He became a communicant of the Church of England without ever losing his pride in his heritage. Still, in England a Jew was a foreigner, an outsider, no matter his religion, his church attendance—or the fact he was born in Bloomsbury. Disraeli himself was actually quite English in the way he romanticized his Asiatic heritage and saw himself as some mysterious wanderer. On the other hand, as a political thinker, he, no less than Froude, found in the English past the moral resources with which to nourish his country.

Young Ben had emotional advantages over Froude. He was the eldest son and had not only a mother but one who doted on him. His father was kind and scholarly and part of an elite literary circle. He saw his son's worth, and had great hopes for his success—in law. Yet Ben was an unruly, noisy, daring child, loved and spoiled, and his parents felt he must go to school at an early age. But it was not easy to decide where. Froude wrote from hard-earned experience: "English boys were rough and prejudiced, and a Jewish lad would be likely to have a hard time among them. No friend of Isaac Disraeli, who knew what English public schools were then like, would have recommended him to commit his lad to the rude treatment which he would encounter at Eton or Winchester. A private establishment of a smaller kind had to be tried as preliminary."

His father wished after that to send him to Eton and then on to university, but "his mother believed that a public school was a place where boys were roasted alive." She had a point. According to Froude, there were no institutions where prejudice had freer play at the beginning of the nineteenth century than the English public school. "The nationality of a Disraeli could neither be concealed nor forgotten, and though he might be called a Christian, and though he might be ready to return blow for blow if he were insulted or ill-used, it is not likely that at either one of our great public foundations he would have met with any tolerable reception. He would himself have willingly run the risk, and regretted afterwards, perhaps, that he had no share in the bright Eton life which he describes so vividly in *Coningsby*." In fact, young Ben's response to bullies was quite different from young Anthony's, and how Anthony must have admired it. Ben learned to box.

Disraeli was a fighter from his youth, first with his fists and later with his tongue. It was absolutely characteristic of him that he studied the art of self-defense and was able as a boy to protect himself. From the beginning his sense of destiny was unwavering. His aim in life was to become the man he knew he could be. Even more extraordinary, he did it his way. He never even attempted to alter his temperament in order to fit in.

As a young man, he was Carlyle's greatest nightmare, a quintessential Dandy. He traveled around the world in his pleated shirts, velvet waistcoats, and colored stockings. With his long hair in curls, "I have also the fame of being the first who ever passed the Straits with two canes, a morning and an evening cane," he wrote home to his mother. "But this was Disraeli—a character genuine and affectionate, whose fine gifts were veiled in foppery which itself was more than half assumed."

For all his fine gifts, his aims seemed impossible. He wanted to be a leader of men. Though he had no land, no "English blood," no pocket borough to ease the way, he was able—finally—to be elected to Parliament. His maiden speech was drowned out. The elaborate oratory of the hustings was not the language of the House of Commons. But he didn't know that yet. His affected expressions that would have been welcome on the campaign trail caused his maiden speech to be received with scorn and laughter that was so loud that he finally realized he would not be able to go on above the hubbub. He paused and then, in a loud and remarkable voice that astounded even those "noisy hounds who were barking the loudest," he made his prophetic declaration: "I will sit down now, but the time will come when you will hear me."

That they will, Dicky Milnes said when Disraeli returned to his seat by his side.

When it came to the question of admitting Jews to Parliament, Disraeli argued no Exeter Hall righteous toleration, he made no excuses for his own Jewish point of view. Christianity was the flowering of the Hebrew religion. To deny Jews entrance into Parliament was to deny Christianity itself. Froude remarked, "He may be said to have brought the Jews into Parliament a quarter of a century before they would otherwise have been admitted there, for the Conservatives left to themselves would have opposed their admission to the end." For a man like Froude who never trusted despondency—even, or perhaps especially, his own— writing this biography of a man as strong as Disraeli was curative.

Disraeli was not born into power, he was not an advocate of any popular measure that had his name on it. "He rose by his personal qualifications alone, and in studying what those qualifications were we are studying the character of Parliament itself." Froude found in Disraeli's early foppishness a useful form of self-protection, a way of joining the world yet protecting himself. It was the major clue to his inner self: "The stripling of seventeen was the same person as the statesman of seventy, with this difference only, that the affectation which was natural in the boy was itself affected in the matured politician, whom it served well as a mask or as a suit of impenetrable armour."

Disraeli did not believe any more than Carlyle that the greatness of a nation depended on material possessions. "He did not believe in a progress which meant the abolition of the traditionary habits of the people, the destruction of the village industries, and the accumulation of the population into enormous cities, where their character and their physical qualities would be changed and would probably degenerate. The only progress he could acknowledge was moral progress, and he considered that all legislation which proposed any other object to itself would produce, in the end, the effects which the prophets of his own race had uniformly and truly foretold."

The biography, besides drawing a psychological and political profile, offers an insight into Disraeli's novels by a contemporary who not only understood but experienced much of the same society and saw the truth of his times in Disraeli's re-creation of an aristocracy of fabulous wealth, sublime manners, and nonchalant duplicity. In Disraeli's novels, dining tables literally groan under the weight of an infinite variety of foods, heavy china, precious crystal. In the glimmering surface and style of fabulous characters at home in their magnificent renovated "Piles" (one of Disraeli's favorite words), what might seem overblown pictures of sumptuosity to later, more proletarian generations was, in certain circles, the way things were.

When Disraeli wrote, Froude described the English aristocracy as being at the absolute height of their magnificence. The industrial age had doubled their already princely fortunes without their having to lift a finger. They were at the top of the world and were objects of universal homage—"partly a vulgar adulation of rank, partly the traditionary reverence for their order, which had not yet begun to wane. Though idleness and flattery had done their work to spoil them, they retained much of the characteristics of a high-born race. Even Carlyle thought that they were the best surviving specimens of the ancient English. But their self-indulgence had expanded with their incomes. Compared with the manners of the modern palace or castle, the habits of their grandfathers and grandmothers had been frugality and simplicity: they had no duties—or none they had been taught to understand. So they stand before us in *Lothair*." Finally Froude could and did offer an analysis of the novel he considered one of the best of his times.

No personal scandals emerge in this biography of Disraeli. Froude gave the same reason he gave in *Caesar,* where the reader is even deprived of the love affair with Cleopatra. The only gossip he allowed about Caesar was that as a young man he was a lion among the ladies (and vaguely, the lads). A dashing figure, he wore his girdle loose and low at the Forum. And later in life his laurel crown served a useful purpose. Caesar liked that it hid his baldness. In Disraeli there is no hint of his early mistress. And his marriage to the older widow that afforded him a larger sphere is handled with the respect Disraeli felt for her and what she had done for him, despite her rather unpolished ways. In both *Caesar* and *The Earl of Beaconsfield,* the reason Froude gave for the lack of indiscretions was that there were no records to document the rumors. He was more than happy to ignore unsubstantiated human folly.

Queen Victoria, by the way, adored Disraeli, allowing him to sit in her presence. Gladstone she loathed, and he had to stand while his politics and his deliberations drove her to distraction. Disraeli requested a title for the pleasure of his extremely devoted wife, and Queen Victoria made her the Viscountess Beaconsfield. Eight years later, in 1876, Disraeli entered the House of Lords, Victoria having made him the Earl of Beaconsfield.

What is remarkable for our purposes about *The Earl of Beaconsfield* is the light it throws on Froude, who, during a time when the nightmares of self-hate returned, found some sort of aesthetic and philosophic comfort in portraying the life of a man who had no inherent physical cowardice that had to be overcome. A man who was not to Eton and Oxford born, who, despite unimaginable hurdles to success in his society, found his lost leader in himself and rose—not only to novels that rank very close to the best of the period, but to prime minister of the country that would always consider him a foreigner.

"Disraeli's life was a romance. Starting with the least promising beginning, with a self-confidence which seemed like madness to everyone but himself, his origin a reproach to him and his inherited connections the least able to help him forward on the course which he had chosen, he had become, at a comparatively early age, by the mere force of his personal genius, the political chief of the proudest aristocracy in the world."

Froude maintained in *The Earl of Beaconsfield* his long-held belief that one could write only about a subject one knew from the inside out. And the clue to Disraeli's inner life, as Froude saw it, was his growing ability to use affectation as a persona, a body armor that protected him personally while it allowed him to persevere and triumph against extraordinary odds in the public sphere. The biography gives us a glimpse as well of Froude, who also traveled in the highest circles and could capture the surge of the moment as it passed:

"They came to call him Dizzy; and there is no surer sign that a man is liked in England than the adoption of a pet name for him. His pungent sayings were repeated from lip to lip. He never courted popular demonstrations, but if he was seen in the streets he was followed by cheering crowds. At public meetings which had no party character he was the favourite of the hour. At a decorous and dignified assembly where royalties were present, and the chiefs of both political parties, I recollect a burst of emotion when Disraeli rose which, for several minutes, prevented him from speaking, the display of feeling being the more intense the lower the strata which it penetrated, the very waiters whirling their napkins with a passion which I never on any such occasion saw exceeded or equaled."

This was the man, as Froude pointed out along with its irony, who came closest to the Carlylean ideal while understanding English politics and society better than the Sage of Chelsea himself. Disraeli personified the otherwise unimaginable for Froude—the hero as parliamentarian.

The Earl of Beaconsfield allows us an important contrast between Froude and Carlyle. There is no doubt that Carlyle was Froude's acknowledged mentor, in spiritual terms his lifelong guide, and that in his public life Froude saw himself as Carlyle's emissary. But they each took the same principles to different ends. Carlyle's antidemocratic sensibilities, combined with his attitudes toward Prussian military might, not to mention his views on slavery and his own early *"Arbeit macht Frei"* repeated ad infinitum in *Past and Present,* are proto-fascistic. All of Carlyle's own works, including Froude's biography of him with Carlyle's anti-Semitic aside concerning Rothschild, were immediately translated into German. The battle scenes from his *Frederick the Great* became required parts of the curriculum in German military schools, as soon as they were published. Froude prophesied that Carlyle would be better appreciated in the future. He was. By the Third Reich. That was where his ideas ended up. It is not without reason that Hitler required sections of *Frederick the Great* be read to him in the bunkers.

Froude's and Disraeli's conservatism, and their respect for Carlyle, was based on conserving old English values of noble obligation, of duty and responsibility, of merry old feudalistic England, where everyone had enough beef to eat, a place to sleep even if in strange surroundings, in days when social strata were clearly defined. Perhaps a Jew, a "foreigner" such as Disraeli, had a better perspective from which to view England's earlier genius—or to be blinded by the glitter of the ideal of feudalism. The same could be said of Froude, who as a young man had turned himself into an outsider before he could appreciate what was lost.

But what about Froude's treatment of the black man, was it all Don Quixote as a Cook's Tourist? Dunn, in an endnote, pointed to passages in *The English in the West Indies* that betray a certain understanding: Froude wrote he came to the opinion long ago in Africa that there were no inherent differences between black and white men. "With the same chances and the same treatment, I believe that distinguished men would be produced equally from both races." But it didn't follow that this could be done immediately. Giving the Negroes the same political powers as the English claimed for themselves would only injure them and aid their sliding back into a primitive condition. After all, his own

"Anglo Norman race has become capable of self-government only after a thousand years of civil and spiritual authority." Before the civil rights movement in America in the 1960s, many Americans who considered themselves nominally liberal thought it would take a hundred years for blacks to find equality. In a young country, a hundred years compares with Froude's thousand. In both it was simply a very long time away. At least it was a far cry from Carlyle's reactionary tolerance of slavery, though one does not wish to make too much a point of it.

What is more central to Froude's vision and reputation is that through his eccentric, often quixotic diplomacy and the passion of his writings, he led his people to see the energy and renewal to be found in emigration, as has been pointed out. He hated war, but his belief that the English-speaking colonies—and he still included the United States among them—would band together at such times of chaos has so far not been disproved. Opposing Gladstone, he made England more conscious of the moral worth of a vital relationship between the colonies and the motherland. "Oceana has accomplished an actual thing,—a good thing I hope," Froude wrote in 1886. "The Colonies are to have the English Flag again with the bar sinister wiped out. The Colonial office paper told me this last night."

Froude underestimated the worth of *The Earl of Beaconsfield*. He wrote it at a time when the old disgust of his first thirty years had returned—in spades. Before the publication of the Carlyle biography Froude was asked by Longman for permission to republish *The Nemesis of Faith*, and he thought of doing it for a while. Now he wrote to Max Müller, "I often dream of it all, and hate myself." It was not the subject matter of his early spiritual autobiography that plagued him. Things had so changed in England by the 1890s that a reason for republication would have been to show younger generations how different the first half of the century was, and how a book that ruined a young man's prospects in 1849 would hardly raise an eyebrow forty years later. It was the disgrace Froude had caused his father by his portrayal of him in *Shadows of the Clouds,* by the scandal of an archdeacon's son writing *Nemesis,* by being expelled from Oxford, by "dropping the 'Rev'd'" from his name. Freeman and other detractors were not alone in remembering. Froude, too, simply could not forgive himself.

During these later years, Froude revisited the past. At Bassenthwaite visiting cousins he saw his mother's old house and stared at the lime tree on which she had carved her initials when a girl. They were still visible, this remaining sign of the mother who had died before his own memory began. There *he* stood by the old lime tree, the only other trace of her left in the world besides those initials.

He wanted to provide some sort of fitting memorial for all of them, his parents and his siblings who died before their time. They had all been buried in the vault attached to the old Dartington church with a decent rail around the spot and a tablet to commemorate their existence. Churches were being renovated by the close of the nineteenth century, and when he went to the spot, he found the burying place obliterated and no one could tell him where it had once been. "The return to oblivion is necessary and in itself not to be complained of—but the process in this case has been rude and rapid." It struck him forcibly that the venerable archdeacon was no longer remembered.

After all, this was Devonshire, his native country, where the name Froude, so rare elsewhere, could be seen on many a headstone in many a parish. Looking at some of those markers in the churchyards of his region, he found he rather liked the sense of being gathered to his own kin. In this he echoed Jane Carlyle when she revisited the churchyard of Haddington during the years of her desperation.

In the summer of 1889, having completed *The Two Chiefs of Dunboy*, he visited a church in Devon that his father had built. He was too ill to walk to the top of the hill to see what had become of it. Fifty years previously he had been there when his father consecrated it. But in a later era, in which architectural style had been thoroughly influenced by the Oxford Movement, and Gothic Revival was the order of the day, the venerable archdeacon was found behind the times. They had pulled down his Protestant church to set up one with a chancel. Even though Anthony realized its loss was no particular architectural deprivation, he wished the Devil would fly away with all the new mason work and let things be as his father had left them. It might have been that summer that he decided to be buried in Devon, in seafaring Salcombe with its hills and wide estuary, where his small yacht was moored and where he found peace away from London.

From Salcombe, as similar to the French Riviera as England gets, in its aspect and often in its climate, a few weeks before his seventy-third birthday, Froude sadly witnessed nature's turbulence, the great blizzard of March 1891. "Four ships were wrecked almost in sight of our windows, and fifty or sixty poor fellows drowned, or lost in the snow after they had struggled ashore. The bodies are even now being discovered as it melts off. Life is very tragic—in spite of political economy and a reformed House of Commons."

I have begged that when I die not a word may be written or said about me that my children can help. And if ever mortal wished for utter oblivion that mortal is I.

—J.A.F.

The Revolution in My Affairs

By the age of seventy-three, there was nothing left for Froude but to sum up. He decided that all private letters to him and from him should be destroyed at his death, or if some remained in the family, they should be destroyed before the deaths of his children. This exactitude was a lesson he learned only too well through Carlyle's inability to take responsibility for his own papers and it was professed by Anthony with a vengeance that might have bordered on the destructive. Those friends who did not destroy his letters, such as Olga Novikoff and John Skelton, were careful of them. Madame Novikoff allowed passages from them to be reprinted in her biography, and Skelton, luckily, did the same at greater length. Ruskin kept Froude's letters, and they have been well edited and published.

When Anne E. Ireland—a writer, lecturer, and daughter of a celebrated biblical scholar, Dr. John Nicholson—wrote to Froude hoping to gain his help on her proposed biography of Jane Welsh Carlyle, he replied coldly. He would soon recant and explain that "my caution was due merely to my regarding you merely as a stranger who had been interested in the story, and I myself have been and am so violently and passionately condemned for having published the Jane Welsh Memoirs that I advise every one who consults me on the subject not to invite me to cooperate unless they wish to draw on themselves the irritation which at present attaches to me exclusively."

The stranger was actually the second wife of the ex-publisher and business manager of the *Manchester Examiner,* Alexander Ireland, a friend of Carlyle and Emerson, and the couple were parents of the future composer John Ireland. Mr. Ireland was one of those displeased by Froude's publication of the memoirs. "Perhaps Mr. Ireland now thinks differently," Froude remarked with appropriate irony. "At any rate I *could* not act otherwise than I did. Pray remember me to him as warmly as he will allow." Ireland had business problems and money worries at the time. In 1886 the *Manchester Guardian* became a supporter of home rule, and the *Examiner*'s liberal supporters went over to that paper. Readership declined and his *Examiner* lost money, passed into other hands, and soon stopped publishing.

Mrs. Ireland, though only in her forties, was suffering from a disease of the heart that she fought valiantly in the last years of her truncated life, while writing the biography of Jane Welsh Carlyle and editing the letters of Geraldine Jewsbury in Froude's possession, to which he allowed her access.

The eighteen unpublished letters to Mrs. Alexander Ireland as she and Froude discussed Mrs. Carlyle were not destroyed, and they give one a rare glimpse into Froude's empathetic kindness, that nurturing quality which many of his friends remarked: Mrs. Ireland was run-down and must take care of herself, he wrote in February 1890. John Bright once told him that the less a person really cared about a subject the better he could speak about it. It was idle for Froude to tell her not to care about Jane Carlyle; still, "Let feelings go their own way and attend first of all to your health."

Another edition of his life of Carlyle was being prepared, and he told her she'd be amused to hear that he had to apply through his lawyers in order to look at the sections of the letters he was accused of transcribing incorrectly.

If Mary and Alexander Carlyle would not let him look at them directly, "I have asked that some indifferent person may be allowed to go over the book with the originals." As executor he could have *"insisted"* on the records being returned, but he was still the gentleman. He preferred to request, and if they refused he would go along with the book as it stood. "I worked for ten years on the letters with a magnifying glass.

I revised the proof with the originals at hand. After the book was published I went over it again and corrected the few misprints which still remained." And in a later letter he mentioned again that Mary Carlyle would neither allow a third party to go over the manuscripts to correct his text nor would she send him a list of errata that he would use and acknowledge as hers. Nothing could be done without "referees to consider my whole treatment of the subject. I cannot submit to this for many reasons. Any referee that I might appoint would have to be informed of the whole story and this is out of the question."

Ill as she was, Mrs. Ireland came to London to lecture on Jane Welsh Carlyle at the end of March. Margaret couldn't attend because she was feverish. Froude could not for different reasons. He would be recognized, and if there was a discussion period after the lecture he might be forced to take part in it, something he wished to avoid—at least for the present. He read the text of Mrs. Ireland's lecture, however, proclaiming it clear, calm, exactly what it should be, "free from all gush and Rhetoric." As well as he knew Jane Carlyle, she had pointed out several things only a woman's eye could see. He added some valuable information without pointing attention to Mrs. Ireland's lacunae: "Geraldine told me that the first mortification after the marriage was a rough repulse." Jane offered Carlyle her help with his writings and he responded as if a mind like hers was incapable of understanding the great issues he was dealing with. "This was at the very outset."

The next month Froude wrote to Mrs. Ireland's husband with sympathy and hopes that Mrs. Ireland's high spirit and powerful constitution would ward off the enemy. He repeated to her husband what he had recently offered her—she being too ill to respond. His publishers were planning to bring out another edition of *The Letters and Memorials of Jane Welsh Carlyle* as soon as the biography was republished. He wanted to have Longman go forward with the biography itself, but with accustomed generosity he proposed postponing the *Letters and Memorials* until after Mrs. Ireland published her biography of Mrs. Carlyle. For Froude, "the present object is that Mrs. Ireland shall recover her health and shall be spared anxiety."

A month later, Mrs. Ireland still ailing, Froude offered the encouragement of knowing of cases like hers that doctors said were hopeless, yet life and strength returned and remained. It was the lecturing that had exhausted her. Not to mention that what he called the "fatal subject" occupying her mind seemed to blight everyone it touched. Let the subject go, he advised, at least until she returned to health. Last summer, "It drove poor Ruskin out of his wits, and he has not yet found his way into them again. Now it is your turn."

Coming out of a bout of madness, Ruskin decided to champion Froude rather than criticize him. Froude had been relieved. He knew Ruskin was thinking of writing something about the Carlyle biography, and Ruskin could be very severe. What might have mitigated against an attack on friend Froude was that Ruskin was more upset by how friend Charles Eliot Norton was acting. Norton had published a second volume of Carlyle's early letters, once more accusing Froude of moral and editorial failure, of having elaborated on facts "with the art of a practised romancer, in which assertion and inference, unsupported by evidence or contradictory to it, often takes the place of correct statement."

Ruskin had recently criticized Froude's *History* in print and earlier had blasted his essays on the English colonies—"I know more about the Colonies than you!" Ruskin's criticism never made a breach in Froude's respect for the man or stopped him from constant concern for Ruskin's health, or his care of Ruskin when it was possible. He had steeled himself for vituperation, which he insisted he would accept, but he was more than pleased when that storm passed. In fact, Ruskin asked him if he could reprint some things from Froude's letters.

At the end of Ruskin's episodic autobiography, *Praeterita,* begun when he gave up his Slade professorship at Oxford, he had a section of *Dilecta* in which he printed certain letters from friends. This Oxford bent toward clever Latin titles has done nothing to bring later generations to Ruskin's lively work. The autobiography was published in sections, and Froude wrote in appreciation of one of them: "I was going into residence at Oriel just when you went up to Christ Church. How vividly you bring the dead to life again! Where are they. Where is it all?"

The letter Ruskin wished to include in his next installment of *Dilecta* was one in which Froude mentioned Hurrell's throwing him into the river when he was a child in order to teach him to swim. "I have such an affectionate and reverend recollection of my eldest brother, notwithstanding his occasional rough handling of me,—he once held me by the legs and stirred the bottom of a ditch with my head—that I would rather not specify him to the public as having pitched me overboard.

"There was another of my brothers in the boat and I am not absolutely sure which of them tumbled me into the water—so let us cut out *eldest* and let *brothers* stand in the plural— But as to me, my character as a boy was a very miserable one—I don't know how I came by it. I have had hard work to mend it even a little, and I do not know that I have essentially succeeded, or indeed whether characters as such admit of mending."

Watch any man through life, he told Ruskin, and one sees that the fruit or flower he throws off year after year can be compared to the organic nature of the apple tree. "Born a crab one remains a crab, though the crab may recover a little from an originally misshaped growth and may become a better specimen of its own kind. In fact I detest *myself:* all life properly conducted is a deliverance from *self,* which is the real Devil and I look forward to the *end* as the final emancipation from bondage, which instead of fearing we ought to welcome."

If Ruskin planned to defend Anthony against Norton's continued assault on his reputation without straining his health, Anthony would consider it heaven-sent, "but you will only give me fresh grief if the interest or the excitement proves mischievous to you." He wrote to Ruskin's caregiving cousin Mrs. Severn to assure there was no danger. Throughout the summer he urged Ruskin not to exert himself. Why stir up that hornets' nest, which was active enough without further prodding? But Ruskin had already written three letters to his dearest Charles containing a series of twelve questions—wild and wacky—in defense of Froude, and he planned to publish them in the next installment of his *Dilecta.*

In this first letter, he used a series of preliminary questions to point out Norton's own misprints—and Norton was guilty of many. Truly, it tempts fate for any writer to make hay over another's typos. Then in the second letter he asked who put it in Norton's head that *he* could understand Carlyle better than Froude and Ruskin. What demon provoked him to write so despairingly of the most deliberate, learned, and religious of European historians? He went on to suggest, in an obviously manic mode, that if the days of dueling hadn't passed, Norton would pay.

There is no doubt that the letters were unbalanced, to say the least. Yet in the final letter, crazy as a fox, Ruskin hit the mark. He asked when Norton had been converted to Carlyle's theories. Which works had Norton studied to the most benefit, he wondered. "In your lectures at Cambridge, on what subjects do you now commend the teaching of Carlyle to your young Americans? On Slavery, Kinghood, Stump Oratory, Hudson's Statuary?—or on the Navigation of the Niagara?"

Norton, saddened by Ruskin's erratic state of mind, responded that Ruskin had given him even more pain than he could have wished to inflict. If Ruskin published these letters, Norton would neither answer his questions or defend himself. He would take the blame. He would allow no semblance of a controversy between them.

Mrs. Severn reported that information to Froude in a way that puzzled him. When Norton said he would take the blame, did that mean he was apologizing to Froude? If Norton thought he had done wrong, he ought to be sorry and to say so. Or if he thought himself in the right, he should explain and defend himself. But of course Froude didn't know the nature of the letters Ruskin wrote him.

Norton, privately, was anything but repentant when it came to Froude. He burned Ruskin's letters: "They were sad, insane outbursts of unbridled resentment at my exposure of Froude's violation of the trust imposed in him by Carlyle." He couldn't have known the letters had already been set in type. But Ruskin was too ill to go on with his *Dilecta,* and they were not published.

Poor Ruskin was not to have the beautiful sunset that Froude wished for him in letter after letter. To Mrs. Ireland, Froude confided, "Nothing is more tragic in the conditions of human life than the death of the mind of the man of genius, which his body survives as an automaton. Swift ended so, and Southey." And so would Ruskin, though Froude still hoped.

He then carefully read Mrs. Ireland's manuscript, *Life of Jane Welsh Carlyle,* and sent his editorial advice. After complimenting her on her tender and sympathetic handling of the "Tragedy" of Cheyne Row, he was obliged to criticize certain points. The first was Mrs. Ireland's hasty writing, with many words omitted and expressions that needed altering: "Remember that you are not writing for a Lecture or a Newspaper. You are writing a Memoir which is to remain and to be studied. I never print anything which I have not written over twice if not thrice, and I always find something to correct. I advise you at least to go over the MS again, pen in hand, and change and prune."

She didn't hint at the real grief at the heart of the matter: "Mrs Carlyle ought to have been a wife and a mother. She was neither. She might have left C. and married. She was strongly tempted." It was in this letter that Froude revealed he knew by whom, but would not name him. Mrs. Ireland leaves the impression that the only thing wrong with the marriage was the clash of temperament and temper. She could respond that Froude had done the same, and he would agree. But he hadn't sought the task that was laid upon him. "Had I undertaken to write Mrs. Carlyle's life myself I must have told the whole truth, or else when I found how the matter stood, have let it alone. I know that you cannot tell in plain words what was amiss, but you might indicate that there was only companionship."

Moreover, "as to the Home Life I miss something which ought to be mentioned. Mrs. Carlyle's nervous system was shattered to pieces."

Carlyle's "tremendous denunciations of everybody and everything, brilliant and intensely interesting as they were to occasional visitors, were unbearable to her who heard the same thing night after night. You indicate very well that he did not and could not understand how ill she was, but you rather *say* this than shew it. The Madhouse was more than a facile expression."

There was nothing guarded in the correspondence as Froude gave her seven points in all, careful and excellent editorial advice. Finally, "In what you say about *myself* I am of course very grateful to you but this I would have you shorten. Clough was immeasurably my superior. You mistake entirely our relative importance."

Mrs. Ireland revised as he suggested and by the end of the month he read the manuscript through again and considered it greatly improved. But again he insisted that for her own sake she must avoid any appearance of attempting to defend him. On every account it was better not to. "I can defend myself effectually if I am ever forced to do it."

It was springtime in Salcombe: "The flowers are coming out. The woods are white with a carpet of anemones and the hedges pink with a mixture of blue bells and crimson Robin. I would send you a basket but they would wither on the way." Despite the good weather, Froude found himself out of sorts once more, and had to give up going personally to the University of Edinburgh to receive an honorary degree, as he had wished.

Still, a month later we find him sailing about the Channel, for as he told Mrs. Ireland he was now feeling stronger than he had in years. Again the characteristic resiliency. He had gone back to his historical work, his life's work, he explained, that he had broken off to tend to Carlyle's papers. Reexamining the twelve volumes of *The History of England,* he unearthed twenty or so typographical errors, and only five substantive errors. Rather than revising the entire series as he had first planned, he found that they stood and it would be better to add a supplementary volume. He wrote *The Divorce of Catherine of Aragon* using newly discovered material that led him to reevaluate the first unfortunate queen and her claims on the throne. That summer as well, the lease on the Moult at Salcombe expired. He would try to buy it. Six months previously he had written of his thankfulness of having "a Molt to move to," even though it was, particularly given his Calvinistic worldview, a sinful extravagance. (He always spelled *the Moult* without the *u.*) Now everything was up in the air. His big house on the hill overlooking the Salcombe estuary and his docked "small yacht" were sold. He would move to another home in the vicinity.

After a shaky reception, Mrs. Ireland's book did well. "The critics know nothing of what they write about. Why should we care what they say?" Besides, "Gladstone's praise must be precious both to you and to Mr. Ireland." Gladstone was equally impressed, ironically enough, by Froude's interpretation of Disraeli.

The last August Froude and his family would spend at the Moult, they found that the dreadful snows of the blizzard of 1891 brought a mournful summer: "The corn rots in the field, the fruit rots unripened on the water and still the winds blow and the rain falls and there is no sign of change."

Froude felt "like a man who has been standing for ten years on the pillory to be pelted with rotten eggs & cabbage stalks. I have taken it all in absolute silence. All storms rage out at last." In that letter he told Mrs. Ireland the best news was that she herself had returned to a semblance of health, and that her heart (in all senses) was sound.

Apparently E. A. Freeman's heart was not. Seven months later, on March 16, 1892, Froude's most vituperative critic died suddenly in Spain. *Schadenfreude* was a term dear to Carlyle. However, one suspects that Froude, a month short of his seventy-fourth birthday, found little joy in the death of a man five years his junior whom he had met only once—on a platform where they both dealt with the Eastern Question from the Russian point of view. (Freeman soon changed his position.)

In Australia, eight years earlier, Froude thanked the colonists, comparing himself to Cinderella at the ball. If he had done anything worthwhile for them, he was prepared to return home and sit by the ashes. When he returned he found, as he told Mrs. Ireland: "The ashes under the life in Cheyne Row are still red hot. Throw water on them and they hiss out in steam, stir them and they burst into flame." Freeman's death, as Waldo Dunn pointed out, probably did nothing other than underscore Froude's own mortality, as he became more and more aware each day that though he had followed his conscience and done what he thought was right, his destiny was to end up always having done things badly. He would end his life as he began it, in the shadow of the clouds. Then, two weeks after Freeman's death, a letter arrived at Onslow Gardens that had all the sparkle of a magic wand:

Dear Mr Froude
    As you are doubtless aware, the Regius Professorship of Modern History at Oxford is vacant by Dr. Freeman's death. I write to you with some hesitation: for on the one hand it may be that you are thoroughly disinclined

for the duties of such a post—though they are not heavy. On the other hand, I do not like to sacrifice any chance of obtaining the services for Oxford of her most famous historian—a feeling to which a recent perusal of Catherine of Aragon *had naturally given great vividness. Pardon me if I have done wrong in asking you to allow me to submit your name to the Queen.*

In any case kindly consider this communication confidential for the present.

Yours very truly
Salisbury

Prime Minister Salisbury's appointment of Froude to replace the man who wished to disembowel him was political and pointed. To some it must have seemed halfway between a scandal and a joke—or to the Oxford-born, a delicious irony. It had actually been through Salisbury's stepmother (and Froude's encouragement through her) that Disraeli had once been urged to offer Carlyle honors. Now Salisbury was at the end of his second ministry, and once more it was his stepmother who urged him to provide her close friend of more than thirty years with a recognition he could enjoy. But did either Lady Derby or Salisbury truly believe that a seventy-four-year-old man would leave the kitchen fire, venture out into a chilly carriage, and go to the ball? Salisbury himself had asked Froude to keep the communication confidential for the moment. They might have thought the honor of being asked would suffice as a happy ending.

Froude didn't even hesitate. His first reaction was to write within the week to Skelton: "The temptation of going back to Oxford in a respectable way was too much for me. I must just do the best I can, and trust I shall not be haunted by Freeman's ghost." He was bidding goodbye to what he called quiet days and quiet work at his own fireside.

However, Froude soon realized that the duties Salisbury said would not be heavy would be astonishingly so, for the likes of him, and expressed second thoughts to his friends. The vice-chancellor (Salisbury was chancellor) and the council were not going to make it an easy return to respectability. Froude read the statutes of the college; the obligations of an Oxford professor had been largely increased since his day. One wonders if he was pointed in the direction of the statute book, or if a combination of cautionary experience added to age had made him take a long look at the letter of the law. In this new world of "new men"—and now "new women," too—professors had not only to lecture but to tutor students on subjects geared to the passing of exams.

Oxford was being turned into an examination mill. O, brave new world. He might very well change his mind, he told Ruskin, so do not spread news of his appointment yet. For if some accommodation could not be made, "I must ask Lord Salisbury to find another poor Slave who will be more Submissive."

One of the stipulations caused no difficulty at all for him: residence at Oxford. Actually, it had been his dream to leave London for Oxford since the first days of his and Henrietta's marriage when the same professorship was delivered—despite Salisbury and his stepmom—into the hands of a different enemy, Goldwin Smith. But the lecture load: He would be required to deliver *forty-two* lectures annually. It would have been a staggering number for one half his age, then and now—and an unthinkable demand for anyone else of Froude's stature. It was an offer made to be refused. He was too old to learn new things and had serious doubts—he phrased it more subtly to the authorities than he had to his friends—about whether to accept the nomination or place it back in Lord Salisbury's hands.

Froude half knew he would get nowhere with his special pleading to the vice-chancellor. Of course he pointed out that the authorities had used their dispensing powers to lighten Freeman's burden, but found it necessary to add, with his customary precise aim at his foot, that he himself could not claim ill health as Freeman had. On the contrary, he was as well and strong at seventy-four years of age as he could possibly hope to be. (He wasn't going to allow them to fault him due to age.) He told them that though the quality of his work hadn't fallen off, he could not reasonably do as much as he used to.

A photograph of him at the time shows him the same tall, handsome, strong-featured man, his hair and side whiskers turned gray to white, his look pensive. An interviewer that summer would visit him at Salcombe and report the sunburnt face and the muscular hands of the tall, well-knit figure, rather dapper in a loose-fitted suit of summer gray. It was impossible to realize he was talking with a seventy-four-year-old man. He was so full of vigor and energy as he spoke that he looked at least ten years younger. The reporter also noticed that ubiquitous long, faraway, almost wistful look and a combination of sadness and severity that played across his face.

By that summer, though he had threatened to place his nomination back in Salisbury's hand, J. A. Froude was Regius Professor of Modern History at Oxford. The vice-chancellor did not relieve him of his forty-two lectures a year, though he did not have to tutor students or directly deal with their examinations. Examinations and *athletics,* of all things. If he were younger he would try to mend the system, turn Oxford back to older ways. He knew that at his age it would be absurd to try. Still, one can almost hear him counsel himself to be reasonable. Ah, those building blocks of history. Forty-three years previously as a rebellious youth he had tried to make Oxford see the sense of new ways. Now he held himself back from storming the barricades as a conservative old man.

Though the authorities certainly would not make things easy for him, they had offered him advice similar to what the authorities in Dublin offered Colonel Goring when he traveled there to ask dispensation to build a chapel and school for his Protestant workers. No to his request for a lighter schedule, but once a professor he might suit himself in the way he implemented the statutes. As if an old dog like Froude would learn to cut corners and do less than his duty in the modern manner. Oxford had refused to do for him what they did for Freeman. Still, the position could be made into a sham if he so chose. "Like much else here, things are ordered for show to take the world in."

On June 16, 1892, Queen Victoria signed Froude's official appointment. He remarked it was the only honor from his country that he ever received.

Number 5 Onslow Gardens would be either let or sold. He had lived there for close to thirty years; one can only imagine the work it would take to pack up his study and his library, not to mention the rest of the house. It was not every man his age who would make such a late transition, even though his two daughters saw to everything. Ashley was building a career in service of the Royal Navy, and Froude was grateful that Margaret and May took the odious business off his shoulders. Perhaps he lacked not only the strength but the heart for removing all memories of those far-gone happy years when Henrietta was at his side.

Froude had never delivered a lecture he hadn't spent weeks preparing, and he remained at Salcombe and did his lectures while his children moved the family, often staying with their relatives in Oxford, Max Müller and his family. By September he wrote that he had worked through summer chained to his post like a convict. "I see daylight now and the actual work which will begin in four weeks will not be difficult, perhaps not even disagreeable."

The Froudes took a house in Oxford, Cherwell Edge (later a Catholic girls' school). It had a good interior and was near the river with open fields about it. However, the outside was hideous, he wrote to Mrs. Ireland. They would try to disguise it with creepers. He told her he believed the university would get more out of him if they gave him freedom to go his own way. Yet he understood that they were a little shy of him and did not know what to expect, so they insisted on the established lines. At any rate, at his age, the connection would be but a brief one. Still, he believed that once they all got used to each other, he and they would get along better than they thought. There he was quite prescient.

The author of *The Nemesis of Faith* would end his life not only as Regius Professor but also as fellow of Oriel College, where he, his father, and his brothers had spent their undergraduate days, and where Newman and Keble had been fellows before him. The former rebel had come back as one of the oldest and, even more curiously, *the* most conservative person in the whole university. If people thought he would join forces, as in the distant past, with those who championed progress, they were sorely mistaken. The youngest son, it would appear, had finally become one of the fathers.

With his professorship came a relaxation of guilt concerning his earlier days. In fact, with the synchronicity that seemed always to attend him, on the first whisper of his appointment, an article on "Book Burning" appeared in the *Daily News* suggesting that the burning of *Nemesis* might be apocryphal, an Oxford myth. A student from Froude's day responded, the Reverend Arthur Blomfield, M.A. Oxon, Rector of Beverstow. It had been his own copy of "Professor Froude's" *Nemesis* that tutor William Sewell took from him and burned forty-three years ago— not in the quadrangle as reported, but in the college hall: "I see him now, with hall poker in hand, in delightful indignation poking at this, to him, obnoxious book . . . I lost my *Nemesis of Faith.* I think I lost 'Faith' in my college tutor, for at least he should have recouped costs."

There was no throwing down this English paper in disgust. Froude clipped the letter and saved it. It obviously amused him.

Froude gave his inaugural address in the fall of 1892. Such an address given by a man who was foisted onto the university to replace his most dangerous critic was certain to be well attended. But from his first words on one can see why students—and townspeople—would continue to flock to his lectures, a new experience for Regius Professors of Modern History. Often professors could number their audience on the fingers of one hand. They had to find bigger rooms for Froude. He drew crowds. His inaugural address, urbane, immediate, refreshingly honest, youthful in its irony, at times downright exciting, was simply a foretaste of what was to come. It was Froude unchained from the disgrace that had attended him. It would appear that self-confidence can have a remarkable effect at any age. He said what he believed, as he always did, but with even greater flow and verve. At seventy-four J. A. Froude came into his own.

He began with a dazzling irony. The cardinals occasionally chose the oldest member of the college as the new pope in hopes of an early vacancy. Sometimes the expectation was disappointed and the most distinguished popes turned out to be men who at election had one foot in the grave. He had no ambition for such a long tenure. He would stay at Oxford as long as he could be useful. He knew he was perhaps the oldest person there that day. If they asked him why he accepted the position at his age, he'd have to tell them he was tempted and he fell. To that laughter rang out. Whatever tension there was in that room had been immediately relieved.

He went on to say he had never heard of a cardinal refusing a nomination due to age or a statesman who would not be willing to be prime minister. There were cheers to this. After all, Gladstone had just unseated Salisbury and returned to office, accepting the prime ministership at the age of eighty-three. If a pope and prime minister did not deem these great offices too heavy for an old man, a professorship of history might innocently be accepted by someone who had made history the study of his life. More cheers when he summed up with crystal clarity concerning his motives: "Briefly, I was offered an opportunity of returning to my old University after a long absence. The temptation was too strong to be resisted."

Then he remembered the Oxford of his day and the breed of men, so many of whom were now gone, such as Keble and Newman, along with the system that produced them. New schools had sprung up and new ways of teaching. Classical languages no longer had their old monopoly. Modern languages were studied. Athletics, once a plaything, was now a serious pursuit, as if the world were to have Olympic games again. The celibate seclusion of college life was gone, and ladies, to the horror of the scholastics, had invaded the sacred premises. This got quite a laugh.

For his part he was there to teach modern history. But there was no such thing. History was one continuous stream from the beginning of time. He had humbly never doubted that. He never believed the human race began anew with the Christian era. He always knew that the modern world inherited languages, law, literature, from earlier ages. That the thoughts of Jews, Greeks, and Romans had helped to mold the minds that came after. Still, the division between old and new was useful. For old civilizations and old creeds wore out. New religions, new impulses, fresh character types neither Jew nor Greek emerged. Scandinavians,

Goths, Huns, Arabs had ideas of their own and initiated a new order. Event piled on event over the entire globe with no visible coherence or purpose. To examine what millions upon millions of human beings really did, what they were really like, was obviously impossible. In his own youth he had been taught that we lived under providential dispensation of which we knew little. The most probable interpretation was that we were in a state of probation, that life was a training ground for human character. As it was with human conduct, so with national conduct. Those nations that followed honesty, frugality, industry, purity, prospered, and those that followed wealth, power, pleasure, were made to know they missed the road. This explanation was too old-fashioned for modern speculation, he realized. But for himself, he still considered it the most reasonable explanation offered.

But he was well aware it all depended on what human life meant to a person. Assume any purpose that conformed to personal inclination, and evidence could easily be found for it. Progress was the rule today. Progress from what to what? He didn't believe medieval Europe was as miserable as it was nowadays pretended or that the distribution of the necessities of life were as unequal then as in the present. There was no doubt today a great deal more liberty, and no doubt good results would arise. But they would not result in bonds of attachment between employers and employees, for affection can't grow where interests are opposed. In his reading of English history he found that there used to be a warmer relation between high and low. Each class thought more of its duties than its interests, and religion was really believed in. In such conditions inequality was natural and wholesome.

He found a way of complimenting his predecessor, as was de rigueur. (The audience must have been holding their breath for how he'd handle that.) Like Dr. Freeman, "who along with his asperities had strong masculine sense," Froude, too, had respect for the method of study at Oxford before the modern changes. It was as good an education as was ever tried. His generation had certain books, the best of their kind and limited in number, which they were required to know perfectly. They learned Greek history from Herodotus and Thucydides, Latin history from Livy and Tacitus, philosophy from Aristotle. They had to learn Aristotle's words by heart, weigh every one of them, and in that way the thoughts and language of illustrious writers were indelibly built into his generation's mind, there to remain.

Then, having acknowledged Freeman, J. Anthony Froude defended himself. He did not wish to boast of his own labors. He had never said much about them, and never would, except for this one occasion when there was a reason for it.

He told the students and dons that during the twenty years in which he worked on the *History of England* he must have read, made extracts from, or copied with his own hand tens of thousands of manuscripts, private letters, secret state documents, minutes of secret councils, often in cipher without a key to it at hand. He had worked in the English Records Office, in archives at Paris, Brussels, Vienna, and Simancas, reading documents written in a half a dozen languages in almost indecipherable scrawls.

He had to cut his way through a jungle of material, for no one had opened the road for him. He had been put in rooms piled to the windowsill with bundles of dust-covered dispatches, and told to make the best of it. Often he found the sand glittering on the ink where it had been sprinkled when a page was turned and had never been turned since. He had been subsequently taunted at times for having mistaken a word. It was likely enough. Given such materials an occasional mistake was not to be avoided, but he thought he made fewer mistakes than a great many people would have done. Be that as it may, he could say with confidence that he added many material facts to the history of the period, though they have been totally unrecognized by most of his critics. Being omniscient already, his critics felt they had no more to learn, he concluded.

Now if he was to be of any use in the present office, he had to follow his own lines. He put it that at his age he could not work in harness with the "athletes" of the new studies. All he could do would be to interest students in aspects of their subjects that were not on the beaten path. He couldn't teach philosophy of history, because he had none. Theories shifted from generation to generation. He saw history as the drama of humanity being played out from age to age. The problems mankind had to solve for themselves have been various and intricate. None more so than what rose in the religious convolutions of the sixteenth century. The wisest and best were divided on the course which duty required, and saints and heroes were found in opposing camps. He would attempt to portray some of them, whether Protestant or Catholic did not matter. Priam and Hector were not less beautiful because one tended to admire Achilles and Ulysses.

For himself, the object of history was to discover and make visible illustrious men and pay them ungrudging honor. And, as usual, he came back to Carlyle, who said the history of mankind was the history of great men. To find these men out, clean the dirt from them, and place them on their proper pedestals was the true function of the historian. There could not be a more noble undertaking, he concluded to resounding cheers.

Everything was all right, he wrote to Ashley the next day. It certainly was. Such a humanly compelling speech isn't delivered every day—anywhere. Everybody from the vice-chancellor to the tutors and the undergrads acknowledged it. If only his stomach would behave itself, all would be well. But his stomach didn't behave. It was the old story of sleepless nights. Still, he'd carry on. So many "Heads, etc., etc." had visited. Turned out he liked Henry Boyd, the vice-chancellor, most of all. He, too, went fly-fishing in Norway.

Those lectures he would deliver over the next two years with an ever greater graceful ease and seamlessness seemed an almost lyrical summing up of his historical career. They were all published: *English Seamen in the Sixteenth Century, Lectures on the Council of Trent, The Life and Letters of Erasmus*. Three books in his last two years. He was reformulating and consolidating what he had learned for the benefit of the young. But again, the flow of his thoughts, the remarkable seamlessness and ease, add a freshness to what he had always upheld. He was an inspired lecturer. His self-confidence and renewed verve cast surprising beams of sunlight even onto the printed page. At the end of his life he was no longer *hating* himself—no matter his serious concerns on the general cause of our fallen natures. His first year as Regius Professor was J. Anthony Froude's very well earned happily-ever-after.

Everything at Oxford had changed, of course, as had he himself, he wrote to friends. At the same time he found his life renewing its old continuity. It was as if the forty years in between had come and gone like a dream. The associations of the place were such that it really did seem to him as if the long years between his university days and his professorship belonged to another person, as if he had been asleep for years and woke to take up the threads of his old existence. For all the ghostly synchronicity of it, he was finally swimming in his element. He found Oxford floating him very comfortably, he wrote to Skelton. "I rather like my life here," he told Mrs. Ireland.

Right before his seventy-fifth birthday, he wanted to see poor Ruskin but could not be absent at the end of term. He was consumed by lectures, committees, and "other such horrors." He was fully engaged in academic life. "The authorities refuse to let me off a single duty, though I pleaded to being 75 years old! because they want to prove that I was old and incapable!! I must not gratify them." Apparently some things stayed the same.

"Old age is very tolerable as long as we can keep in health and work," he told Mrs. Ireland. "My Oxford life agrees with me. I have plenty to do. The students come about me in considerable numbers and their fresh bright faces and minds give me back my own youth. My only trouble is to find myself treated as so awful a personage, but I manage to put them tolerably at their ease."

He did that by giving his students access to him, his family, his new home. There was tea for them and theirs—men and women—any day they wished. Except Saturday afternoon, when he held a special seminar for the study of British state papers relating to the Reformation for a select group of students. One of them remembered those days, looking out the windows of Cherwell Edge to the many boats and canoes gliding by on the river, while a small group of deeply interested students were gradually learning to know, understand, and revere this ardent and painstaking teacher.

Froude realized he was best with the very young students and the very old dons; those in the middle, making their own local career, did not much like the intrusion among them of a professor who had a position outside the university. Still, he interfered with nobody and "I dare say we will do very well in time."

He didn't have much time left. He was hardly unaware of the callous way in which he was overworked at Oxford. He had no illusions. "It will kill me, Margaret," he told his daughter, "but it is worth the price."

By his second year at Oxford, the underlid of his right eye—so often cauterized—would droop, giving him, along with his slightly stooped shoulders and his heavy academic schedule, a weary as well as a far-off look. His decline, what seemed to be a slow winding down, was noticed. Not that anything was made easier for him. He finished his second year with the lectures on Erasmus that some say finished him.

At the end of May 1894, the term over, he returned to Salcombe. He had just celebrated his seventy-sixth birthday and was not feeling well. Still, he was able to go out yachting on several occasions. By the middle of June he was not only ill but appeared to be in a rather alarming decline. His regular doctor, as well as one called in from Plymouth, was consulted. Both agreed that he had an internal disorder that was going to be fatal, though not painful. That stomach problem of his had been serious all along. When told the truth, Froude responded, "Well, if my time has come I shall not complain; I have had my innings." At the end, it looked as if Oxford athletics had rendered him a metaphor.

His suffering came in the shape of what was called great nervous prostration. As times he was not himself at all—or to be more accurate he had suddenly aged beyond recall and could no longer control his demons when they struck. Two registered nurses attended him, as well as his doctor. His characteristic resiliency allowed him some days of reprieve, but that excitability did not lessen, and though his days were numbered, his summer was long.

In September, Margaret moved him downstairs into the library so that he could have more cheerful surroundings there among his books. He was wheelchair-bound by then, and it was easier as well to move him around on the downstairs level. On a good day that month, he made out a final will, short and succinct. Ashley and Margaret were his coexecutors. He had already provided much for his children, and he parceled out what remained. All his private papers and unpublished manuscripts were to be destroyed. And he underscored the destruction of "all such letters, papers and memorials of or relating to the late Mrs. Jane Welsh Carlyle" that he had not published in his lifetime together with "any unpublished manuscripts" relating to either of the Carlyles. Apparently there were secrets he did keep.

The night of Thursday the eighteenth of October was the last time he recognized Margaret, Ashley, and May. He then went off on his own. The night nurse woke his three children at five the next morning and informed them their father was dying. They got out of bed and went to him. Then he appeared to rally slightly. His children did not leave him that day. And all through Friday night they held vigil. One can only wonder what the three of them thought, what they said to each other, watching the man who for all of them had been the one constant parent, lying there dying, his books lining shelves all around him. They had not only witnessed but understood the ups and downs of his "checquered" career, as he so long ago phrased it. He was their father and he was their great man passing. On Saturday morning, October 20, 1894, without returning to them, yet with no struggle or further nervous excitability, J. Anthony Froude passed peacefully. He died in his library at Woodcot, Salcombe, his children by his side.

If you go to Salcombe today, you'll hear the same story that was in Froude's obituary. People will point to the big pink house on the hill, where Froude had spent so many years, and talk, not of Froude by name—though a small road is named for him there—but of Tennyson's visits to "a friend who lived at the Moult." In Froude's declining years he developed a way of speaking of last things that had a certain stark poetry. The real character of a people is nowhere gleaned with more unconscious completeness than in their cemeteries, he said. "Philosophise as we may, few of us are deliberately insincere in the presence of death." To Ruskin he wrote, "It is rather forlorn, this winding up of life. One's friends fall off one after the other: and those that are left turn wrinkled and yellow—while the vital juice dries out of our own veins." He spoke most probably in a similar vein to Tennyson, before and after their short-lived falling-out. Tennyson predeceased him and Froude wrote in homage of him to his son.

One can visualize Tennyson, an old man, after one of those visits—and one of those conversations—with Froude, sailing from the Salcombe estuary, and as the Salcombe legend goes, writing "Crossing the Bar." The kernel of truth is there, if not the dressing. Sunset and evening star and let there be no mourning when they pull out to sea.

Froude's death was widely reported, and the appreciation that so often eluded him in his lifetime poured forth. Part of a poem in his memory published in the *St. James Gazette* observed that now when heroic memories pass like sunset shadows from the grass, when England's children cry and stir, each for herself, and few for her, we may think tenderly of one who told, like no unworthy son, her history and championed the younger, braver, finer England he saw.

Certain things he spoke from his grave. His will was one. Had not Waldo Dunn gained the confidence of Ashley and Margaret, Froude might have succeeded in obscuring all but the many books and essays he had published. But they trusted Dunn, and both Ashley and Margaret, like their grandfather the archdeacon, lived till their mideighties. In the twentieth century they attempted to accede to their father's wishes, yet on their own authority they determined he should not go gentle into that good night—or into that complete obscurity which Carlyle spoke of so often, and which Froude attempted to provide for himself. One might well ask why Froude didn't destroy everything before his health failed. Death at one's own hand is a bit tricky, even for the stubborn. Had his breakdown been of a different sort, he might very well have accomplished his ends during lucid final days. He had another concern, as well, exhibited in his Cuban journal. He had to leave enough for his family to protect their name, should it become necessary.

In accordance with his wishes, his funeral was carried out as simply as possible. Had Dean Stanley—Froude's old Oxford friend whom Emerson remembered at Delmonico's as one of that splendid generation—still been alive, Westminster Abbey would have been offered as it had been for Carlyle. But that was not Anthony's destiny.

On Thursday, the twenty-fifth of October, Anthony's funeral cortege left from his Salcombe home. At twelve noon the mourners walked behind the plain closed hearse to Holy Trinity Church, where the first part of the office of the dead was said by the vicar. Then the procession went to the Salcombe cemetery, where the conclusion of the burial service was read. The polished oak coffin was lowered into a plain open grave.

Prince Edward Albert sent his condolences to Oxford, and the Professor of Holy Scripture, Professor Shanday, commemorated Froude at services. Those that could not be at the funeral sent flowers—so many flowers. First among them Mary Sackville-West, the Countess of Derby (Lord Derby had predeceased his old friend). Then, the Countess of Ducie, the Earl of Carnarvon, the Countess of Carnarvon, Jacob Bright, the provost of Oriel, countless others—including old Sir George Gray, who was in England. That very summer, before facing his end, Froude had thought of another trip to the Pacific colonies with Sir George. Flowers, too, from his American admirer, Bret Harte.

Certainly James Anthony Froude was prepared for the final voyage. And if anyone did pray for oblivion, truly it was he. His destruction of his own papers is one of the reasons that he remains "the last great Victorian awaiting revival," as A. L. Rowse put it. Most of his books are out of print. And even though lip service is paid to *Thomas Carlyle* as one of the greatest biographies in the English language, the wear and tear of more than a century of niggardly criticism, aided by its author's being ignored by the academy, has taken its toll. Perhaps more than anything, his political perspective has obscured him. J. A. Froude was anything but politically correct, even in his time. Yet that contemporary expression itself indicates it is not the quality of the thought or the circumstances that infuse it that holds one's interest today, the way it once did. We tend toward quick decisions based on how an issue is represented to us in a sound bite. And we don't really discuss as much as we direct our point of view at the other without needing to hear what we assume will be the retort. It often gets loud, but it rarely illuminates.

Pendulums swing. And this biography, published 111 years to the month after Froude's death, comes out at a time when many of the contrarian issues he brought to public scrutiny are—quite suddenly—once more being discussed: emigration, faith, evangelical concerns, the bonding together of English-speaking peoples in wartime. Beyond it all, the very nature of democracy itself. What Froude saw in his visits to the United States was the old Puritan spirit, a great people who thought of duty, community, and country beyond material gain. "When I am most despondent about the future of mankind I can always comfort myself in thinking of America," he wrote to Boston publisher James Fields in 1879. One wonders what he would say of us today. What he would say about the two-party system that he believed cared more about their own internal wars than protecting their country. About greed, corruption, globalization, the immense disparity between the captains of industry (CEOs) and the ruthless downsizing of their work-forces. Has all this brought us to the edge of the decline of yet another Roman republic, as he saw was the case with all democracies? We, too, began with vigor and earnestness; shall we too decline in luxury? What-ever our opinions of the serious national concerns of our day, perhaps it is time to read Froude again.

But of course, it was the opposite of revival that Froude wished. Here is what the man whose literary and worldly accomplishments spanned his century wrote and directed his children to place on his tombstone, what he counted not unworthy:

In memory of
James Anthony Froude, M. A.
Regius Professor of
Modern History, Oxford.
Son of the Rev. R. H. Froude
late Archdeacon of Totnes
Born at Dartington
April 23, 1818.
Died at Salcombe
October 20, 1894.

With those last words, he hoped, in all finality, to honor his father and end his story.

AFTERWORD

"The pleasure to me is in the writing of the book," Froude said, and I certainly can echo his words as I complete this biography of a man who in his personal life, writings, and public actions both influenced and reflected his century to a dramatic and unparalleled degree. I came to him, as most who remember him have, through his biography of Carlyle, a monumental achievement, and asked the question most do. How could a man who had such psychological insight and whose prose is perhaps the best I have ever read—as alive today as when it was written—be so forgotten? I realize now that it was mainly through his own wishes. Still, I admit to having had no compunction in lifting the veil once more and revealing the man who was such a pivotal political and literary figure in his own time. Part of his destiny was that most of the important issues of his day were reflected in the way he lived his life.

For Froude, style was the by-product of expressing oneself as clearly and as honestly as possible—and I agree with him. However, the vitality of his prose itself reached out to me past the page and past opinions that often differed from my own, affording such unmitigated pleasure that I could not help myself from wanting to learn more about him, to forge beyond those two anonymous initials "J.A." and that unusual last name, too close for comfort to *Freud* (which, by the way, I now mispronounce as *Froude*.)

It became a voyage of discovery. Though I knew Anthony Froude to be a great prose artist, I had no idea I would be taken past the bounds of literature and the Carlyle biography with its subsequent scandalous controversy to South Africa, Australia, New Zealand, the West Indies, Cuba, and the States, to the inner workings of the Liberal and Conservative cabinets, to new thoughts concerning democracy, to Russian ladies and Benjamin Disraeli, to fly-fishing, and to personal tragedy.

The voyage also took me to the many libraries, librarians, and archivists I would like to thank for their courtesy and kind help: from Gerard Tracey, archivist of the Birmingham Oratory, to the staffs, librarians, archivists, and trustees at the Bodleian Library, Exeter College, Keble College, and Balliol College at Oxford University, the British Library, the John Rylands University Library of the University of Manchester, the Exeter Central Library, Hatfield House, the Folger Shakespeare Library, the Houghton Rare Book Library at Harvard, the Beinecke Rare Book and Manuscript Library at Yale, the New York Public Library, the Butler Library at Columbia, the Huntington Library, and the Pierpont Morgan Library, among others, for their permission to read, for exchange of information, and for permission to quote from their records. And finally to Colin Harris and his associates at the Bodleian for the trouble they took in rushing the unpublished letters from Froude to Max Müller to me at the last moment.

Two biographies of Froude precede mine: Herbert Paul's *Life of Froude* published in 1906 and Waldo Dunn's two-volume *James Anthony Froude* published in the 1960s. Paul's is an intellectual history written by an historian who had seen Froude in the flesh and whose Oxford was a generation or so removed from Froude's. He brings the contemporary reader a bit closer to the Oxford mind of Froude's day.

Margaret and Ashley Froude appear to have given limited access to Paul, but they trusted Dunn and in the earlier half of the twentieth century gave him access to their father's primary records—letters, journals, diaries, the unpublished autobiography of his early life—as well as remembering their father in conversation. Without Dunn only the barest bones of Froude's life would have remained, since Froude had willed that all papers be destroyed in his children's lifetime. The primary material in Dunn's two-volume biography is invaluable; the scholarship meticulous. If Dunn saw everything in Froude's "chequered" history in the most favorable light, it is a natural consequence of dedicating his working life to rescuing Froude from the distortion of his reputation caused by the Carlyle controversy.

I would like to thank as well those friends and colleagues who have supported me as I researched and wrote. First and foremost, my friend William S. Peterson. As no good deed goes unpunished, in the years that have followed my graduate work under his direction, I have often looked to him for his insight and advice. I am once more indebted to his intelligence and generosity, from his extensive knowledge of everything from church history to book design, to his taking the time from his own work to read and criticize an earlier version of this biography. I also received and am grateful for generous encouragement and support from Reynolds Price, Phillip Lopate, William McBrien, Paula Uruburu, Iska Alter, Joann Krieg, Vivian Gornick, Alan O'Day, Hedley Sutton, Daniel Hungmin Park, Nicole Buscemi, and Adrian Thompkins. I'd like to thank Ileene Smith, who showed such early enthusiasm for this project. I am particularly indebted to my editor, Alexis Gargagliano. Her insight and significant editing and support have been invaluable. Heartfelt thanks as well to my literary representative, Harriet Wasserman, for her encouragement and belief in the value of this biography from inception.

I thank Hofstra University for released time and travel grants as I worked on this biography. As always, Hofstra's support is very much appreciated. The book could not have been completed in a timely manner without a National Endowment for the Humanities Fellowship for College Teachers and Independent Scholars, 2004–2005, which allowed me a year away from my teaching and administrative duties in order to devote myself fully to the completion of *J. Anthony Froude*. I am more than grateful for their support; the NEH, however, is in no way responsible for the content of this biography.

ABBREVIATIONS

Author's or editor's last name or item's title is generally used to cite books and articles. Primary material in libraries and certain books use the following abbreviations:

BL   Manuscripts in the British Library, London. With permission of the British Library.

CL   *Collected Letters of Thomas and Jane Welsh Carlyle*, Duke/Edinburgh edition.

Dunn I   *James Anthony Froude: A Biography 1818–1856.*

Dunn II   *James Anthony Froude: A Biography 1857–1894.*

EC   Manuscripts at Exeter College Library, Oxford. With permission of the Rector and Fellows of Exeter College, Oxford.

F & C   Dunn, *Froude and Carlyle: A Study of the Froude-Carlyle Controversy.*

Folger   The Folger Shakespeare Library, Washington, DC. JAF letters; William Bodham Donne to Mrs. Kemble. With permission of the Folger Shakespeare Library.

F-R   Viljoen, *The Froude-Ruskin Friendship.*

Harvard   The Houghton Library, Mary Aitken Carlyle Letters; Charles Eliot Norton Letters; John Ruskin Letters. By permission of Harvard University.

Ireland   18 Letters of JAF to Mrs. Alexander Ireland, with permission of the Beinecke Rare Book and Manuscript Library, Yale University.

Jowett Papers   Letters of Benjamin Jowett at Bailliol College, Oxford. By permission of the Jowett Copyright Trustees.

KC   Keble College, Oxford, 36 Letters from Archdeacon Froude to John Keble, 1823–1855. By permission of the Warden and Fellows of Keble College, Oxford.

Kerry   "A Fortnight in Kerry," Part I and Part II, 217–307, *Short Studies on Great Subjects*, II

MM   Letters between JAF and Friedrich Max Müller, Special Collections and Western Manuscripts, Bodleian Library, Oxford. By permission of the Bodleian Library, University of Oxford.

OK   Stead, *The M.P. for Russia . . . Olga Novikoff.*

Oratory   Letters between John Henry Newman and the Froude family at the Birmingham Oratory, Edgbaston. By permission.

OxCR   "The Oxford Counter-Reformation," reprinted in *Short Studies on Great Subjects,* IV.

Rylands   The John Rylands Library. JAF letters to Mrs. Gaskell. By permission of the John Rylands University Library, the University of Manchester.

Shadows   All quotes from "The Spirit's Trail," the first of two novellas in *Shadows of the Clouds,* by Zeta.

S Wilberforce   Bodleian Library, Oxford. S. Wilberforce Deposit, Keble Correspondence, Newman Correspondence, Bodleian Library, Oxford, by permission of Special Collections and Western Manuscripts.

Yale   Manuscripts at Beinecke Rare Book and Manuscript Library; Osborn Files; George Eliot and G. H. Lewes Collection; Lady St. Helier Papers, by permission.

NOTES

Sliding Toward Tasmania

2 "lived and breathed": Dunn I, 72.
4 "the twentieth century": Harper, 5.
4 "was an ass": Dunn I, 13.
5 "rest of us": ibid., 16.
6 "to the bank": ibid., 13.
7 "make me at all": ibid., 12–21.
8 "soon to face": ibid., 26–28.
8 "older than themselves": Oratory, Oct. 28, 1827.
9 "holes in my face": Dunn I, 31–34.
9 "college stairs": *Shadows,* 29.
10 "dogs cannot": ibid., 36.
11 "John Henry Newman": Wilfred Ward as quoted by Faber, 46.
12 "in the flesh": Oratory, June 20, 1835.
12 "road of duty": JAF, OxCR, 242.
12 "to my ear": *Nemesis,* 117.
13 "lead him out of it": KC, Nov. 26, 1834.
14 "to the Provost": Oratory, Feb. 28, 1836.
15 "bygone days": ibid., Mar. 7, 1836.
15 "of his life": Brendon, 19.
15 "surrounded us": Dunn I, 18.
16 "at any rate soon": Oratory, June 2, 1823.
16 "under such circumstances": S Wilberforce, ms. c. 7, fols. 65–66.
16 "same disposition": Dunn I, 19.
18 "such a quarter!": Oratory.
19 "*do* feel." S Wilberforce, ms. c. 7, fols. 57–58.
19 "suddenly free": Dunn I, 47.
20 "rest of him": *Shadows,* 44.
20 "*was* nothing": ibid., 45.
20 "nothing else": ibid., 46.
20 "unbridled fun": ibid., 16.
20 "broken flower": ibid., 2.

21 "suddenly shining": Dunn I, 51.
21 "the best": Sidebotham, Dorothy Margaret, "The Life and Thought of Richard Hurrell Froude and His Influence on the Oxford Movement of 1833," MA Thesis, University of Manchester. April 1971.
21 "rapid decline": to Keble, Oratory, July 26, 1855.
22 "his father": *Shadows,* 32–33.
22 "next to him": Dunn I, 60–61.
23 "few days": Oratory, Sept. 11, 1838.
23 "you at all": Harper, 215.
23 "he tough?": Dunn I, 60–61.
24 "one before": *Shadows,* 57. In the novella, the archdeacon is Canon Fowler, his son, Edward Fowler.
24 "been plunged": Dunn I, 57–60.
24 "as a man": Brendon, 6.
25 "by it": KC, William Froude to Keble, 1839.
25 "should order": KC, Bristol, 1839.
26 "he feels": ibid.
26 "the porch": OxCR, 269.
26 "my place": Dunn I, 58–59.
26 "so long": *Shadows,* 76.
28 "be subdued": KC, Mar. 8, 1841.
28 "saintly person": Dunn I, 63–66.
29 "should part": ibid., 67.
29 "Oxford movement": OxCR, 259.
29 "the flame": ibid., 235.
30 "our own": Dunn I, 70–71.
31 "a Tractarian": see OxCR, Letter III. John Henry Newman, 4:272–93.
31 "before him": ibid.
32 "and bishoprics": Dunn I, 72–75.
32 "semi-monastic life": Pattison, 189–90.
34 "most historians": OxCR, Letter V, "The Lives of the Saints," 4:315–39.
34 "ought not": Oratory, Nov. 9, 1844.
35 "the Tractarian party": to R. W. Church, Oratory, Dec. 23, 1884.
36 "the ages!": *Nemesis,* 43–44.
36 pseudonym Zeta: The book is composed of two stories. It is the first, "The Spirit's Trials," a thinly disguised autobiographical novella, that is the one referred to throughout as *Shadows.* Of lesser interest is the second story, "The Lieutenant's Daughter."
37 "end forever": *Shadows,* 42.
37 "greater ones": Dunn I, 236–37.
37 "in the book": Jowett Papers, Oct. 29, 1847.
38 "made to you": EC, Exeter, July 8, 1847.
38 "*to me*": EC, Dartington, Dec. 14, 1847.
39 "or not": Dunn I, 99.
39 "auto or otherwise": Mulhauser, I:244.
39 "not a treatise": Dunn I, 149.
39 "be so heinous": ibid., 126.
40 "inside out": ibid., 131.

41 "and Christian": EC, Ash Wednesday, 1849.
41 "J.A. Froude": ibid., Feb. 24, 1849.
41 "any opinion": ibid., J. L. Richards to JAF, Feb. 27, 1849.
42 "to you": EC to Froude.
42 *"of infidelity"*: Dunn I, 232–33.
43 "see them": EC, Apr. 10, 1849.
43 "his God!": Dunn I, 226–27.
44 "had gained": ibid., 147–48.

YES AND NO

45 "to rise": Dunn I, 235–36.
46 "him good": Müller, 397–99.
47 *"Cambridge Review"*: Dunn I, 101–2.
48 "sexual imagination": See Susan Chitty's fascinating study *The Beast and the Monk.*
48 "hard floor": Chitty, 84.
48 "Blachford Mansfield": ibid., 52–53.
49 "and survived": ibid., 17.
49 "French novel": Jowett Papers, Dec. 13, 1847.
49 "passionate throbbings": Kingsley, *Yeast,* 145–46.
50 "many men": Dunn I, 137.
50 "at Eversley": Chitty, 201.
50 "the Tracts": Chitty, 54.
51 "future direction": ibid., 121–22.
51 "too many": Kingsley, *Yeast,* 28–29.
52 "was bearing": Dunn I, 148.
52 "active men": ibid., 152.
53 "strange to him": ibid., 161.
53 "strange elfin beauty": to Walter Mantell, Jan. 22, 1859, Dunn II, 596.
54 "of others": Dunn I, 160–61.
54 "forth reeling": Eliot, 15.
55 "day long!": Dunn I, 154.
55 "about yourself": Yale, Jan. 17, 1858.
56 "possess it": ibid., Sept. 26, 1858.
56 "second present": ibid., Mar. 13, 1859.
56 "don't wonder": Dunn I, 161–62.
57 "wife, 1849": ibid., 162.
57 "of mustard": ibid., 166.
57 "and ungraceful": ibid.
58 "determined to try": merged passage, Dunn I, 168.
58 "promising Margaret": Georgina Margaret Froude was her full name; she was always called Margaret.
58 "in those years": ibid., 169.
58 "open to me": ibid., 169–70.
59 "as himself": ibid., 146.
59 "nothing whatever!": *CL,* 24:13.
60 "we did": Dunn I, 146.

60 "my own person,": EC, Apr. 10, 1849.
61 "fully occupied": Dunn I, 170.
61 "by scribbling": ibid., 186.
61 "more enjoyable": ibid., 171–72.
61 "the leaves": Yale, Sept. 25. Froude never dated his letters by year.
61 "Please don't": Dunn I, 174.
62 "he them": ibid., 196.
64 "unheroic times": Dunn I, 185.
64 "as *Shadows*": Anthony was indebted to Spinoza for this crew.
65 "got it back": Dunn I, 167.
66 "personal resources": ibid., 16–17.
66 "kind friends": KC, Feb. 14, 1837.
66 "powerful engines": ibid., Nov. 26, 1834.
67 "but surely": Dunn I, 181.
67 "own punishment": ibid., 184.
67 "occupy me": ibid., 185.
68 "very doubtful": Oratory, Jan. 25, 1860.
68 "speak of it": Letter of William to Newman. See Harper, 82.
69 "sweet gentleness": Oratory, April 24, 1856.
69 "I say more?": Dunn I, 192.
69 "of it": ibid., 193–94.
69 "his example!": Lowry, 139–40.
70 "breathe it to him": MM, December 23, 1853.
70 "give up": Yale, Osborn Files. Apr. 14, [no year].
72 "to say": Dunn I, 278–79.
73 "supremacy were unjust": *History of England,* 2: 383.
74 "moral crime": ibid., 1:446. Years later, Froude would reevaluate Catherine of Aragon on the basis of other records that came to light.
74 "adequately bridge": ibid., 1: 61–62; also see 208.
75 "James Anthony Froude": Paul, 152.
75 "pure erudition": Strachey, 196–97.
76 "but his own": Folger, Sept. 4, 1856.
77 "think of it": Dunn I, 195.
78 "gather on them": Dunn II, 273.
78 "to the same": ibid., 274.
79 "the special rule": Dunn I, 20.
79 "of the State": ibid., 200–201.
80 "of discord": *Shadows,* 24–25.
80 "vivid presence": Oratory, Feb. 23, 1859.
81 "has nothing": Dunn II, 566.
81 "his name": Dunn I, 200–201.

THE PERFECT MARRIAGE

83 "to this": Dunn II, 282.
84 "own hands": Kingsley, *Charles Kingsley,* 2:306.
84 "near London": Folger, June 10, 1860.
85 "Waldo Dunn": See my Afterword for Dunn's role in preserving J.A.F.'s papers.

85 "second mother": Dunn II, 295.
86 "pigmy body": ibid., 286.
86 "as a fault": "Obituary.—Mr John William Parker, Jun.," *Gentleman's Magazine*, 222.
86 "rejected it": Maurer, 215.
87 "earlier volumes": *History of England*, 7: viii.
88 "to thine": From *Fraser's*, May 1862, reprinted in "Death of Mr Froude," by Edward Albert, *The Salcombe Times*, Oct. 27, 1894. The entire poem reads:

TOGETHER

Sweet hand that, held in mine,
Seems the one thing I cannot live without,
The soul's one anchorage in this storm and doubt,
I take thee as a sign
Of sweeter days in store
For life, and more than life, when life is done,
And thy soft pressure leads me gently on
To Heaven's own Evermore.
I have not much to say,
Nor any words that fit such fond request:
Let my blood speak to thine and bear the rest
Some silent heartward way.
Thrice blest the faithful hand
Which saves e'en while it blesses; hold me fast:
So near the better land.
Sweet hand, that, thus in mine,
Seems the one thing I cannot live without,
My heart's one anchor in life's storm and doubt,
Take this, and make me thine.

88 "I suppose": Dunn II, 290.
88 "European history": ibid., 292.
89 "my darlings": ibid., 293–94.
90 "offer myself": ibid., 294–95.
90 "of the family": ibid., 250–51.
90 "of his life": Dunn II, 297.
91 "as granite": Skelton, 160.
91 "over a skull": Woolf, 4.
91 "imperfectly believed": *My Relations with Carlyle*, 7.
92 "dare to love": ibid., 4.
92 "all things and subjects": *F & C*, 194.
93 "concerning persons": Maurer, 224.
93 "object of jealousy": Rylands, Oct. 21, 1863.
93 "the management": Skelton, 130.
94 "to Froude": ibid., 245–46.
94 "ever known": ibid., 121.
94 "credit for!": Folger, 299, April 1860.
95 "March Frasers?": BL, Feb. 9, 1869.
96 "your article": Skelton, 127–28.

97 "really a sin": T.C. to R.B., 1856.

97 "be right": Skelton, 129–30.

97 "my poetry": Dunn I, 328.

98 "public life": Folger, Ramsgate, Aug. 25 [n.y.].

99 "uses it": Conway, 2:185.

99 "one name": Moncure Conway, "Working with Froude on *Fraser's* Magazine," *The Nation,* Nov. 22, 1894, p. 402.

99 "historically so": Newman, *Apologia,* 298.

100 "Roman Catholicism": OxCR, 377. In "The Oxford Counter Reformation," Froude acknowledged that Kingsley's feelings toward Newman had, perhaps, been embittered "by the intrusion of religious discord into families in which he was interested."

101 "his studies": Oratory, Dec. 29, 1859.

101 "country's religion": ibid., Jan. 31, 1860.

101 "incredible trial": ibid., Mar. 16, 1864.

101 "sorry for Papa": Harper, 154.

101 "his imagination": ibid.

101 "love her": Oratory, Feb. 7, 1864.

102 "vow celibacy": ibid.

102 "no good": ibid.

102 "its hopelessness": ibid., Dec. 29, 1859.

104 "given him": Dunn I, 306–7.

104 "making converts": Newman, *Apologia,* 105.

104 "the Armada": to Lady Salisbury, Dunn II, 310.

105 "satisfactorily believed": Dunn II, 310.

105 "calling by the name": ibid.

105 "my spirit": Cecil, 33.

105 "mischief-making": ibid., 215.

106 "political dialogues": see "Mary Sackville-West" in the 2004 *Oxford Dictionary of National Biography.*

107 "to be": *Life in London,* 2:230–32.

108 "into quiet": *Letters and Memorials of Jane Welsh Carlyle,* 2: 271–72.

110 "is dead": Markus, 222–23.

110 "her home": *Life in London,* 2: 255–67.

111 "be made": ibid., 274–75.

112 "ballot box": Heffer, 359.

113 "even conceivable": *CL,* 6: 222.

113 "criticism indeed": When he began his *History of England,* Anthony had some copies of the two introductory chapters printed and "sent them about for criticism." Though the process wasn't a pleasant one, and what one critic praised, another rejected, he got something from the process, he told Max Müller, "especially from Carlyle who though he barked loud enough at what he did not like, was warm and genial and hearty. His remarks were numerous, most of them valuable, and all, I need not say, very amusing." There was nothing warm or amusing in the old man's brutal words more than a decade later as J. A. Froude concluded his monumental series. One can only wonder if what Anthony once wrote to Müller still held in this instance: "In general I trust other people's taste, but I stick to my own judgement."

113 "of Froude": Paul, 136–37.

113 "hang entranced": Strachey, 191–202.

114 "been regurgitated": Rowse, *Glimpses of the Great,* 232.

114 "not to be": Froude wrote a preface to and published Carlyle's *Tour in Ireland* after Carlyle's death.

115 "with facts": Skelton, 144.

115 "Scottish students": "Calvinism," *Short Studies,* 2:19.

115 "than I": *F-R,* July 27, 1874, 132.

116 "theatrical ourselves": Kerry, 2: 226–28.

118 "for the day": ibid., 250–56.

121 "out of Derreen": Skelton, 151.

121 "singular people": Kerry, 2: 259–307.

121 "pleasing aspects!": BL, Nov. 1871.

122 "among themselves": Skelton, 151.

122 "or comfort": Carlyle, *The Correspondence of Thomas Carlyle and Ralph Waldo Emerson* 2: 353.

123 "me as well": Dunn I, 373–77.

123 "Lord Overstone's?": ibid., 384.

124 "for ignorance": Dec. 2, 1872, in Dunn, 379.

125 "not impossible": ibid., 381.

125 "to seed": ibid., 385.

127 "in London": ibid., 388.

127 "*absolutely* alone": BL, Mar. 13, 1874.

127 "present resource": Skelton, 152–53.

Confronting the Labyrinth of Modern Confusion

131 "against it": *Life in London,* 2: 348–51.

132 "like witchcraft": Carlyle, *Reminiscences,* 210.

135 "burnt nothing": ibid., 2nd edition, Preface.

135 "year after year": *F & C,* 21.

135 "better today": Dunn II, 390.

137 "concern in it": "England and Her Colonies" and "The Colonies Once More," *Short Studies,* 2:180–216 and 397–438, respectively.

138 "the expenditure": Dunn I, 290.

139 "resist temptation": ibid., 437.

140 "J. A. Froude": Folger, YC, 986, PM, July 10, 1874.

141 "principal street": "Leaves from a South African Journal," *Short Studies,* 3: 477–558.

141 "should do": Dunn I, 396.

142 "almost white": "Leaves from a South African Journal," *Short Studies,* 3: 512.

143 "to itself": ibid., 527–28.

144 "to discharge": Dunn I, 414–15

145 "use to him": ibid., 419, quoting Paul, 277.

145 "*urge* it": Dunn I, 422.

146 "as that": ibid., 424.

149 "a figure": ibid., a letter to Margaret, 428–40.

149 "with me": Skelton, 153.

149 "financial compensation": Dunn II, 443.

149 "been followed": ibid., 447.

151 "sad tranquillity": ibid., letters to Margaret, 427–40.

151 "old opinion": Skelton, 158.

151 "of others": Paul, 344–45.

THE HERO AS BIOGRAPHER

154 "explicitly revealed": OK 1: 294–95.

155 "Nicholas Kiréeff": OK 1: 205–6.

156 "*have Constantinople*": ibid., 442.

156 "accurate knowledge": Dunn II, 449.

156 "being done": ibid., 450.

156 "gentle animal": Conway, 2:183.

158 "a boy!": Carlyle, *Reminiscences,* 42.

160 "a Wife": *CL,* 2: 20; Markus 87–97.

161 "very laughable": *CL,* vol. 2.

162 "been crushed": *First Forty Years,* 1:156.

162 "so unsufferable?": *CL,* 2: 481.

162 "your love!": ibid., 450.

162 "your head": ibid., 471.

164 "loved him—": *CL,* 3: 360–61.

164 "destroy you?": ibid., July 29, 1825.

165 "suffering now": Markus, 152.

165 "of it all": *My Relations with Carlyle,* 22–23.

168 "extreme youth": *F & C,* 242.

168 "Carlyle's illness": *My Relations with Carlyle,* 24.

169 "to the adventurous": Harris, *My Life and Loves,* 2: 296–97.

170 "you expect?": ibid., 168.

171 "imperious mistress": *My Relations with Carlyle,* 19.

171 "in my power": Carlyle, *The Life of John Sterling,* 229.

172 "all to me": *My Relations with Carlyle,* 31.

172 "natural growth": *Life in London,* 1: 34.

173 "readily assented": *Reminiscences,* 31.

173 "told them": *Life in London,* 2: 478.

174 "relieved and easy": *My Relations with Carlyle,* 32.

174 "so 'reticent'": Harvard, Nov. 20, 1875, no. 989.

175 "in the world": *First Forty Years,* 1: 320–21.

175 "revolting a faith": Harvard, Nov. 20, 1875, no. 976.

176 "not fair!": ibid., May 11, 1879, no. 986.

176 "or me!": ibid., Oct. 20, 1885, no. 6194.

176 "Froude's capacity": Norton, *Letters,* 1: 461–62.

176 "my Uncle": Harvard, Feb. 2, 1876, no. 978.

177 "was pleasanter": ibid., Nov. 6, 1877, no. 982.

178 "own cheques": *F & C,* 61.

178 "infirm years": see Carlyle's Will and Codicil, *F & C,* 277–86.

178 "thought it fair": His own brother, Dr. John, an executor to the will, thought Mary needed greater compensation. When Carlyle bought five one-thousand-pound Russian bonds—he, like Froude, sided with the Russians over the Turks—Dr.

John convinced him to give one of them to Mary. She would also have, he told her, the things at Cheyne Row willed to him. But he did nothing in writing, and since Dr. John died before Carlyle, his inheritance was divided between all the nieces and nephews.

178 "an injustice": *F & C,* 63.
179 "exists anywhere": ibid., 77.
179 "Thomas Becket": Articles appearing in *Nineteenth Century* and then collected in *Studies,* 4:1–230.
179 "Mr. Freeman": All quotes from the above article when not cited in Dunn as well.
180 "I have said": Dunn II, 466–67.
181 "Strachey wrote": Strachey, 197.
182 "better of him": ibid., 294.
183 "for her": *F & C,* Froude's memorandum of Oct. 16, 1881, 298–303.
184 "her hands": ibid., 34–36.
185 "from me": ibid., 291.
186 "their shadows": *First Forty Years,* 1: 368.
187 "heroic faith": All quotes from Carlyle's "Boswell's Life of Johnson" of 1832. *Miscellaneous Essays,* 4: 67–131.
189 "than joy": July 13, 1874, "Last Letters," 243.
190 "a life": *First Forty Years,* 1: 368.
190 "*in love*": ibid., 284–85.
190 "of it": ibid., 368–69.
191 "me time": Markus, 112.
191 "ungovernable fury": *My Relations with Carlyle,* 21–23.
192 "of character": *First Forty Years,* 1: 364–67.
193 "between them": ibid., 2: 23.
193 "his disappointment": ibid., 2: 31.
193 "at Craigenputtock": ibid., 2: 443.
194 "no longer": ibid., 2: 464.
194 "to predict": ibid., 2: 478.
194 "of her cousins": Harvard, Aug. 9, 1882, no. 991.
195 "left there": OK, 2: 326.
197 "be done with it": Carlyle footnotes, *Letters and Memorials of Jane Welsh Carlyle,* 2:104–6.
199 "at all": Harvard, Sept. 26, 1883, no. 992.
201 "him so": OK, 1:536.
202 "give you": Dunn I: 569–70.
203 "was great": OK, 2: 327.
205 "the poet": *Life in London,* 2:170–74.
205 "her home": Norton, *Reminiscences,* 53.
207 "himself desired": *Life in London,* 2: 404–6.

The Unstrung Bow

211 "effects produced": *F-R,* Nov. 13, 1884, 29.
212 "own convictions": ibid., Nov. 3, 1884, 28.
212 "his past": Margaret and Ashley allowed Dunn access to his autobiography, and he published it in sections in the first volume of *James Anthony Froude.*

213 "the globe": *F-R,* Nov. 13, 1884, 30.
215 "or the other": ibid., Dec. 24, 1879, 9.
216 "American children?": Dunn II, 457.
217 "were exceptional": Froude to Ashley, from Ashley Froude's introduction to the school edition of *English Seamen in the Sixteenth Century.*
217 "in one week": *Oceana,* 382.
218 "healthy alone": ibid., 147–48.
218 "not enough": ibid., 67.
219 "the low": ibid., 73.
219 "Year's morning": ibid., 72–73.
220 "seabirds": Froude called them "gulls," and his critics made a point that they were actually storm petrels or Mother Carey's chickens.
220 "a relief": ibid., 92.
220 "its best": ibid., 88.
221 "own likeness": ibid., 188.
222 "no more": Dunn II, 521.
222 "me bewildered": *Oceana,* 111.
222 "further present": ibid., 157.
223 "the multitude": ibid., 204–5.
224 "metaphorical parts": ibid., 153.
224 "in the world": ibid., 153–55.
225 "of responsibility": ibid., 170.
225 "decided part": ibid., 165.
225 "more afterwards": ibid., 166–69.
226 "valued more": ibid., 195.
228 "to desolation": ibid., 319.
228 "son's manners": Dunn II, 520.
228 "as down": *Oceana,* 290–91.
229 "feel distressing": ibid., 345.
229 "at *Frisco*": ibid., 357.
230 "was California": ibid., 358–59.
231 "the consequences?": ibid., 360.
231 "home there": ibid., 364.
231 "Americans themselves": ibid., 374.
232 "and westward": ibid., 380.
232 "modern shape": ibid., 375.
232 "to know it": ibid., 393.
232 "let it happen": ibid., 354–55.
233 "a spiritual one": ibid., 354–57.
233 "good as another": ibid., 341.
234 "answer, 'Impossible'": ibid., 223–24.
235 "mid-twentieth century": The discussion of Maria S. Rye is based on and greatly indebted to Marion Diamond's fine study "Emigration and Empire."
235 "without wind": Skelton, Aug. 2, 1885, 188.
235 "for inferiority": *Oceana,* 328.
236 "we recommend": Dunn I, 537–38.
236 "for them": OK, 2: 90.
237 "exposing it": Dunn I, 538.

237 "for it": *West Indies,* 275.
237 "or another": Dunn II, 542–43.
238 "at hand": ibid., 545.
238 "at all": *F-R,* 38.
238 "deserve it": ibid., 34.
239 "to her": ibid., 55.
239 "a parallel": *F & C,* 305.
240 "human hearth": Norton, *New Princeton Review,* culled from Norton's list, 17–18.
240 "Froude's misprints": Harvard, Aug. 28, 1886, no. 6199.
240 "to no avail": An irony of the situation is contained in a letter Mary sent to Norton, Sept. 26, 1882: "I should greatly like to read your *Reminiscences* and hope that I may still do so in print. I am correcting the Froude Volumes . . . and hope to send them off [to you] next week. . . . The first volume is much more full of errors than the second. The 'Jane Welsh Carlyle' part was printed from a copy which I made long ago," Harvard, no. 992.
241 "of me!": *F-R,* Apr. 10, 1886, 44.
241 "to bear": ibid., Nov. 29, 1886, 64.
242 "and *irremediable*": ibid., Dec. 2, 1886, 67.
242 "old love affairs": See Dunn, *F & C,* for the documentation of the legal matters.
242 "become detestable": *My Relations with Carlyle,* 70.
243 "certificate *grandson*": *F-R,* Apr. 10, 1886, 44.
243 "into silence": *West Indies,* 25.
244 "Barbadian afflictions": ibid., 105.
244 "the enemy": ibid., 191–92.
246 "the Chinaman": *Oceana,* 203–4.
247 "sorry for her": ibid., 296–97.
248 "they grew": ibid., 43.
251 "in these parts": *West Indies,* 261–66.
251 "not show": ibid., 289.
251 "gentleman abroad": ibid., 295.
252 "spoils all": Dunn II, 545–53. All diary entries quoted are from these pages.
252 "hear them": *West Indies,* 297.
253 "blue devils": ibid., 319.
254 "only indifferently": *My Relations with Carlyle,* 8–9.
254 "of hope": ibid., 7–8.
256 "too late": ibid., 39.
256 "it myself": ibid., 38.
256 "private kind": ibid., 27.
256 "to go on": ibid., 28–29.
258 "perish everlastingly": *West Indies,* 252–53.

THE WORLD ACCORDING TO THE MUSLIM, THE IRISHMAN, AND THE HEBREW CONJURER

259 "stern approval": *F-R,* June 25, 1889?, 86.
260 "should it?": ibid., Mar. 5, 1890.
260 "skin eruptions": Dunn II, 564–65.
262 "with it": OxCR, 254–55.

262 "by another": Skelton, 205.

264 "appalling spectacle": ibid., 148.

264 "much care": *Two Chiefs,* 170.

265 "their fortunes": ibid., 366–67.

266 "entertaining companions": ibid., 304–6.

266 "do so": Skelton, 205.

267 "at advantage": ibid., 203–4.

267 "about anything": *F-R,* 95.

267 "about nothing": ibid., 73.

268 "up the millions": *Life in London,* 2: 284.

268 "detested Jews": *Beaconsfield,* 84.

268 "to his country": ibid., 3.

270 "as preliminary": ibid., 13.

270 "in *Coningsby*": ibid., 15.

270 "half assumed": ibid., 34.

271 "hear me": ibid., 71.

271 "to the end": ibid., 155.

271 "Parliament itself": ibid., 4.

271 "impenetrable armour": ibid., 19.

273 "in the world": ibid., 178.

273 "or equaled": ibid., 234.

275 "spiritual authority": ibid., 613.

276 "those initials": *F-R,* 58.

276 "rude and rapid": ibid., 95.

276 "House of Commons": Skelton, 215.

The Revolution in My Affairs

278 "me exclusively": Ireland, Sept. 20, 1889.

279 "still remained": ibid., Feb. 8, 1889.

279 "very outset": ibid., Mar. 22, 1890.

279 "spared anxiety": ibid., Apr. 18, 1890.

279 "everyone it touched": ibid., May 9, 1890.

280 "correct statement": *Early Letters,* 2: Preface.

280 "than you!": *F-R,* July 27, 1874, 132.

280 "is it all?": ibid., Mar. 8, 1886, 34–35.

281 "to welcome": ibid., May 31, 1889, 78–79.

282 "by Carlyle": ibid., June 25, 1889, 87.

282 "and Southey": Ireland, Apr. 14, 1890, not 1891 as attributed.

282 "still hoped": "Stormy days clean up, sometimes in a brilliant sunset—but it is sad when the bright day ends so mournfully," he wrote of Ruskin's madness to Max Müller.

283 "relative importance": ibid., Oct. 11, 1890.

284 "to Mr. Ireland": ibid., July 21, 1891.

284 "at last": ibid., Aug. 26, 1891.

284 "into flame": ibid., Oct. 7, 1890.

285 "Salisbury": Dunn II, 575.

285 "Freeman's ghost": Skelton, 216–17.

286 "more Submissive": *F-R,* Apr. 15, 1892.

287 "world in": Dunn II, 582.

287 "his family": Ironically, the Max Müllers now lived in the home once owned by another of Froude's critics, Goldwin Smith.

292 "resounding cheers": Speech republished in "Professor Froude at Oxford," *Exeter Gazette,* Oct. 1892. Kindly provided by Devon Library and Information Services of Exeter Central Library.

292 "etc., etc.": Dunn II, 581–82.

292 "life here": Ireland, Mar. 7, 1893.

292 "gratify them": *F-R,* Apr. 12, 1893, 126.

293 "their ease": Ireland, May 1, 1893.

293 "painstaking teacher": Dunn II, 585.

293 "in time": Ireland, May 1, 1893.

293 "worth the price": Dunn II, 579.

294 "by his side": "Death of Mr Froude," Albert Edward, "Death of Mr. Froude," *The Salcombe Times,* Oct. 27, 1894, Devon Library and Information Services.

295 "of death": *West Indies,* 323.

295 "own veins": *F-R,* Oct. 16, 1889, 98.

295 "their mideighties": Margaret died in 1935; Ashley in 1949.

296 "Bret Harte": "Funeral of Professor Froude," *Exeter Gazette,* Oct. 26, 1894, Devon Library and Information Services.

297 in 1879: Harvard, Autograph File, May 6 [1879].

SELECTED BOOKS AND ARTICLES

Allingham, H., and D. Radford, eds., *William Allingham: The Diaries*. London: The Folio Society, 1990.

Bate, W. Jackson, *Samuel Johnson*. Washington, DC: Counterpoint, 1998.

Blake, Robert, *Disraeli*. Garden City, NY: Anchor Books, Doubleday and Company, Inc. 1968.

Boswell, James, *Life of Johnson*. Edited by R. W. Chapman. Oxford and New York: Oxford University Press, 1980.

Brendon, Piers, *Hurrell Froude and the Oxford Movement*. London: Paul Elek, 1974.

Carlyle, Alexander, and James Crichton-Browne, *The Nemesis of Froude: A Rejoinder to James Anthony Froude's "My Relations with Carlyle."* New York and London: John Lane: The Bodley Head, 1903.

———. *New Letters and Memorials of Jane Welsh Carlyle.* New York and London: John Lane: The Bodley Head, 1903.

———. *New Letters of Thomas Carlyle.* New York and London: John Lane: The Bodley Head, 1904.

Carlyle, Thomas. "Boswell's Life of Johnson," *Critical and Miscellaneous Essays,* vol. IV. London: Chapman and Hall, Ltd., 1894.

———. *The Collected Letters of Thomas and Jane Welsh Carlyle*. Edited by Kenneth J. Fielding et al. North Carolina: Duke University Press, 1970–present. Ongoing.

———. *The Correspondence of Thomas Carlyle and Ralph Waldo Emerson, 1834–1872*. Edited by Charles Eliot Norton. 2 vols. Boston: Osgood & Co., 1883.

———. *Critical and Miscellaneous Essays: Collected and Republished*. London: Chapman and Hall, Ltd., 1895.

———. *Early Letters of Thomas Carlyle. 1814–1826*. Edited by Charles Eliot Norton. New York and London: MacMillan and Company, 1886.

———. *Letters and Memorials of Jane Welsh Carlyle*. Edited by James Anthony Froude. New York: Charles Scribner's Sons, 1900.

———. *The Life of John Sterling*. London: Chapman and Hall, 1851.

———. *Reminiscences*. Edited by James Anthony Froude. New York: Charles Scribner's Sons, 1900.

———. *Reminiscences*. Edited by Charles Eliot Norton. London: J. M. Dent and Sons Ltd., 1972.

———. *Reminiscences: A New and Complete Edition.* Edited by K. J. Fielding and Ian Campbell. Oxford and New York: Oxford University Press, 1997.

Cate, George Allan, ed. *The Correspondence of Thomas Carlyle and John Ruskin.* Stanford: Stanford University Press, 1982.

Cecil, David. *The Cecils of Hatfield House, an English Ruling Family.* Boston: Houghton Mifflin Company, 1973.

Chitty, Susan. *The Beast and the Monk: A Life of Charles Kingsley.* New York: Mason/Charter Publishers, Inc., 1975.

Conway, Moncure Daniel. *Autobiography: Memories and Experiences.* London, Paris, and Melbourne: Cossell and Company, 1904.

Darwall-Smith, Robin. *The Jowett Papers: A Summary Catalogue of the Papers of Benjamin Jowett (1817–1893).* Oxford: Balliol College Library, 1993.

Diamond, Marion. *Emigration and Empire: The Life of Maria S. Rye.* New York and London: Garland Publishing Inc., 1999.

Disraeli, Benjamin. *Lord George Bentinck: A Political Biography.* London: Colburn and Company Publishers, 1852.

Dunn, Waldo Hilary. "Carlyle's Last Letters to Froude." *The Twentieth Century,* Jan. 1956, 45–53; Mar. 1956, 255–63; June 1956, 591–97; Sept. 1956, 241–46.

———. *Froude and Carlyle: A Study of the Froude-Carlyle Controversy.* Port Washington, NY: Kennikat Press Inc., 1969.

———. *James Anthony Froude: A Biography 1818–1856.* Oxford: Oxford at the Clarendon Press, 1961.

———. *James Anthony Froude: A Biography 1857–1894.* Oxford: Oxford at the Clarendon Press, 1963.

Eliot, George. *Selected Critical Writings by George Eliot.* Edited by Rosemary Ashton. Oxford: Oxford University Press, 1992.

Faber, Sir Geoffrey. *Oxford Apostles.* London: Penguin Books, 1954.

Froude, Hurrell. *Remains of the Late Reverend Richard Hurrell Froude, M.A., Fellow of Oriel College.* Edited by John Henry Newman and John Keble. London: Rivington, 1838, vols. 1 and 2; 1839, vols. 3 and 4.

Froude, James Anthony. *Caesar; a Sketch.* London: Longmans, Green, and Company, 1879.

———. *A Dialogue on the Life and Actions of King Henry the Eighth.* London: Parker, Son, and Bourn, West Strand, 1861.

———. *The Divorce of Catherine of Aragon.* New York: Charles Scribner's Sons, 1899.

———. *The Earl of Beaconsfield.* New York: Harper and Brothers, 1890.

———. *The English in Ireland in the Eighteenth Century.* London: Longmans, Green, and Company, 1874.

———. *The English in the West Indies, or The Bow of Ulysses.* London: Longmans, Green, and Company, 1888.

———. *English Seamen in the Sixteenth Century: Lectures Delivered at Oxford, Easter Terms 1893–4.* New York: Charles Scribner's Sons, 1906.

———. "A Few Words on Mr. Freeman: A Letter to the Editor," *Nineteenth Century,* April 1879, 618–37.

———. *Historical and Other Sketches.* Edited by David H. Wheeler. New York: Funk and Wagnalls, 1883.

———. *History of England from the Death of Cardinal Wolsey to the Defeat of the Spanish Armada.* New York: AMS Press, Inc., 12 vols. 1969. (Reprinted from the edition of 1862–70.)

——. *John Bunyan*. English Men of Letters Series. Edited by John Morley. New York: Harper and Brothers Publishers, 1889.

——. *Lectures on the Council of Trent*. Port Washington, NY: Kennikat Press, 1969.

——. *Life and Letters of Erasmus: Lectures Delivered at Oxford 1893–4*. New York: Charles Scribner's Sons, 1895.

——. *My Relations with Carlyle*. Freeport, NY: Books for Libraries Press, 1971.

——. *The Nemesis of Faith*. London: John Chapman, 1849.

——. *Oceana, or England and Her Colonies*. New York: Charles Scribner's Sons, 1886.

——. *Shadows of the Clouds*. By "Zeta." London: John Ollivier, 1847.

——. *Short Studies on Great Subjects*. 4 vols. London: Longmans, Green, and Company, 1894.

——. *Thomas Carlyle: A History of the First Forty Years of His Life, 1795–1835*. 2 vols. London: Longmans, Green, and Company, 1882.

——. *Thomas Carlyle: A History of His Life in London, 1834–1881*. 2 vols. New York: Charles Scribner's Sons, 1884.

——. *The Two Chiefs of Dunboy, or an Irish Romance of the Last Century*. New York: Charles Scribner's Sons, 1889.

Froude, William. *The Papers of William Froude, M.A., L.L.D, F. R.S., with a Memoir by Sir Wescott Abell, K.B.E*. London: The Institution of Naval Architects, 1955.

Goetzman, Robert. *James Anthony Froude: A Bibliography of Studies*. New York and London: Garland Publishing, Inc., 1977.

Guiney, Louise Imogen. *Hurrell Froude: Memoranda and Comments*. London: Methuen and Company, 1904.

Hardinge, Arthur. *The Life of . . . Fourth Earl of Carnarvon 1831–1890*. Edited by Elisabeth Countess of Carnarvon. London: Oxford University Press, 1925.

Harper, Gordon H. *Cardinal Wiseman and William Froude*. Baltimore: John Hopkins Press, 1933.

Harris, Frank. *My Life and Loves*. Edited by John F. Gallagher. 5 vols. New York: Grove Press Inc., 1963.

Heffer, Simon. *Moral Desperado: A Life of Thomas Carlyle*. London: Weidenfeld and Nicolson, 1995.

Himmelfarb, Getrude. "A Forgotten Worthy," *New York Review of Books,* June 25, 1964, 9–10.

Ireland, Mrs. Alexander. *Life of Jane Welsh Carlyle*. New York: Charles L. Webster and Company, 1891.

Jenkins, Roy. *Gladstone: A Biography*. New York: Random House Trade Paperbacks, 2002.

Kaplan, Fred. *Thomas Carlyle: A Biography*. Ithaca, NY: Cornell University Press, 1983.

Kingsley, Charles. *Charles Kingsley: His Letters and Memories of His Life*. Edited by His Wife. London: Kegan Paul Trench and Company, 1888.

——. *Yeast; a Problem*. London: J. M. Dent & Sons, 1859.

Lowry, Howard Foster, ed. *The Letters of Matthew Arnold to Arthur Hugh Clough*. London and New York: Oxford University Press, 1932.

Markus, Julia. *Across an Untried Sea*. New York: Knopf, 2000.

Maurer, Oscar Jr. "Froude and *Fraser's Magazine,* 1860–1874." *Texas University Studies in English,* vol. 28, 1949, 213–43.

Mozley, Anne, ed. *Letters and Correspondence of John Henry Newman*. 2 vols. London: Longmans, Green, and Company, 1891.

Mozley, Reverend T. *Reminiscences, Chiefly of Oriel College and the Oxford Movement*. London: Longmans, Green, and Company, 1882.

Mulhauser, Frederick L. *The Correspondence of Arthur Hugh Clough*. Oxford: Oxford at the Clarendon Press, 1957.

Müller, Friedrich Max. *Auld Lang Syne*. New York: Charles Scribner's Sons, 1901.

———. *The Life and Letters of the Right Honourable Friedrich Max Müller. Edited by His Wife*. London and Bombay: Longmans, Green, and Company, 1902.

Newman, John Henry. *Apologia pro Vita Sua: An Authoritative Basic Text of the Newman-Kingsley Controversy Origin and Reception of the Essays in Criticism*. Edited by David J. DeLaura. New York and London: W. W. Norton and Company, 1968.

———. *The Idea of a University*. Edited by Frank M. Turner. New Haven and London: Yale University Press, 1996.

Norton, Charles Eliot. *Letters of Charles Eliot Norton with Biographical Comment by His Daughter Sara Norton and M. A. DeWolfe Howe*. 2 vols. Boston and New York: Houghton Mifflin Company, 1913.

———. "Recollections of Carlyle," *The New Princeton Review*, July 1, 1886, 1–19.

———. ed., *Reminiscences*. London: J. M. Dent and Sons, Ltd., 1972.

O'Day, Alan. "Media and Power: Charles Stewart Parnell's 1880 Mission to North America." Historical Studies, 22: 202–21.

Park, Joseph Hendershot. *British Prime Ministers of the Nineteenth Century: Policies and Speeches*. New York: New York University Press, 1916; London: Oxford University Press, 1950.

Pattison, Mark. *Memoirs*. London: MacMillan, 1885.

Paul, Herbert. *The Life of Froude*. London: Sir Isaac Pitman and Sons Ltd., 1905.

Pope-Hennessy, James. *Monckton Milnes: The Years of Promise 1809–1851*. New York: Farrar, Straus and Cudahy Inc., 1955.

Pope-Hennessy, Una. *Canon Charles Kingsley: A Biography*. London: Chatto and Windus, 1948.

Rowse, A. L. *Froude the Historian: Victorian Man of Letters*. Gloucester: Alan Sutton, 1987.

———. *Glimpses of the Great*. London: Methuen, 1985.

Ruskin, John. *Praeterita: The Autobiography of John Ruskin*. Oxford and New York: Oxford University Press, 1983.

Skelton, John. *The Table-Talk of Shirley: Reminiscences of and Letters from Froude, Thackeray, Disraeli, Browning, Rossetti, Kingsley, Baynes, Huxley, Tyndall, and Others*. Edinburgh and London: William Blackhead and Sons, 1895.

Stead, W. T. *The M.P. for Russia. Reminiscences and Correspondence of Madame Olga Novikoff*. London: Andrew Melrose, 1909.

Stephen, Leslie. *The Life of Sir James Fitzjames Stephen*. South Hackensack, NJ: Rothman Reprints Inc., 1972.

Strachey, Lytton. *Portraits in Miniature and Other Essays by Lytton Strachey*. New York: Harcourt, Brace and Company, 1931.

Turner, Frank M. *John Henry Newman: The Challenge to Evangelical Religion*. New Haven and London: Yale University Press, 2002.

Viljoen, Helen Gill, ed. *The Froude-Ruskin Friendship*. New York: Pageant Press Inc., 1966.

Willey, Basil, *More Nineteenth Century Studies: A Group of Honest Doubters*. New York: Columbia University Press, 1969.

Woolf, Virginia. *Carlyle's House and Other Sketches*. Edited by David Brackshaw. London: Hesperus Press Ltd., 2003.

INDEX

ABOUT THE AUTHOR

JULIA MARKUS is the author of several novels, including the award-winning *Uncle,* and two previous biographies, *Dared and Done: The Marriage of Elizabeth Barrett and Robert Browning,* and *Across an Untried Sea,* which deals with women of genius in the nineteenth century. She is professor of English and director of Creative Writing at Hofstra University.

ILLUSTRATION CREDITS

John Henry Newman, John Keble reproduced by the kind permission of the Warden and Fellows of Keble College, Oxford; Hurrell Froude, Thomas Mozley, and J. H. Newman at Oriel College Common Room, reproduced by the kind permission of the Provost and Fellows of Oriel College, Oxford; Jane Welsh Carlyle, "the worst," Geraldine Jewsbury with Jane Welsh Carlyle, Carlyle with niece Mary Aitken, Mary Aitken and Alexander Carlyle in 1879, and Froude the young rebel used with permission of the University Archives and Columbiana Library, Columbia University; William Froude, by permission of The Image Works, Inc.; Mary Sackville-West, Lady Derby, with the kind permission of the Marquess of Salisbury; "Who Shall Rule?" and "Critics," *Harper's Bazaar*'s 1872 and *Punch,* 1870 respectively; "Leghorn," by kind permission of the Birmingham Oratory; "Sir George Grey's House," in *Oceana,* by permission of Scribner; Charles and Fanny Kingsley, by permission of *Country Life;* Totnes, author's photograph; "He Is Not Dead but Sleepeth," Jane Welsh, Edward Irving, E. A. Freeman, Olga Novikoff in court dress, Harriet Bush, F. Max Müller, private collections.